Bill Barnes
2/5/98

GALILEE

GALILEE

HISTORY, POLITICS, PEOPLE

RICHARD A. HORSLEY

TRINITY PRESS INTERNATIONAL
Valley Forge, Pennsylvania

Trinity Press International, P.O. Box 851, Valley Forge, PA 19482-0851

Library of Congress Cataloging-in-Publication Data

Horsley, Richard A.
    Galilee: history, politics, people / Richard A. Horsley. – 1st ed.
        p.   cm.
    Includes bibliographical references and index.
    ISBN 1-56338-133-8 (cloth : alk. paper)
    1. Galilee (Israel)—History. 2. Jews—History—168 B.C.-135 A.D.
    3. Judaism—History—Post-exilic period, 586 B.C.-210 A.D.
    I. Title
DS110.G2H63   1995
956.94'5–dc20   95-34935
                                                                      CIP

Printed in the United States of America

95   96   97   98   99   10   9   8   7   6   5   4   3   2   1

CONTENTS

❧

Acknowledgments

❧

Special appreciation to Laura Whitney and her staff at the Andover-Harvard Library and to Gayle Pershouse and her staff at the Episcopal Divinity School–Weston College Library for their assistance and patience with me in ransacking their collections; to research assistants Marcus Aurin, Heather Kapplow, John McCosh, and particularly John Stevens, of the University of Massachusetts in Boston, for hundreds of hours devoted to search and discover missions; to Ann DiSessa and Judi Roberts, multi-competent staff at the University of Massachusetts Boston for the many ways in which they facilitated this project; to Mordechai Aviam for expert, suggestive guidance through the topography and archaeology of Galilee; to Ellen Aitken, Jennifer Berenson, Mimi Bonz, Bernadette Brooten, Denise Buell, Sam Han, Cynthia Kittredge, Helmut Koester, Shelly Matthews, Barbara Rossing, and Demetrius Williams for the fresh explorations and critical discussions of history and society in early Roman Galilee in a doctoral seminar at Harvard Divinity School; and to Allen Callahan, Rob Doran, Obery Hendricks, Doug Oakman, Andy Overman, Jim Pasto, Pat Tiller, Larry Wills, and especially Neil Silberman, for a critical reading of some or all of the chapters and for any number of important suggestions.

INTRODUCTION

୶୨୧ଡ଼

Two major religions originated in ancient Galilee. Both rabbinic Judaism and Christianity stem from and lay claim to ancient Israelite traditions that were cultivated in Galilee as well as in Judea and Samaria. According to the Christian Gospels, Jesus, who was recognized by his followers as the Messiah and whose "hometown" was Nazareth, carried out his ministry primarily in Galilee, with headquarters in Capernaum, at the northern end of the Sea of Galilee. According to rabbinic traditions, following the destructive Roman suppression of two widespread revolts in Judea, the rabbis and other Judeans relocated in Galilee where they established academics and compiled first the Mishnah and later the Jerusalem Talmud. When Christianity became the established religion of the Roman empire, Galilee became part of the "Holy Land" along with Judea and Jerusalem, with successive generations of pilgrims flocking to sacred sites such as Nazareth and Capernaum. Similarly, Jews have traditionally considered Galilee part of Eretz Israel, with many a town or village being the revered site of some great rabbi's tomb. The rise of Islam, of course, produced yet another prophetic religion whose faithful considered this territory holy.

More recently, renewed pursuit of the historical Jesus, critical studies of rabbinic literature, and intensified archaeological explorations have led to revived interest in Galilee. Questions about Jesus' teachings and activities required information regarding the context of his ministry. His aphorisms suddenly seemed to lack meaning without some life-situation they might have addressed. Like the sayings of Jesus, the rulings of the rabbis no longer seemed satisfying when taken as abstract teachings to anyone, anywhere, anytime. And archaeologists found material evidence of urban as well as rural life, Greek as well as Hebrew and Aramaic language, and seemingly pagan as well as Jewish symbols in the decor of synagogues.

Previous understanding of Galilee was ill-prepared for this sudden revival of interest and information. In the general cultural as well as academic division of labor, Galilee belonged to a largely Christian biblical studies and the parallel period of Jewish studies. Biblical studies, of course, developed in a Christian theological environment geared to training an educated clergy. Not surprisingly, the focal issues and conceptual apparatus had much to do with the explanation and rationalization of the rise of "Chris-

I

tianity" out of "Judaism" — for example, with why and how the Jews had generally not received Jesus as the promised Messiah, while he had been recognized by Gentiles who came to form most of the early churches. Galilee, of course, while the place of Jesus' origins and ministry, figured only as the location of the first stage in his ministry. The more important site, ultimately, was Jerusalem, scene of the climactic events and the center from which the Christian mission radiated out into the wider world.

Thus Galilee was understood in the context of a grand scheme of Christian origins. It was not until a transference was made from insights into the history of science that we came to recognize that ancient Galilee, like ancient Judaism generally, was constructed as part of a dominant historical "paradigm" that defined the key issues and legitimate interpretations of biblical and other studies of the origins of Christianity. Thus the first step toward serious historical investigation of ancient Galilee would be to discern the principal features and functions of the dominant paradigm according to which "Judaism," with its Pharisees and synagogues, and Jesus and his followers, as the founders of "Christianity," have been constructed in European-American culture and scholarship.

The Paradigm of Christian Origins

The dominant paradigm has something to do with an embattled Christianity in a secularizing Western Europe. Not surprisingly, Christian theologians felt a bit defensive after the provocateurs of the French Revolution threatened to strangle the last king in the entrails of the last priest. Not only that, Enlightenment reason had steadily chipped away at the scriptural basis of the faith. As a matter of self-defense in a rationalistic modernity, much of the Gospel narratives had to be relinquished as myth. Only by sacrificing the seemingly irrational and mythic could the remainder be salvaged as a solid basis of spiritual or ethical teaching on which the individual believer could still stand. The great "demythologizing" debate was really just the culmination of decades of retreat into the rational and to a scientifically defensible basis on which one could finally stake one's authenticity — or the final surrender to the imperial claims of reason to define reality. Religion became confined primarily to a private, individual spiritual realm, ostensibly separate from economic enterprise and political participation alike.[1]

The nineteenth century must have been difficult for Christian theologians to live through. In the generation of the Revolutionary War in America, deists such as Thomas Jefferson, as well as Congregationalist preachers such as Samuel Langdon, still appealed to biblical text and history as propounding a model of civil government, not simply edification for individual piety. At least by the mid-nineteenth century among German scholars, however, Christianity and its scripture were purely spiritual and the very foundation of a religion that was no threat to a citizen's participation in the nascent German state. Christianity was also universal, open to and uniting any and all individuals in the realm of the spirit. But there was a hitch. Such a Christianity needed an Other. And that Other was "Judaism," which played the role of the exclusivist-particularist-ritualistic and "political" religion over against the ethical-spiritual and universalistic Christianity.[2]

During the last generation some of the more seriously objectionable and dispensable aspects of this paradigm were "corrected." For example, in the embarrassment and ecumenical (at least for the "Judeo-Christian tradition") spirit in the aftermath of the Holocaust, Judaism was no longer "Late Judaism," which had been replaced in the historical succession by "Early Christianity." Scholars now recognized that "Judaism" was in the "early" stages of its development at the same time as "Christianity." Yet the basic conceptual components of the overall paradigm remained. "Judaism," in Christian scholarly discourse, was still characterized as nationalistic-political and particularistic-exclusivistic, limitations that early "Christianity" finally broke through, in the fullness of time, to universalism and a purified individual spirituality. The divine plan and God's will for ethical universalism were fulfilled in Jesus' ministry and especially in the Pauline mission. Jesus challenged the particularism, ritual obsessions, and self-righteousness of Jewish priestly and Pharisaic religion. Paul then pioneered the breakthrough into fully universalistic religion.

While there is now widespread recognition of the more blatant ways in which biblical exegesis and the construction of the historical "background" are determined by this paradigm, it still dominates the fields of biblical interpretation and Jewish history. Focus is still on the individual and the religious as separate from other dimensions of life, perhaps not surprising given that professional practitioners are now located in religion departments as well as theological schools. Although with all sorts of qualifications and variations, "Judaism/Jewish" is still counterpoised with "Hellenism/Hellenistic." Hellenism introduced a kind of universalism into the ancient world, but Judaism resisted and rebelled in pursuit of its own particularism and residual nationalism.[3] After Judaism's "failure" to adjust interactively with Hellenism, the Pharisees and their heirs, the rabbis, focused Judaism ever more rigorously on the Law. Moreover, the Pharisees, one of the "sects" and the principal leadership of Judaism, were instrumental in developing a Law-focused piety based in the synagogue that was also concerned with purity and boundary maintenance. The synagogue, under Pharisaic (and then rabbinic) leadership, provided the requisite alternative to sacrifices in the Temple once the latter had been destroyed by the Romans.

This established scholarly paradigm supplied the lens through which scholarly interpreters read the Christian Gospels, which in turn ostensibly confirmed the paradigm. Matthew, Mark, and Luke all portray the scribes and Pharisees, "from every village of Galilee," as the leaders of "*their* synagogues," sitting "on Moses' seat" as the "teachers" of the Law, including highly particularistic and ritualistic matters such as detailed purity codes (see esp. Matthew 23; Mark 2:1–3:6; 12:38–40; Luke 5:17).[4] Jesus not only challenges the casuistry of the scribes and Pharisees, but he also breaks through the particularism and exclusivism by reaching out to the Gentiles. The trips back and forth across the Sea of Galilee in Mark are read as bridging the "Jewish" side in Galilee itself and the "Gentile" side across the sea in Gaulanitis and the Decapolis.[5] Key passages in the Synoptic Sayings Source "Q" used by Matthew and Luke are interpreted as prophetic pronouncements of judgment against "Judaism" (or "all Israel"), with the pilgrims and disciples now representing the new universal religion over against the exclusive and decadent old one.[6]

Problems and Persistence of the Paradigm

In a number of its key aspects this paradigm has been challenged as inappropriate or even counter to the literary and, more recently, the archaeological evidence from antiquity. It is increasingly recognized, for example, that religion was not a separate sphere of life, but embedded with political-economic forms. Most prominently, the Temple was the dominant political-economic institution as well as the center of worship in ancient Judean society. In my own case, what became unavoidably clear in reading the Jewish historian Josephus was that "Jewish nationalism" under whatever rubric ("the Zealots," the "politics of holiness," and so on, along with the concept of "the Jewish war") not only merged under one concept a number of distinctive movements and protests, but also obscured a sort of "class conflict" that prevailed in late second-temple Palestine.[7]

Nevertheless, even when recognizing that a certain set of evidence runs counter to a component of the dominant paradigm, scholars still tend to revert to the paradigm, often finding some way to restate or nuance the aspect now requiring "updating." For example, some who recognized that the modern concept of "the Zealots" (as a long-standing movement agitating against Roman rule) was not supported by the evidence claimed from Josephus still wrote of "Jewish nationalism" or "the politics of holiness."[8] Or, although I recognized the class conflict in the distinctive diversity of "Jewish" movements previously merged under "the Zealots" or "Jewish nationalism," I failed initially to discern the regional differences hidden behind the dominant paradigm.[9]

Several ways in which the dominant paradigm comes under suspicion, yet is finessed or glossed over, are directly related to historical constructions of Galilee. Recognition that there was no evidence for "the Zealots" in Galilee did not lead to questioning the modern scholarly concept.[10] The realization that no evidence for Pharisees' activity in Galilee exists outside of the Christian Gospels (New Testament scholars already having learned not to trust the narrative "editorial" sections in the Gospels as reliable historical evidence) did not lead to serious questioning about the Pharisees' role in the synagogues in Galilee. After all, the Pharisees were assumed to be the rabbis' immediate predecessors. And since the rabbis had taken over the leadership of "Judaism" after the destruction of the Temple in 70, they therefore must have begun to take over in Galilee in the immediately preceding years, even though we cannot be sure that they were active there during Jesus' ministry a few decades earlier (around 30 C.E.).

Furthermore, archaeological evidence that synagogue *buildings* were not built in Galilean villages prior to the third century C.E. did not lead to questioning the existence of the *synagogue* as the distinctive form of "Judaism" under Pharisaic leadership; instead it merely led to a shift in focus from building to community. Since, by definition, the synagogue — as *the* form of the religion of Judaism following the destruction of the Temple — was headed by the Pharisees, therefore it must have developed just at this time. Thus Mark and Matthew already know of "*their* [the Jews'] synagogues."[11] Or, as archaeological excavations in Galilean cities stimulated excitement about how "urbanized" and "cosmopolitan" Lower Galilee must have become (without, of course, attending carefully to exactly when), an "urbanized" Lower Galilee near Nazareth and Capernaum meant that Jesus was rooted less in Jewish particularism and more in the "cosmopolitan" (i.e., "Hellenistic") atmosphere of Lower Galilee.[12]

Reversion to the previously dominant paradigm, however, is not the only or the most obvious alternative. Were it not for the interest invested in the standard view of things, discovery of discrepancies between ancient evidence and modern constructs would press inquiry further into just how far-reaching the discrepancy might be. Part of our problem, of course, is that with the recent explosion of knowledge and specialization of research, no one is conversant with the several aspects of the old paradigm that may have become problematic. A cursory survey of only those aspects already mentioned is sobering.

With regard to the Pharisees (and the rabbis as their presumed successors), the problems go far beyond the lack of evidence for their activity in Galilee in the first half of the first century C.E. For example, it is not at all clear when, if ever, the rabbis, presumed to be the Pharisees' successors, were placed in control or took charge of Jewish life in Palestine. Much of our previous "knowledge" of the rabbinic academy at Jamnia may turn out to be rooted in or projected onto a "legend of origins."[13]

The problems with the "synagogues" as the Jewish counterparts and competitors of the Christian "churches" go beyond the late dates of buildings. The local assemblies or congregations to which the terms *synagōgai* and *knesset* refer in New Testament and rabbinic texts had far more than mere religious functions. Moreover, far from being their leaders, the Pharisees or rabbis would appear not even to have been members of such local assemblies for the most part.

To look more closely at the Gospel of Mark, in which Jesus supposedly bridges the boundary between "Jews" and "Gentiles" into a more universal "Christian" religious community, there is nothing to indicate that the Galilee (west) side of the sea is "Jewish" and the east side "Gentile." The adjective *ioudaios* is missing in the narrative, and *hoi ioudaioi*, "the Judeans," except for what is apparently a regional reference in 7:3, occurs only in the charge against Jesus, which was also inscribed on his cross, "the king of the Judeans" (15:2, 9, 12, 18, 26). Obviously the prevailing paradigm has determined this standard "reading" of Mark, presumably with the assumption that *synagōgai* referred to Jewish religious buildings in Capernaum and other villages where Jesus had been teaching and healing.[14] Such "dominant paradigm" readings of Mark and other early "Christian" literature simply ignore just how problematic is the evidence for when and how Galilee became "Jewish." Jewish scholars who are aware of the historical contingencies both before and after the first century C.E., on the other hand, attribute much more significance for the emergence of Jewish culture and institutions in Galilee to subsequent developments, such as the migration of numbers of Judeans, including priestly families and early rabbis, into Galilee following the Roman suppression of the two revolts in 66–70 and 132–135. Of course, if "Judaism" with all its supposed nationalism and exclusivist purity codes that established unbridgeable boundaries against the Gentiles was not yet fully developed and well established in Galilee, it is inappropriate to believe that the Gospel of Mark portrays Jesus as mediating between Jews and Gentiles in the establishment of a universalistic religion.

Not surprisingly, the greatest discrepancies between the dominant paradigm and the historical realities in Galilee emerge in connection with the principal dichotomies of the paradigm, that is, the divisions between "Jewish" and "Hellenistic" and between "Jewish" and "Christian." A critical review of the evidence (in chapter 4) suggests that no community or movement in Galilee understood itself as "Christian" over against "Jewish" until the fourth century. The standard dichotomy between "Christian" and "Jewish" may thus be virtually irrelevant to Galilee until that time. The problems with the other standard dichotomy, "Hellenistic" versus "Jewish," are not so clear-cut, but still suggest that the old paradigm blocks rather than facilitates historical understanding.

"Hellenistic" culture and its impact on "Jewish" culture is usually located in the cities founded in Palestine under the Hellenistic and Roman empires and is also closely associated with "urbanization."[15] Clarification of the historical situation in the eastern Mediterranean under Hellenistic and Roman empires suggests that both the concept of "urbanization" and the idea of cities as centers of "Hellenistic" cultural influence on indigenous culture, while pertinent, simplify and distort affairs in early Roman Galilee.

Before the Romans took control of the eastern Mediterranean, the area had been ruled for nearly three centuries by Hellenistic empires. Galilee in particular had been ruled and taxed for a century by the Ptolemaic regime and for nearly another century by the Seleucid regime before coming under the Hasmonean high-priestly regime in Jerusalem. Galileans had thus been in contact with Greek as the language of imperial administration for two centuries before experiencing an interlude (probably) of Hebrew or Aramaic under the late Hasmoneans, and before Herod, Antipas, and the Romans reverted to Greek as the official language. During this time Hellenistic cities such as Scythopolis, Ptolemais, and Tyre had politically and culturally dominated the areas surrounding Galilee. Whether an imperial administrative center such as Sepphoris or a *polis* such as Scythopolis, these Hellenistic political forms were already composite or mixed realities, with Greek-derived political forms and language superimposed on indigenous aristocracies and cultural forms.[16] Rarely was there a complete suppression of native culture and people and their replacement by pure Greek forms and style.

Thus the crucial factor in dealing with Hellenistic influence in a given case is the class division between the ruling strata (whether imperial administration, city council, or "native" ruler) and the indigenous peasantry they ruled. Insofar as local ruling groups were part of the overarching Hellenistic empire, they stood on a continuum of greater or lesser assimilation of/into Hellenistic political and cultural forms. Although the early Hasmonean rulers posed as the deliverers of distinctively Judean religious-political traditions and although they ruled subject peoples according to "the laws of the Judeans," they relied increasingly on mercenary troops, reached accommodations with the Seleucid rulers, and adopted Hellenistic forms of administration. Herod, followed by his son Antipas, apparently set up a standard Hellenistic-style administrative apparatus. The people ruled by these regimes had thus been continuously subject to Hellenistic influence in varying degrees since Alexander the Great. Even their Judean rulers brought Hellenistic influences along with and probably confused with Judean influences. It is therefore unlikely that much of historical significance will be generated by applying the opposition of "Hellenistic versus Jewish" to Galilee in early Roman times apart from the political-economic relations between the people concerned.

The concept of "urbanization," as used recently with regard to ancient Galilee, is similarly problematic.[17] To put matters simply, in the Hellenistic and Roman empires, urban and rural are inseparable correlates. An urban settlement did not raise its own food. A city was economically dependent on the surrounding countryside (e.g., Scythopolis) or on its *chōra* along with a certain degree of commerce (e.g., Tyre). Indeed, many cities in the eastern Mediterranean originated and/or continued as royal cities or political-economic(-religious) administrative centers of the rulers ("native" at one level, imperial at another); Jerusalem is a prime example. Thus the same factor of class division between rulers and ruled emerges as the key to urban versus rural as well as to Hellenistic versus Jewish. Except possibly for the formative generation of early Israel, it is difficult to discern any time during which Galileans or other Israelites were not subject to a royal and/or administrative city or cities. The appropriate historical question would not be whether an area was urban(ized) or rural but the proximity and intensity of interaction between city and village, and at times the degree of cultural-ethnic difference between rulers and ruled.

Given the above, it seems appropriate to refocus matters on the question of whose interests were represented in the politically, economically, culturally–dominant cities, how those were expressed, and how they affected the Galilean populace. That is, in contrast with the principal dichotomies that dominate the received paradigm of Christian origins, life in ancient Galilee would appear to have been structured according to a division between Hellenistic-Judean-Roman rulers based in cities and the vast majority of people living on the land, whose background and culture has yet to be determined very clearly.

Approach and Reconceptualization

Given the increasing awareness of the discrepancies between the dominant paradigm of Christian origins and historical realities in second-temple Palestine generally and Roman Galilee in particular, a twofold task presents itself. It may be necessary to "de-construct" some of the received standard "knowledge" of ancient Judean and Galilean life. Correspondingly, it may be possible to discern some of what has been "subjugated knowledge" (Foucault) of life in Galilee and its relations with the institutions and forces impinging on it. It would surely be naive to imagine that such an endeavor would suddenly be completely free of the previously dominant paradigm of Christian origins. Indeed, it is surely more realistic that fresh inquiry must proceed with critical awareness and periodic criticism of its own standpoint, concepts, and procedures.

In refocusing an approach and reconceiving a conceptual apparatus with regard to ancient Galilee, one consideration is to bring the discourse of biblical and Jewish studies into closer conversation with the discourse of other fields. Bountiful resources in the academy, including archaeology, historiography, political science, historical sociology, anthropology, cross-cultural studies, and ethnographical studies, may be helpful. Biblical scholars and Jewish historians have only begun to utilize the "social sciences" in exploration of their subject matter. It is already clear, however, that ancient Judea, Galilee, and the larger empires of which those districts formed a part would be grouped with "traditional agrarian societies" or "aristocratic empires." Broad cross-cultural sociological, anthropological, or other social-science studies such as those by Gerhard Lenski or John Kautsky may prove illuminating of both the broad structural dynamics in ancient Palestine and the relations between particular groups, such as the high priests and the scribes/Pharisees.[18] Lenski, for example, has already been utilized fruitfully in analyses of Hebrew biblical history. Simply to adopt a model of an "agrarian society" such as Lenski's and then test how it fits ancient Judea would not serve to illuminate ancient history so much as to provide yet another test of the model. More helpful in the long run, I believe, will be to work back and forth dialectically between our sources for ancient Judea and Galilee (critically considered) on the one hand, and comprehensive comparative studies such as Lenski's and Kautsky's on the other. The goal would be to construct an analysis focused as specifically and precisely as possible on social relations in ancient Judea and Galilee. In anticipation of such a procedure in the following chapters, it may be useful to highlight some of the issues that emerge from the comparison of such general models and such evidence as we have for ancient Palestine.

Since religious and other cultural matters are embedded in the basic political-economic structures and institutions, a first priority among procedural principles, perhaps, is to recognize the fundamental social forms of social formation. The vast majority of people would almost certainly have belonged to cross-generational families with some sort of rights to land in semi-autonomous villages and towns.[19] Those who ruled and taxed the Galileans would have been based in a temple-state, a Roman client-state, or a city with jurisdiction over the villages and towns.

In traditional agrarian societies, the economic differences between the ruling aristocracies and the people, mostly agricultural producers, are far greater than in modern industrial societies, and the cultural gulf similarly far wider. Recent historical and comparative studies emphasize that to characterize the relations between rulers and villagers as "functional" is to impute a reciprocity that did not exist. It is not clear what villagers received in "exchange" for their economic produce taken as taxes, rents, or religious dues.[20] For ancient Galileans and Judeans the costly (in terms of revenues derived from the people's produce) construction of roads and monumental buildings illustrate the relationship. The Roman roads were primarily for imperial military purposes, not for local commerce, and were of marginal importance for the peasantry. Among the many temples built or rebuilt by the Herods, the massive temple area in Jerusalem was, among other functions, used as a public gathering place and as the site of pilgrimage festivals. The temples to Caesar in Caesarea and Panion and the theater in Sepphoris probably had no public functions that directly involved villagers. Aristocracies accumulated wealth not so much for investment as for display. Such was the function of the Temple in Jerusalem and the palace-fortresses of Herod at key sites around Palestine and the palace-fortress of his son Antipas in Tiberias. To come full circle in appreciation of such a system, "the open display of great wealth, by making the gap between the aristocracy and lower classes visible, serves the function of making it all the wider and more unbridgeable."[21]

In certain important respects the distance between the Galileans and their rulers was not as extreme as usual among "aristocratic empires." While rulers and ruled are often peoples of different "societies," as was the case with the Romans and subject peoples such as the Judeans and Galileans, the Galileans shared a common Israelite cultural heritage with the Hasmoneans and later high-priestly rulers in Jerusalem. Moreover, while generally class differences are so great between aristocracies and peasantries that no "class conflict" results, the cultural heritage shared by the Judean priestly aristocracy and the Judean and Galilean people was likely a factor in the conflicts that persisted throughout late second-temple times.[22] Recognition that peasants "do not generally share the religious and moral assumptions of the aristocracy" and are particularly suspicious of the aristocracy's claim of religious sanctions for their own rule[23] forces us to question characterizations of ancient "Judaism" as monolithic.[24] The persistent conflict that focused on the Temple and high priesthood among Galileans as well as Judeans arose out of what is at least an ambiguity: perhaps more than usual among traditional agrarian societies, the Galilean and Judean peasantry had come to value, as well as resent, the Temple, priesthood, and scribal traditions as central institutions of Israel, perhaps particularly over against the increasing presence of alien rule and political culture.

Nevertheless, the differences between the two principal levels was such that affairs in Galilee fit the generalization that, by and large, "politics takes place not between classes but within classes."[25] Our major sources for Galilee all confirm this. Josephus focuses throughout on political affairs among the ruling groups — Romans, Herodians, high-priestly families. Peasants enter the narrative only when they make sufficient trouble so that the rulers are compelled to send out the military to restore proper social order. The Gospels portray Jesus and the disciples as moving among the villages, but avoiding the cities — until the face-off in Jerusalem, of course. The rabbis, although not exactly "rulers," are careful to distinguish themselves as a cultural elite from the peasants. Because local communities also had their politics, the investigations below will include discussion of "the politics of the people," as well as the affairs of the elite.[26] That most politics took place within the classes is the rationale for the division of material into parts 2 and 3. However, due to the unusual degree of political conflict between the "classes" in ancient Judea and Galilee, which was rooted in the fundamental political-economic-cultural relationship between rulers and ruled in Roman Palestine, the treatment in virtually every chapter will be necessarily relational.

Were we extraordinarily rigorous with respect to our conceptual apparatus, we would avoid such abstract standard modern social scientific terms as "society" until we reached clarity on just what referent such a term might have in Roman Palestine. Would "Galilee" ever have been comprehendible as a "society"? Nor do more old-fashioned, but still commonly used concepts such as "state" or "country," let alone "nation," fit traditional aristocratic empires. And it is by no means clear that they have "governments" in the modern sense of that word.[27] Pending the emergence of more appropriate terms, however, we may have no choice but to continue with such concepts while remaining aware of the necessity of negotiating around them as we examine ancient Galilee in Roman times. While reminding ourselves that villages and towns were the fundamental form of local community, we can utilize terms such as "state" or "regime" to suggest that power relations took the form of institutions semi-separate from the rest of the "society" being "governed" or "administered."

Perhaps the most striking thing about Galilee in late second-temple and Roman times is the frequency with which the particular rulers and ruling institutions changed, from the Seleucid regime to the Hasmonean temple-state to Herod's kingship plus high priesthood to the client rulership of Antipas without the temple-state to "urbanization" — all in the course of little more than 200 years. Because, given the prevailing power-relations, the rulers and form of rule could affect affairs in Galilee dramatically, it is important to attend closely to historical developments in or impinging on life in Galilee. For this reason, the investigation begins with a review of historical developments, part 1, with further elaboration of the structure of political-economic-cultural relations in parts 2 and 3.

To regain some sense of the whole, it is necessary to conduct historical inquiry across a number of disciplines, such as archaeology, textual interpretation, history, sociology, and anthropology. Recent expansion into new fields of inquiry and the corresponding specialization of research can be helpful in restoring a certain balance of perspective and knowledge in a subject area traditionally cultivated by biblical studies. For example, Israeli scholars have recently produced extensive analyses of the military history of the temple-state under the Seleucids, the Hasmoneans, and Herod. Such studies attend to data that scholars of religion tend to ignore, but which may be important for a more complete view of social relations. Yet the tendency for fields to subdivide, specialize, and proliferate (as in current biblical studies) is contrary to an understanding of the whole. Thus at the risk of being somewhat conversant in several but really competent in none, I will attempt to draw upon interrelated and overlapping disciplines in posing questions, analyzing evidence, and generally exploring what we do and do not know about affairs in ancient Galilee.

To summarize briefly the approach and conceptual apparatus: to avoid the problems that the received paradigm of Christian origins presents in understanding ancient Galilee, I am pursuing (provisionally) an alternative view of Palestine in general and Galilee in particular. This alternative view includes both social-structural and historical dimensions. It assumes, moreover, that religion is embedded in fundamental social forms such as village or temple-state, and that individual persons are embedded in fundamental social forms such as families, villages, priesthood. The fundamental political-economic-religious structure entailed a primary division between rulers and ruled, which was complicated by variations in the configuration of rulers and changes in regional relations. Throughout the Roman period people in local semi-autonomous communities lived and labored under the claims and oversight of two or more layers of rulers, imperial and regional. The configuration of the layers of rulers and their claims shifted from time to time according to the Roman disposition of the various districts of Palestine.

In broad social-structural and historical terms, then, Galilee appears somewhat as follows during Roman times: In late second-temple Judea proper, the primary division between the high-priestly rulers with their scribal "retainers," on the one hand, and the peasantry grouped in towns and villages, on the other, continued as it had under the Persian and Hellenistic empires. Once the Romans conquered the area, however, this hierarchy was complicated by the imposition of Herod and then Roman governors above the high-priestly aristocracy. Galilee, which had been directly under imperial administration for centuries, came under the Judean high-priestly regime for a century, compounded by Herod's rule during the latter decades of that time. Although recently subjected to Jerusalem rule, the Galileans during this century would have shared to a degree a common Israelite cultural heritage with (the Judeans and) their high-priestly rulers. For most of the first century C.E. the Romans set Herodian client-rulers over (all or part of) Galilee. The (re-)building of cities by Antipas would likely have made a dramatic economic and cultural impact on the Galileans. Two changes resulted from the two major revolts of 66–70 and 132–135 and their suppression by Rome. Both the Jerusalem high-priestly regime and client rulers were replaced by an "urbanization" of administration, placing the countryside under the jurisdiction of the major "cities," region by region. The migration of Judeans to Galilee, in particular the location of rabbinic academies in Sepphoris and Tiberias, restored the direct interaction between elite or official cultivators of Israelite cultural traditions and the popular cultivation of Israelite traditions.

The attempt to avoid the conceptual apparatus of the previously dominant paradigm of Christian origins poses the problem of what terms to use instead in certain key connections. Since there is such thin evidence of any community in Galilee prior to the fourth century that would have understood itself as "Christian" as distinct from "Jewish" or Israelite, "(Jewish-) Christian" can simply be avoided. Very likely there were communities of Jesus-followers in Galilee at least in the first century C.E. As indicated in the traditions they may have left, such as in the discourses of the Synoptic Sayings Source "Q" or the Gospel of Mark, the Jesus-followers understood themselves as a renewal movement of Israel, however critical they may have been of the Jerusalem rulers, institutions, and representatives. I will also avoid the term "Judaism" with reference to Palestine because of the considerable diversity of literature and groups there, and because anything that could qualify as "religious" was embedded in social forms and institutions that are inseparably also political and economic. Thus it makes more sense to proceed in terms of those social forms and institutions, such as the temple-state, the Judean and Galilean villages, and distinctive groups such as the Qumran community and the Pharisees.

With reference to the people living in late second-temple and Roman Palestine, it makes sense to follow the available sources. Early rabbinic literature such as the Mishnah uses "Israelites" in reference to the people living in Galilee. Josephus almost always uses "Galileans" with reference to the villagers and townspeople of Galilee. Only rarely does he use the term "Judeans" (*ioudaioi*) as inclusive of Galileans. Most of his references to "Judeans" are to people living in (or coming from) Judea. The Gospel of Mark does not use "Judeans" with reference to people in Galilee (7:3 appears to be a regional reference, "the Pharisees and all the Judeans"). While the terms "Jews" and "Jewish" seem to have clear referents when used of people and cultural expressions in diaspora communities of the wider Hellenistic-Roman world, they do not allow much precision in reference to the diversity in Palestine. This is partly a regional and partly a historical problem. My tentative approach will be, with close attention to the sources, to use "Judean" for *ioudaioi* unless it clearly has a broader reference. It also makes sense to use "Judeans" for people from Judea who were stationed in or moved to Galilee, at least into the second century C.E., insofar as they may have had some social-cultural differences with indigenous Galilean residents. By late antiquity, of course, when the differences between indigenous Galileans and those whose ancestors had migrated from Judea were less important, such a distinction may not matter. By late antiquity in Palestine, therefore, the terms "Jews" and "Jewish" can be used somewhat synonymously with the term "Israelites" in rabbinic literature. That is the time at which our sources allow Galileans to be absorbed into another term and to disappear from history.

Sources

One of the principal subjects of this book is what we do not know about Galilee — or rather, except for what Josephus tells us about the revolt in 66–67 C.E. and for what the rabbis tell us about case laws from around 200 C.E., we do not know very much directly about Galilee and Galileans. Ironically, the longest chapter in this book concerns the period and issues about which we know the least; hence the necessity of reasoning our way through the lack of solid information about who the Galileans were prior to the Hasmonean takeover and about how and to what degree they came to participate in the temple-community based in Jerusalem. Of the four major sources of evidence, I will make detailed use of three.

Most extensive and most important are the histories of the Jewish historian Josephus, which make critical use of his accounts all the more essential. That Josephus played such an instrumental role in Galilee during the great revolt of 66–67 makes his accounts of those events more valuable and, at the same time, more problematic. Critical historiography on Josephus continues to grow in scope and sophistication, illuminating his use of sources and his own agenda, as well as his blatant biases and exaggerations. Recent reviews of Josephus's life and historiography have revised the conclusions of pioneering studies.[28] It is sometimes possible to compare Josephus critically with his sources and for many incidents and issues he conveniently provides two different accounts.

Precisely because the principal potential utility of the investigations below will be in interpretation of the Christian Gospel traditions and of the figure of Jesus, I will generally avoid using the Gospels as sources for life in Galilee. The use of synoptic or Johannine Gospel traditions as historical sources for Galilee is just as problematic as using them as sources for the historical Jesus. Currently the scholarly pendulum seems to be swinging back toward the sense that the Gospels, particularly Mark and the Synoptic Sayings Source "Q" used by Matthew and Luke, provide some reliable reflections of social life in Galilee. Luke, of course, seems the least trustworthy; he often writes patterns from elsewhere in the Hellenistic-Roman world into scenes set in Galilee. To construct a picture of Galilee without steady use of and reference to the Gospels, therefore, I will draw on them only occasionally, such as when they provide the primary or only source for a particular matter, when they suggest a general pattern, or when some Jesus-saying offers a commentary on some matter established by other evidence.

Early rabbinic literature is becoming more and more important for historical investigations as rabbinic scholars produce increasingly sophisticated critical methods of evaluating the materials. Christian scholars have begun to heed admonitions not simply to assume that rabbinic literature provides evidence for late second-temple "Judaism," particularly for the Pharisees, on the assumption of continuity between the latter and the later rabbis. Jacob Neusner has demonstrated how rabbinic literature can rather be used critically to discern certain rulings and concerns of sages several generations prior to the compilation of the Mishnah, even some as early as the end of second-temple times.[29] Others have demonstrated how to utilize particular kinds of rabbinic materials such as case law as evidence for social relations contemporary with or just prior to the generations in which the rabbinic source can be dated.[30] Depending on the kind of material and the degree to which it may be judged to reflect or even repeat popular customs or practices, it may be possible to extrapolate back to earlier generations on the assumption of the conservatism of standard popular customs.

Archaeological reports now complement literary sources. Archaeology, of course, because of the difficulty of establishing chronological sequence, can delineate evidence only in very general "strata" (often of a century or more). Nevertheless, despite the limitations of chronological precision, historians must warmly welcome the new evidence, given the paucity of literary evidence for most periods in Galilee. To date, most of the findings are from middle to late Roman times. Even limited evidence from earlier periods, however, makes possible determinations such as continuity of settlement in certain locations and more informed speculation regarding regional patterns of culture.[31]

◆ *Part 1* ◆

HISTORY

Chapter 1

THE ROOTS OF
GALILEAN INDEPENDENCE

✺

For the mountains are a refuge from soldiers and pirates, as all the documents bear witness, as far back as the Bible.

— FERNAND BRAUDEL

Israelite Origins in Galilee

Toward the beginning of his account of the popular insurrection in Galilee in 66–67 C.E., the Jewish historian Josephus writes glowingly of the land and people:

> With this limited area, and although surrounded by such powerful foreign nations, the two Galilees have always resisted any hostile invasion, for the Galileans have always been numerous and warlike; never did the men lack courage nor the country men. For the land is everywhere so rich in soil and pasturage and produces such variety of trees, that even the most indolent are tempted by these facilities to devote themselves to agriculture. In fact, every inch of the soil has been cultivated by the inhabitants; there is not a parcel of waste land. The cities, too, are thickly distributed, and the multitude of villages, thanks to the fertility of the soil, are so densely populated that even the smallest of them contains above fifteen thousand inhabitants.
>
> (*B.J.* 3.41–43)

The self-styled "general" is obviously exaggerating the qualities and numbers of the people he claims to have led in resistance to Roman rule. He nevertheless places his finger on distinctive features of Galilee and its inhabitants evident from our earliest sources.

Indeed, in the first glimpse we catch of the earliest Israelite tribes in Galilee, the archaic Song of Deborah portrays the people as fiercely independent, fighting for their land against the Canaanite kings striving to subject them.

> The peasantry prospered in Israel, they grew fat on plunder,
> because you arose, Deborah, arose as a mother in Israel....

> To the sound of musicians at the watering places,
> there they repeat the triumphs of the LORD,
> the triumphs of his peasantry in Israel....
> The people of the LORD marched down...against the mighty....
> The chiefs of Issachar came with Deborah,...
> Zebulun is a people that scorned death;
> Naphtali too, on the heights of the field.
> The kings came, they fought,
> at Taanach, by the waters of Megiddo.
> The torrent Kishon swept them away,...
> March on, my soul, with might!
>
> —JUDGES 5:7, 11, 13, 15, 18, 19, 21

Summoned by the prophetess Deborah, the Israelites came down from the hill country to face the professional armies of horses and chariots defending the fortified Canaanite cities in the plain, such as Megiddo. They were victorious when their God Yahweh sent a torrential rainstorm that caused the chariots to become bogged down in the mud or immobilized by a flash flood.

The Galileans' recurrent struggles to resist domination by various outside rulers, moreover, had much to do with the location and topography (and productivity) of their land. The few passages in the Hebrew Bible that mention Galilee refer variously to some part of the hilly and mountainous area west and northwest of the Sea of Galilee toward the coastal plain near the Mediterranean Sea, or even more narrowly to the mountainous region later known as Upper Galilee.[1] Most likely the Hebrew term *ha-galil* was a secondary shortening of an original *galil ha-goyim*, "circle of the peoples" (Isa. 9:1/8:23; quoted in Matt. 4:15; cf. 1 Macc. 5:15).[2] "Circle of the peoples" was likely a reference to the "peoples," "city-states," and other rulers who surrounded and competed for political-economic domination in the area (or possibly to the shifting petty kingships and fiefdoms within the area). The name "Galilee" thus combines political and geographical reference to land and people subject to changing pressure or domination by the nearby kingships or grander empires periodically competing for control of northern Palestine.

The topography of Galilee is closely related to its political geography. Southern or "Lower" Galilee is a series of valleys and ridges ascending gradually from the western coastal plain into the interior, then dropping dramatically in elevation to the Jordan valley and the lake (Sea of Galilee) in the east. Northern or "Upper" Galilee is more mountainous and less accessible. The western valleys were the natural hinterland for the coastal cities such as Acco/Ptolemais and Tyre, which dominated further into the region when they were politically strong. But, as can be noted in other places such as Switzerland in European history or the Berbers in North Africa, the rugged terrain meant that the peasantry who eked out a living in the upland valleys could more easily maintain a certain independence, particularly in periods when the surrounding regimes were weak.[3] Thus, whatever the historical period, topography is a major factor in Galilean history, abetting the hill people's periodic efforts at resisting incorporation into the more complex societies based in the surrounding valleys and plains.

Correspondence from a number of local Palestinian rulers preserved in the Egyptian imperial archives discovered at Amarna provide some fascinating glimpses of affairs in and around Galilee in the fourteenth century B.C.E., just prior to the appearance of Israelites in the area.[4] A few princes or kings, who were also vassals of the Egyptian pharaoh, held uneasy sway at points around "the circle," at Tyre and Acco on the coast, at Megiddo and Taanach in the great plain just to the south, and at Hazor in the Huleh valley just below Upper Galilee. Aiab, head of Ashteroth, objected to the pharaoh that the king of Hazor had seized three of his towns (El Amarna [EA] 364). Abimilki, the ruler of Tyre, complained of encroachment on his territory by the same "king" of Hazor in alliance with Zimreda of Sidon, suggesting that their spheres of domination met or overlapped somewhere in Upper Galilee (EA 148).

Most fascinating in this diplomatic correspondence are the many references to the *hapiru*, who posed a threat to the rule of the local princes.[5] These *hapiru*, clearly groups of people with differing ethnic origins, stood outside the main social structure of areas dominated by the fortified cities. They had formed bands larger than the usual gangs of brigands, more like the Cossacks on the southern frontiers of Russia or the Haiduks in the Balkans in early modern times. The local princes of Palestine complained to the pharaoh that the *hapiru* raided their territory, but some of those local princes had in effect hired bands of *hapiru* as mercenaries or border guards.

The decline of the Egyptian imperial regime during the Amarna age and the resulting competition for dominance among local Palestinian princes led to a disintegration in the complex social order centralized in fortified cities such that *hapiru* peasants previously subject to those cities were able to establish more independent communities in the hill country. This disintegration of the dominant political order may have provided the context in which Israel emerged as an independent people in the hill country of Palestine. According to recent historical reconstructions, the Israelites started in Galilee, as further south, in the twelfth century B.C.E. when fugitives or rebels from Canaanite kingships moved into the previously unsettled or sparsely settled hill country.[6] Hazor, north of the Sea of Galilee, was a well-established Canaanite city, as indicated in Judges 4:2 and in the Amarna archives. Excavations at Hazor show that the city was destroyed in the Late Bronze Age and that the early Iron Age settlement there was little more than a village.[7] Indeed, archaeological digs in the area suggest a general cultural break just at this time, although the changes occurred over a lengthy period. Archaeologists may be able to show that, like the tribes of Ephraim and Manasseh in central Palestine, the clans of Naphtali and Zebulun established new settlements in the Galilean hill country independent of domination by established kingships.[8]

The early Israelites would have used the rugged terrain to advantage in maintaining their independence of political domination and economic exploitation by Canaanite rulers in their fortified cities. Each clan, village, or group of settlements (the *mishpahah* in Hebrew) in a given valley would have been more or less self-sufficient economically, further grounding their valued independence. Establishing and maintaining that economic self-sufficiency and independence, however, would have required a great deal of cooperation within the clan or village, for example, to terrace the steeper slopes for farming. In the Song of Deborah, the phrase traditionally translated "heights of the field" (*meromei saheh*, Judg. 5:18) is a reference to just such terracing among the clans of Naphtali.[9]

Despite their passion for independence, however — or perhaps because of it — the Israelite clans and tribes, which were separated from one another by rough terrain and considerable distances, had to cooperate across village, valley, clan, and tribal lines as well as within the villages. This cooperation was based on their common loyalty to Yahweh and their covenantal bonds with one another. Peasant militia from six different tribes respond to Deborah's call: Ephraim, Machir (later Manasseh?), and even Benjamin, from the hill country south of the great plain, along with Zebulun, Naphtali, the tribe of the prophetess Deborah and the military leader Barak, and Issachar, which may originally have lived in the hill country of Galilee as well. Moreover, the cursing of other tribes or units (Reuben, Gilead, Dan, Asher, and Meroz; Judg. 5:15–17, 23) for not responding to the emergency of their "kin" in Galilee is clear indication of established expectations of intertribal solidarity over against potential domination by outside rulers. Covenantal bonds among clans and tribes both defined and held together "the people of Israel," which was historically visible perhaps only when they made common cause in defense of their mutual freedom from alien rulers in a series of emergencies during the twelfth and eleventh centuries B.C.E. (Judges and 1 Samuel 3–7). Perhaps the most famous, led by Gideon of the Abiezrite clan in Manasseh, again involved the northern tribes of Naphtali and Zebulun, along with Asher (Judges 6–8; esp. 6:35). One episode in the Gideon story also makes clear that the people were to remain free of an Israelite king and of foreign rulers since Yahweh was the actual king of Israel (Judg. 8:22–23; cf. 1 Sam. 8:1–18). Otherwise, when not engaged in common battles against outside threats or celebrating a "covenant renewal" (Joshua 24), "Israel" existed concretely in its multiple independent villages or clans scattered over the hill country of Galilee and the more southerly areas of central Palestine.

Subordination to Monarchy and Temple in Jerusalem

In an irony of history, the Israelites resorted to kingship in order to generate a centralized military force to resist domination by the Philistines. At first kingship was a revolutionary action against unwanted hierarchical domination. Biblical narratives portray the kingship of both Saul and the young David as initiated by popular acclamation or "anointing" (*messiah*) and as conditioned by the continuing approval of the people (1 Sam. 8, 10:17–27; 2 Sam. 2:4; 5:1–3; cf. 1 Kings 12).[10] Both the Philistine threat and the power struggle between the house of Saul and the nascent kingship of David took place in the south and may not have involved the vital interests of the Galilean tribes. Nevertheless, the latter appear to have been implicated and involved as part of "all the tribes/elders of Israel" or "all the people," whether in acclaiming or anointing Saul and David as kings (1 Sam. 10:24; 11:15; 2 Sam. 5:1–3) or in the battles against the Philistines or, closer to home, against the Ammonite siege of Jabesh-Gilead (1 Sam. 11:1–11).

The tribes of Israel came to regret anointing David as king. The politically shrewd *messiah* moved step by step with the help of his non-Israelite mercenary troops to establish his power over Israel. First, he conquered the non-Israelite stronghold of Jerusalem as the capital from which he ruled and to which he brought up the ark of Yahweh, symbol of Israel's covenantal unity under God (2 Sam. 5:6–10; 6:1–5). Then, in addition to holding off the Philistine threat, he conquered any and all principalities on the periphery of Israel, whether or not they posed a threat (e.g., 2 Sam. 8; 11:1). Once David became comfortable with his concubines, however, he was driven from Jerusalem by a widespread insurrection, apparently involving all the tribes, led by David's son Absalom (2 Samuel 15–19). But no sooner had he suppressed the rebellion with his mercenary troops and consolidated his position within his own tribe of Judah than, a second time, "all the people of Israel [except Judah] withdrew from David and followed Sheba son of Bichri" (a Benjaminite; 2 Sam. 20:1–2). This time the Galilean tribes were clearly involved, at least as a result of the suppression of the revolt by David's mercenary army. Sheba "passed through all the tribes of Israel to Abel of Beth-maacah," a district town in northernmost Naphtali near Dan, to which the royal mercenaries set siege. Legend has it that a "wise woman" of the town persuaded the rest to sacrifice Sheba to save the town from sure destruction by David's ruthless army (2 Sam. 20:14–22). Thus the Deuteronomic history indicates that the Israelites were decisively disillusioned about their messiah ruling by military might from Jerusalem. Precisely by means of his mercenary army, however, David had the Israelite tribes under effective control.

Once Solomon won the power struggle for succession, he installed an unabashedly imperial monarchy. In the ancient Near East, a royal temple was a necessity for a monarchy, providing grounding in the sacred cosmos and divine legitimation for political-economic domination. Solomon proceeded to have a temple built in Jerusalem, in which the ark of Israel was installed, with the understanding that now the king and Temple mediated between Yahweh and Israel (1 Kings 6–7). The Temple itself, not to mention Solomon's own palace, which was twice the size of the Temple and fortress cities throughout the realm, was a major building project requiring vast resources of wealth and labor. In a traditional agrarian society, the only source for either one was the people. Thus Solomon instituted both a taxation system to generate revenues to support the regime and to pay for building materials and expertise, and a system of forced labor to generate the manpower for his massive construction projects, with both headed by a newly established bureaucracy (1 Kings 4–5). All Israel was subjected to both tribute and forced labor. The impact, however, may have been most severe on the Galilean tribes. Faced with a serious "balance of payments" problem, Solomon resorted to ceding to Hiram, king of Tyre, "twenty cities in the land of Galilee" — along with their people, of course — in payment (1 Kings 9:10–14). The free peasantry had now become mere dispensable pawns subordinate to Solomon's grand scheme for the glorification of his imperial capital.

Given the sharp repression of resistance to the increasingly heavy hand of the monarchy under David and the Pharaoh-like demands for produce and labor by Solomon, it is not surprising that Israel rose in rebellion when Solomon died, with only Judah and Benjamin remaining under the Davidic monarchy (1 Kings 12). The principal issue was the forced labor imposed to build the Temple. "Israel" then came together under a more limited and conditional kingship. For two generations, at least, any attempt by the son of the previous king to establish a dynasty was met with a popular and/or military uprising, the first led by Baasha of the tribe of Issachar (1 Kings 15:27). When Ahab did manage to succeed his father Omri and consolidate power in a more grandiose monarchy, however, the prophetic bands led by Elijah and Elisha organized popular resistance and finally succeeded in touching off another military-led insurrection (1 Kings 17–19; 2 Kings 1–10). The popular resistance, however, could not sustain itself indefinitely, and by the eighth century all we hear are the voices of individual oracular prophets such as Hosea and Amos. That is, not only did the Israelites decisively reject the rule of monarchy and Temple in Jerusalem, but seemingly out of a continuing sense that political-economic power should only be conditional, they resisted attempts to consolidate monarchic power and particularly the combination of severe economic exploitation and foreign cultural impositions by Ahab.

Special note should be taken of the Elijah–Elisha events and traditions in several respects. Several of the principal stories in the Elijah–Elisha cycle (see esp. 1 Kings 18–19; 2 Kings 1–2; 9) provide windows onto organized and sustained popular resistance to oppressive rule and foreign cultural influences. The story in 1 Kings 18 in particular attests a vivid ideal of a free Israel (of twelve tribes) that could be revived, an ideal that could become the rallying symbol for more active resistance to oppressive rule. The stories of Elijah and Elisha suggest that they were moving widely through the different tribal areas performing healings and organizing (bands of prophets, *bene-nabi'im*). Although their own places of origin are Tishbe in Gilead and Abel-meholah in Manasseh, respectively, Elijah and Elisha moved through Galilee and beyond, as indicated in the stories (1 Kings 17; 2 Kings 4), suggesting that at least some places there would have been affected by and would remember their activities. Finally, their activities and their movement of resistance left a considerable *memory* in the tradition. Behind and within the material in the Deuteronomic history are cycles of popular stories, suggesting that if such material commands so much attention in the history sponsored by the rulers, it must have been an even more prominent memory in popular traditions.[11]

Anticipating subsequent developments, we should also note the differences between the Galilean tribes and those in the central hill country during the independent existence of the kingdom of Israel. Ephraim and Manasseh were always the most prominent tribes. The northern Israelite monarchy itself, moreover, was always located in the central hill country, at first primarily at Tirzah, then at the newly built capital of Samaria. Thus the Galilean tribes were always somewhat removed from and subordinate to political power centered in the functioning capital. Although cult centers were built at Dan in the far north as well as at Bethel, along the border with the kingdom of Judah, the most important holy places and/or symbolic political-religious centers of Israelite covenantal coherence were always in the south — at Shiloh, Gilgal, and especially Shechem. Partly because of its geographical characteristics, "the circle of the peoples" had always been an area of shifting political jurisdictions and influence. In fact, for a period during the second generation of the kingdom of Israel's existence, Ben Hadad, king of Damascus, had conquered and controlled "Ijon, Dan, Abel-beth-maacah, and all Chinneroth, with all the land of Naphtali" (1 Kings 15:16–21). In the experience of Israel as a political power, the Galilean tribes must have been somewhat peripheral. Subsequent history would exacerbate that.

The Separation and Isolation of Galilean Israelites

In the standard histories of ancient Israel, the fall of Samaria to the Assyrian empire in 722 (–720) is the decisive event at which point the independence of the kingdom came to an end. A far more decisive event for the history of the Israelite clans and tribes in Galilee was 733–732, when "King Tiglath-pileser of Assyria came and captured Ijon, Abel-beth-maacah, Janoah, Kedesh, Hazor, Gilead, and Galilee, all the land of Naphtali" (2 Kings 15:29). Tiglath-pileser's own inscription mentions the towns of Merom and Yiron in Upper Galilee and Hannathon, Kana, and Jotbah in Lower Galilee.[12]

How Tiglath-pileser's conquest of Galilee is interpreted, particularly the clause "and he carried the people captive to Assyria," is of crucial significance for understanding the subsequent history of Galilee. The key question is whether there was any continuity of the Israelite population into Persian, Hellenistic, and Roman times.

Arguments that Galilee was devastated and virtually its entire population deported have been revived recently on the basis of surface surveys of pottery at numerous sites in Lower Galilee.[13] The implications of this possibility are that after being almost completely depopulated under the Assyrians, Galilee was resettled largely by non-Israelites in Persian and Hellenistic times. The non-Israelite population would then supposedly have been Judaized in some way after the Hasmoneans took control of Galilee in 104 B.C.E. (see chapter 2).

Yet continuity of the Israelite population seems far more likely, despite the fragmentary evidence and the often inferential interpretation on which the hypothesis is based.[14] The Deuteronomic historians write that a decade later, in 722–721, "the king of Assyria captured Samaria [and] carried the Israelites away to Assyria" (2 Kings 17:6, 23).[15] Official Assyrian annals say somewhat the same thing, only about the treatment of Samaria in 732: "All its ["Omri-land's"] inhabitants and their possessions I led to Assyria" (*ANET* 284). Yet from context it is clear that this does not even mean all the inhabitants of the capital city, Samaria, for there were sufficient officers and military left to replace Pekah with Hoshea as king and to yield a sizable tribute to the Assyrians. It seems clear that when the Assyrians conquered Samaria and other capital cities in Syria-Palestine, they deported primarily the rulers, their principal officers, their artisans, and other royal servants and retainers (just as the Babylonians did in Jerusalem in 587–586; 2 Kings 24:13–17; cf. Jer. 52:28).

The Assyrian annals mention explicitly that from the thousands of prisoners deported (27,290 from Samaria) they integrated sizable contingents of professional chariot warriors or cavalry into the imperial armies (*ANET* 284–85).[16] Other Assyrian records, moreover, make clear that the Assyrian emperors had special interest in using the skilled dependents of conquered rulers for their own purposes: Aramaic-speaking scribes in the imperial bureaucracy, artisans and builders in restoration of temples, merchants in the expansion of international (imperial) trade, goldsmiths and other smiths in the decoration of palaces and temples.[17] It is possible that either regular peasants or "royal peasants" of conquered rulers were also deported to serve as imperial gardeners, vintners, and shepherds. The deportees from a given region, however, would appear to have been primarily the skilled scribes and artisans and military along with the ruling families and/or royal officers themselves. Thus, if as many as 13,520 prisoners were removed from Galilee by the Assyrians in 732, one would think first of the military and royal officers stationed there. The figures of 625 or 650 deportees from towns such as Hannathon, Yotba, Kana, Aruna, and Merom (*ANET* 283) would have included military or other royal officers, if those were fortified administrative centers, as well as peasants. The bulk of the Israelite population, however, that is, the vast majority of the peasantry, would have been left on the land. That a productive population was left is presupposed by the Assyrians creating a province with their own administrative officers to gather taxes and keep order in the area (as also mentioned in the official annals).[18]

Those whom the Assyrians deported from Galilee, moreover, may not even have been Israelite administrators and their dependents. Since early in the ninth century, the Syrian regime in Damascus had periodically invaded and controlled at least northern Galilee and other parts of Israel (1 Kings 15:17–21; 2 Kings 10:32–33; 13:3, 7, 22). At points the Israelite regime in Samaria was able to regain control of these territories (2 Kings 13:25; 14:25, 28). The account of the Assyrian conquest of Galilee in 733–732 (2 Kings 15:29), in addition to having a somewhat garbled list of which towns and territories were taken, does not indicate whether they were taken from the regime in Samaria or from that in Damascus. The least problematic reconstruction of the pertinent Assyrian inscriptions and of the events themselves indicates that Syria had already taken control of much of Israel's territory, including Galilee.[19] Thus "the people carried captive to Assyria" would have been Syrian officers and their dependents, not Israelites. And there is no reason to think that the Syrians any more than the Assyrians or Babylonians would have deported the Galilean villagers.[20]

Following the Assyrian conquest (assuming continuity of the Israelite population), the Israelites in Galilee had a history separate and different not only from the Judeans, but also from the Israelites in the central hill country. (The difference in subsequent historical experience would be all the more dramatic if there were no continuity of Israelite population and later Galileans were non-Israelite.)

First, for the next six centuries the imperial administrative arrangement was separate and often different for Galilee. Following their conquest, the Assyrians incorporated the area west of the Jordan and from the great plain north, including all Galilee, into a separate province of the empire administered from Megiddo, with the Trans-Jordan area and the coastal plain as the separate provinces of Gilead and Dor, respectively. This is the reference in Isaiah 9:1, in which the awareness of the legacy of tribal Israel is still vividly in mind: "In the former time he brought into contempt the land of Zebulun and the land of Naphtali, but in the latter time he will make glorious the way of the Sea, the land beyond the Jordan, Galilee of the nations." When the rest of the kingdom of Israel fell to Assyria in 722–720, it was apparently combined with the coastal plain as a separate province. For at least the next 400 years the successor empires, the Babylonian and the Persian, continued this provincial organization, with Galilee and Samaria under separate administration, and Judah becoming yet another separate administrative district of the great Satrapy "Beyond the River" (Euphrates). To provide support for the Phoenician cities needed in their sea war with the Greeks, the Persians may have transferred frontier villages from the administration of Megiddo to Tyre or Sidon, but there is no reason to suspect that Galilee would have come under Jerusalem or Samarian jurisdiction during the Persian period.[21]

Second, the Assyrian conquest would presumably have had less of an impact on the people of Galilee than on the Israelites under the continuing jurisdiction of Samaria, given the previous political structure and the arrangements imposed on the two districts, respectively. Ancient empires did not generally interfere directly in the culture of the subject people, except by deporting and resettling governing elites. The capital of the kingdom of (northern) Israel was Samaria, in the central hill country, there having been no dominant city in Galilee itself as the traditional center for a ruling elite. When the Assyrians conquered Samaria, they imposed a new, foreign ruling class on the area subject to that city (2 Kings 17:24). As the Deuteronomic historians complain, the resettling of foreign peoples in Samaria created a good deal of cultural-religious syncretism, including some alteration in social customs in that district. In Galilee, by contrast, the Assyrians apparently simply replaced the deported royal Israelite officers with Assyrian officers, with the administrative headquarters located at Megiddo, south of Galilee. This left the remaining Israelite village communities relatively free to conduct their local affairs according to indigenous customs, without much interference by a Galilean ruling class concerned to establish its own authority in the area.

A third difference emerged from a combination of previous history and Persian (and subsequent) imperial policy. The Persians, like the Hellenistic and Roman empires after them, ruled through native aristocracies, including previously existing kingships and priesthoods. In the case of Judah, they restored the ruling families that had been deported by the Babylonians when they conquered Jerusalem in 598 and 587. Similarly in Samaria, while its origins are even less clear, a client regime governed locally under the Persians.[22] Thus both Judah and Samaria were ruled by "native" aristocracies that claimed to be the traditional legitimate rulers of the land — whatever the majority of people thought. Since no such ruling group had ever existed in Galilee and none apparently emerged under the Persians, no such arrangement was made there. The area was simply administered by imperial officials in Megiddo.

This last difference became the basis for the different treatment of Galilee, in comparison with Judea and Samaria, by the Hellenistic empires that successively dominated Palestine after the conquest by Alexander the Great. Recognizing "the Jews" as an *ethnos*, a "people" or "nation" under their own hereditary rulers,[23] the Ptolemaic regime based in Egypt and the later Seleucid regime based in Antioch did not at first pursue an aggressive policy of Hellenization in Judea, including the establishment of Hellenistic cities. The initial treatment of Samaria became more complicated at the outset. Recent reconstructions of Samaritan history suggest that the capital city must have been punished for its resistance, and a Hellenistic city founded in its place. The "native" elite, however, must have resettled the ancient site of Shechem and established the temple on Mount Gerizim in order to claim the support of the inhabitants of the area.[24] For much of the Hellenistic period, therefore, Samaria must have had both a Hellenistic city-state and a native elite in the center of the country.

Developments were very different in Galilee. On the one hand, in the areas surrounding Galilee itself, the Hellenistic emperors founded several cities: Ptolemais (Acco) on the Mediterranean to the west and Scythopolis (Beth Shean) in the Great Plain to the south, and the cities in the Decapolis to the southeast. It is unlikely that these cities would have had a major impact on peoples in Galilee. There is no evidence that they had political-economic jurisdiction or control over any section of Galilee, which was presumably under Ptolemaic and later Seleucid imperial administration. Under the Hellenistic regimes, then, the Galileans were not governed by a native aristocracy on the one hand, and were not subjected to newly founded Hellenistic city-states on the other, although some Hellenistic cities were founded nearby. While the Ptolemaic regime was unusually rigorous in its economic exploitation of the subject territories and while other Hellenistic regimes founded cities in their territories, the Hellenistic empires were no different from other ancient empires in interfering little in local affairs of villages and towns.[25] It therefore seems safe to assume that local social-economic-religious life in Galilee was allowed to continue according to indigenous customs and traditions, presumably of Israelite provenance.

Jerusalem and Galilee after Solomon

After the decisive Israelite rejection of the imperial Davidic monarchy involving forced labor to build Solomon's Temple, there were three points historically at which Jerusalem might again have exerted some influence on life in Galilee. Yet it appears that Galilean historical experience continued to be separate and different from Judea and Jerusalem for many centuries after the Galilean and other northern Israelites asserted their independence of Jerusalem.

First, during the political vacuum in the wake of Assyrian decline in the late seventh century, the youthful king Josiah not only centralized political-economic-religious power in Judah, but reasserted Davidic rule in the north. At Bethel and elsewhere in "the cities of Samaria" he destroyed the "high places," defiled the altars, and slaughtered the priests (2 Kings 23:15–20). The question is whether such carnage would have evoked the appreciation and loyalty of ordinary people in the north because the cult centers were royal Samarian or Assyrian institutions economically burdensome to the peasant producers. Insofar as Josiah's policy in the north was the same as in Judah itself — to destroy local centers of loyalty in order to centralize power in the monarchy and Temple in Jerusalem — it seems much more likely that such actions would only have evoked popular resentment of Jerusalem. According to the Chronicler's history, after the fall of Samaria to Assyria, when the earlier reforming king Hezekiah of Judah "sent word to all Israel...through the country of Ephraim and Manasseh and as far as Zebulun" summoning the people to keep the passover in Jerusalem, the northerns simply "laughed [the couriers] to scorn and mocked them" — although a few "humbled themselves and came to Jerusalem" (2 Chron. 30:1–10). Josiah's "reform" apparently did reach into Galilee ("as far as Naphtali," 2 Chron. 34:6–7; "from Geba to Beer-sheba," 2 Kings 23:8; and control of the district of Megiddo, 2 Kings 23:29). Jerusalem's period of influence over the north was limited, however, twenty years at most. Not long after Josiah's death in 609, the Babylonians conquered Jerusalem twice, in 598 and 587. The second time they destroyed the Temple and took the ruling elite into exile in Babylon. The brief interlude of possible Jerusalem influence in Galilee under Josiah, then, would hardly seem to have laid the basis for any Galilean loyalty to Jerusalem as cultural and cultic center.

Second, the Persian restoration of the exiled ruling class in Jerusalem in the late sixth century might have offered an opportunity for it to gain influence outside its own district of Judah. Pursuant to its policy of restoring native ruling groups and renewing indigenous laws and customs, the Persian regime sponsored the rebuilding of the Temple in Jerusalem.[26] The earliest governors of Judah, such as Zerubbabel, were descendants of the Davidic dynasty. The restoration, however, was initially unsuccessful, resisted by both the governing elite in neighboring districts, such as the Samarians, and the ordinary Judeans who had remained on the land when the rulers were deported by the Babylonians. Even once the Temple was rebuilt, toward the end of the sixth century, there were power struggles between rival priestly groups, and struggles and shifting alliances between the most powerful priestly families in Jerusalem and powerful families in nearby areas, such as the Tobiads, based east of the Jordan. By repeated exertion of its own power through its representatives Ezra and Nehemiah, the Persian regime was eventually able to check the struggles between the most powerful priestly factions and to mitigate their exploitation of the peasantry.[27] Only toward the end of the fifth century, however, do our fragmentary archaeological and literary sources give evidence of a stable situation in Jerusalem, that is, only about a century before the conquest by Alexander the Great.[28]

Ezra and Nehemiah, the imperial "reformers," achieved stability in the ruling circles of Jerusalem, moreover, not simply by checking the self-interest of local officials and powerholders (a typical problem in widespread empires), but by drawing sharp lines of exclusiveness around the legitimate powerholders in Jerusalem, who were basically those who had returned from exile. Partly to block repeated alliances between the Jerusalem and neighboring elites, Nehemiah prohibited intermarriage with neighboring peoples, including not just the Samarians or Phoenician traders, but also "the people of the land" — the ordinary nonpriestly Judean people who were not descendants of those who had been among the former ruling groups restored to power by the Persians.[29] There thus seems to be little or no basis for imagining some sort of missionary program whereby Jerusalem priestly groups attempted to influence Israelites in the north. The Jerusalem priestly elite were too involved with their own power struggles and with their own self-definition. The emphasis on exclusiveness by Ezra and Nehemiah, which placed even the ordinary people of Judah in a position of secondary rights, hardly seems an appropriate basis on which to unify a wider range of Israelite peoples.

Third, a major difference between the historical experience of the descendants of former Israelites in Galilee and the Judeans of late second-temple times is that the former did not go through the traumatic crisis of the sudden attempt at forced Hellenization under the Seleucid emperor Antiochus IV Epiphanes (175–167 B.C.E.) and the successful popular revolt against both their own Hellenizing priestly aristocracy and the Seleucid armies (167–152). Galileans' experience of "Hellenism" would have been primarily of two sorts: Ptolemaic and then Seleucid administrators or their agents engaged in tax collection; and whatever influence filtered into the area from Scythopolis or Ptolemais. In neither case did Hellenism pose a direct or sudden threat to the traditional way of life. Judeans had been sheltered from direct Hellenistic cultural influence for some time because of the imperial regimes' toleration of their traditional way of life under the Temple and high priesthood. The sudden, officially sanctioned, and militarily enforced transformation of the traditional Judean polity led by some of their own priestly aristocracy proved an intensely traumatic experience for the Judeans, scribes, lower priests, and peasants alike. This trauma was the watershed from which flowed the resurgence of apocalyptic literature in Judea, such as Daniel.

This collective trauma also helps explain the intensity with which the Judeans eventually fought against the Seleucid troops in liberating themselves from imperial rule. The "Maccabean Revolt" was a highly unusual and unprecedented experience of a people mobilizing and organizing themselves to fight for their very lives. The revolt included an unusual bonding of the people across class (priests, scribes, peasants) and village lines. It left memories of having successfully resisted domestic and imperial oppression that could, along with the apocalyptic spirit, inspire subsequent resistance. Although there would likely have been considerable resentment against the Temple and high priesthood prior to the revolt, the experience of "liberating" and rededicating the Temple may well have established or renewed popular attachment to the Temple in Judea. The Maccabean Revolt also resulted in the appointment to the high priesthood of the Hasmoneans, heroes of the struggle against Seleucid rule with widespread popular following in Judea.

None of this, however, would have been experienced directly by the Galileans, who were removed in distance and had been under separate jurisdiction for centuries. Nor do we have evidence of anything in Galilee comparable to the Hellenizing reform carried out in Jerusalem or the sharp imperial repression of the traditional way of life there. We can only imagine that the Galilean descendants of former Israelites might have been sympathetic with other descendants of former Israelites in their bid for independence. With regard to the Hellenizing reform and the Maccabean Revolt, however, and with regard to the entire history of former Israelites in Palestine since Solomon's death, Galileans had experienced a separate and distinctive history.[30] That history had involved periodic assertion of independence of urban rulers, including several centuries earlier a sharp rejection of Jerusalem rulers and their temple.

A comparison of the different historical developments in Judea and Samaria under the Persian and Hellenistic empires with those in Galilee dramatically illustrates the respective situations at the end of the second century B.C.E. Temple and Torah, often taken as the key institutions of "Judaism," provide a telling focus for the comparison. As indicated in numerous passages of the Torah, Yahweh the God of Israel was worshipped at many specially sacred sites (as well as, presumably, in periodic local celebrations in ordinary villages) in the land of Israel throughout the monarchic period. It was primarily after the rebuilding of the Temple in Jerusalem that claims appear in (now biblical) Judean literature that the Jerusalem Temple is the only legitimate site for such worship. Thus service of the God of Israel in the central hill country ("Samaria") and Galilee was solidly established for centuries and continued into Persian and Hellenistic times quite apart from developments in Jerusalem. Nevertheless, while the second Temple and high priesthood gradually established a certain hegemony in Judea, and at least some people in the central hill country finally (late fourth century) rebuilt Shechem and established their own temple on Mount Gerizim,[31] no central city or temple (that we know of) was established by the indigenous people of Galilee.

Similarly, the Judean priesthood(s) and scribal elite compiled or wrote what came to be the Torah and other literature used to legitimate and guide affairs in the temple-community centered in Jerusalem and to claim primacy for Jerusalem as a center of Israelite traditions. The Samaritans, apparently in reaction to the destruction of their temple at Gerizim late in the second century B.C.E., formulated their own version of the Torah, or Pentateuch, that claimed primacy for Gerizim.[32] With no indigenous aristocracy or scribal elite corresponding to those in Jerusalem and Shechem, however, the Galileans did not develop any corresponding sacred literature so far as we know. On the other hand, we also have no evidence that either the Judean or the Samaritan sacred literatures were propagated in Galilee. It is highly likely, however, from what we know of agrarian societies under foreign rulers, that Israelite traditions continued to be cultivated independently in the popular oral traditions of Galilee.

Chapter 2

GALILEE UNDER
JERUSALEM RULE

❧

The law of the emperor stops at the hedge of the village.
— VIETNAMESE FOLK-SAYING

After many centuries during which it was not connected with Jerusalem, Galilee suddenly appears under Jerusalem rule in early Roman times. How did this change come about? Modern assumptions often obscure the historical relations between Galilee and Jerusalem in late second-temple times. Treatments of Galilee often focus primarily on religion. Scholars who view Galilee as already largely "Jewish" emphasize how it was finally reunited with its "cultural and cultic matrix."[1] Those who view Galilee as largely Gentile prior to Hasmonean rule interpret Josephus's report of the takeover as a "conversion" to Judaism, perhaps even a "forced conversion."

Earlier constructions of Hasmonean history as a religious crusade by the Maccabean armies abolishing idols in its territory and forcibly Judaizing neighboring peoples depends heavily on certain passages in 1 Maccabees. First Maccabees, however, was written with an archaizing ideology to legitimate the Hasmonean dynasty as the divinely favored latter-day deliverers of Israel.[2] Thus that ideology should not be imposed uncritically onto the events of Hasmonean expansion, certainly not onto events that happened after the writing of 1 Maccabees.[3] Furthermore, the concept of religious conversion may be an anachronism when applied to ancient Judean history, since in a traditional agrarian society there was no such thing as a religion, separate from the basic political-economic institutions, to which people could "convert."

Since religion was inseparable from the political-economic dimensions of life — the Temple stood at the apex of a temple-state, the High Priest was the head of state — we cannot adequately understand the Hasmonean takeover in Galilee and subsequent Jerusalem rule of the district without a comprehensive investigation that includes the political and even the military along with the religious dimensions.

The Rise and Expansion of the Hasmonean State

Prior to and immediately after the Maccabean Revolt, the community of Judeans governed by the Jerusalem temple-state, under the watchful eye of the Seleucid regime, extended no more than a day's walk in any direction from the Temple. The ethnically homogeneous population may not have exceeded 100,000. The Hasmonean leader of the revolt against Seleucid suppression of the Judean way of life, Judah the Maccabee ("The Hammer") was little more than a leader of popular guerrilla operations against the Seleucid imperial armies, and his brothers Jonathan and Simon were local officers of the Seleucid imperial administration. Two generations later, Simon's grandson Alexander Janneus was the most powerful head of state in the area. He and his successors ruled virtually all of Palestine, from Upper Galilee in the north to Idumea in the south, Perea and the Decapolis across the Jordan River in the east, and the whole Mediterranean coast except Ascalon in the west. The ethnically and culturally diverse population of nearly one million was ruled by a king/high priest who recruited an ethnically diverse administration from powerful families of the subject districts. The Hasmonean takeover of Galilee was part of a dramatic transformation whereby the Hasmoneans were able to consolidate political-economic-religious power in Judea as a result of the Maccabean Revolt against Seleucid imperial rule, and then to extend their rule over most of Palestine.

The rise and expansion of the Hasmonean state in Palestine should be understood in the context of the decline of Seleucid power in the region. As the imperial regime's military power and diplomatic influence in an area declined, principalities previously under imperial control competed for influence and domination in the area. This had happened in Palestine before. After the Amarna age, when Egyptian power subsided in the area and the small Canaanite kingships became locked in exhausting internecine warfare, the Israelite tribes asserted their initial independence as a people. In the late seventh century B.C.E., as Assyrian power declined, Josiah expanded Jerusalem's influence temporarily into Samaria and as far as Galilee. In the second century B.C.E. the military resources of the Seleucid regime based in Syria were stretched thin in response to several revolts by subject peoples. The imperial regime was further weakened by the struggles of rival claimants to power. That weakness, in turn, led ambitious local strongmen to expand their own regional power by playing one side against the other or by playing a Seleucid pretender against the increasing Roman influence in the eastern Mediterranean.[4]

The absence of a dominant imperial power in Syria-Palestine lasted for nearly a century, until the Romans took firm control of the area. Initially the Hasmoneans in Judea were only one of several rival regimes competing for influence. The Seleucid decline left an opening for a resurgence of

Nabatean (Arab) power to the east of Judea, and created a vacuum in which Zeno Cotylas and his son Theodorus, rulers of Philadelphia (Rabbat Ammon), could exert effective control of other cities of the Decapolis (Josephus, *Ant.* 13.235, 356, 393; *B.J.* 1.60, 86). To the north the Itureans were engaged in a similar expansion of power from their base in the mountains of Lebanon. In the latter part of the second century B.C.E. they extended their control over much of Galilee as well as Gaulanitis, Auranitis, and Batanea to the east.[5] In southern Palestine, the Hasmoneans steadily consolidated their control of Judea itself and then extended their rule to neighboring districts as well.

Only the visionaries who produced the fantastic dreams in Daniel and other apocalyptic literature would have imagined that organized resistance to the Seleucid imperial suppression of the traditional Judean way of life would eventually lead to Judean independence. It did so, however, in a way the more irenic sages (*maskilim*, Dan. 11:33) did not anticipate or approve. As leaders of resistance against the Seleucid forces, Judah, Jonathan, and Simon generated a widespread popular following in Judea as heroic defenders of the sacred Judean traditions (such as the biblical memories of the liberation and autonomy of the Judean people that dominate 1 Maccabees). After years of guerrilla warfare against Seleucid armies they also built up a sizable and experienced fighting force that other Judean factions as well as the imperial armies had to reckon with. When first Jonathan (in 152 B.C.E.) and then Simon (in 142 B.C.E.) obtained recognition by the Seleucid regime as high priest, the high priesthood and temple-state underwent a significant change. With the appointment of upstart military leaders instead of members of the aristocratic Zadokite Oniads, in whose family the office had been hereditary, the basis of high-priestly power shifted from sacred tradition to military force. As a high-ranking Seleucid imperial officer ("First Friend of the King"), whose military forces were desperately needed by the emperor, the Hasmonean high priest was in a position to play one rival Seleucid against another to expand Hasmonean-Judean power. The decree proclaimed to the great assembly of Judeans in 1 Macc. 14:28–49 (and inscribed on a stela erected in the Temple), which legitimated Simon as ruler (*hegemon*) and general (*strategos*) as well as high priest,[6] indicates that the Hasmoneans had risen to power on the basis of the military forces under their command and the wealth acquired from booty and territory taken. By means of this decree the Hasmoneans consolidated their power in Judea, both in the direction of temple affairs and in governing the country and maintaining its "security" by means of fortresses and garrisons. Significantly, the decree also forbade any opposition to the Hasmoneans. This consolidation of power in the hands of Simon amidst the wider context of Seleucid decline set the stage for Hasmonean expansion.[7]

The early Hasmoneans extended their control only to adjacent districts, perhaps primarily for strategic reasons. They placed garrisons of loyal

Judeans in fortresses such as Gezer and took control of key cities such as Joppa. In the first major territorial expansion, Jonathan brought the three districts of Samaria just to the north of Judea under his rule, not by force of arms but by skillfully playing one rival Seleucid faction against another, as already noted (1 Maccabees 9–11). Judean literature from the early Hasmonean period, such as fragments of the historian Eupolemus, express expansionist ideals in their reconstructions of ancient history, portraying David as having "led an army against the Idumeans and the Ammonites and Moabites and the Itureans and the Nabateans...and Phoenicia, whom he compelled to pay tribute to the Judeans" (in Eusebius, *Praep. Evan.* 9.30.3–5).[8] A principal motive of Hasmonean expansion may have been to establish Judean rule in the rest of Palestine as had the prototypical Judean king David.

Actual wars of conquest began under John Hyrcanus after 129 B.C.E., when the Seleucids could no longer effectively inhibit Hasmonean expansion. Hyrcanus appears to have taken the first major step in this direction when, with 3,000 talents of silver taken from the tomb of David, he hired foreign mercenaries, an unprecedented act, according to Josephus (*B.J.* 1.61; *Ant.* 13.249 — at least since the Jewish Persian governors such as Nehemiah; cf. Neh. 2:9). Josephus also reports that Hyrcanus amassed great wealth from his economic exploitation of Judea, thus building a secure fiscal basis for expansion of his rule into new territory (*Ant.* 13.273).[9] In addition to making attacks across the Jordan to the east, Hyrcanus captured Shechem, destroyed the Samaritan temple at Mount Gerizim, and, after the prolonged siege, utterly destroyed the city of Samaria (*B.J.* 1.61–63; *Ant.* 13.249, 254–56).[10] Judging from the severity of the devastation in both cases (*B.J.* 1.65; *Ant.* 13.281), it seems likely that Hyrcanus was attempting to eliminate any possible rival political-religious center of power in Samaria or Gerizim. The report that Hyrcanus enslaved the inhabitants of Samaria is credible, given the lack of reference to any "leading men" of Samaria being active in political affairs until well after the Roman-sponsored restoration of the city (*B.J.* 1.166, 213, 229, 302–3; *Ant.* 18:88–89; 20:118–36). Having destroyed the temple on Gerizim and the city of Samaria, Hyrcanus apparently intended to rule the whole district directly from Jerusalem. By taking Scythopolis and "laying waste the whole country south of Mt. Carmel," Hyrcanus extended his control in central Palestine up to the frontier of Galilee (*B.J.* 1.64–66; *Ant.* 13.275–81).

The Hasmoneans then expanded further north into Galilee as well as south into Idumea. According to Josephus's sequence of events, Hyrcanus brought Idumea under Hasmonean rule after destroying the Samaritan temple at Mount Gerizim but prior to conquering Samaria, Scythopolis, and the Great Plain (*B.J.* 1.63; *Ant.* 13.257–58). Hyrcanus's son Aristobulus extended Hasmonean rule into Galilee in 104 B.C.E., defeating the Itureans who had taken control when the Seleucid regime could no longer dominate the area. Finally, another of Hyrcanus's sons, Alexander Janneus (103–76 B.C.E.), in extensive military campaigns subjected several nearby Hellenistic cities, so that the area ruled by the Hasmonean regime was virtually the same as that under Solomon's rule centuries earlier.[11] It seems likely that in extending their rule over additional territories (as in their Greek names and titles, such as "the Philhellene"), Aristobulus and Alexander Janneus were imitating the pattern of Hellenistic kings — as well as the Judean prototype of the Davidic or Solomonic kingdom. A central feature of Hellenistic kingship was "to reign over as much territory as possible and to subjugate other peoples."[12] Some of the primary concerns of Judean literature of the Hasmonean period were the justification of the Hasmonean conquests and debates about what should be done with the subject peoples.[13]

The Hasmonean-Judean state that ruled Galilee after 104 B.C.E. was thus much larger and more powerful than the tiny temple-state in the immediate environs of Jerusalem under the Persian and Hellenistic empires. When the Romans re-established imperial domination, they "liberated" most of the Hellenistic cities from Hasmonean-Judean rule. Yet the decrees of Caesar and the Roman Senate (cited by Josephus) confirming Hyrcanus II and his descendants in "the powers and privileges enjoyed by their forefathers" clearly indicate the political-economic power the Hasmoneans had built up in Palestine.[14]

> It is my wish that Hyrcanus, son of Alexander, and his children shall be Ethnarchs of the Judeans and shall hold the office of High Priests of the Judeans for all time in accordance with their ancestral customs [194]; ... and whatever high-priestly rights or other [pecuniary] privileges exist in accordance with their laws, these he and his children shall possess by my command [195]. ... That his children shall rule over the Judean nation and enjoy the fruits of the places given them [196]. ... That both Hyrcanus and his sons shall be High Priest and priests of Jerusalem and of their nation with the same rights and under the same regulations [nomima] as those under which their forefathers uninterruptedly held the office of priest [199]. ... These men shall receive and fortify the city of Jerusalem [200]. ... That [the Judeans] in the second year shall pay the tribute at Sidon, consisting of one fourth of the produce sown, and in addition, they shall also pay tithes to Hyrcanus and his sons, just as they paid to their forefathers [203]. ... For the city of Joppa, Hyrcanus and his sons shall pay tribute, collected from those who inhabit the territory [206]. ... As for the villages in the Great Plain, which Hyrcanus and his forefathers before him possessed, it is the pleasure of the Senate that Hyrcanus and the Judeans shall retain them with the same rights as they formerly had. Also the ancient rights which the Judeans and the High Priests and the priests had in relation to each other should continue, and also the (pecuniary) privileges which they received by vote of the people and the Senate. As for the places, lands [chōras], and farms, the fruits of which the kings of Syria and Phoenicia, as allies of the Romans, were permitted to en-

joy by their gift, these the Senate decrees that the ethnarch Hyrcanus and the Judeans shall have [207–9]. (*Ant.* 14.194–95, 196, 199, 200, 203, 205–9)

The traditional "rights and privileges" that the Romans confirmed to the Hasmonean regime were those of rule over and taxation of the people under their jurisdiction. To the Romans and to Hellenistic authors generally, "Judea" and "the Judeans" referred to the whole area of Palestine headed by the Judean temple-state.[15] The reference to the Great Plain makes clear that the Hasmonean dynasty was here confirmed in control of its wider territory, which (once the previously conquered Hellenistic cities were restored to independence by Rome) still included the districts of Idumea, Perea, Samaria, and Galilee, as well as Judea proper. However vague the phrase "Hyrcanus and the Judeans" (in 14.207 and 209) may seem, it is clear from these decrees that the people in the different districts of Palestine were politically-economically-religiously subject to the Hasmonean regime. Specially relevant to the relation between Hasmonean regime and Galileans are the three references to "their own/ancestral laws (or customs or regulations)": they are understood as legitimating and defining the "rights and [economic] privileges" of the high-priestly rulers of the Judeans (14.194, 195, 199).

Concerning Conquest, Conversion, and Cultural Identity

Not until the Hasmonean expansion was Galilee, along with other districts of Palestine, referred to as part of "Judea."[16] How Galilee became linked again with Jerusalem and Judea is a crucial question for the subsequent history of Galilee as the context of Jesus' ministry and the context in which rabbinic Judaism took root in late antiquity.[17] On this question where so much is at stake, however, our sources are fragmentary and even cryptic. Precisely when evidence is limited, moreover, historical reconstructions rely more heavily than usual on modern interpreters' assumptions and interests. Historical inquiry and reconstruction must therefore include a critical review of modern concepts as well as the limited evidence for this crucial transition in Galilee.

Much of the disagreement about what happened when the Hasmoneans took over Galilee has focused on two major issues. First, how the incorporation of Galilee under the Hasmonean state is understood depends on the cultural background of the Galileans and their previous relations with Jerusalem and Judea. Two alternatives have dominated debate: (a) the inhabitants of Galilee had become predominantly Gentile/pagan after the Assyrians (supposedly) deported the Israelite population; or (b) Galilee had become heavily, even predominantly Jewish over the centuries prior to the Hasmonean annexation. As discussed in chapter 1, however, a more precise social-political analysis leads to a more precise alternative, that is, that during second-temple times most inhabitants of Galilee were descendants of the northern Israelite peasantry. The second issue, usually based on the assumption that the Galileans were largely Gentile/pagan, is whether the Hasmonean takeover in Galilee involved a military conquest and/or a religious conversion (and whether the conversion was voluntary or forced). The concepts of conquest and conversion, however, may not be appropriate to the Galileans under the Hasmonean regime.

Who Were the Galileans in Second-Temple Times?

The competing views of who the Galileans were in second-temple times prior to Hasmonean expansion are based on problematic texts, even on different readings of the same key texts.[18] Some read the report in 1 Macc. 5:21–23 to mean that Galilee was already Jewish, while others cite it as evidence that only a few thousand Jews lived in the southwestern corner of Galilee near Ptolemais at the outset of the Maccabean Revolt, the rest of Galilee presumably having been Gentile/pagan. The account in 1 Macc. 5:21–23 of Simon's military mission to rescue "brothers" under attack in western Galilee, however, cannot be taken at face value.[19] The parallel sequence of places named indicates that 1 Maccabees 5 and 2 Maccabees 10–12 follow a common source.[20] But Simon's expedition to Galilee is missing in 2 Maccabees and the brief account in 1 Macc. 5:21–23 is lacking in detail characteristic of 1 Maccabees generally and duplicates motifs from Judas's mission to Gilead in the immediately following paragraphs. Thus the account in 1 Macc. 5:21–23 has long since aroused skepticism about its historical veracity.

Several of the other texts adduced in support of the view that Galilee was "Jewish" in Hellenistic times and even supportive of the Hasmoneans are similarly problematic.[21] For example, the report in 1 Macc. 9:2 of the Seleucid general Bacchides marching into Judea via the road to *Galgala*, encamping at (the untranslatable) *maisaloth tên en 'arbelois* and capturing it, is often read as indicating that Galileans or Galilean Jews fought against Bacchides in support of their Judean compatriots.[22] Only by reading this passage through Josephus's paraphrase of it in *Ant.* 12.421, however, can it be taken as a reference to Galilee.[23] A more critical explanation of this problematic passage is that after Bacchides came into Judea he camped not "at Arbela in Galilee," but at the "ascents" (*mesiloth* in Hebrew) in "the hill country of Beth-el" (*har-beth-el* in Hebrew; cf. 1 Sam. 13:2; Josh. 16:1), just to the north of Jerusalem, precisely where he was headed to confront Judas.[24]

The key text pertaining to the identity of the Galileans (as well as to the question of their conquest or conversion) is Josephus's brief account of the Hasmonean takeover.

In his reign of one year, with the title of "Philhellene," [Aristobulus] made war on the Itureans and acquired a good deal of their territory for Judaea and compelled the inhabitants, if they wished to remain in the country, to be circumcised and to live in accordance with the laws of the Judeans.... Strabo also testifies on the authority of Timagenes,"...He acquired additional territory [*chōra*] for [the Judeans] and brought over to them a portion of the Iturean nation." (*Ant.* 13.318–19)

The "territory acquired for Judea" must have been (part of) Galilee.[25] Hyrcanus's conquests had reached as far as Samaria and Scythopolis, right to the frontier of Galilee. Except for Gaulanitis, which was secured by Aristobulus's brother and successor Alexander Janneus, all other territories controlled by the Itureans were still intact well over a half-century later when the Romans finally assigned Batanea, Auranitis, and Trachonitis, as well as Ulatha and Panaeas, to Herod (*Ant.* 15.342–64). The sudden appearance of numerous coins of Alexander Janneus in the Hellenistic stratum at the village of Meiron confirms that Hasmonean rule became effective in Upper Galilee with his reign.[26] If we take Timagenes at face value and/or do not differentiate between the Itureans and "the inhabitants" of the country, then the Itureans must have comprised a substantial portion of the population when Galilee was taken over by Aristobulus.[27]

A third reading of this account by Josephus makes more sense historically. Sources for the Itureans suggest that they were based further north, in Lebanon, and that, while they had moved into control of Galilee after the decline of Seleucid power, in the area they had not settled there.[28] Thus Josephus's own account can be read as a clarification of his source(s), Strabo-Timagenes. Writing as an outside observer, Timagenes had assumed that Galilee was Iturean because it was ruled (at least for a time) by the Itureans (just as the Romans later considered Galilee as part of Judea because it was ruled from Jerusalem). Josephus's "correction" distinguishes between "the inhabitants...in the land" (*chōra*) and their previous rulers, "the Itureans," on whom Aristobulus made war and from whom he wrested territory for Judea. The contrast with Josephus's earlier account of Hyrcanus's conquest of Idumea is instructive. There Hyrcanus had "subdued the Idumeans" and "permitted them to remain in their country" (*Ant.* 13.257). In Galilee, on the other hand, the inhabitants were different from their Iturean rulers when the Hasmoneans took control.

Who were those inhabitants of Galilee in second-temple times? Unless new evidence surfaces, we cannot know for certain. Given the long history of domination by various empires, the population was most likely mixed to some degree. The texts previously cited in support of arguments that the inhabitants were mostly Jewish/Judean do not stand up to critical scrutiny. Yet no positive evidence has been produced that Galilee was inhabited largely by Gentiles/pagans prior to Roman times. If, on the other hand, we assume some continuity of the population since Assyrian times, then an appreciable portion of the Galileans must have been descendants of northern Israelites, since the Assyrians had apparently deported only the administrative officers (see chapter 1).[29]

Were the Galileans Conquered and/or Converted?

Whether the Galileans were conquered and/or underwent a (forced or voluntary) conversion focuses on the same Josephan account of the Hasmonean takeover of Galilee. This question, however, proves inappropriate to the situation when we probe the ancient political-economic-religious relations involved.

A comparison with the Hasmonean takeover of Idumea, a somewhat analogous situation for which we have more evidence, may be instructive. The two principal accounts from Josephus are:

> Hyrcanus also captured the Idumean cities of Adora and Marisa and, after subduing all the Idumeans, permitted them to remain in their country so long as they had themselves circumcised and were willing to observe the laws of the Judeans [tois ioudaiōn nomois]. And so, out of attachment to the land of their fathers, they submitted to circumcision and to making their manner of life conform in all other respects to that of the Judeans. And from that time on they have continued to be Judeans. (Ant. 13.257–58; cf. B.J. 1.63)

> Now Hyrcanus had altered their form of government [politeia] and made them adopt the customs and laws of the Judeans [ta ioudaiōn ethē kai nomima]. (Ant. 15.254)

Two non-Josephan fragments supply comparisons on the Idumeans:

> Judeans are those who are so naturally by origin. The Idumeans, on the other hand, were not originally Judeans, but Phoenicians and Syrians, having been subjugated by the Judeans and having been forced to undergo circumcision, so as to be counted among the nation [ethnos] and keep the same customs, they were called Judeans. (Ptolemy the Historian)[30]

> The Idumeans are Nabateans, but owing to a sedition they were banished from there, joined the Judeans and shared in the same customs with them. (Strabo, Geogr. 15.2.34)

Critical examination and comparison of the accounts by Josephus (B.J. 1.63; Ant. 13.257–58) and Ptolemy the Historian leave no reason to doubt that Hyrcanus conquered Idumea by military action. Josephus's principal accounts about John Hyrcanus's treatment of the Idumeans follow in sequence his summary reports of Hyrcanus's military expeditions against cities and their territories across the Jordan to the east and his conquests and destruction of Shechem and Gerizim to the north. The marked increase in the numbers of Idumeans mentioned in Egyptian papyri in the late second century B.C.E. may well be correlated with displacement and flight in the wake of Hyrcanus's attacks.[31] Less clear is whether the Book of Jubilees (esp. chaps. 36–38) corroborates Hyrcanus's military conquest of the Idumeans.[32]

Galilee also was taken by military conquest. As Seleucid control of the area weakened, the Itureans extended their sway over northern Palestine, while the Hasmoneans expanded their rule northwards from Judea into Samaria and the Great Plain. In appropriating additional territory for Judea, Aristobulus "made war on the Itureans," who had only recently taken control of Galilee. Even after the Itureans were pushed back, Aristobulus's successor Alexander Janneus engaged in a continuing three-way struggle for control of the area with Cleopatra of Egypt and her renegade son Ptolemy Lathyrus based in Cyprus.[33] In contrast to the Idumeans, however, the Galileans themselves were not defeated by the Hasmoneans' Judean or mercenary armies. Rival regional rulers engaged in military battles in Galilee. The Galileans themselves were not subject to military attack; rather, control over them was the objective of the regimes competing for dominance of the area.

This struggle between rival regional rulers for control of Palestine provides the concrete political-economic context in which we can consider whether the concept of religious conversion (forced or voluntary) is appropriate to the historiographic accounts and the likely treatment of the Galileans by the Hasmonean regime. Again the key text often interpreted in terms of religious conversion is Josephus's report that the "Philhellene" Hasmonean king Aristobulus, after acquiring a good deal of the Itureans' territory for Judea, "compelled the inhabitants, if they wished to remain in their country, to be circumcised and to live in accordance with the laws of the Judeans" (*Ant.* 13.318–19).

The standard concept of religious conversion would appear inappropriate to cases that involve a shift in the political-religious status of a whole people. Religious "conversion" ordinarily assumes religion as separate from political-economic life and implies a deep sense of change in the religious convictions of an individual.[34] A recent proposal for broadening the concept of conversion so that it includes "practice of the Jewish laws, exclusive devotion to the God of the Jews, and integration into the Jewish community," while based primarily on diaspora materials, may enhance the interpretive possibilities of "conversion" for the Galileans and Idumeans under Hasmonean expansion.[35]

Again, comparison with the Hasmoneans' treatment of the Idumeans may illuminate their treatment of the Galileans. Recent interpretations of Hasmonean expansion into both Galilee and Idumea in terms of "conversion" to "Judaism," whether forced or voluntary, are based on a broadly synthetic combination of the sources. The intricate arguments for a gradual and "voluntary conversion," although sharply critical of Josephus's accounts, are nevertheless problematic and unconvincing.[36] One such argument contends that, while forced conversion usually means only a surface acquiescence in the new religion by "the converted," it was effective and lasting for the Idumeans insofar as "the Idumeans as a whole supported the Jews in their later wars with the Romans."[37] There are a number of indications, however, that regardless of whether it was voluntary or forced, the Idumeans' "conversion" was not especially effective.

Josephus himself gives several indications that the Idumeans did not in fact "conform their manner of life in all respects to that of the Judeans and from that time on continued to be Judeans" (*Ant.* 13.258). His brief reference to Hyrcanus's having altered the Idumeans' *politeia* (*Ant.* 15.254) is part of an account about how nearly a century later a prominent Idumean was still leading resistance to adoption of Judean customs.

> Costobar was an Idumean by race [*genei*] and was one of those first in rank among them, and his ancestors had been priests of Koze, whom the Idumeans believe to be (a) god. Now Hyrcanus had altered their polity and made them adopt the customs and laws of the Judeans. When Herod took over royal power, he appointed Costobar governor of Idumea and Gaza, and gave him (in marriage) his sister Salome.... [But Costobar] did not think that it was proper for him to carry out the order of Herod, who was his ruler, or for the Idumeans to adopt the customs of the Judeans and be subject to them. (*Ant.* 15.253–55)

The "conversion" of the Idumeans cannot have been very complete. If a prominent figure such as Costobar, a high-ranking Herodian officer already assimilated into the world of Hellenistic power politics, was still surreptitiously loyal to Idumean traditions, then Idumean villagers were probably even more attached to their own ancestral Idumean customs.

As in the story about Costobar, so also in several other accounts Josephus refers to the inhabitants of Idumea as "Idumeans," that is, as different from "Judeans." At points he even refers to the Idumeans as a "people" or "nation" (*ethnos*) distinct from "Judeans" (e.g., *B.J.* 1.123, 4.231). In contrast to the rival Judean groups or parties engaged in the revolt against Rome, the Idumeans appear distinctive, with their own indigenous tribal structure: "a turbulent and disorderly people" (*ethnos*), whose multiple chieftains could muster large bands of fighting men "hastily from the countryside" (*B.J.* 4.228–35, 517–20). These matter-of-fact descriptions suggest that the Idumeans did not become integrated into the Judean temple-community and did not become *Ioudaioi* ethnically. Rather they remained a separate *ethnos* with their own traditional social structure.[38]

The claim that the Idumeans "supported the Jews in their later wars against the Romans" depends upon an oversimplified synthetic picture of "Judaism," "Jews," and the "wars against the Romans." Josephus's accounts of the protests and insurrections following Herod's death in 4 B.C.E. do not indicate any Idumean involvement.[39] The insurrections were rather popular outbursts of long pent-up resentment of Herodian tyranny touched off by Archelaus's and the Romans' repressive measures. Josephus's accounts of the great revolt of 66–70 C.E. have limited numbers of Idumeans responding to calls for help from Judean peasant forces in Jerusalem to fight against the high priests who were attempting to negotiate terms with the Romans (*B.J.* 4.228–35, 326–33, 345–53, 517–26, 566–72; 6.378–81). The conflict in 66–70 was primarily between the high priests, Herodians, and their Roman backers on the one hand, and insurgents from the Judean populace on the other. Idumeans were involved primarily in attacks on their Jerusalem rulers, with a smaller number remaining in the only fortified city, Jerusalem, to face their imperial rulers' attempt at reconquest. While we can reasonably detect anti–high priest, anti-Herodian, and anti-Roman motives behind these events, they offer no indication of a previous religious conversion.[40] The limited evidence for Idumea under Hasmonean rule thus suggests that any supposed conversion of the Idumeans must have been ineffective. The Idumeans maintained active resistance to observance of Judean laws, continuing devotion to the Idumean god Koze, and practice of indigenous Idumean customs. Their integration into the Judean temple-community appears to have been minimal.

Josephus gives similar indications for Galilee. Although "the Judeans" is inclusive of people in Galilee in a few passages, Josephus ordinarily differentiates "the Galileans" from "the Judeans." Indeed, at points he even indicates that the Galileans were a separate *ethnos* from the Judeans (*B.J.* 2.510, 4.105). Galileans supposedly worshiped the same god as the Judeans. There are numerous indications, however (as we shall see in subsequent chapters), that distinctive Galileans traditions and customs continued long after the Hasmonean annexation. There would appear to be some question, therefore, about the degree of the Galileans' integration into the Judean temple-community as well.

Rather than debate the historical reality and effectiveness of conversion of the Idumeans and the Galileans, however, we should recognize that the concept itself, even in an expanded version, is not appropriate to Josephus's and others' accounts or to what happened when the Hasmoneans expanded their rule into Idumea and Galilee. If we think in concrete social-historical terms, of course, this is not surprising. In contrast to an individual or a family being integrated into a Jewish community in the diaspora, including observance of the Jewish law and exclusive devotion to the one God, the integration of the whole Idumean or Galilean people into Judean society would have required a major program of "re-socialization," if not massive social engineering. Clearly a concept of religious conversion does not adequately encompass all of the ethnic, cultural, and political-economic facets involved when a whole people or the inhabitants of a whole area are suddenly brought under the control of new rulers.

The Inclusion of Galilee in the Judean Temple-State:
Toward a More Comprehensive Approach

To understand what the extension of Hasmonean rule meant for life in Galilee, including the religious dimension, we must attend more fully to political-economic relations between the Hasmonean state and Galilee. As noted above, the Hasmoneans took over Galilee as one of the major steps in the extension of their rule over most of Palestine. In the decades after Aristobulus pushed the Itureans out of the area, Alexander Janneus reasserted Hasmonean control of Galilee and engaged in continuing wars of conquest, including areas on the frontiers of Galilee.

In order to defend the frontiers of their expanded kingdom as well as to maintain control over the Galilean populace, the Hasmoneans established garrisoned fortresses, both in the center and on the periphery of Galilee.[41] That Ptolemy Lathyrus failed to capture the town shortly after Alexander Janneus succeeded Aristobulus suggests that Sepphoris (probably the principal administrative town in Galilee) was already fortified and defended by Hasmonean troops (*Ant.* 13.338). The numerous coins of Alexander Janneus unearthed by archaeologists in the villages of Upper Galilee are further signs of the Hasmonean military presence along the frontier with Tyre and the Itureans.[42] The Hasmoneans thus must have established and maintained a half-dozen larger or smaller garrisoned fortresses around Galilee as part of their overall system of security and administration. That Aristobulus II, moving to oppose Hyrcanus II as the reigning king/high priest in 67 B.C.E., quickly gained control of twenty-two fortresses, not counting the major royal fortresses of Alexandrium, Hyrcania, Machaerus, and the Jerusalem citadel (*Ant.* 13.416–29), suggests that the Hasmonean regime had upwards of thirty fortresses that they used to control and administer the various districts of their realm as well as to protect against attack along the frontiers.[43]

The Hasmoneans also must have placed their own trusted officers (Alexander Janneus's "friends," *Ant.* 13.422) in charge of the fortress towns and administrative centers such as Sepphoris. How the Hasmoneans governed Galilee may become clearer by comparison, again, with how they dealt with Idumea. According to Josephus, Herod got his start in the political affairs of Palestine under his father Antipater, scion of a powerful Idumean family and the skillful and trusted minister of Hyrcanus II. Less known is that Antipater's father Antipas had been appointed military governor (*strategos*) of all Idumea by Alexander Janneus. Such men were not only "Idumean by birth [*genos*]," but "in the front rank of the people [*ethnos*] by ancestry, wealth, and other advantages" (*Ant.* 14.10; *B.J.* 1.123). Once the Idumean Herod had become the Romans' client-king in Judea, moreover, he in turn appointed Costobar, head of another powerful, aristocratic Idumean family, as the governor of Idumea and gave him his sister in marriage (*Ant.*

15.253–54). In short, the Hasmonean rulers in Jerusalem made political alliances with powerful Idumean families. Insofar as Idumean society still retained its traditional tribal structure (see above), the rest of the Idumean people could be expected to follow the lead, or be subject to the power, of the most prominent families.

Galilee, however, had no indigenous aristocracy. The area had apparently been administered (land and livestock registered and produce collected as taxes) through imperial officers stationed as far away as Alexandria and their agents closer to the scene in Acco-Ptolemais, or Sepphoris, or other fortresses maintained by imperial regimes such the Ptolemies.[44] The establishment of Hasmonean rule in Galilee would thus have meant the imposition of a Judean-Hasmonean aristocracy.[45] Most of the Hasmonean officers placed in Galilee would probably have been Judeans, trusted officers receiving choice assignments as rewards for faithful service. It is also possible, since one-third to one-half of the Hasmonean armies under Alexander Janneus were mercenaries (*B.J.* 1.93; *Ant.* 13.377) and Alexander became embroiled in sharp conflict with influential circles in Judea/Jerusalem, that he may have deployed non-Judean officers there as well.[46]

That the Hasmonean regime governed Galilee and other areas over which they had extended their rule provides a connection in which the specific language of Josephus's accounts of Hasmonean takeover of Galilee and Idumea can be more adequately understood. In both cases the inhabitants, writes Josephus, were required to live "according to the laws of the Judeans." Josephus generally uses "the laws (or customs) of the Judeans" in a comprehensive sense, for traditional regulations of all aspects of social life (political-economic-religious).[47] Reading sources such as Josephus and the history of ancient Judea generally in terms of the modern Western separation of politics and religion may have led to misunderstanding in this regard. The relationship between the Persian or Seleucid imperial regime and the temple-state at the head of the Judean temple-community was by no means analogous to a separation of church and state. The temple-state carried out political-economic functions inseparable from its religious functions. When the Seleucid emperor Antiochus III granted a "charter" to the Judean *ethnos* and the temple/high-priestly government early in the second century B.C.E., he was following earlier Persian imperial policy:[48] "All members of the nation shall be governed [*politeiesthosan*] in accordance with the ancestral laws [*kata tous patrious nomous*]" (*Ant.* 12.142; cf. Ezra 7:14). Since at least Persian times political-economic-religious-cultic affairs in Judea had proceeded according to the traditional laws of the Judeans under imperial acknowledgment and legitimation. In Hellenistic culture the ancestral laws of the Judeans or the laws of Moses were understood as laying out the *politeia*, the constitution or government of the Judean temple-state, as evident in the account by Hecataeus around 300 B.C.E.[49] If the account in *Ant.* 15.254 was our only source, we would conclude that Hyrcanus was forcing a change in their form of government (*politeia*) on the Idumeans. Probably we should read the initial account, *Ant.* 13.257, couched in terms of the Idumeans "observing the laws of the Judeans" in somewhat the same sense.

As noted above in connection with Caesar's decrees confirming the Hasmonean rule in Palestine, "the laws (or customs) of the Judeans" pertain to "the rights and privileges" of the Hasmoneans, that is, they define political-economic-religious relations between the Hasmonean rulers and their subjects. Josephus's references to the Galileans' subjection to "the laws of the Judeans" by Aristobulus should be read in the same sense. It meant political-economic-religious subordination to the Hasmonean high priesthood in Jerusalem.

Josephus confirms this interpretation in a passage that can only be understood as an intentional and highly significant expansion on his source 1 Maccabees (and not simply a piece of sloppy historiography). Whereas 1 Maccabees (10:29–30, 38) cites a decree by the Seleucid Demetrius I, rejected by the Hasmonean Jonathan, remitting taxes and adding three districts from the province of Samaria (and Galilee), Josephus has Jonathan accept the decree that "three toparchies be attached to Judea, [namely] Samaria and Galilee and Perea" (*Ant.* 13.49–50). The effect, then, is to transform what was originally a subordination of three small districts in Samaria to the Jerusalem high priests (1 Macc. 10:38) into a legitimation of subsequent Hasmonean expansion:

> I also permit them [the Judeans] to use the ancestral laws and observe them, and wish that those in the three nomes being attached to Judaea be subject [to these laws] and that this [vis., the imposition of the law] be the responsibility of the high priest, so that not a single *Ioudaios* have any temple to revere other than the one in Jerusalem. (*Ant.* 13.54)[50]

Subjection of the Galileans and others to "the laws of the Judeans" meant, in effect, subordination to the Hasmonean temple-state in a political-economic way inseparable from its religious dimension.

The otherwise puzzling requirement that the Galileans and the Idumeans undergo circumcision as a prerequisite to remaining in their land can also be more adequately understood in a more comprehensive political-economic way. Presumably both Idumeans and Galileans (whether they were descendants of Israelites or Itureans) already practiced circumcision.[51] Insofar as circumcision was a sign of membership in the Jewish/Judean covenant community (cf. *Barn.* 9:6),[52] then the Hasmonean requirement for peoples newly incorporated into the Judean temple-community to be (re-)circumcised is comprehensible as a sign of being joined to the "body-politic."[53]

This move by the Hasmoneans to require the peoples of annexed territory to live "according to the laws of the Judeans and be circumcised" would appear to be unprecedented in Judean (biblical) history and unwarranted in "the laws of the Judeans" as known from the Torah. On the other hand, insofar as the Hasmoneans, drawing on Davidic-Solomonic precedents, viewed these territories as properly subject to Jerusalem rule, then it would have seemed only appropriate to bring the inhabitants under the ancestral laws of the temple-state. It is also possible that the Hasmoneans were adapting a standard practice of the Hellenistic empires. Whereas the Persian imperial regime had sponsored the codification of indigenous people's or temple-state's laws, as in fifth-century B.C.E. Judea, the Ptolemies and Seleucids sponsored, and under Antiochus Epiphanes forced, the abandonment of the ancestral laws or polity in favor of one modeled on Greek patterns. Ironically, the second- and third-generation Hasmoneans, descendants of the leaders of the popular rebellion to restore the ancestral laws against Antiochus IV Epiphanes' attempt to abolish the ancestral *politeia* (see 1 Macc. 2:19; 3:29; 6:59; 2 Macc. 4:11; 6:1; 8:17; 11:25), were now requiring peoples of subjected areas to accept new laws, the laws of the Judeans.

Additional related facets of the Judean-Hasmonean takeover in Idumea and Galilee may be imagined on the basis of some cross-cultural comparisons.[54] In the early eighteenth century the Ashanti kingdom extended its rule over both the related Akan peoples and the non-Akan peoples in West Africa (modern Ghana). Included in their rule of the conquered peoples was a conscious policy of acculturation. However, they politically incorporated primarily the peoples with whom they shared a "kinship" and some common customs. They used the kinship and common traditions as political propaganda to unite local peoples against European domination as well as to legitimate their own rule.[55] Because of their segmentary social system, the Ashanti even integrated some of the subject peoples into their lineage system by manipulating ancestral traditions. The Nuer effected a similar incorporation or integration of much of the neighboring Dinka people — thus explaining more satisfactorily the decline in Dinka population, originally thought to be due to war casualties, and the increase in Nuer population, originally thought to be a cause of the conquest instead of the result.

Neither the Idumeans nor the Galileans (nor the Itureans) would appear to have been integrated into the Judean *ethnos*, which was presumably not a segmentary social system. As noted above, Josephus repeatedly refers to both as separate from the Judeans, indeed as forming separate *ethnoi*, and indicates that the Idumeans at least retained their own tribal social structure. Kinship and shared traditions, however, would appear to have been factors in the incorporation of both Idumeans and Galileans under the Hasmonean-Judean temple-state, at least from the Judean side. Both the Arabs and the Idumeans (Edomites) were believed to have descended from Abraham, the former through Ishmael, the latter through Esau. The Book of Jubilees provides a window onto the common background that Judean intellectuals may have believed they shared with the Idumeans.[56] Jubilees offers reassurance of Rebecca's maternal love and Jacob's and Esau's fraternal love (chap. 35) on the one hand, while — contrary to biblical (Torah) narratives — having Jacob alone receive the blessing, from Abraham as well as Isaac, while Esau receives only a curse (chaps. 20, 26; 36:12–20), on the other. After the sons of Jacob finally defeat the sons of Esau, "they made peace with them and placed a yoke of servitude upon them so that they might pay tribute to Jacob and his sons always... and the children of Edom have not ceased from the yoke of servitude... until today" (38:10–14). Clearly this construction of the history of origins in Jubilees could have served as a legitimation of Judean domination for Judean readers. Yet it is conceivable that an appeal to common ancestry and fraternal relations may have been constructed for Idumean consumption as well. We can only imagine what the Idumean construction of the common genealogy may have been. Presumably similar appeals to common ancestry and traditions would have been used both to legitimate Hasmonean rule and to emphasize shared cultural traditions with the Galileans, who were simply brought under Hasmonean rule, and not conquered, as were the Idumeans. It is also possible that many Galilean and Idumean villagers may have found common ground, rooted in such shared traditions, with Judeans and their Hasmonean high priests as effective opponents of and alternatives to their previous Hellenistic imperial rulers.

The situation of the Galileans required to live according to the laws of the Judeans would have depended to a considerable degree on their cultural background. If, like the Idumeans, they were of non-Israelite background, then their indigenous traditions and customs would have differed substantially from those of the Judeans and the Hasmonean state. If, on the other hand, most Galileans were of Israelite background, they would supposedly have worshipped the same God of Israel and shared certain Israelite traditions with the Judeans and the Jerusalem temple-state. As descendants of northern Israelite tribes the inhabitants of Galilee would have shared with the Judean temple-state traditions such as the exodus story, the Mosaic covenant (including the sabbath), stories of independent early Israel prior to the Solomonic monarchy and its temple, and certain traditions akin to some of those subsumed in the Judean Torah and early sections of the Deuteronomic history (including circumcision, ancestor legends, victory songs). Even traditions stemming originally from northern Israelite history, such as the Song of Deborah or the Elijah–Elisha story-cycle, would have been shared with Jerusalem insofar as they had been adapted for use in the Deuteronomic history.

Nevertheless, even as descendants of Israelites, the Galileans would have found "the laws of the Judeans" different from their own indigenous customs and traditions. Although Galilean customs were rooted in some of the same Israelite traditions as the laws of the Judeans, they had under-gone more than eight centuries of separate development. In addition to their own distinctive local customs and traditions, the Galileans would have held very different understandings of some of the shared traditions, such as the Elijah–Elisha stories. Moreover, "the laws of the Judeans" were pre-sumably the official Jerusalem traditions shaped according to priestly and scribal interests under the Judean temple-state, whereas the Galilean cus-toms would have been popular traditions. As noted above, "the laws of the Judeans" were the official laws defining and legitimating the polity of the Judean temple-state. The Temple itself, temple dues, and rule by the high priesthood would all have been foreign to the Galileans, whose ancestors had rebelled centuries earlier against the Solomonic monarchy and Temple. Thus the Galileans, like the Idumeans, would have experienced the laws of the Judeans superimposed on their own customs as the means to define and legitimate their subordination to Jerusalem rule.

Their shared roots in Israelite traditions provided a basis for the incor-poration of Galileans under the Judean temple-state, with varying degrees of change or friction depending on variations in the local village customs. Yet centuries of separate historical experience, divergent development of traditions, and different social locations meant that a distinctively Gali-lean social life would have continued under Hasmonean rule. As in Idumea, so in Galilee, the existing social forms and customs would have remained in place. Local family and communal affairs would have been conducted according to the Galileans' own customs and traditions. The Galileans' living "according to the laws of the Judeans," probably pertained primar-ily to their political-economic-religious relations with the temple-state in Jerusalem.

It would be unrealistic to imagine that the extension of Hasmonean rule over Galilee resulted in a sudden or thorough conformation of social life in Galilee to "the laws and customs of the Judeans." For the Galileans either to have conformed their local communal affairs to Judean laws, of-ficial or unofficial, or to have become well integrated into the Jerusalem temple-community as the Judeans had over many centuries, would have required an intense program of social engineering. Agents of "secondary socialization" or "re-socialization" would have had to intervene across the fundamental class and regional division between the Jerusalem temple-state and local village community. For that to have happened, the officers or re-tainers of the Hasmonean government (under command or on their own authority) would have had to undertake a program of resocialization of the Galileans into the Judean laws as well as a detailed application of the Judean laws to local community life. Josephus portrays the Pharisees as having exercised a function of promulgating "regulations" (*nomima*) for the Judean people under John Hyrcanus and again under Alexandra Salome. Thus the degree to which Galileans would have assimilated Judean laws and customs and become integrated into the temple-community would have depended on the amount of attention from the Hasmonean rulers and/or the amount of active intervention in village affairs by the legal-scribal retainers of the Hasmonean regime such as the Pharisees or other scribal groups. Evidence of the survival of tribal social structure in Idumea and the case of Costobar indicate that the Hasmoneans did not mount such a program in Idumea. A survey of the subsequent history of the Hasmonean regime and its governing activities suggests that little such effort could have been made in Galilee.

From Hasmonean Rule to Roman Conquest

While the Hasmoneans continued to govern Galilee "in accordance with the laws of the Judeans," efforts to press the Galilean villagers to assimilate Judean laws and customs must have been slow and sporadic during the forty years prior to the Roman takeover in 63 B.C.E. Certainly little by way of instruction in the Judean laws and cultivation of loyalty to the Temple could have been accomplished during the chaotic reign of Alexander Janneus (103–76 B.C.E.), immediately following the takeover of Galilee. He continued the policy of requiring (at least some) subjected people "to adopt the ancestral customs of the Judeans" (*Ant.* 13.397). But whatever energies Alexander did not exhaust in new military conquests must have been devoted to the extensive resistance he evoked among his own people, particularly from the scribal or "retainer" class through which his regime would supposedly have governed the populace. Josephus's reports of the virtual civil war raging in Jerusalem and Judea suggest that Pharisees and other retainers were likely among the thousands Alexander killed, the 800 he brutally crucified, and the 8,000 who fled into exile for the remainder of his reign (*Ant.* 13.372–83). Alexander does not appear to have been interested in pressing the Judean laws on recently subjected peoples in any case. As noted earlier, shortly after his father John Hyrcanus had imposed "the laws of the Judeans" on the Idumeans, Alexander appointed as military governor of Idumea not a prominent Jerusalem priest or sage well versed in the laws, but the head of a prominent Idumean family only recently brought under the jurisdiction of those laws (*Ant.* 14.10).

Alexander's wife and successor Alexandra Salome (76–67 B.C.E.), on the other hand, made peace with the Pharisees. In fact, according to Josephus, the Pharisees became the virtual administrators of the state (*Ant.* 13.398–41). Given the political position and program of the Pharisees (explored further in chapter 6 below), it is at least conceivable that during Alexandra Salome's reign the Hasmonean regime spearheaded more rigorous application of Judean laws in Galilee and other recently annexed areas. Nevertheless, the Pharisees were not the only force in her administration. Like her husband, "she recruited a large force of mercenaries" and she left

Alexander Janneus's "friends" and other officers in charge of the numerous fortresses around the realm (*Ant.* 13.408–9, 416–17, 422).

It is difficult to discern how the prolonged and repeatedly disruptive Roman conquest of Palestine could have done anything other than slow or even weaken the integration of Galilee under Jerusalem rule — although it might at points have driven some Galileans to make common cause with the Judean peasantry against the Roman forces and their client rulers in Jerusalem.

Pursuant to their standard policy of governing native peoples indirectly, through the native aristocracy or local ruler, the Romans confirmed the Hasmonean dynasty in power soon after their initial conquest in 63 B.C.E.[57] The division of the people into five separate districts by the proconsul Gabinius in 57 B.C.E. was no exception to this policy, since the districts were to be governed by aristocratic councils (*synhedria*; *Ant.* 14.90–91; *B.J.* 1.169–70). After a year or two, however, Gabinius restored centralized rule by the Hasmonean regime from Jerusalem (*B.J.* 1.178). Julius Caesar's decrees cited earlier (dated 48–47 B.C.E.) confirmed Hyrcanus II and his descendants in the office(s) of Ethnarch and High Priesthood of the Judeans along with the rights and privileges they held in accordance with the traditional laws (*Ant.* 14.193–210). Those rights and privileges were "rule over the nation of Judeans" and enjoyment of the produce of the territories subject to them. For the people, however, this meant not only paying taxes to Hyrcanus and his descendants, but also rendering tribute to Rome (one-fourth of the produce sown every second year). Galileans, Idumeans, and other subjects of the Hasmoneans were here apparently included among "the Judeans" for the political and economic purposes of imperial rule. But the "rights and privileges" mentioned are not those of "Judeans" generally, let alone those of Galileans.[58] The implications for Galileans were simply that they were to continue under Hasmonean rule, and to be taxed by the regime in Jerusalem as well as by the Romans, through the regime in Jerusalem. Roman rule would thus have made Jerusalem rule seem all the more burdensome.

Moreover, the prolonged rivalry among the principal leaders in Rome and the great Roman civil war dragged Galileans, like virtually all other peoples of the eastern Mediterranean, into its wake. The "civil war" between rival Hasmoneans that had begun prior to the Roman conquest was perpetuated by the shifting favors of one or another of the rival Roman leaders, such as Pompey and Julius Caesar. The impact on Galilee was direct as well as indirect. A major battle was fought near Mount Tabor in southeastern Galilee (*Ant.* 14.102; *B.J.* 1.177). More ominously, around 53–52 B.C.E., Cassius, in an expedition to check the rival Hasmonean forces opposed to Hyrcanus II, enslaved "thirty thousand" people at the town of Tarichaeae/Magdala along the shore of the lake (*Ant.* 14.120; *B.J.* 1.180). The military campaigns raging through the land and the extraordinary demands for taxes levied to support such campaigns also caused social chaos for the peasantry. The eruption of banditry is usually an important barometer of social chaos. Josephus reports that "the brigand-chief Ezekias was ravaging the district on the Syrian frontier with a large troop" (*stifei*) (*B.J.* 1.204; *Ant.* 14.159). He also mentions a major stronghold of brigands in the hills and caves at Arbela, near the Sea of Galilee a few years later (*B.J.* 1.304–5; *Ant.* 14.415). Given the selectivity of ancient historiography, those were probably only the most prominent among dozens of local brigand bands in Galilee.[59]

Another result of the initial stages of Roman domination of Palestine was the emergence of strong repressive rule from Jerusalem. The ambitious Idumean aristocrat Antipater, already the force behind High Priest Hyrcanus II, had cultivated favor with Julius Caesar, who appointed him as "governor [*epitropos*] of all Judea" (the term, in official Roman parlance, for the whole of Palestine subject to Hyrcanus; *B.J.* 1.199; *Ant.* 14.199). Antipater, in turn, designated his sons to be military governors (*strategoi*): Phasael in Jerusalem and environs, and Herod, the future "king," in Galilee (*B.J.* 1.203; *Ant.* 14.158). The Galileans were thus the first among Herod's future subjects to become acquainted with his repressive practices. Among his early exploits were the vigorous suppression of the banditry along the Syrian frontier and the energetic collection of a special levy of taxes by Cassius (*Ant.* 14.159–60, 168–71, 274; *B.J.* 1.204–6, 210–11, 220–21).

The first few decades of Roman domination in Palestine would thus have weakened the authority of Jerusalem and the temple-based Hasmonean high priesthood in Galilee. By adding to the people's tax burden, by exacerbating the civil war between rival Hasmonean factions, and by sponsoring brutal repressive measures, the Romans produced chaos and alienation among the Galileans, whose subjection to Jerusalem rule they had confirmed.[60]

The prolonged war by which Herod conquered his kingdom would hardly have eased the integration of Galilee under Jerusalem rule. The Romans, eager to consolidate control of the eastern Mediterranean, particularly Syria-Palestine, as a buffer against the threatening advance of the Parthians in the East, appointed Herod king in "Judea." Almost simultaneously the last Hasmonean rival, Antigonus, allied himself with the Parthians. Herod's conquest of his kingdom and the widespread resistance he encountered are thus mixed in with the attempts of Antigonus and the Parthians to gain control. Not only were Galileans subjected to three more years of periodic warfare, but there was widespread popular resistance to Herod and his powerful partisans in Galilee.

The recent claim that the opposition to Herod in Galilee came primarily from the Hasmonean nobility, starting with the "brigand-chief" Hezekiah, so that there "was no widespread involvement of the whole population,"[61] lacks both evidence and historical credibility. Josephus gives no indication that the resistance Herod encountered at different points involved the same people, let alone that their "leaders, Hezekiah and the others, were aristocrats."[62] Indeed, that the mothers of the murdered brigands were appealing to Hyrcanus (*Ant.* 14.263–68) appears to contradict the claim that the brigands were Hasmonean nobles. The mothers could hardly have appealed to the rival Hasmonean ruler. Moreover, the concept of a "native" "land-owning" nobility does not fit the historical situation of Galilee under the last of the Hasmoneans as the Romans took control in the eastern Mediterranean. Like other ancient Near Eastern client-states, the Hasmonean regime had high-ranking and intermediate officers who administered political-economic affairs.[63] The basis of their power and wealth was their office in the regime. They would have had little or no support in the countryside as a basis for sustaining the decade-long struggle against Herod that this hypothesis imagines.

A careful reading of Josephus's accounts indicates two different levels of resistance to Herod's conquest in Galilee: a feeble short-lived effort by "the garrisons of Antigonus" and a more persistent popular resistance. According to Josephus, in his initial campaign to take control of the area Herod "set out to reduce the remaining strongholds of Galilee and to expel the garrisons of Antigonus" (*B.J.* 1.303; cf. *Ant.* 14.413). These strongholds, less elaborate and formidable than Alexandreion or Masada, were among many Hasmonean fortresses at various points in the land which Aristobulus and his sons had held or retaken periodically over the previous three decades. The garrisons were apparently experienced troops, perhaps mercenaries, who had remained loyal to Aristobulus and his sons or who simply joined Antigonus's cause (see, e.g., *B.J.* 1.117; *Ant.* 13.417, 427; 14.83, 89). The garrison at Sepphoris simply fled before Herod's advance, says Josephus. The ensuing stories in both of Josephus's histories, however, appear to be somewhat confused. In both he has Herod immediately launch a campaign against the brigands dwelling in caves near Arbela, but then Josephus reports on a regular military engagement in which the left wing of Herod's battle line is nearly routed by the enemy's right wing (*B.J.* 1.304–5; *Ant.* 14.415–16). After narrating Herod's victory and dispersal of the enemy across the Jordan River, his payment and dismissal of his troops to winter quarters, and the refortification of Alexandreion, Josephus finally tells of Herod's actual attack against the cave-dwelling brigands (*B.J.* 1.306–9; *Ant.* 14.417–21). Thus the pitched military battle narrated between the two introductions of the cave-dwelling brigands probably refers to resistance by some of those garrisons of Antigonus, resistance that ended with their dispersal across the Jordan.

The remainder of Josephus's accounts of resistance to Herod apparently have to do with various popular groups. The dramatic story of Herod's massacre of the cave-dwelling brigands, which Josephus tells with great relish, gives the impression that the brigands had been active in the area for some time and were well entrenched with families in their inaccessible caves along the steep cliffs. When finally "smoked out" of their caves, they "prefer death to slavery!" (*B.J.* 1.309–13; *Ant.* 14.421–30). But no sooner had Herod turned back to his large-scale military campaign against Antigonus than "the usual promoters of disturbance in Galilee" slew the general he had left in charge. That Herod "fined the towns a hundred talents" in retaliation indicates that this "rebellion" against Herod was popular and widespread (*B.J.* 1.315–16; *Ant.* 14.432–33). Some time later, in yet another widespread insurrection inspired by a victory of Antigonus, "the Galileans rebelled [*apostantes*] against the powerful [*dynatoi*] in their country and drowned those who were partisans of Herod in the lake" (*Ant.* 14.450; cf. *B.J.* 1.326). This time the Galileans' insurrection was paralleled in much of Judea and Idumea.

One begins to wonder just what Josephus meant at the beginning of his narratives of Herod's conquest that "all Galilee" had gone over to Herod (*B.J.* 1.291; *Ant.* 14.295). Obviously "all Galilee" did not include the ordinary people. Probably Josephus was referring to the people who, to his aristocratic mind, "counted," that is, the *dynatoi*, or powerful ones. At least some of the former Hasmonean officials and allies in Galilee, accepting the inevitable, had gone over to Herod's side immediately. But many ordinary Galileans and Judeans alike had by this time sufficient experience of Herod's ruthless treatment to resist the imposition of his rule. Judging from Josephus's reports, the popular resistance to Herod and the (formerly Hasmonean) "powerful ones" who joined his side was unusually persistent in Galilee.

As Herod's conquest of greater "Judea" brought the sixty-plus years of Hasmonean rule to an end in Galilee, it is difficult to discern just how and when, except perhaps during the decade of Alexandra Salome, there would have been sufficient domestic peace and energy for the Hasmonean regime to concentrate on integrating Galileans under Jerusalem temple/ high-priestly rule and the Judean laws.

Herod's Reign in Galilee

Despite Josephus's extensive accounts of Herod's reign, we have much less direct evidence for Galilee under Herod's rule than under Hasmonean rule.[64] We must extrapolate from indirect evidence to the likely effects of Herod's policies and practices on relations between Galileans and Jerusalem. The results would appear to be mixed. On the one hand, Herod left the Temple, the high priesthood, and the Judean laws intact. His repressive rule, moreover, ensured a prolonged period of social stability in which those priests and scribes could have cultivated their interests, along with the laws of the Judeans, among the Galileans and others. On the other hand, the effects of Herod's political-economic and cultural-religious practices may have compromised the authority of the Jerusalem-based institutions and undermined their effectiveness for Galileans as perhaps for Judeans themselves. The following outline of basic historical developments here will be supplemented by fuller discussion of the Temple, high priesthood, and Pharisees in chapter 6.

After taking over the Hasmonean fortresses in Galilee, Herod would have garrisoned them with his own troops, headed by loyal officers. The "king" who added some massive fortresses of his own to those already established by the Hasmoneans — Masada and Herodium being among the most famous — did not leave any district of his realm without elaborate security measures. In addition to the fortresses already in place along the frontiers of Upper Galilee, the new colony of cavalry Herod established at Gaba in the Great Plain was probably aimed at Galilee (*B.J.* 3.36; *Ant.* 15.294). Following the Hasmonean lead, Herod simply took over Sepphoris as the principal administrative fortress and town from which to rule and tax Galilee (*B.J.* 2.56; *Ant* 17.271).

While Herod left the Temple and high priesthood intact, he made them into instruments of his own rule. As the crowning jewel of his massive building program throughout his realm, he rebuilt the Temple in grand Hellenistic-Roman style, doubling the size of its outer court and raising its height (*B.J.* 1.401; *Ant.* 15.380–402).[65] A virtual fortress itself, the rebuilt Temple was in turn dominated by the fortress he erected next to it. Somewhat analogous to Solomon's Temple, besides being a dedication to God, the lavishly rebuilt Temple was a monument to Herod's own glory, a monumental institution of religio-political propaganda. Among other things, "round about the entire Temple were fixed the spoils taken from the barbarians, and all these King Herod dedicated, adding those which he took from the Arabs" (*Ant.* 15.402). And since the completion of the Temple "coincided with the day of the king's accession," a glorious anniversary festival was celebrated for the double occasion (*Ant.* 15.423).

Although it continued in command of the elaborate religious-economic-juridical temple apparatus (albeit with drastically reduced power), the high priesthood became not only an instrument of Herod's rule but subject to his whim as well. After the upstart Hasmonean family had replaced the Zadokite Oniads at the head of the temple-state, the high priesthood had again become hereditary. To lend some minimal legitimacy to his rule, Herod initially surrounded himself with Hasmonean associations, primarily by marrying Mariamme the daughter of Hyrcanus II, whom he brought back from Parthia to an honored place at court (*Ant.* 15.11–21).[66] Having drastically reduced its powers, Herod also undermined the legitimacy of the high priesthood by installing priestly families from Babylonia or Egypt and others of his own choosing into the high-priestly office. Not surprisingly, one of the principal cries of the Judean crowd in Jerusalem after the death of Herod was for the removal of the high priest appointed by Herod and the installation of someone "more lawful and pure" (*Ant.* 17.207–8; *B.J.* 2.7). Thus if the high priesthood and temple-based government or the Hasmonean dynasty in particular had gained a degree of loyalty among Galileans earlier in the first century, Herod's treatment of the high priesthood would have only undermined it.

Like the new high-priestly incumbents, the Pharisees were also active politically during Herod's reign. Contrary to the recently prominent thesis that the Pharisees withdrew from "political" affairs into conventicles of piety under Herod, they merely experienced a "demotion" in status and political influence, given the higher level of Herodian administration above them.[67] Josephus's reports indicate their continued involvement in political affairs despite their refusal to sign loyalty oaths to Herod and Rome (*Ant.* 17:41–46).[68] Presumably the Pharisees continued their professional role as what Josephus calls experts in (the most accurate interpretation of) the laws of the Judeans, which Herod also left intact, along with the Temple and high priesthood. Because of their loss of status officially, Pharisees and other scribes or teachers could well have been all the more active in seeking influence among the people. Nevertheless, our only literary evidence for the Pharisees during this period has them hovering around the Herodian court maneuvering for influence (*B.J.* 1.571; *Ant.* 17.41–46). If they were active in Galilee under Herod, we have no record of it.

While Herod apparently left the traditional laws and customs of the Judeans in place, he did not observe them himself. In fact he did much that would have undermined the traditional social-religious ethos. In addition to rebuilding the Temple in Jerusalem, Herod carried out massive building projects throughout his realm, all in Hellenistic-Roman style. Most significant, there was "no suitable spot within his realm which he left destitute of some mark of homage to Caesar" (*B.J.* 1.407). In closest proximity to Galilee was the temple of white marble Herod built and dedicated to Caesar at Paneion, near the site of ancient Dan and the site later of Caesarea Philippi.

Herod also sponsored athletic games, again in honor of Caesar, and built a theater and amphitheater (and hippodrome? *Ant.* 17.255) at Jerusalem, decorated with inscriptions concerning Caesar and trophies of his own military victories (with offensive images). When the Judeans objected to his violation of traditional customs, some even forming a conspiracy against him, he instituted sharply repressive measures to control the population, including a network of informers and an expanded series of fortresses throughout the country (*Ant.* 15.267–95, 366). He further instituted a law that thieves should be sold into slavery to foreigners, which violated the traditional laws (*Ant.* 16:1–5). Josephus, himself a member of a wealthy and dominant priestly family, knew well the implications: "Departing from the traditional customs, [Herod] gradually corrupted the ancient way of life…and neglected those things which had formerly induced piety in the masses" (*Ant.* 15.267). If the social order that Herod maintained through repressive tyranny created a stable situation in which others may have been cultivating the traditional laws of the Judeans, then Herod's cultural and legal program subverted those same traditions.

Two stories in Josephus suggest that peoples subject to rule from Jerusalem under Herod continued to live according to their own indigenous laws, whether in areas such as Idumea and Galilee ostensibly subjected to observance of the Judean laws by the Hasmoneans, or in areas brought under Jerusalem rule by Herod himself. The story about Costobar, noted above, dramatically illustrates how Idumeans not only continued their own religious practices but actively resisted the laws of the Judeans nearly a hundred years after their supposed subjection (*Ant.* 15.253–55). That Herod punished his brother-in-law and governor of Idumea because he had secretly protected Hasmonean partisans at the siege of Jerusalem, not because he resisted the Judean laws, also indicates that Herod was not particularly concerned to press for Idumeans' conformation to "the laws of the Judeans." An analogous situation probably existed among the Galileans, who became subject to the Judean laws nearly a generation after the Idumeans. The Galileans and Idumeans may have been governed from Jerusalem according to the traditional Judean laws, just as the Judeans were. But that does not mean that the Galileans or Idumeans would have abandoned or changed their own customs in favor of the Judean laws. Herod would not have pressed the issue.

Josephus also reports that Herod planted a large "village" in Batanea as a buffer against the unruly former raiders in Trachonitis. There he settled a large band of equestrian Jews from Babylonia. Because he had exempted the colony from taxation, however, "people from all parts who were devoted to the ancestral customs of the Judeans" also settled there (*Ant.* 17.25–26). Thus directly to the east of Galilee was located a distinctly "Jewish" settlement. Yet the original nucleus of the "village" were Babylonian Jews, whose "ancestral customs" would have differed considerably from those that developed in and around Jerusalem. Although not free of Herod's taxation, other villages and towns, particularly in outlying districts such as Galilee, were free to continue social life according to their own local traditions and ancestral customs.

The general effect of Herod's rule on all subject peoples was extreme economic burden and hardship. As noted earlier, the Roman conquest and confirmation of Hasmonean "rights and privileges" had meant a double level of taxation for the people. The Roman imposition of Herod as client-king added yet a third layer of taxation, for the Temple and the priests did not suddenly forego their revenues. Herod's taxes must have been unusually heavy in order to support his demonstrative munificence to the imperial family and Hellenistic cities, his extensive and lavish court that utilized several palatial fortresses, his vast program of cultural buildings and military fortresses, and the centerpieces of his building projects, the temples to

Caesar and the rebuilt Temple in Jerusalem. The people complained of the burden, and once or twice, particularly when drought and famine struck, Herod had to back off temporarily. But the general level of taxation resumed and the overlapping layers continued.[69] The effect on the peasantry in Galilee, as elsewhere, was increasing indebtedness and even alienation of their ancestral lands, as they were unable to support themselves after rendering up percentages of their crops for tribute to Rome, tithes and offerings to priests and Temple, and taxes to Herod.

At Herod's death, Galileans, like his other subjects, moved quickly to protest and to assert their independence. Because of the distance to Jerusalem, few Galileans could have taken part in the clamor by the Jerusalem crowd for the lessening of taxes, the release of prisoners, and the appointment of a more righteous high priest. Nor could they have participated in the violent clash initiated by the troops in the temple courtyard during the passover celebrations (*B.J.* 2.4–13; *Ant.* 17.200–218). During the festival of Pentecost several weeks later, however, "a countless multitude flocked in from Galilee," as well as from Idumea, Perea beyond the Jordan, with the native people of Judea predominant in numbers and ardor. "It was not the customary ritual so much as indignation which drew the people in crowds to the capital" (*B.J.* 2.42–44; *Ant.* 17.254–55). The roots of that indignation ran far deeper than the provocative actions by Roman troops asserting their control. Assuming that we can trust Josephus's report that Galileans joined in this protest, it indicates that Jerusalem (and the temple courtyard as the public gathering place) was important to Galileans at least as the locus of political power, as the capital from which they were ruled. As in the appeal by the mothers of the Galilean brigands slain by the young Herod, the Jerusalem Temple was where they went to protest injustice.

Far more widespread and significant than the Pentecost protest was the Galilean assertion of independence, at least in the area of Sepphoris. The principal head of the insurrection in Galilee was Judas, son of the brigand-chief Hezekiah, who had been killed a generation earlier by Herod.

> This Judas got together a large number of desperate men (his considerable multitude of followers) at Sepphoris in Galilee and there made an assault on the royal palace, (and having seized all the arms that were stored there, he armed his men) and made off with all the property that had been seized there. (*Ant.* 17.271; cf. *B.J.* 2.56)

Josephus's parallel report that "he attacked other aspirants to power" suggests that the insurrection was more widespread than the movement led by the popularly acclaimed king Judas son of Hezekiah in the area around Sepphoris.

There is thus little reason to believe that Galilean attachment to the Temple and high priesthood or their assimilation of Judean laws would have advanced much under Herod's heavy hand. Indeed, the Temple and high priesthood probably lost some of their already threatened legitimacy among Judeans as well as among Galileans during Herod's reign. The popular uprisings that erupted in every major district of Herod's realm, in Perea and Judea as well as in Galilee, were not movements to restore the Temple and the Torah, as was the Maccabean Revolt. Nor did they take the form of a popular election by lot of high-priestly officers, as did the Zealots (proper) in northwest Judea in the winter of 67–68.[70]

Instead, as Josephus reports, in each case the insurgents acclaimed one of their number as "king" (*Ant.* 17.271–85; *B.J.* 2.56–65). In the present context we must move beyond the observation that these movements were informed by a tradition of popular kingship attested in Judean biblical traditions (of Saul, David, Jehu, and so on).[71] We must appreciate also what these traditions and movements stood against. The tradition of popular kingship would have been different from and opposed to traditions that served to legitimate either the Temple or the Torah. There appears to have been a revival of interest in kingship tradition among literate groups as well just at this time, perhaps also in reaction to illegitimate Roman-sponsored Herodian kingship.[72] The literate speculation about a coming anointed one envisaged the king as "the son of David" (Psalms of Solomon 17). Popular kingship, however, even if it had included the Davidic motif, would not necessarily have been distinctively "Judean," since David had been an Israelite hero as well as a Judahite one, and since popular kingship had preceded David as well as continued on in northern Israel long after David's time (esp. Jeroboam, Jehu). Thus the revolt in Galilee, like those in Judea and Perea, was probably an Israelite assertion of independence of the principal institutions of Jerusalem rule as well as of Herodian tyranny.

Chapter 3

GALILEE BETWEEN
ROMAN RECONQUESTS (4 B.C.E.–67 C.E.)

༄

Aristocratic societies are not like modern societies, not only because they are not modern, but because they are not societies.... The aristocracy (and those attached to it in the towns, like servants and low-level bureaucrats) and each village are separate communities or societies.

— JOHN KAUTSKY

I and my associates had been commissioned by the Jerusalem assembly to press for the demolition of the palace erected by Herod the Tetrarch, which contained representations of animals. Capella and the (council of) ten refused. Jesus son of Sapphias, however, the ringleader of the sailors and destitute class, joined by some Galileans, set the whole palace on fire...and then massacred all the Greek residents in Tiberias.

— JOSEPHUS

Rome struck decisively against any subject people who had the audacity to reassert their freedom (cf. *B.J.* 2.53; *Ant.* 17.267). In response to the popular insurrections in Galilee, Perea, and Judea following Herod's death in 4 B.C.E., Varus the Legate of Syria assembled a massive army of Roman legions and auxiliary troops from the cities and client-rulers in the surrounding area to put down the rebellion. According to Josephus's accounts, the main force proceeded toward Judea proper to secure the city of Jerusalem as well as the countryside. A detachment was sent "to fight against the Galileans who inhabit the region adjoining Ptolemais." Josephus reports in both accounts that the Roman troops captured and burned the city of Sepphoris and enslaved the inhabitants (*B.J.* 2.68; *Ant.* 17.288–89). Since recent archaeological probes in Sepphoris itself have found no clear evidence of massive destruction at this time,[1] it may be that the punitive Roman strike into the area, including the enslavement of the people, was against the surrounding villages in which the insurrection led by the popular king Judas, son of Hezekiah, was clearly based (*B.J.* 2.56; *Ant.* 17.271–72).

It is surely significant that Josephus's reports of the Roman reconquest distinguish regional peoples and movements, such that "the Galileans" are not identified with or closely associated with "the Judeans" in revolt further south, let alone with "the Judeans in Jerusalem" itself. In suppressing the rebellion in Galilee as elsewhere, the Romans terrorized the populace as a means of intimidation and imperial control. In the environs of Sepphoris and in places such as Emmaus, the villages were burned, the people sold into slavery, and thousands of rebels publicly crucified in a systematic "search and destroy" strategy (*B.J.* 2.70–75; *Ant.* 17.291–95). It is clearly pertinent to the movement catalyzed by Jesus of Nazareth and the literature it eventually produced (the Gospel traditions) that Galileans in the area around Sepphoris, particularly those in villages such as Nazareth, experienced the terrorizing violence of Roman troops in retaliation against their aspirations for independence.

Once the Romans decisively suppressed the popular rebellions following the death of Herod, they divided Herod's realm among his sons. Judea proper, along with Samaria, was set under Archelaus, while Galilee and Perea were given to Antipas (4 B.C.E.–39 C.E.). With the exception of a brief period under Herod's grandson Agrippa I (41–44 C.E.), Galilee remained under separate political jurisdiction from Judea through the rest of the first century C.E. After being subject to Jerusalem rule for only a hundred years, Galilee was thus politically no longer under the jurisdiction of the Temple and high priesthood for the final seventy years of the second-temple era. This leaves us wondering just what authority the Temple continued to have among Galileans and what influence the high priests and their representatives such as scribes and Pharisees continued to wield in a territory now subject to a client-king of the Romans. Since there is precious little evidence on this issue, it would be well not simply to make assumptions on the basis of the political-religious structure of the Hasmonean and Herodian regimes. In fact, the two Roman reconquests of Galilee and Judea that frame this period served not to enhance the opportunities for further integration of Galilee into the Judean temple-community, but to limit and, finally, to eliminate them.

Far from being culturally unified in a common "Judaism," moreover, the Herodian rulers and the Jerusalem priestly aristocracy were now rivals competing for influence with the Romans as well as for revenues from their economic base, the peasantry of the various districts of Herod's old kingdom. A closer look at the few brief reports of rulers and events in Galilee prior to the great revolt in 66 suggests little by way of forces that would have unified Galileans with the dominant institutions in Jerusalem, specifically the Temple and the high priesthood. Josephus's far more extensive accounts of the revolt in Galilee in 66–67, in fact, indicate regional fragmentation within Galilee itself as well as a continuing resistance to manipulation and control from Jerusalem.

Galilee under Antipas, Roman Governors, and the Agrippas

For the previous century Galilee had been implicated in certain events that pertained primarily to their Jerusalem-based rulers, such as the wars between rival Hasmoneans and Rome's appointment of Herod as king of Judea. With the appointment of Antipas, Galilee came under separate political jurisdiction from Judea proper. It is important, therefore, to distinguish between events distinctive to Galilee along with those events in Jerusalem that influenced Galilee, on the one hand, and events that pertain only or primarily to the history of Judea and Jerusalem, on the other. We should also not misread Josephus's reports that a Galilean was instrumental to an event to mean that that event involved Galilee.

The most important example is the organized resistance to the Roman tribute in 6 C.E., when Judea came directly under a Roman governor, organized by what Josephus calls "the fourth philosophy" among the Judeans (the other "philosophies" being the Pharisees, the Sadducees, and the Essenes). This was an apparently nonviolent movement of "tax resistance" by people acting on the firm belief that God was their exclusive lord and master, hence they could not submit to something tantamount to acknowledging Caesar as lord (*B.J.* 2.118; *Ant.* 18.4–6, 9–10, 23–24). Confused by Josephus's association of this early resistance to the Roman tribute with later resistance to Roman rule, particularly the Zealots proper, who emerged in Jerusalem during the great revolt (in 67–68), modern scholars constructed a picture of a long-standing, widespread, and well-organized movement of national liberation which they labeled "the Zealots." Moreover, because "the fourth philosophy" was led by "the teacher" (*sophistēs*) Judas of Galilee, whom many scholars supposed to be identical with Judas son of Hezekiah, the Galilean popular king in 4 B.C.E., the movement was thought to have originated in and/or been prominent in Galilee.[2]

Unlike Judea, however, Galilee was not suddenly disrupted by imposition of direct Roman rule in 6 C.E.; it had already acquiesced to the rule of Antipas, so far as we know. Moreover, the very name "Judas of Galilee" indicates not that Judas was active *in* Galilee but that he was originally or reputedly *from* Galilee. We have no way of knowing whether Judas of Galilee or "the fourth philosophy" had any influence in Galilee. In any case, whether "the Zealots" were prominent in Galilee can now be recognized as a nonissue historically.[3] Most of the events or movements figuring in debates about how "revolutionary" Galilee was actually occurred in Judea during a period when Galilee was under separate political jurisdiction and would be only indirectly relevant to affairs in Galilee.

Following the Roman devastation of the area around Sepphoris and enslavement of the people in retaliation for the uprising led by the popular king Judas in 4 B.C.E., Antipas rebuilt and fortified the city to be "the ornament of all Galilee" and called it Autocratoris, that is, "imperial city" (*Ant.* 18.27). The rebuilt city was apparently Antipas's initial capital, and the city became a center of Roman political and cultural influence, remaining steadfastly loyal to the Romans and a focus for Galileans' resentment, as evident in Josephus's account of events in 66 (*Vita* 38–39, 104, 346–48). After rebuilding Sepphoris, however, Antipas set about founding the completely new city of Tiberias on the shore of the lake as his new capital. It is clear from the names of his officials and their descendants that Tiberias was a "royal" city and another center of Roman political-cultural influence (*Vita* 32–35).

It has often been assumed that Antipas was a "Jewish" ruler, and it was recently even claimed that he depicted himself on his coinage as "a pious Jew."[4] This assumption and claim, of course, depend on the more general assumption that Galilee was basically "Jewish." We have no evidence, however, regarding how Antipas's subjects may have viewed representations on coins. Non-Judean as well as Judean descendants of former Israelites would supposedly have shared the tradition of Mosaic covenantal prohibition of images. While the aniconic coinage of Antipas may be an indication of his diplomacy as a ruler, it does not reveal much about his piety.

A more telling question is whether Antipas did anything to foster either observance of "the laws of the Judeans" or continuing relations between Galileans and the Temple in Jerusalem. On this question, the indications from literary evidence are negative. Three of Josephus's reports fairly clearly suggest that, if anything, Antipas was oblivious to the religious-cultural sensitivities of his subjects and/or that the Jerusalem authorities and their representatives had little or no influence over Antipas. First, Antipas apparently built his new "royal" administrative city on the site of a graveyard, which was contrary to Judean tradition (*Ant.* 18.38). Second, the royal palace was lavishly decorated with representations of animals in a style forbidden by "the laws" (*Vita* 65; again a basic covenantal prohibition in general Israelite tradition as well as in the Torah). If the construction of Tiberias is any indication, Antipas was not particularly sensitive to the beliefs of his subjects, let alone ready to foster the cultivation of Torah in Galilee. Third, Antipas again simply flouted the Judean laws in marrying his brother Philip's wife Herodias (*Ant.* 18.136; cf. Lev. 18:16; 20:21). In the same context Josephus writes pointedly that "some Judeans" viewed the subsequent destruction of Antipas's whole army by the Arab king Aretas (in retaliation for Antipas's divorcing his daughter in order to marry Herodias) as divine vengeance for Antipas's execution of John the Baptist (*Ant.* 18.109–19). Apparently Antipas had developed a reputation for violating the Judean laws and was viewed as deserving of divine judgment by those whose opinion would have been important and known to the aristocratic priestly historian Josephus, that is, priestly and/or scribal elements in Jerusalem.[5]

It may not be by accident that there is no indication that Antipas was involved in "Jewish affairs" in the same official way as the three later Herodian rulers, Agrippa I, Herod of Chalcis, and Agrippa II, who were entrusted with authority over the Temple, temple vessels, high-priestly robes, and/or appointment of high priests (*Ant.* 19.274–75, 297, 313–14; 20.15–16, 179, 203, 213). In the only historically credible report that Antipas visited Jerusalem, it was with Vitellius the Legate of Syria, clearly to smooth over the offense caused by Roman troops crossing Judean territory on a mission of retaliation against the Arab king Aretas's defeat of Antipas's army (*Ant.* 18.109–15, 120–24).[6] Finally, it is difficult to imagine that Antipas would have facilitated his Galilean subjects' relationship with the Temple and high priests. Tithes and offerings to priests and Temple, an economic demand on the Galilean peasant producers, would have competed with Antipas's own demands for tax revenues — and his needs for the latter must have been considerable given his massive building projects at Sepphoris and Tiberias.

Nor, on the other hand, did the Romans' client-ruler Antipas attempt to foster the development (from the top down) of a regional and/or ethnic identity in Galilee parallel to what supposedly emerged in Judea much earlier, focused in the Temple and high priesthood.[7] Judean attachment to the central institutions, of course, had taken centuries to develop. The Maccabean Revolt and Maccabean literature both reflect popular Judean concern for the Temple as well as for the traditional way of life generally. Although the later Hasmoneans lost support among much of the Judean population and Herod undermined the legitimacy of both the Temple and the high priesthood, the move by the Zealots proper (a coalition of villagers from northwest Judea) to hold a popular election of high-priestly officers in 67–68 indicates continuing popular attachment to priestly leadership of the people.[8] Antipas's reign was far too brief for comparable centralized Galilean institutions to emerge.

More decisively, the imperially imposed structure of political-economic relations in Galilee (see further chapter 7) worked against a development parallel to the earlier one in Judea. Whatever Antipas's intention, the founding of a new capital in the middle of his reign merely set up a rivalry between Tiberias and Sepphoris for political-economic prominence in Galilee (*Life* 36–39). Moreover, judging from the names of the most prominent men in Tiberias and Sepphoris's loyalty to Rome during the great revolt in 66, the leading residents of the cities were Hellenistic-Roman, that is, of different cultural background (as well as political-economic position) from the Galileans. "Herod's" birthday banquet in the account of John the Baptist's execution in Mark 6 portrays not Galilean village leaders, but the principal figures of the realm (*hoi prōtoi tēs galilaias;* cf. *hoi prōtoi* of Tiberias, Josephus, *Life* 64, 67; and *hoi prōtoi* in another administrative list, *Ant.* 18.273) along with the "great ones" (barons or inner circle; cf. Dan. 5:23) and military officers in a typical court scene (Mark 6:21, 27). In this case the terms used for the military officers give away the Hellenistic-Roman character of Antipas's court and administrative cities, as well as its limited scale: *chiliarchos*, the standard term in the eastern empire for "commander of a thousand," and *speculator*, Latin loan word best known in connection with the imperial guard in Rome.[9] In the political-economic structure of things, moreover, the building and maintenance of these cities depended on heavy taxation of the Galileans. Thus no common Galilean regional political and/or ethnic identity could develop — unless, of course, we mean the sharp hostility Josephus found directed against both Tiberias and Sepphoris by the people he refers to as "the Galileans" (*Life* 30, 39, 273–80, 390–92, and so on).

We must draw somewhat the same conclusions about the effects of the reign of (Herod) Agrippa I on Galilee, despite his representation in modern scholarly literature as more of a pious Jew than either Herod the Great or Antipas.[10] It is clear that he was highly ambitious and extremely extravagant, and that his many years of cultivating imperial aspirants and freedmen in Rome, particularly Gaius (Caligula), paid off handsomely for the rights of Jews in Hellenistic cities such as Alexandria, as well as for his own spectacular rise to power under the emperors Gaius and Claudius. Gaius awarded him both the territory of Philip to the north and east of Galilee in 37 C.E., and then Galilee and Perea when Antipas was deposed in 39. Claudius gave him Judea and Samaria as well in 41. It might be imagined that even though his reign was brief, since he died in 43, his own supposed loyalty to Jewish traditions may have led to greater cultivation of those traditions in Galilee. Critical examination of Josephus's accounts, however, indicates that under Agrippa I affairs in Galilee were no different than they were under Antipas, in whose administration he had served briefly as the "market warden" (*agoranomos*) in Tiberias.

Agrippa himself was almost never in Galilee. He was in Rome, where he had been raised and educated "with the circle of Claudius" (*Ant.* 18.165), from the time he was given Galilee in 39 until he was also granted Judea and Samaria in 41, and thereafter resided primarily in Caesarea, with largely ceremonial appearances in Jerusalem.[11] In Agrippa's absence, Galilee continued to be ruled, as it had been under Antipas, from Tiberias by a Hellenistic-style administration at the center of which were Agrippa's brother Aristobulus, his friend and prefect, Helcias, and "other very powerful members of the (Herodian) house" (*Life* 37; *Ant.* 18.273). In the highly dramatic face-off between "the Judeans" and the legate of Syria, Petronius, who had been ordered to place a statue of Gaius in the temple, these Herodian officials mediated between the protesting people and the imperial official. But these Herodian officials were the rulers of Galilee, concerned for their own positions so dependent on the social order necessary to produce crops for taxes and tribute, not the leaders of the people, whose protest had apparently been initiated by Judeans (*Ant.* 18.261–63, 274; *B.J.* 2.184–87, 192, 199). The same fundamental cultural as well as political-economic division between rulers and ruled continued as under the Hasmoneans, Herod, and Antipas.

After Judea was included in his territories, Agrippa I made visits to Jerusalem now and then for festivals from his preferred residence in Caesarea, much as the Roman governors had done. He does seem to have been heavily involved in the politics of the Temple and high priesthood. In the short span of his authority, first over appointment to the high priesthood, he deposed and appointed high priests three times (*Ant.* 19.293, 313–16, 342). There appears to have been a resurgence of high-priestly aggressiveness just before and during the reign of Agrippa, perhaps because of a power vacuum when no Roman governor was appointed after Pontius Pilate was removed in 37.[12] Agrippa's crackdown on the nascent movement of Jesus' followers (more likely for civil disorder than "persecution" specifically for their religious beliefs), the execution of James the brother of John, and the arrest of Peter likely pleased the priestly aristocracy (probably "the Judeans" referred to in Acts 12:1–3). But Agrippa apparently also clashed with high-priestly circles over other issues and was severely criticized (e.g., by the rigorist Jerusalemite Simon in *Ant.* 19.332–34).

Josephus writes that Agrippa "scrupulously observed the traditions,... neglected no rite of purification, and no day passed for him without the prescribed sacrifice" (*Ant.* 19.331). That statement, however, comes at the conclusion of a flattering paragraph in which Josephus compares Agrippa in highly favorable terms with Herod, but falsely so on two of the three major points of comparison. From the rest of Josephus's accounts it is clear that, except for his more benign demeanor, Agrippa was much like Herod in those two major ways. Agrippa may have piously observed purification rites and sacrifices for the benefit of Judeans in Jerusalem and represented the interests of diaspora Jewish communities in imperial politics (*Ant.* 19.279, 288). Like his grandfather, however, he lavished grandiose gifts on Hellenistic cities, particularly Berytus, and sponsored extravagant festivals in honor of Caesar as well as theatrical and gladiatorial entertainment (*Ant.* 19.330, 335–37). Again like Herod, his extraordinary munificence to Hellenistic cities came at the cost of heavy taxation of the peoples he ruled (*Ant.* 19.252).

There are several other indications that Agrippa's "Jewish piety" may have been more cosmetic and sporadic than substantive. A critical examination of rabbinic references to King Agrippa reveals a man concerned for his personal prestige and honor, whose only participation was in showy ceremonial acts in the Jerusalem Temple.[13] While his coins from Jerusalem have no images, those from other cities bear the image of Caesar or even of Agrippa himself. He also apparently had images made of his young daughters, images that became the focus of obscene demonstrations by auxiliary troops from Caesarea and Sebaste when he died. The most telling indication is clearly the epiphany he staged for his courtiers and administrators at the spectacles in honor of Caesar at Caesarea. Appearing in the theater dressed in silver brilliantly illumined at daybreak by the first rays of the rising sun, he was addressed as a god (*Ant.* 19.344–45). It is worth noting that those same people mourned his death a few days later, and not his Judean or Galilean or other subjects, judging from Josephus's narratives. Thus we may justifiably conclude that Agrippa's scrupulous sacrificing and purifications in Jerusalem were one side of a pattern of cultural-religious relativism or pluralism, a pattern perhaps typical of the Hellenistic world. But there is no indication that the side exhibited to his Judean subjects in Jerusalem would have carried over into his sponsoring support of the Temple and cultivation of "the laws of the Judeans" in Galilee.

After Agrippa I's death, a relative power vacuum ensued in Galilee, with frequently changing political jurisdictions and divisions. After Agrippa I (39–43) Galilee came under a Roman governor for the first time, when Cuspius Fadus (44–45 c.e.) was made "procurator of Judea and of the whole kingdom" (note the distinction; *Ant.* 19.363). He was followed by the Alexandrian Jew Tiberias Alexander (46–48) and Cumanus (49–52), whom Tacitus places over Galilee only (*Ann.* 12.54), while Josephus has him clearly in charge of Judea and Samaria as well (*B.J.* 2.223–46; *Ant.* 20.103–36). Felix followed in 52, and he and his successors Festus (60–62), Albinus (62–64), and Florus (64–66) continued as governors over western Galilee (i.e., around Sepphoris), apparently as part of "the rest of Judea" (*B.J.* 2.252) after Nero transferred eastern Galilee, around Tiberias and Tarichaeae, to Agrippa II in 54.

One possible manifestation of this political vacuum was Cumanus's failure to take prompt action in the case of some Samaritans' killing of (a) Galilean(s) on the way to a festival at Jerusalem. Josephus says that Cumanus treated the Galilean "notables' " entreaty on the matter simply as "less important than other affairs on his hands" in his first history, although he attributes Cumanus's inaction to bribery by the Samaritans in his later account (*B.J.* 2.232–33; *Ant.* 20.119).

Compounding the political vacuum created by the Roman administrative division of Galilee and the frequent changes in rulers, both the successive Roman governors and Agrippa II must have been utterly preoccupied with the increasingly chaotic affairs in Jerusalem and Judea. With the partial exception of the escalating sequence of violence starting with the murder of the Galilean(s) on pilgrimage to Jerusalem under Cumanus, all of the events and movements recounted by Josephus took place in the south, none of them in Galilee. The Roman governors had all they

could possibly handle in Judea, suppressing increasingly epidemic outbursts
of banditry, popular prophetic movements, assassinations by the terrorist
Sicarii ("Daggermen"), rival gangs of ruffians sponsored by various high-
priestly families, and popular protests over outrages often caused by the
governors' own insensitivities.[14] Agrippa II, now in charge of high-priestly
appointments and in the thick of Jerusalem politics, seemed obsessed with
deposing and appointing high priests one after another. The scene in Galilee forms a striking contrast. Nothing in Josephus's extensive accounts of
the turmoil of these years or in any other source suggests that Galilee experienced any of these movements or agitations, other than the increase in
banditry that would account for the sizable groups already in existence at
the outbreak of the great revolt in 66.

Although the Romans placed political-economic administration of Galilee in the hands of Herodian client-rulers or Roman governors after Herod's
death, the Temple-based high-priestly government in Jerusalem still had a
strong interest in the area. We can imagine that the Jerusalem authorities
and/or their representatives, such as scribes and Pharisees, continued to
press their interests and influence in Galilee, but we have no evidence — unless we give credence to certain materials in the Christian synoptic Gospels.
The Gospel of Mark (followed with variations by Matthew and Luke) represents the Pharisees and, to a more limited extent, the scribes, as active in
Galilee opposing the ministry of Jesus. Clearly the picture in Mark 2:1–3:6
of the Pharisees watching Jesus' every move cannot be taken at face value.
Ancient governments, unlike many modern regimes, did not keep their subjects under regular surveillance.[15] More noteworthy as historical evidence
may be what are called the woes against the scribes and Pharisees in the
Synoptic Sayings Source apparently used by Matthew and Luke (Q/Luke
11:37–52) and the pre-Markan "pronouncement stories" in which Jesus
puts down the Pharisees' accusations and challenges (e.g., Mark 7:1–13;
10:2–9). Both of these early sets of synoptic Gospel materials criticize or
condemn the scribes and Pharisees for the effects of their religiously rooted
social-economic activities on the Galilean people.[16] Unless we were to reason that the social-political-religious roles in which these gospel materials
portray the scribes and Pharisees are reminiscences from their activities in
Galilee one or two generations earlier, under Herod, then here is credible
evidence for their presence in Galilee during the first half of the first century C.E. The credibility of these gospel materials as evidence is enhanced by
Josephus's reports about how quickly and energetically the Jerusalem high-
priestly government asserted their claim to control affairs in Galilee after
the outbreak of the revolt in 66, as well as by their delegation of mostly
Pharisees as representatives of the Jerusalem priestly government's interests
in Galilee.

Prior to the outbreak of the great revolt in 66 we have very little evidence
for the Galilean people themselves. Extant literary sources make reference

to only two events in this period which involved Galileans, both indirectly in relations to Judeans and/or the Jerusalem temple. While the pertinent accounts are most suggestive, they are also extremely difficult to interpret. In both Josephus's and Philo's accounts of Gaius's order for Petronius to erect his statue in the Jerusalem Temple, Galilean peasants would appear to have been involved. Josephus's accounts, like that of Philo, are heavily overlaid with "Jewish apologetics" focused on "the Judeans'" pacifist stance and readiness for martyrdom, if necessary, in defense of their sacred traditions. Moreover, as mentioned above, the protests appear to have been initiated by Judeans who appealed to Petronius at Ptolemais before he went to Tiberias to consult with Agrippa's courtiers (*Ant.* 18.263–68, 269–72; *B.J.* 2.192, 193). Nevertheless, it is those officials in Tiberias, that is, the rulers of Galilee, whom Josephus has voice concern about the land still being unsown, hence a prospect of no harvest from which the tribute would be taken. That suggests that there may well have been a "peasant strike" of some scope underway in Galilee itself, whatever the type and extent of the Judeans' protest. Hence we may well have in Josephus's accounts an indication that on this occasion ordinary Galileans made common cause with Judeans when faced with a threat to the basic covenantal principles they shared from ancient Israelite tradition. Of course, the Galileans' motives may have been more complex. Given their likely residual grievances against Roman rule, Gaius's provocative order and the major military expedition underway to implement it may have proven too much to abide silently. The other event, the Samaritan murder of the Galilean(s) headed toward Jerusalem for a festival, resulted in a major crisis in relations between the Roman governor and the respective Judean and Samaritan indigenous aristocracies. What lies behind the incident, however, is of potential relevance for relations between the Galileans and the Jerusalem temple. The presupposition is that at least some Galileans journeyed to Jerusalem for festivals (as Josephus says explicitly in his second account, *Ant.* 20.118). Some relationship with Jerusalem institutions must have developed among Galileans despite the evident inattention from Jerusalem rulers since late Hasmonean times. Precisely because the evidence is so fragmentary and difficult to interpret we must explore the character of the relationship between Galileans and Jerusalem institutions further in chapter 7.

The fullest literary evidence for activities among Galileans themselves stems from the traditions about Jesus and his followers in the Christian Gospels. We can readily imagine how the economic and cultural impact of Antipas's building activities early in the first century and then the political power vacuum created by the rulers' neglect of Galilee in mid-century may have contributed to the origin and development of the movement(s) that found expression eventually in the Gospel of Mark and the Synoptic Sayings Source Q. Certainly both of those documents of Gospel literature have a certain historical verisimilitude with the conflictual structure of political-economic-religious relations among Rome, Jerusalem, Tiberias, and the Galilean people. Both represent Jesus as founding a movement that stands over against the Jerusalem-based authorities in a renewal of Israel reminiscent of both Moses and the northern Israelite hero Elijah. To keep this study manageable, however, it seems better to draw only sparingly on Jesus-traditions.[17]

Aristocratic Strategy and Historiography on the Great Revolt

Josephus's Historiography and the Structure of Imperial Rule

With the eruption of the great revolt against Roman rule in 66 we suddenly move from a paucity to a plethora of evidence for Galilee. Both the value of and the problem with Josephus's accounts of events in Galilee from the summer of 66 to the summer of 67 stem from the fact that Josephus himself was one of the principal actors in those events. Thus, while he often provides "eyewitness" reports, his accounts are not only apologetic but self-glorifying and self-serving in the extreme. Moreover, because he first led the resistance against Roman reconquest in Galilee (or so he claims), but then deserted to the Romans and assisted in the reconquest of Jerusalem, he has much to explain about his own and other aristocrats' role in the great revolt.

Josephus himself raises our suspicions. He leaves inconsistencies both within and between his two lengthy accounts of events in Galilee. His first account, in books 2–4 of *The Jewish War*, begins with Josephus himself being sent by the provisional government in Jerusalem as commander to organize the defenses in Galilee and focuses on an elaborate self-portrait as the ideal general. With the exception of the siege of Jotapata (at which he deserted to the Roman side), however, this first account has only one brief portrayal of Josephus actually engaged in combat against Roman troops (3.59–64).[18] The later account in his autobiographical *Life* is utterly self-justifying, even to the point of claiming that he and the priestly aristocratic council in Jerusalem were just pretending to be making preparations to fight the Romans. Yet in contrast with the earlier account, the *Life* has a few more portrayals of Josephus actually fighting, against Roman or "royal" (Agrippa II's) troops (*Vita* 114–21, 373–80, 394–97, 398–406).

The "Jewish Revolt" is usually constructed — and Josephus's accounts of it read — as a nationalist revolt against Roman rule by the Jewish people generally, with emphasis often on the instigation of the revolt by the religiously inspired "Zealots" of Judaism. To the degree that there was disagreement within Jerusalem or Judea, the sides are then labeled "the war party" and "the peace party."[19] The tendency is then to attempt to figure out which side Josephus was really on, and to distribute credit and discredit to his two accounts accordingly.[20] Such previous critical assessments of Josephus's historiography, however, were done with limited attention to the determinative importance of the political-economic structure of the imperial situation in Roman Palestine. In order both to critically assess our principal source, Josephus, and to appropriately reconstruct the events about which he writes, it would be well to review the fundamental structure and dynamics of the imperial situation,[21] as well as to review the events leading up to the outbreak of the popular insurrection in Jerusalem, Judea, and Galilee.

The fundamental political-economic-religious division in ancient Palestine was, as in any traditional agrarian society, that between rulers and ruled, in this case, between the wealthy and powerful high-priestly and Herodian families centered in Jerusalem and the villagers and townspeople in the rest of the land. As we have noted, this division was complicated in first-century Palestine by the establishment of (rival) Herodian rulers in Sepphoris and Tiberias. It would be misleading to think simply in terms of Roman rule over against Jewish society, given the Roman policy of "indirect rule" through native kings and aristocracies generally, and Roman practice in Palestine in particular. Rome sent governors, who maintained order, but Judea was still ruled by/through the high priesthood/Temple government in Jerusalem, while Galilee and Perea were ruled (during most of this period) by Herodian client-rulers. Indeed, Rome held its client-rulers responsible for maintaining social order as well as rendering the tribute, and proceeded to punish them severely if matters got out of hand, as illustrated by the conflict between Judeans and Samaritans under Cumanus, mentioned above. It is increasingly clear that the hostilities that erupted in the summer of 66 C.E. were primarily between groups of ordinary Judeans and their high-priestly and Herodian rulers and creditors, with the Roman troops called in to suppress the insurrections. Once insurrections had erupted, however, the Judean aristocracy was caught in a very difficult situation. Not only were they desirous of restoring their own control as the ruling class of Judea, but the Romans held them responsible. Flight was simply an admission of failure. Virtually the only alternative, given the structure of Roman imperial rule, would have been to attempt to regain control of their people and negotiate with the Romans.[22] Josephus's accounts of his own actions and motivations should be read against just this structure of the situation.

A brief review of the initial events of the revolt in Jerusalem in the summer of 66 may help in placing the ideology and apology of Josephus's accounts in perspective so that we can utilize them more critically in reconstructing subsequent events in Galilee. Jerusalem had been slipping into increasing anarchy for several years. Banditry had become virtually epidemic in the countryside in the aftermath of drought, famine, and the resultant indebtedness and hunger. The principal high-priestly families, with their hired gangs of thugs, not only were feuding among themselves, but had become predatory, seizing by force from the threshing floors the tithes intended for the ordinary priests (*Ant.* 20.180, 206–7). Completely frustrated at the high priests' continuing collaboration with the Romans, a group of sages/teachers called Sicarii or "Daggermen" turned to assassinating key high-priestly figures (*B.J.* 2.254–57).[23] Despite the fact that the population of Jerusalem was as dependent on the Temple/high-priesthood system as the high-priestly aristocracy was on their Roman sponsors, blatant abuses by the last Roman governor, Florus (64–66), finally provoked outright defiance and organized resistance. One group captured the fortress of Masada, killing the Roman garrison. The priests conducting services in the Temple refused to continue the sacrifices for Rome and the emperor (*B.J.* 2.408–10).

Despite the efforts by the high priests, the Herodian aristocracy, and the leading Pharisees to control the populace, a spontaneous insurrection was gaining momentum. The insurgents attacked not only the Roman garrison and reinforcements from Agrippa II's troops, but their own priestly aristocracy as well. They set fire to the high-priestly houses as well as to royal palaces. They burned the public archives in order to destroy records of debt. They killed not only the whole Roman garrison, but also members of the priestly aristocracy, such as the former high priest Ananias and his brother Ezekias (*B.J.* 2.411–53). The Herodian and high-priestly families, along with leading Pharisees and other wealthy and powerful figures such as Josephus, took refuge in the upper city or took asylum in the inner court of the temple, with the lower city and temple area in the hands of the insurgents (*B.J.* 2.422; *Vita* 20). This situation continued throughout the summer and into the fall. When the Roman troops under Cestius finally came to retake control of Jerusalem, and the priestly aristocracy attempted to open the gates to them, the insurgents drove the Roman legions away from Jerusalem and completely out of the country (November 66; *B.J.* 2.517–55).

This is the context in which we must understand Josephus's accounts of affairs in Galilee in general and of how he came to be sent to take charge there in particular. In the *Life* Josephus writes that as he "consorted with the high priests and the leading Pharisees...we saw the people in arms and,...being powerless to check the revolutionaries,...we professed to concur in their views" (21–22). Even more after the defeat of Cestius, "the principal men of Jerusalem," recognizing their precarious situation amid well-armed revolutionaries, attempted to control by pretending to lead.

> Being informed that the whole of Galilee had not yet revolted from Rome, ...they dispatched me, with two other priests, to induce the disaffected to lay down their arms and to impress upon them the desirability of reserving these for the picked men of the nation. The policy was for them to have their

weapons constantly in readiness for future contingencies, but to wait and see what action the Romans would take. (*Vita* 28–29)

That account may well be "apologetic." But the strategy it articulates would be completely consistent with the position and role of regional aristocracies in the Roman empire, where they were held responsible for the behavior of their subjects.

The same aristocratic strategy can be detected in Josephus's earlier account of the formation of a provisional government by the high priests who remained in Jerusalem (*B.J.* 2.562–68).[24] All we have to do is "read between the lines" in the context of the situation in Jerusalem sketched above. According to this account, at the assembly supposedly held in the Temple after the Roman forces were driven out, the principal leaders of "those who defeated Cestius" were not included among those appointed as "generals to conduct the war," while the renegade priestly aristocrat Eleazar was sent to Idumea (where he would supposedly be neutralized and relatively harmless). Placed in key positions, particularly in Jerusalem, were stabilizing priestly aristocrats. Josephus confirms this in subsequent indications that the key commander in Jerusalem, the high priest Ananus, was hoping to moderate and was indeed actively suppressing the more revolutionary elements in the countryside (as in *B.J.* 2.651, 652–54). If the real strategy of Ananus and his associates is not clear at the end of book 2, then it becomes much more so during the struggles against the Zealots and in Josephus's own key indication in his encomium on Ananus in book 4 (esp. 4.319–22). That the priestly aristocrats were taking charge in an attempt to moderate the situation and assert some control of their society (which was their historical social-political-religious role) is explicitly articulated already in the *Jewish War*, and cannot be dismissed either as a late appearance only in the *Life* or as simply an "apology." That Josephus and his priestly cohorts were sent to Galilee basically to assert control of the situation seems clear on the basis of both reports, however self-serving they may be.

Jerusalem's Reassertion of Authority over Galilee

That a council in Jerusalem, particularly a high-priestly one, sent commanders to Galilee at all indicates that, upon the withdrawal of effective Roman power in the summer of 66, Jerusalem authorities immediately asserted their claim to control of Galilee (*B.J.* 2.562–68). Jerusalem had not held political jurisdiction over Galilee for seventy years. Yet in the minds of the provisional government in Jerusalem headed by high priests, Galilee, like Idumea, belonged under their jurisdiction. Josephus's lengthy accounts of the attempt to replace him provide further evidence that in the minds of priestly aristocrats and leading Pharisees the commanders over Galilee would be delegated from Jerusalem (*B.J.* 2.626–31; *Vita* 189–335). Thus events in Galilee in 66–67 cannot be understood in terms of a simple opposition of pro- and anti-Roman; we must also consider reassertion of Rome's interests by the provisional high-priestly government in Jerusalem. Whether the Romans could make their authority effective, of course, was quite another matter.

The basis of whatever power Josephus wielded in Galilee was his own little army, which he claims was 4,500 mercenaries and a "body-guard" of 600 (*B.J.* 2.583).[25] Even if those figures are typically inflated, and even if they were identical with the brigands he paid in Galilee, the point is the same. Rarely did he use these troops in action against Roman or royal forces (e.g., 2,000 infantry, *Vita* 116–17). But he regularly used them to control areas and affairs in Galilee. He boldly claims to have "taken by storm" the principal cities of Gabara, Sepphoris (twice), and Tiberias (four times) and to have deployed 10,000 of his own *hoplites* against Tiberias at one point (*Vita* 82, 321–31). He mentions repeatedly that he had left a commander with troops to maintain control of Tiberias (*B.J.* 2.616; *Vita* 89, 272). His troops and bodyguard were always with him, dismissed only for the special occasion of the sabbath (*Vita* 159). He claims to have enjoyed the support also of significant numbers of "the Galileans" in arms, but he always relied basically on his own mercenaries in which he had complete trust (note the distinction, e.g., in *Vita* 240–42, 243). Josephus was also able at least to neutralize the potentially rival fighting forces, the large bands of brigands that had formed in different regions of Galilee. He coopted them and the peasants simultaneously by persuading the latter to pay the former to serve as mercenaries — who took their orders from him (*Vita* 77–78).

One significant way in which Josephus utilized his mercenaries, a standard procedure in ancient politics, was in effect to hold hostage a number of local Galilean leaders. In his second account of events in Galilee, which is less pretentious and idealizing than the self-portrait of "the ideal general and governor," he more candidly explains that those Galileans who were his "friends" dining with him and serving as envoys to Jerusalem (while under guard), were basically magistrates ("those in office") taken as hostages for the loyalty of the district whom he could also use to legitimate his decisions (*Vita* 79, 228; cf. *B.J.* 2.570).

The Multiple Conflicts in Galilee, 66–67 C.E.

The situation in Galilee when Josephus arrived was anarchy, at least from his point of view. From Josephus's accounts, read in the light of the usual Roman "scorched earth" practices (particularly in punitive reconquests), it is evident that Roman troops to a degree created their own opposition.[26] If social-economic conditions were similar to those in Judea or to portraits in the synoptic Gospel tradition, it is understandable that banditry was on the increase in Galilee as well as in Judea. But we have no way of knowing whether any genuinely insurrectionary activity was already underway in Galilee. In any case, as in previous Roman conquests of Palestine, the process began in the northwest, with western Galilee. Marching against Chabulon, the Roman governor of Syria Cestius Gallus found it deserted (its inhabitants had fled to the hills), but pillaged and burned the town. "He next overran the district, sacking everything in his path and burning the surrounding villages and returned to Ptolemais" (*B.J.* 2.504–5). Whether any organized opposition existed before, "the Judeans" then attacked the troops he had left behind. Sepphoris welcomed the return of Roman power. But "all the rebel and brigand elements in the district" (likely formed or reinforced by those fleeing the Roman advance) "fled to the mountain in the heart of Galilee which faces Sepphoris and is called Asamon . . . and were quickly defeated . . . by the heavily-armed legionaries" (*B.J.* 2.510–12). The Romans then proceeded southward toward Jerusalem, "seeing no further signs of revolt in Galilee."

But insurrection there was, contrary to that simplistic statement. And it was not merely a resurgence of excitement in response to the defeat of Cestius's troops by the Judeans when they withdrew from Jerusalem the next fall. What Josephus found was not simple anti-Roman activity but multiple conflicts, including regional tensions, rural hostility against the ruling cities, and class conflict within the cities, which complicated the questions of acquiescence to Roman and/or Agrippa's rule and acceptance of Jerusalem's authority. Anticipating further discussion of these dynamics in later chapters, we can delineate briefly the principal conflicts manifest in Josephus's accounts of events in Galilee from late 66 through the summer of 67. In almost every instance, the overt conflicts that erupted in 66–67 were rooted in long-standing tensions or even social structural conflicts understandable from the history sketched in this and the previous chapter.

Sepphoris

Of the rival capitals, Sepphoris, "the greatest city of Galilee," remained unequivocally loyal to Roman rule (*Vita* 346). An administrative center under the Hasmonean and Herodian regimes, it had been rebuilt by Antipas after 4 B.C.E., and was either his capital or a Roman administrative city, independent of Jerusalem. Josephus and/or the Jerusalem provisional government attempted to assert their authority there. But the Sepphorites steadily resisted, at one point refusing to listen to either Josephus or the priestly Pharisaic delegation sent from Jerusalem to replace him (*Vita* 123–24). While waiting for the Romans to retake control in Galilee, they even hired the brigand-chief Jesus and his horde of several hundred as mercenaries to protect them (*Vita* 104–11). It is difficult to discern just what sort of mutually manipulative game Josephus was playing with the Sepphorites. He claims at one point to have been, in effect, a mediator mitigating the overall conflict, making it easier for Sepphoris as the only unit remaining unequivocally loyal to the Romans to maintain their position, and he reaches a mutual "understanding" with Jesus and their brigand-protectors (*Vita* 30–31, 107–11). Is it in that connection that he could have been "inveigled into (further) fortifying the city," which was already a fortress (*Vita* 347; *B.J.* 2.61; cf 3.34)? Yet at other points he claims to have taken Sepphoris by assault twice (*B.J.* 2.646; *Vita* 82, 374, 395–96).

The city's pro-Roman stance clearly exacerbated its fundamental social-structural conflict with "the Galileans." Josephus claims to have found manifestations of this as he arrived, then to have used the Galileans' hatred of the Sepphorites for his own purposes, while trying to mitigate its extreme effects (*Vita* 30, 107, 374–77). The further implications of this conflict between Sepphoris and the peasants it ordinarily "governed" were not long in reasserting themselves. When the Romans finally sent troops to protect the city, the latter also became a basis from which to reclaim control of the countryside. Both infantry and cavalry "made constant sallies and overran the surrounding country...devastating the plains and pillaging the property of the countryfolk, invariably killing all capable of bearing arms and enslaving the weak" (*B.J.* 3.59–63, 110).

Tiberias

Founded by Antipas only a half-century earlier, Tiberias had experienced perhaps only a decade of direct Roman rule and never had come under Jerusalem's political jurisdiction. Directly under Agrippa II since 54, Tiberias suffered a demotion in status and power, being now only head of a toparchy, like Tarichaeae, and no longer the "royal" capital of its early days, as it was under Antipas and Agrippa I. The statement Josephus places in the mouth of his rival historian and Tiberian intellectual, Justus son of Pistus (Latin names), likely articulates a genuine resentment about this loss of status, both in general and over against Sepphoris in particular (*Vita* 37–39). This loss may also have played a part indirectly in the motivation of the Tiberians' attack on villages subject to the nearby "Syrian" cities of Hippos and Gadara at the very outset of the insurrection (*Vita* 42, 341–42). Since there is no evidence that Tiberias was a particularly "Jewish" city, it is unlikely that these Tiberian attacks were part of a systematic Jewish retaliation against the surrounding Syrian cities for the massacre of Jews in Caesarea, as Josephus suggests in the *War* (2.457–60).

Tiberias was divided primarily along class lines: "the respectable citizens," or "ten principal men," headed by Julius Capellus, on the one hand, and "the riff-raff," or "party of the sailors and the poor," led by Jesus son of Sapphias, on the other (*Vita* 32–35, 64–67, 69, 296). Josephus claims that his rival Justus headed up a third party, although we never see it in action (*Vita* 36). Capellus and the "leading men" are consistently pro-Roman and pro-Agrippa, at several points attempting to arrange for Agrippa's troops to take control of the city. Eventually they manage to flee to the king in the Roman camp and throw themselves on Vespasian's mercy (*Vita* 34, 155; *B.J.* 2.632, 3.453–54).[27] Jesus and his followers burned and looted the royal palace and killed "all the Greeks" in the city at the outset, and finally led active resistance to the Roman troops at Tiberias and then at Tarichaeae at the end (*Vita* 66–67; *B.J.* 3.450, 457–59). Apparently these two parties struggled for control of Tiberias throughout the brief period of the "revolt" in Galilee. There appears to have been either a pitched intra-city war or a "purge" by one side or the other as the Roman legions finally retook control of Galilee (*Vita* 353).

The struggle between the two principal factions in Tiberias is compli-cated and confused in Josephus's narratives by his principal concern, his own control of the city. Much of his overall narrative, in fact, is concerned with how he repeatedly had to reassert that control (*Vita* 155–74, 317–35; *B.J.* 2.632–46). He claims to have taken it by storm four times (*Vita* 82). After taking control initially, moreover, he left an officer named Silas as "commander" in charge of affairs in the city (*Vita* 89; *B.J.* 2.616). Jose-phus's attempt to control Tiberias is clearly part of a general agenda of the provisional government in Jerusalem, headed by high priests and in-creasingly influenced by leading Pharisees such as Simon son of Gamaliel. This is evident first in Josephus's conference with the "council and principal men of the city" in which he pressed upon them the orders of the "Jeru-salem council" that the royal palace be demolished because it contained "representations of animals . . . forbidden by the laws" (*Vita* 64–65). The Jerusalem council's agenda of controlling Tiberias along with other areas of Galilee is further evident in the priestly Pharisaic envoys' lengthy negoti-ations there to replace Josephus as commander (*Vita* 271–303). Whether it was the same as the Jerusalem council's agenda, Josephus also had his own agenda, which he had repeatedly to disguise over against popular interests. That agenda, clearly, was to work in alliance primarily with Capellus and the upper class of Tiberias, who were loyal to Agrippa, while keeping them (as long as possible) from reestablishing Agrippa's control so that he could assert his own and/or Jerusalem's authority. As he says clearly at several points, he had to disguise his real intentions. But his ultimate strategy is nevertheless evident in such actions as his placing of the loot taken from the royal palace in the hands of Capellus and the principal councillors to hold in trust for the king (*Vita* 68–69, 296).

The relationship between Tiberias and "the Galileans," finally, is more complex than the unqualified opposition Josephus reports between Sep-phoris and "the Galileans." The Galileans made common cause with the lower-class Tiberians, led by Jesus son of Sapphias, in the burning and looting of the royal palace, which the upper-class Tiberians were attempting to protect (*Vita* 64–67). Moreover, Josephus's report that some Tiberians together with some Galileans accompanied him in an attack against Sepphoris is credible, given the Tiberians' jealousy of their rival capital city (*Vita* 107). Yet "the Galileans...had the same detestation for the Tiberians that they had for the Sepphorites" (*Vita* 384). That historically rooted resentment was directed at Tiberias insofar as it had been the ruling city from which they were dominated, that is, at the ruling group and officials of the city, as is clear from Josephus's documented tirades against his rival Justus, who (along with his brother) apparently had some official position. "The Galileans, resenting the miseries which he had inflicted on them before the war, were embittered against the Tiberians" (*Vita* 392). Indeed, "the Galileans had cut off his brother's hands on a charge of forging letters prior to the outbreak of hostilities" (*Vita* 177). It is also significant to note Josephus's argument in the last passage (174–77): precisely because of the potential violence of the Galileans, it is important to play along with (and coopt) their passion for independence — until the appropriate social order can be reestablished, of course.

Gabara

Situated in the hills about ten miles north of Sepphoris, Gabara was the third of the "chief cities of Galilee." Although it was never the capital city, it must have been the principal administrative center in northwestern Galilee to be included regularly in a list with Sepphoris and Tiberias (*Vita* 82, 123, 203).[28] As social unrest escalated in the summer of 66, some Gabarans, along with some people from Soganae, Tyre, and Gadara (?) attacked Gischala to the northeast, which attacked them in return (*Vita* 44). Later, Gabara formed a lasting alliance with Gischala under the leadership of John son of Levi, Simon, the leading citizen of Gabara, having become John's close friend and associate (*Vita* 123–24). Unless we dismiss the report as part of Josephus's overblown claims of support by "the Galileans," Gabara apparently had the same conflicts with the peasants in its district as did Sepphoris and Tiberias (125). If the "house of Jesus" was anything like Josephus describes, "a great castle as imposing as a citadel," then there must have been some extremes of wealth and power in the region. Gabara seems steadfastly to have resisted Josephus's control. Although Josephus claims to have taken it by storm, he does not claim to have fortified the city, but only the village of Soganae not far away. As Vespasian began the reconquest of Palestine, his "first objective" was Gabara. Finding it without combatants, "he slew all the males who were of age...and also burned all the surrounding villages and towns," enslaving the (remaining) inhabitants (*B.J.* 3.132–34).

Tarichaeae

Like Tiberias, Tarichaeae (=Magdala) was the center of a toparchy (regional administrative district) under Agrippa II. As what must have been the largest town along the lake before Tiberias was built, it may well have been an administrative center also under Hasmonean and Herodian regimes. It seems to have been Josephus's most comfortable "headquarters" and most reliable ally during his activity in Galilee (*Vita* 97, 159–60, 276, 304). That is not surprising since information that Josephus gives in passing indicates that the concerns of the dominant Tarichaeans paralleled his own (and those of the Jerusalem elite). In dealing with Tarichaeae it is important to note Josephus's careful distinction between the residents of the town itself, or at least the dominant ones, and both the peasants from the surrounding area and activists or refugees from other towns such as Tiberias, who gathered in or around Tarichaeae at crucial points and were far more ready to offer resistance to Roman/royal rule or Josephus's command (*B.J.* 2.598–602). "The indigenous residents had from the beginning not wanted to fight," but became caught between the surrounding peasant or the Tiberian lower class's interest in independence and the inevitable Roman reconquest (*B.J.* 3.492, 500–501). Vespasian appears to have recognized this in his disposition of the captives when he restored the residents to their town (*B.J.* 3.532–35). Two of the "principal men" of the town, Dassion and Janneus son of Levi ("the most powerful man of the Tarichaeans") were "very special friends of the king" and were still safely in place (*Vita* 131; *B.J.* 2.597). Josephus entrusts them with goods that had been taken from one of the king's high officers in an ambush, to be returned in good time. Josephus appears not only to have been on good terms with the Tarichaeans, but to have depended on their support particularly in dealing with Tiberias (*B.J.* 2.635–41; *Vita* 97–98).[29]

Gischala

The regional differences become more pronounced when we come to Gischala, even if the multiple social conflicts are less complex. While undoubtedly smaller than Tarichaeae, Gischala was nonetheless an important regional town (*polichne*, *B.J.* 4.84). In addition to being situated in the rugged northern hill country of Upper Galilee, remote from the capital cities of Sepphoris and Tiberias, it lay on the frontier with the territory controlled by Tyre. There had been a history of conflict along this frontier, particularly between the northern Galileans and Kedasa, a large fortified village (and ironically probably formerly Kedesh in the territory of Naphtali). Such conflict apparently erupted anew in the summer of 66 (*B.J.* 2.459, 4.105). As is often the case in a frontier region during intense social unrest, there were numerous fugitives in the area (*B.J.* 2.588, 625; *Vita*

372). At the very outset of the widening social disorders, Gischala had been attacked by peoples from the surrounding towns of Gabara and Sogane, to the southwest in Galilee, Tyre to the north, and Gadara (?) around the lake to the southeast. Such is the context in which the people of Gischala, under the leadership of John son of Levi, struck out at their attackers and rebuilt and fortified their town (*Vita* 43–45).

Such is also the origin and basis from which John of Gischala became Josephus's principal rival for the leadership of Galilee and eventually one of the leaders of the resistance in Jerusalem. It is impossible to separate what transpired in Gischala and "Upper Galilee" from John's rise and maneuvers for prominence in Galilee more generally. John may even have started as a brigand, for it is in just such circumstances that threatened communities (or even cities such as Sepphoris) look to strongmen for protection and leadership. However respectable or unrespectable his origins, John built a sizable band of followers partly out of those numerous fugitives from the Tyrian villages (*B.J.* 2.587–88).[30]

John's initial conflicts with Josephus were basically struggles between local autonomy or leadership and control of local matters from above. As Josephus admits at points, John and the Gischalans had already fortified their town; it was not done on his instruction, as he claimed elsewhere (*Vita* 45, 89; cf. *B.J.* 2.575, 590). The most obvious case of such a struggle between local power versus control from the commanders appointed by the Jerusalem council is the seizure of the imperial grain stored in the villages of Upper Galilee, a case in which John ostensibly sought and received approval for his action from the "higher authorities" (*Vita* 71–73). Does the technical term "his district" (*eparchia*) in this account indicate that Josephus and the two other priestly governors were administering Galilee in districts assigned to local prefects (*eparchoi*)? Or might it mean even that John had been appointed prefect in charge of (part of) Upper Galilee by the provisional government in Jerusalem, with Josephus and his cohorts being charged only with Lower Galilee? Josephus complains about John's seizure of the grain for the same reason he complains about John's ingenious scheme to supply pure oil for the Jewish inhabitants of Caesarea Philippi in return for considerable revenue: John outmaneuvered him to bolster his own personal and/or local power as opposed to Josephus's stated design to bolster his own personal and/or regional power.

John's and Gischala's next step was to compete with Josephus for influence in the rest of Galilee. Josephus tells at length how John lobbied for support in Tiberias. At one point the struggle almost came to active conflict between John's men and the mercenaries Josephus had left in the city to maintain control (*B.J.* 2.614–20; *Vita* 84–96). Josephus claims to have checked John's challenge to his own dominance by threatening to confiscate the property and burn the houses of anyone in any city who continued to cooperate with John (*B.J.* 2.624–25; cf. *Vita* 368–72, placing this much later). Yet John continued to build support and make alliances in Tiberias and elsewhere. John and the Gischalans apparently reversed their earlier conflict with Gabara and forged a lasting alliance with Simon, the leading man of the city, having become John's friend and associate (*Vita* 123–24, 235).

John finally began cultivating influential figures in the Jerusalem council. Josephus was already closely allied with the high-priestly families. Jesus son of Gamala, who had formed a sort of duumvirate with Ananus, was supposedly "an intimate friend" (*Vita* 204). Thus it is not surprising that John formed links with the leading Pharisees who were playing an increasingly important role in the provisional government. As Josephus narrates at length, eventually a basically Pharisaic delegation was sent to replace him in command of Galilee.[31] Now two competing sets of commanders claimed to represent Jerusalem's authority over Galilee, each with different connections in Galilee, sometime in the same city. The struggle for domination in Galilee made for strange alliances. The peasants of Gischala, united with the Tyrian refugees-turned-brigands under John's leadership, forged alliances both with their former enemies the Gabarans (who, interestingly enough, were afraid of the peasants in their own district), and with the lower-class party as well as the scribal official Justus in Tiberias. Moreover, they then began cooperating with a basically Pharisaic delegation from Jerusalem.

Other Conflicts

Most difficult to assess and reconstruct is what was happening among the Galilean peasantry — or rather, the peasants of Lower Galilee, since in Upper Galilee our information pertains mainly to the Gischalans. It is clear in both accounts that "the Galileans" ordinarily refers to the peasantry, that is, people from the countryside (*chōra*), either in a given area or in all of Galilee (e.g., *B.J.* 2.602, 621–22; 3.199; *Vita* 102, 243), often in distinction from the city people, the Sepphorites and/or Tiberians.[32]

The issues are unusually muddled because Josephus made "the Galileans" the centerpiece of his self-defense in the *Life*. He asserts *ad nauseam* that "the Galileans" had such affection for and loyalty to him that they were more concerned for his safety than for the loss of their villages and families (84, 124, 198). He repeatedly has them entreat him to let them take vengeance on his opponents in Tiberias and particularly on John and Gischala (99, 102, 368). When the delegation comes from Jerusalem to relieve him of his command, "the Galileans" supposedly acclaim him as "the benefactor and savior of their country" (244, 259; note the typical Hellenistic-Roman terms). Throughout all this self-justifying rhetorical narcissism, however, it never occurs to Josephus to include any explanation of the basis of such adulation by peasants whom he wrote about with

such disdain in his political histories. In fact, except for the fictional report about recruiting an army of 100,000, he gives no indication of having
recruited, organized, armed, aided, or defended any Galileans. Although
he claims to have taken armed Galileans under his command at two or
three points, he apparently never led them in an actual military engagement (see *Vita* 107–8, 212–13, 242–65). On the other hand, he provides
plenty of examples of (1) how he used the Galileans as pawns in his own
agenda of attempting to control Sepphoris and Tiberias and to thwart the
influence of John of Gischala, and (2) how, while using the Galileans, he
did not trust them, hence did not arm them when asked and kept their
magistrates or leaders as hostages under guard (79, 228). Thus, in order
to reconstruct what the Lower Galilean peasantry may have been doing
in 66–67, we must sort critically through Josephus's apologetic rhetoric with extreme skepticism about his claims, utilizing as evidence only
those passages that cannot be reduced to or explained away as his own
rhetoric.[33]

As noted above, the Roman troops surely created some of their own opposition with their "scorched earth" practices. Their punitive sacking and
burning of villages would have created numbers of fugitives who swelled
the ranks of the brigands or "rebels." Such Roman terrorization of the
peasantry, however, merely exacerbated and ignited the social conflicts that
already existed in Galilee. As noted already in connection with the cities,
well before the unrest became serious in 66 or Josephus came to Galilee, "the Galileans" were resentful at Sepphoris and Tiberias because of
how they had been treated by their rulers/administrators (*Vita* 30, 39,
177). Thus it is not surprising that they took the opportunity of the withdrawal of effective Roman or royal rule to vent their hostility against those
they apparently viewed as exploiters (e.g., *Vita* 66–67, 374–78, 381–84).
Furthermore, there is no reason to doubt and, given the structure of the imperial situation, good reason to believe Josephus's reports that one motive
for the Galileans' hostility against Sepphorites and (upper-class) Tiberians
was the latter's loyalty to Rome and/or Agrippa II, that is, the people's
ultimate rulers. One incident illustrates the opposition:

> The principal men from the council [of Tiberias] had written to the king
> inviting him to come and take over their city. The king promised to come,
> writing a letter in reply, which he handed Crispus, a groom of the bed-
> chamber, a Jew by race, to convey to the Tiberians. On his arrival with
> the letter he was recognized by the Galileans, who seized him and brought
> him to me. The news created general indignation and all were up in arms.
> On the following day large numbers flocked together from all quarters to the
> town of Asochis... loudly denouncing the Tiberians as traitors and friendly
> to the king, and asking permission to go down and exterminate their city.
> For they had the same detestation for the Tiberians as for the Sepphorites.
> (*Vita* 381–84)

The Galileans' opposition to their ultimate rulers, the Romans, and their client Agrippa was, in the very structure of the situation, connected with their hostility to their immediate rulers in the capital cities.

Insofar as the peasants were armed, they had done it themselves.[34] Although apparently not all were armed (*Vita* 368), Josephus certainly encountered a people in arms. Yet there is nothing to indicate major or frequent attacks against the cities or any other targets, and it is difficult to believe that there would have been except for Josephus's restraining influence. The only insurrectionary activity for which we have evidence appears to have been local and ad hoc.

> Some adventurous young men of Dabaritta [village on the western slope of Mount Tabor] lay in wait for the wife of Ptolemy, the king's overseer. She was travelling in great state, protected by an escort of cavalry, from territory subject to the royal administration, into the region of Roman dominion, when, as she was crossing the Great Plain, they suddenly fell upon the cavalcade, compelled the lady to fly, and plundered all her baggage. They then came to me at Tarichaeae with four mules laden with apparel and other articles, besides a large pile of silver and five hundred pieces of gold. (*Vita* 126–27)

We can imagine that other such actions took place, but have no evidence.

The Galileans' insurrectionary activity was clearly distinct from, if at points similar to, the actions of the large bands of brigands that formed from the social turmoil. The situation in Lower Galilee appears to have been different from that in and around Gischala, if we can trust Josephus in this respect. Under John's leadership the Gischalans and the local bandit gangs had joined forces. The situation in Lower Galilee was complicated by the different interests of (and responses to the anarchy by) the city of Sepphoris and the machinations of Jerusalem's commander on the scene, Josephus. As noted above, Sepphoris had hired the large troop under the brigand-chief Jesus as mercenaries for its protection (against the Galileans and/or Josephus) and Josephus managed to persuade "the multitude" (precisely where he does not say) to pay other brigands, apparently primarily to leave them alone.

The brigands of Lower Galilee thus appear not to have been a revolutionary force, at least after the initial skirmishes against the Roman troops sent to put down the insurrection in the summer of 66. In ordinary times peasants usually lived in a certain symbiosis with the small gangs of bandits in their area. But with the large bands of brigands left in Galilee in the later summer of 66, it is likely that some "Galileans" were anxious about "the brigands," as Josephus reports (*Vita* 206). Galileans in villages around the city of Sepphoris may have feared the huge horde of brigands under Jesus, whom Josephus left free to operate. Elsewhere in Galilee the villagers may have feared the very brigands Josephus had ordered them to pay for "protection." Insofar as we can trust Josephus's accounts, the peasantry of

Lower Galilee do not appear to have made common cause the large hordes of brigands.

The peasants of Lower Galilee seem to have been insurrectionary in two principal ways, neither of which involved organized and active revolutionary activity. First, realizing at least temporarily a typical peasant dream, they lived for a time independent of their rulers. With Roman (or Agrippa's) military power temporarily absent, they effectively exerted their independence of imperial or royal officers and administrative apparatus in Sepphoris and Tiberias (and Gabara and Tarichaeae?). The Sepphorites clearly felt threatened by this peasant anarchy, hiring Jesus and his company until the Romans could send a garrison to protect them. And in Tiberias the Galileans joined forces with the party of sailors and the poor led by Jesus son of Sapphias, at least in the attack on the royal palace. But so far as we know there was no organized massive assault on either capital city.[35]

Second, although there is no way we can estimate and evaluate percentages of participant peasants or villages, clearly a number of villages and/or individuals offered resistance to the Roman reconquest of the area. Understandably, as the Romans advanced, devastating the land and slaughtering or enslaving the peasantry, many fled to fortress towns or mountain strongholds. For example, whatever Josephus's role may have been, there was major resistance and a major siege necessary at Jotapata, north of Sepphoris. Judging from the few heroes of that fight mentioned by Josephus, many of the combatants there were from surrounding villages such as Saba and Rumah (*B.J.* 3.229–33). In Japha, "the largest village in Galilee," close by Nazareth, the inhabitants advanced to meet the Romans and offered heroic resistance (*B.J.* 3.289–306). At Tarichaeae, resistance was offered primarily by Galileans from the surrounding area, not the residents themselves (*B.J.* 3.492–502). And at Mount Tabor "a vast multitude" again offered resistance to the Roman reconquest (*B.J.* 4.54–61).

The Galileans' relation to Josephus, finally, cannot have been anything like what Josephus claims. His own reports, both of how he treated them and of how they opposed him, utterly undermine the credibility of his claim of their unflinching devotion. Josephus clearly established some sort of working relationship or alliance with at least some of the peasants of Lower Galilee. He exploited their hostility against Sepphoris and Tiberias for his own purposes, as he emphasizes repeatedly. Whatever the basis of their opposition to John of Gischala and the town of Gabara, he coopted it in his power struggle with John. When in western Galilee, at least, he made his headquarters in villages such as Cana, Asochis, and Japha. Was common opposition to Sepphoris a sufficient basis for this cooperation? The basis of their tacit acceptance of his presence may simply have been the mercenaries he always had with him. And tacit acceptance may have turned to grudging acceptance, since the support of a few hundred professional soldiers (Josephus surely exaggerates when he claims thousands) would have been a considerable drain on a local agrarian economy. It is likely moreover, that Josephus sent his troops out foraging through the countryside for food more than the one time he mentions (*B.J.* 2.634).[36]

Whatever his working relationship with the Galileans, Josephus clearly did not trust them. In this connection his own professional troops play one of their more important roles. Just as the Romans, in standard practice, took hostages from Sepphoris to secure the loyalty of the city (*Vita* 31; cf. *B.J.* 3.31), so Josephus retained a number of Galilean magistrates (*hoi en telei*) as hostages for the loyalty of the Galileans (*Vita* 79).[37] They traveled and dined with him, and he claims, at least, that he used them as a council to help legitimate his decisions. Most telling is his report of his use of "thirty Galileans of the highest repute" as emissaries to the Pharisaic priestly delegation sent to replace him: "I instructed them to pay their respects to the deputies, but to say not a word more. To each of them I attached a soldier whom I could trust, to watch them and see that no conversation took place between my emissaries and the other party" (*Vita* 228). One suspects that the reason Josephus then sent an armed escort of 500 men with the delegation of 100 "leading men" of Galilee was not simply for their protection during the journey (*Vita* 266–68). Upon their return to Galilee, not surprisingly, those delegates then reported to the Galileans exactly what Josephus wanted them to hear (309–11). With the aid of his mercenaries, Josephus was clearly manipulating the leading men and the "magistrates" of the Galileans.

Nor, apparently, were the Galileans particularly taken in by the manipulative commander from Jerusalem. Interspersed with his grandiose claims to their undying affection are several reports of how they anticipated, distrusted, challenged, or opposed him. While he was negotiating with the principal men of Tiberias, the Galileans were helping loot and burn the royal palace (*Vita* 66). They distrusted his favoritism to and protection of the foreign nobles of the king (149–52). They were not fooled by his supposedly secret plan to return goods they had plundered to Agrippa's finance officer (*B.J.* 2.595–97; *Vita* 126–31). They (apparently correctly) suspected that his ultimate intention was "to betray the country to the Romans," did not place much stock in his protestations to the contrary, and (he says) tried to kill him (*Vita* 132–48; *B.J.* 2.598–610). It would thus appear from Josephus's own accounts of events that "the Galileans," far from being devoted to him, were suspicious of his motives and resistant to his leadership, while in certain ways cooperative when it suited their own concerns.

It is clear from this survey that there was no unifying ideology and no coherent, let alone unified, anti-Roman "revolt" in Galilee in 66–67 C.E. There were rather a number of interrelated conflicts, most of them local or regionally based. While Sepphoris remained steadfastly pro-Roman, Tiberias was split between its pro-Agrippa elite and a more insurrectionary popular faction. "The Galileans," by which Josephus refers mainly to the peasantry of Lower Galilee, focused their hostilities on Sepphoris and the ruling class of Tiberias, while making common cause with the popular faction of Tiberias in opposition both to Roman or royal rule and to the commander sent from Jerusalem. Between the toparchy capital Tarichaeae and the surrounding peasantry there was less conflict despite different degrees of interest in "revolt" from royal rule. In Upper Galilee, John of Gischala led a sizable coalition of forces, uniting the peasants of his native town with a brigand-horde of refugees from the Tyrian frontier, and challenged Josephus effectively for influence in Galilee.

With the notable exception of the "principal men" of Tiberias and those who dominated affairs in Tarichaeae, all of these different groups, for different reasons, successfully resisted Josephus's attempts to assert Jerusalem's (or his own) authority in Galilee. The utter failure of Josephus's mission to maintain control in Galilee, as documented even through his self-serving accounts, indicates just how fragmented and independent the various areas or cities of Galilee were and how little authority was commanded in Galilee by the high priestly–Pharisaic council in Jerusalem or the commander it sent, whether to organize the area's defenses or, more likely, "to induce the disaffected to lay down their arms."

Chapter 4

GALILEE AFTER
ROMAN RECONQUEST

⚜

Galilee, Galilee, you hate the Torah. In the end you will be victimized by [Roman] oppressors.

— RABBI YOHANAN B. ZAKKAI

[The Judean sages] are rude and know little Torah.

— RABBI YONATAN

In the post–Bar-Kokhba era we read of conclaves held at Usha and Beth Rimmon, but these were apparently emergency meetings only and the authority of those assembled was at most of a moral and religious nature. Contrary to what is often maintained in scholarly literature, such gatherings and a supposed national institution representing the entire Jewish community have little in common.... The Sanhedrin was no longer functional, not even in an altered form, in the second and third centuries.

— LEE I. LEVINE

Roman reconquest of Galilee in the summer of 67 was swift and devastating. Prior to the massive military campaign led by Vespasian, contingents of Roman troops had begun the punitive process of burning and pillaging the villages and either slaughtering or enslaving the villagers (see, e.g., *Vita* 213–14; *B.J.* 3.61, 110). By his own admission, Josephus and his mercenaries offered little or no protection to the people. As the Roman conquest began in earnest, Josephus simply fled to Tiberias (*B.J.* 3.127–31). Even where the Romans encountered no resistance, as at Gabara, they killed or enslaved the populace and devastated the countryside ("all the villages and countrytowns in the area"; *B.J.* 3.132–35). By July the more defensible fortified villages such as Japha and Jotapata were taken after brief sieges. Shortly thereafter Tiberias opened its gates to the Romans, who then quickly took Tarichaeae. There remained only some "mopping up" operations on less accessible places such as Mount Tabor and Gischala in Upper Galilee, which were taken by November.

89

A considerable percentage of the Galilean peasantry must have been killed or taken away as slaves and numerous villages and towns destroyed in the course of the Roman reconquest. Even when we take Josephus's exaggerations into account, the numbers of those slain or enslaved must have been high. In Japha, where no males were spared except infants, he has 15,000 slain, 2,130 women and infants enslaved, while in Jotapata he has 40,000 killed (*B.J.* 3.304–6, 336–39). Of those captured in and around Tiberias and Tarichaeae, he has 1,200 elderly killed, 6,000 youths sent as slaves to work on Nero's pet project, digging the canal at the isthmus of Corinth, and 30,000 more sold as slaves (*B.J.* 3.540–41).[1]

Some sixty years after the great revolt of 66–70, Judeans again rebelled against Roman rule.[2] Yet nothing indicates that the Bar Kokhba Revolt of 132–135 C.E. involved Galilee directly. The titles Sepphoris received under Antoninus Pius, *autonomos, pistē,* and *filē,* suggest that it again remained steadfastly pro-Roman. No coins, texts, or archaeological digs suggest insurrectionary activity or Roman repressive action in Galilee. The active rebellion, and the Roman devastation in suppressing the revolt, appear confined to Judean territory. One could project at most a certain unrest, perhaps in sympathy with the Judeans. Yet because of the proximity of the second revolt to Galilee, we must consider the impact its aftermath may have had on life in Galilee.

The period after the great revolt of 66–67 saw both the consolidation of early Christianity and the rise of rabbinic Judaism. Yet there is very little evidence for either one in Galilee itself. This makes it all the more important not to assume a state of affairs on the basis of previous constructions of those religions, but to reexamine the evidence or lack thereof for affairs in Galilean society in the late first and second centuries C.E.

Galilee under Direct Roman Rule

Following the Roman reconquest of Galilee in 67, the western region continued under direct Roman jurisdiction as part of the Roman province of Judea. The area around the lake was returned to Agrippa's rule before it, too, reverted to the province of Judea, and its people came directly under Roman rule for the first time. After the Bar Kokhba Revolt the province was renamed Syria Palaestina. Around 120 C.E. the province was upgraded from praetorian to consular status, with many of the appointees high-ranking Romans.[3] Despite the recent revolt, Roman rule from the governor's seat in Caesarea was apparently not much more rigorous than before. Rome's principal concern was the collection of tribute. As elsewhere in the empire, the Roman governors relied on provincial administrative officials and initiatives from below.[4] As Rome phased out its reliance on client-rulers, villages previously organized in toparchies were placed under the cities' jurisdiction for taxes and other administrative purposes. This process may have proceeded more slowly in Galilee than elsewhere. Indeed, the lack of evidence from Galilee, in contrast to the surrounding areas, for dating (of documents, for example) by the city era suggests that the Galilean cities were relatively unimportant administratively. Nevertheless, all of Lower Galilee was placed under Sepphoris and Tiberias, probably by the time of Hadrian, and remained so until Byzantine times. Upper Galilee (Tetrakomia) remained outside of either city's area, under the administrative authority of a representative of the provincial governor. After the Bar Kokhba Revolt the Romans stationed the Sixth Legion at Legio, with the Plain of Jezreel as its land, just south of the territory of Sepphoris.

Galilee was apparently not taken as imperial land after the revolt of 66–67. Debate about whether the whole land of Judea was made into imperial estates has revolved around the report that Vespasian had instructed his Roman officers "dispose of [*apodōsthai*] all the land of the Judeans. For he did not found there a city of his own, but kept the countryside [*chōra*] for himself" (*B.J.* 7.216). Recent inclination is to believe that only the land of the rebels was confiscated.[5] One would suspect that the Romans would have followed the same practice in Galilee. It does not appear, however, that large numbers of Galilean peasants became tenants on imperial land.[6] Nothing in early rabbinic literature reflects the closer supervision by a representative of the Roman governor one would expect in that case.[7] As we shall discuss further in chapter 9, mishnaic laws assume that households farming their own family inheritance was the usual situation in the second century. Some of those householders had become wealthy and had others in their debt. But nothing suggests that the Romans had changed the status of Galilean land and/or peasants in general following the great revolt.

Economic pressures on the Galilean peasant producers may have been lighter when Galilee came under Roman administration (either directly or indirectly through the cities of Sepphoris and Tiberias). After Agrippa II's death all of Galilee came under Roman administration, presumably thereafter with no taxes to be paid to a client-ruler. With the destruction of Jerusalem and the Temple, moreover, the institutional base for high-priestly enforcement of tithes and offerings to priests and temple dissolved. Even if collection had been inefficient in the decades before the revolt, enforcement virtually disappeared after the destruction of Jerusalem. Rome, of course, still expected its revenues. In addition to the traditional tax on crops from the land (which was waived only for wealthy collaborators with Rome such as Josephus; *Vita* 429) Rome levied a *tributum capitis*, which was felt to be unusually burdensome. Gamaliel II complained that this "poll-tax," which was apparently higher in Syria and Judea than in other provinces, was "one of the things by which the government oppresses Israel" ('*Abot R. Nat.* 8, 4).[8] After the destruction of the Temple, moreover, Rome imposed a special punitive tax of two drachmas on all "Judeans" as a replacement of the former Temple tax.[9]

While overall tax burdens may have been somewhat less, Roman military presence and the economic burdens that presence entailed increased after the revolts. Earlier, of course, any military presence in Galilee would likely have been the officers of Herod, Antipas, or the Agrippas. After the revolts Rome kept an unusually large military force of two legions plus auxiliaries in the province of Judea, one of them stationed just south of Galilee in Legio. They maintained cohort-size fortresses at Tiberias and Sepphoris (as suggested by rabbinic stories), as well as at Tel Shalem, south of Beth Shean.[10] The Romans generally held the area in which its military forces were stationed responsible for its economic support, the implications for Galilee being obvious, given the Sixth Legion stationed in the adjacent great plain. The increased Roman military presence in Galilee also brought with it demands for both *annona*, exactions of goods, and *angariae*, or "service to the state." Although both of these demands were originally made on an ad hoc local basis, they escalated into what was virtually another form of regular taxation during the third century. When it needed them, moreover, the army would simply take supplies of bread or wine or animals (*t. Bek.* 2.2; *t. Ḥal.* 1.4).[11] In addition to seizing the peasants' draft animals for food, the soldiers might expropriate them for transport or other work (*m. B. Meṣ.* 6:3). And the Romans could simply draft gangs of workers from the populace when needed (*m. B. Bat.* 9:4; *t. Ohol.* 9.2; *t. Yebam.* 14.7).[12] One of the likely purposes of this expropriation of asses and local peasants was the building of roads in the area. From the first century to the third, the Roman military built roads connecting Sepphoris with Legio to the south, Ptolemais to the west, and likely Tiberias and Scythopolis to the east.[13] Except for the presence of the Roman military and their often onerous demands on the people, however, Roman administration was haphazard and somewhat remote, the governors for the most part remaining in their comfortable coastal villas at Caesarea.

As important as the consolidation of Roman and urban rule for its effect on life in Galilee, of course, was the destruction of the Temple and the end of the high priesthood in Jerusalem. Galilee had been subject to Jerusalem rule from 104 to 4 B.C.E. and then subject to continuing influence from the Temple and priesthood for another seventy years prior to the great revolt. Even in the decades prior to the revolt of 66, affairs in western Galilee were governed (at least partly) through the priestly aristocracy in Jerusalem. It seems likely that the Temple had asserted at least some claim on the resources and loyalty of eastern Galilee also, either in cooperation or competition with the regime of Agrippas II. Although the sudden destruction of the Temple and high priesthood would have had less of an impact on the Galileans than on the Judeans themselves, there would nevertheless have been important implications for social-religious life in Galilee. On the one hand, as noted already, no longer would demands for Temple dues have been actively pressed upon the Galileans. On the other hand, the destruction of the Temple and high-priestly government meant the disappearance of the institutions that had attempted to hold the Galileans together with the Judeans under one political-economic-religious system. No longer would scribes and Pharisees be officially delegated by an established governing institution to teach and/or apply the Judean laws to aspects of Galilean social-economic life. The destruction of Jerusalem and the Temple, of course, also displaced the priests, scribes, and Pharisees, descendants of whom eventually relocated in Galilee and created what became rabbinic Judaism (see below). But nothing corresponding to the temple regime, however weak it had become toward the mid-first century, would emerge that could exert the same political-economic-religious influence and pressure on the people to live according to the laws of the Judeans. The historical situation had changed dramatically as a result of the Romans' destruction of the Jerusalem Temple in 70.

Once the Romans granted them control over the whole areas of western and eastern Lower Galilee, respectively, Sepphoris/Diocaesarea and Tiberias came to dominate affairs in Galilee even more than they had as the administrative instruments and/or residences of Antipas and the Agrippas. Both received from Rome the recognized privileges of "autonomy," such as the minting of coins. By the time of Hadrian, Sepphoris had become Diocaesarea, presumably with the correspondingly even more complete Roman orientation that entailed. If the theater illustrates the Roman political culture already established in Sepphoris in the first century, the extensive Dionysiac mosaic discovered recently in a large villa attests to the thriving Hellenistic-Roman culture likely dominant in Diocaesarea during the second and third centuries. Legends on coins from the time of Caracalla illustrate the pride as well as the dependency of the city: "Diocaesarea the Holy City, City of Shelter, Autonomous, Loyal, Friendship and Alliance between the Holy Council and the Senate of the Roman People." As the apparatus through which the empire was administered, the heads of cities such as Tiberias and Diocaesarea would have collected the tribute for Rome as well as the revenues from which the cities themselves lived.[14]

By late antiquity Galilee, and particularly Tiberias, the seat of the patriarchate as well as of rabbinic academies, had become some of the principal centers of international Jewry. Sages even came from Babylon to study there. Jews from elsewhere in the diaspora wanted to have their bones reinterred there. Just how the center of Jewish life and learning shifted from Judea to Galilee has been the subject of intense recent investigation and discussion. While the emergence of rabbinic circles is an important part of the story, it was by no means the only influence on the ensuing history of Galilee.

The Development of Rabbinic Influence in Galilee

After the Roman suppression of the Bar Kokhba Revolt in 132–135 in Judea, Galilee became the center of rabbinic activity and in time the principal basis of rabbinic Judaism in Palestine. The key historical questions are just how quickly rabbinic authority emerged and what influence the rabbis had on life in Galilee. On these questions some major reevaluation of previous historical constructions is now underway.

According to the standard view enshrined in textbooks, reference works, and the fields of Jewish studies and Christian origins generally, following the destruction of Jerusalem the Pharisaic party or sect emerged as the nation's leaders and laid the foundations of rabbinic Judaism.[15] The great Yohanan ben Zakkai gathered the surviving Pharisees at Jamnia/Yavneh, where he had received permission from Vespasian to found an academy that succeeded the Sanhedrin in Jerusalem as the authoritative governing council of the nation. In order to pull the nation together again after the disastrous destruction of Jerusalem and the Temple, Yohanan and the council at Jamnia took a number of key steps to consolidate or reconstitute Judaism. Focus on sacrifices and the special sanctity of priests was replaced by emphasis on the study of the Torah and teachers with the title of "rabbi." The authority previously vested in the Temple was now transferred to the synagogues in a series of liturgical reforms in the synagogue services. To protect the community from the threat of competition from without, they excommunicated the Christians (=*minim*), purged the scriptural canon of all works written in Greek and of all apocalyptic literature, and turned generally inward toward the Jewish community and away from the outside world. Then, following the Roman defeat of the Bar Kokhba Revolt in Judea, the rabbis transferred their council to Galilee, thereafter the center of rabbinic Judaism in Palestine, where the Mishnah and later the Palestinian Talmud were compiled.

This synthetic picture of the pivotal and comprehensive historical role of "Jamnia" is coming unraveled in recent years.[16] Because there has been so much scholarly historical "con-fusion" on the basis of extremely limited and fragmentary evidence, it is necessary to reexamine critically virtually every major component of this standard older construction of the origins of rabbinic Judaism at Jamnia. In the increasing recognition that the process by which "formative Judaism" eventually took form lasted many centuries we must also acknowledge that major components of the eventual outcome did not originally belong together. According to their own repeated testimony, the rabbis had virtually no authority among the people in Galilee at the time the Mishnah was compiled, around 200. Far from having been the leaders of the local synagogues, the rabbis were not particularly interested in them, neither the Mishnah nor the later Talmuds having much of anything to say about synagogues (or the Mishnah even about prayer). The triumph of the rabbis "over the indifference of the masses . . . was not earlier than the seventh century C.E."[17] There is no evidence that the Romans ever formally placed the rabbis politically in charge of affairs in Palestine or Galilee. The emergence of Judah the Prince as the "Patriarch" in Galilee around 200 may have been an ad hoc arrangement, with the "patriarchate" not being formally constituted until the late fourth century under the "Christian emperors" shortly before it came to an abrupt end early in the fifth century. Meanwhile, there is no evidence of any self-conscious split between "Judaism" and "Christianity" in Galilee in the first or second century, let alone any "excommunication" of "Christians" as heretics.

The same critical studies that are dismantling the standard old construction of the formation of rabbinic Judaism, however, are also helping us discern a rough outline of the steps by which the rabbis came to exert influence on social life in Galilee.

The notion that the Pharisees-become-rabbis under the leadership of Yohanan ben Zakkai set up a rabbinic academy (and a new Sanhedrin) at Yavneh to provide guidance for Judaism almost immediately after Jerusalem and the Temple were destroyed is based solely on the rabbinic story of Yohanan's miraculous escape from Jerusalem under siege by the Roman army.[18] The four somewhat different versions of Yohanan's escape in late rabbinic literature all appear to be developments of the same basic story. After having himself smuggled out of Jerusalem, Yohanan goes immediately to Vespasian and greets him prophetically as king. When the general finds out that Nero has died and he has indeed been made emperor, he offers to grant Yohanan a request. In three versions of the story, Yohanan asks to be allowed to start a school at Yavneh.

The problems of this story start with its historical credibility. Titus was the Roman general who conducted the siege of Jerusalem, his father Vespasian having already become emperor in Rome. This story of Yohanan, moreover, is closely paralleled by Josephus's story of his own escape from the siege of Jotapata and prophetic greeting of Vespasian as emperor. What we have in four variants is thus not a reliable report of a historical event, but a standard story (of a miraculous escape from a city under Roman siege and an interview with the emperor-to-be) which the rabbis made into a foundational legend for the academy they started at Yavneh. But this foundational legend provides no evidence for when such an academy was started or for what function it served or for whether it had any authority or influence in Palestine. It is also notable that the story does not say anything about a council actually being established at Yavneh.

Other sources, however, may provide a sense of a more concrete foundation for the subsequent development of rabbinic authority. Yavneh, along with the nearby towns of Azotus and Lydda, was precisely where the Romans settled wealthy and prominent Judean families who had either collaborated with or surrendered to the Romans during the great revolt, as Josephus makes clear (B.J. 4.130, 444). This fertile area toward the Mediterranean coast had traditionally been royal land under the direct dictates of king or emperor. After Herod's death, Yavneh and Azotus became the basis of his sister Salome's income of sixty talents a year, and she in turn bequeathed the territory to Julia, wife of Augustus (B.J. 2.98; Ant. 17.321; 18.31). This area was thus evidently at the disposal of the Romans as a basis for resettling the prominent Judean families who had a stake in restabilizing the imperial order. Among the prominent Judeans who apparently received large estates here were Eleazar ben Harsum, whom legends have in possession of huge tracts of land (including numerous villages) worked by tenants or slaves (y. Dem. 4.28b; y. Ta 'an. 4.69a; b. Yoma 35b), and (Rabbi) Gamaliel, whom tradition honors as the second head of the academy after Yohanan (m. B. Meṣ. 5:8).

There is thus direct continuity between the "leading Pharisees" who played prominent roles in the provisional government of Jerusalem in 66–68 (see chapter 3), the leadership of the academy at Yavneh, and the tannaitic rabbis who attempted to influence affairs in Galilee after the Bar Kokhba Revolt of 132–135. That is, Rabbi Gamaliel was the grandson of Gamaliel, the "teacher of the law" and influential Pharisee in the Jerusalem Council in Acts 5:34, and son of Simon son of Gamaliel, the prominent Jerusalemite Pharisee who, along with other Pharisees, was attempting to control affairs in Galilee (including the removal of Josephus; Vita 190). And Rabbi Gamaliel was supposedly the predecessor (and ancestor) of the dynasty of "patriarchs" (Judah the Prince, Gamaliel III, Judah II, Gamaliel IV, Judah III) who wielded considerable power (and headed a rabbinic academy?) in Galilee in the third century. Although we have precious little evidence for what the proto-rabbis were actually doing in Yavneh, it is clear that they enjoyed a solid economic base, some of them at least with extensive estates, and a social-political base among other prominent Judean families, from which to seek wider influence in Judea and, later, in Galilee.[19]

Given the paucity of our sources it is difficult to discern the degree to which features of later rabbinic Judaism — such as the study of Torah as the new cult and the rabbis and the new priests — was prefigured already among the leading Judean figures who gathered in Yavneh in the first two or three generations after the destruction of Jerusalem and the Temple.[20] Not only is the evidence sparse for the role of particular leaders such as Yohanan ben Zakkai or Eliezer ben Hyrcanus, but we cannot even determine the character and function of the gathering at Yavneh. It seems unlikely that it was a nascent political institution; it is even uncertain whether we should call it an academy. Perhaps it was simply an assembly of the surviving priests, scribes, sages, Pharisees, and others ready to cooperate in "putting the pieces back together" in the wake of the Roman reconquest. Probably the list of Yohanan's disciples in m. 'Abot 2:8–14 represents just this composite gathering at Yavneh: Eliezer ben Hyrcanus, a Pharisee; Yose, a priest; Simeon ben Nathaniel, an *am ha'ares;* Eleazar ben Arakh, a mystic. Increasingly clear is that the old generalization about the rabbis being primarily a continuation of Pharisaism is a simplification at best. Critical analysis of early rabbinic traditions reveals that opinions attributed to the Yavnean figure Eliezer ben Hyrcanus have strong similarities with traditions of the Pharisaic "houses," or disciples of Hillel and Shammai, while neither accord well with later rabbinic concerns. On the other hand, the traditions attributed to Yohanan ben Zakkai, whom no source identifies as a Pharisee, bear similarities both to earlier scribal concerns and to the later rabbinic agenda.[21]

The assembly or academy at Yavneh would thus appear to mediate the agenda of the scribes and sages generally more than the particular concerns of the Pharisees to the later generations of rabbis. The scribes generally, and not simply the Pharisees, would have been displaced by the destruction of the temple-state apparatus by the Romans. The scribes generally would have had both the professional expertise and the personal-political calling to continue the cultivation of "the (ancestral) laws of the Judeans," all the more so after the loss of the Temple. And early traditions of Yavnean figures are represented as engaged precisely in activities that were typically scribal (and not peculiar to the Pharisees): giving rulings on legal cases, calendrical matters, and certain religious and social disputes. Some of these cases were of general concern to the whole society; others were local matters. The rabbis based at Yavneh already had at least some contact with Galilee. They offered opinions or decisions on legal cases in places such as Meiron, Sogane, Tiberias, and particularly Sepphoris. On the other hand, whereas the earlier scribes and Pharisees functioned as the legal experts and interpreters of the temple-state, no credible early traditions represent the Yavnean leaders as (in some way official) representatives of the Roman government.

The destruction entailed in the Bar Kokhba Revolt would undoubtedly have had a direct impact on the nascent rabbinic movement and an indirectly if not direct impact on Galilee. It has been claimed that a massive number of Judeans from a devastated Judea migrated north into Galilee in the aftermath of the Bar Kokhba Revolt. Such a claim, however, appears to rest principally on the presuppositions through which the extremely limited and indirect evidence is interpreted. The literary evidence is nothing more than the rather indefinite settlements of rabbinic schools at Usha or Beth Shearim in western Lower Galilee (*Gen. Rab.* 97; *b. Roš Haš.* 31a–b). The archaeological evidence for claims of major influx of population into Upper Galilee is the growth of the village of Meiron in the middle and late second century and for corresponding claims about Lower Galilee is the growth of Beth Shearim in mid-second century.[22] That population growth in certain towns must be due to immigration from Judea is based on the "building of synagogues" in the third century, for which we have evidence of only two or three until later centuries. Although some migration took place, the evidence is simply not strong enough to support the hypothesis of a massive migration of people from Judea to Galilee in mid-second century.[23]

The tradition that a rabbinic school reestablished itself in western Lower Galilee in the aftermath of the Bar Kokhba Revolt, however, does seem credible historically. According to rabbinic literature itself, circles of rabbis left Judea during or after the Bar Kokhba Revolt and settled on the western border of Galilee at Usha, and then at Shefar ʿam and Beth Sheʿarim (*Gen. Rab.* 97; *b. Roš Haš.* 31a–b), before establishing themselves more prominently in the cities of Sepphoris and Tiberias later in the second century.[24] Eventually many reestablished themselves as wealthy landowners in Galilee, as Gamaliel had been in Judea, or enjoyed the patronage of wealthy landowners.[25] Thus, whereas the Roman destruction of Jerusalem in 70 eliminated the institutional base from which Judean influence in Galilee was orchestrated, the Roman devastation of Judea in suppression of the Bar Kokhba Revolt led the remaining social-cultural leadership of Judea to relocate in Galilee.[26]

The early rabbis had very little interaction with or influence upon social-economic-religious life in Galilee. Their own testimony in the case law of tannaitic literature (Mishnah and Tosefta) indicates this clearly.[27] Actual rulings by the early rabbis cover a very limited range of issues, such as the calendar, vows, mixed kinds (of crops), and particularly purity and tithes. Certain issues were apparently not brought to the early rabbis because they lay out of their jurisdiction. The disposition of corpses, synagogue proceedings, and sabbath observances were local matters resting on traditional customs and local community leadership. Civil and criminal cases were decided by local courts, not rabbinic deliberations. Rabbinic rulings in areas such as mixed kinds, purity, and tithes were not simply "religious" and related directly to the economic struggles of the people for a livelihood. It is precisely here that the early rabbis' own witness is strikingly clear: their rulings were by and large disregarded.

Many early rabbinic texts assume, and some state explicitly, that ordinary people were not observing the purity codes, which would have been difficult to keep in mind during normal productive activity as well as highly complex (e.g., *m. Bek.* 4:10; *m. Tohar.* 7:3; 10:3). The rabbis had an explanation for why the people were unobservant: "Simply because the peasants [*amme ha-aretz*] are not versed in the rules concerning the shifting of what is unclean" (*m. Tohar.* 10:1) and the other intricacies of purity. Even poor priests were suspect (*m. Ter.* 9:2). The rabbinic rules limiting the ways crops could be sown ("mixed kinds") and forbidding crops in the seventh year imposed unwelcome economic hardships on the peasants. Not surprisingly, such rules went unobserved. Apparently the rabbis moved away from earlier fanatical tactics of enforcement, such as destroying the unobservant farmers' "mixed" crops to declaring them "ownerless," that is, fair game for others' use (*m. Šeqal.* 1:2). Disregard of the sabbatical year was apparently as common as failure to tithe (*m. 'Abot* 5:9; *t. 'Abod. Zar.* 7 [8].10). Those who profited from breaking the sabbatical taboos were deemed to have forfeited certain religious and civil rights (*m. Sanh.* 3:3; *m. Roš. Haš.* 1:8). One definition of a peasant (an *am ha-aretz*) is one who does not tithe properly, and many a peasant was regarded as breaking one or another of the obligations for "firstlings" or "heave-offerings" or "the poor-tithe" (*t. 'Abod. Zar.* 3.10; cf. *m. Bek.* 4:7–10). Rules against keeping small cattle were also widely ignored (*t. B. Qam.* 8.14; *t. B. Meṣ.* 2.33; 5.7).

The only areas of life where there was not such resistance by or conflict with the Galilean people were in regard to matters such as keeping the calendar and observance of sabbath, set festivals, and circumcision. In calculating the calendar, the rabbis may have performed a welcome function. But the lack of conflict on such matters as sabbath, yearly festivals, and circumcision, which were all traditional and dependent on local custom, hardly points to the acceptance of rabbinical authority. Indeed, the early rabbis appear to have remained somewhat aloof from the peasantry whose impurity they suspected and whose practices they distrusted.[28] "Morning sleep and midday wine and children's talk and sitting in the assemblies of the peasants put a man out of the world" (*m. 'Abot* 3:11). It has been suggested that the early rabbis may even have lost influence with the people for a time after the move to Galilee, where they at first would have lacked a firm economic and political base and where they had no history of interaction with or authority over the people.[29] In any case, the witness of the Mishnah itself, compiled around 200 c.e., and other early rabbinic evidence indicates not only that the early rabbis did not govern or provide leadership in Galilee, but that they were virtually without authority or influence during the first few generations of their presence there.

The Patriarchate and Rabbinic Influence in Galilee

That the rabbis eventually gained some influence in Galilee in the course of the third century may not be due solely to their own adjustments and compromises. It appears that rabbinic circles established their influence first in dependence upon and then in struggles with the unprecedented institution of the patriarchate, which became prominent Galilee in the third century.

The authority wielded in Galilee and beyond by Judah the Prince (*nasi*) emerges in our sources at the beginning of the third century.[30] The Christian theologian Origen, who lived close by in Caesarea for twenty years, commented on the political power wielded by Judah.

> Now that the Romans rule and the Jews pay the two drachmas to them, we who have had experience of it know how great is the power wielded by the ethnarch among them and that he differs in no way from a king of a nation. (Secret) trials are held according to the law, and some are condemned to

death. And though there is not full permission for this, still it is not done
without the knowledge of the ruler. (*Ep. ad Afric.* 20, 14)

Rabbinic literature makes the relationship between Rabbi Judah and the
emperor "Antoninus" (probably Caracalla) legendary, suggesting that the
principal basis of Judah's power in Palestine and his authority in the Jewish
diaspora was his personal friendship with the emperor. Recent imperial history may have set the context, for in appreciation for Jewish backing during
a power struggle in 193, the emperor Severus made a number of favorable
gestures toward Palestinian communities. Judah, apparently exploiting the
newly favorable imperial disposition, obtained grants of land for himself,
increased civic rights for Tiberias, and other favors.[31]

Judah also appears in rabbinic sources as the virtual king described
by Origen, with great influence on social and economic as well as cultural affairs.[32] In the area of religious observance, which of course also
impacted certain social-political affairs and economic (agricultural) life, in
addition to determining the calendar, he tried to minimize the severity of
days set aside for mourning the destruction of the Temple and granted
the large Hellenistic cities of Palestine preferred status vis-à-vis the Jewish law. He exerted more direct influence in the society by controlling the
(ordination and) appointment of local judges, although many villages, such
as Simonias, just west of Nazareth, dismissed or protested the designated
candidates.[33] Judah and his successors in the patriarchate were also engaged in fundraising, apparently including collection of tithes, although
nothing indicates a role in the collection of taxes for the Romans.[34] The
patriarchs also employed a kind of private police force. Conceivably the
most important basis of his power within the society was his cultivation of
and intermarriage with the wealthy families. Capping this meteoric rise to
power by Judah the Prince is the sudden appearance in rabbinic sources of
claims that Hillel had been of Davidic descent,[35] that is, as a way of tracing
the latter-day *nasi*'s lineage back to David the *nasi*.

All of that, however, does not mean that Judah the Prince was, in effect, the governor or ruler in Galilee, certainly not with anything like
the political-economic power possessed by Herod or Antipas. The Roman
empire had long since moved away from indirect rule through native aristocracies or strongmen. Rabbinic texts offer no explicit evidence that Judah
was in some way appointed by the Romans. If he had been the governor or
ruler, he would not have pressed for Tiberias to be granted the status of a
colonia, for that would have diminished his own power and prestige. Collection of regular taxes, of course, would have been handled by the city
councillors, especially after Rome "urbanized" imperial rule by administering areas such as Galilee through cities such as Sepphoris and Tiberias.
Moreover, if Judah had been the designated governor, he would have had
no need for a private police force.[36]

Nevertheless, the degree of power and influence wielded by Judah the Prince and his successors in the third century was utterly unprecedented. There is no mention of anything of the kind for Simeon b. Gamaliel in the mid-second century or for Gamaliel earlier. The term *nasi* occurs rarely in tannaitic texts and is not used as a title applied to any rabbi in particular until the few references to Rabbi Judah "the Prince." Only later rabbinic texts use the term as a title for other tannaitic rabbis, usually those in the lineage of Hillel. Other uses of *nasi* in tannaitic texts are nontitular, for example, for a rabbi "lifted up" among his colleagues for a particularly fine explanation (*t. Pesah.* 4.13–14).[37] Gamaliel is reported only to have control over the calendar and the appointment of teachers in connection with the academy. He is reported to have gone to the Roman governor in Syria to "receive authority," but that was probably simply for "permission to teach" (*m. 'Ed.* 7:7). There is no indication that his reported journey to Rome was in an high administrative capacity (*m. Ma'aś. Š.* 5:9), any more than was Josephus's journey to Rome at a very young age (to defend some fellow priests sent to Rome for trial "on a trifling charge"; *Vita* 13–16). His journeys within Palestine were largely on private business, and he and his son Simeon may well have enjoyed prestige because of their wealth as well as their learning. Tannaitic texts simply have both Gamaliel and his son Simeon dealing with the same sorts of cases as other rabbis, such as purity laws or cancellation of vows. And they make no mention of administrative powers, such as appointing judges, ordaining rabbis, collecting funds, or even presiding over the Sanhedrin.[38] The political-economic power enjoyed by Judah the Prince was something dramatically new that had emerged in special new circumstances toward the beginning of the third century.

That the emerging "patriarchate" wielded such power in Galilee, however, does not mean that the rabbis, at whose head the *nasi* supposedly stood, had suddenly established their authority as well. The bases of the patriarch's power were independent of the rabbinic circles, in the close personal relationship with the emperor, above, and in wealth and interconnections with other wealthy families based apparently in the principal cities in and around Galilee. The rabbis' self-portrayal in the Mishnah as having little influence with the peasantry of Galilee, discussed above, simply confirms that the suddenly powerful patriarchate was not (primarily) dependent upon or rooted in rabbinic authority.[39] Some rabbis supported the patriarch, some were even in his service. But many rabbis criticized Judah the Prince and/or his successors for decrees regarding tithing, for appointment of incompetent judges based solely on their wealth, or for their own fiscal greed at the expense of the people's welfare. Rabbi Hiyya refused to recognize Judah's prerogatives and openly flaunted his rulings (*b. Qidd.* 33a; *b. Mo'ed Qat.* 16a–b). The rabbis clearly felt that Judah had moved too quickly, assumed too much power, and asserted his authority in areas where there was no precedent.[40]

Within the rabbinic traditions themselves, interestingly, those who cooperated with the patriarch appear as the leading sages of their generation, while those who criticized the patriarch appear as lesser sages. Moreover, the latter either worked outside of the main centers of rabbinic activity or lived and worked in Tiberias, when the patriarch was based in Sepphoris.[41] These "coincidences" in rabbinic traditions suggest that nascent rabbinic authority in Galilee, including authority within the rabbinic movement itself, was based in the de facto power of the patriarchate, and not the other way around. Later in the third century the patriarchs became somewhat detached from and peripheral to rabbinic circles.

Thus it may be through their initial dependence upon and then struggle with the patriarchs' political-economic power in the course of the third century that rabbinic circles both achieved more institutionalized form in permanent academies in Sepphoris and Tiberias and became somewhat more involved with the social life of the Galilean peasantry. In the second half of the third century the rabbis also appear to have relaxed their emphasis on purity and tithing, areas in which the people of Galilee had strongly resisted their authority. In such ways the rabbis gradually gained more influence with the people. Nevertheless the rabbis' role in Galilee during the second and third centuries was primarily "academic," their influence among the people minimal, and their political authority apparently still marginal.[42] The rabbis' orientation was not to the villages of Galilee. After moving to Galilee they quickly established their base in the cities. The authority was dependent to a considerable extent on the patriarchs. Indeed, from the mid-third century, when the patriarchate had moved to Tiberias, into the early fourth century, the leading rabbis in the Tiberian academy were priests from Babylon.[43] That, along with the emergence of Tiberias as an important Palestinian necropolis for diaspora Jews, suggests that by the late third century the rabbis were oriented as much or more to Jewry around the Roman empire and beyond as to local affairs in Galilee. "In the third and fourth centuries C.E. the rabbis were an elite class in Jewish society of Roman Palestine."[44]

The most remarkable product of the early rabbis in Galilee, presumably promulgated under the leadership of Judah, was the Mishnah.[45] Debate among rabbinic scholars is not likely to reach consensus in the near future regarding what the precise agenda and purpose of the rabbis may have been in the gathering and promulgation of this voluminous material. Both the structure and substance of the Mishnah, however, indicate that its framers worked out of a tradition distinctively oriented to the Judean Temple and priesthood. While speaking through the persona and style of the scribes turned rabbis, the Mishnah advocates a religious-economic program important to the priests. Well over half of the tractates pertain directly and almost only to the priests and Temple services, while many others that concern primarily scribes or householders are also pertinent to the priests and/or Temple indirectly. The Mishnah's conception of the holiness of the land and the means by which the land and its produce could be sanctified clearly stands in continuity with the Jerusalem Temple and priesthood. Economically, the center of interest is the village, made up of households as the units of agricultural production. But village life and produce are aligned to the Temple as the center of holiness. Part of the crops the land produces, given the application of the peasants' labor, is still reserved for the priests. Unclear from the Mishnah itself (or any other source) is whether any system of collection and distribution of tithes was set up once the Temple and its administrative apparatus were destroyed. Yet it is clear that the rabbis attempted to set themselves into the priests' stead as the beneficiary of the tithes.[46]

Rabbis, Christian Pilgrims, and Galileans

Galilee after the destruction of the second Temple has often been discussed primarily in terms of religions and their rivalry. It seems highly questionable, however, whether the division and conflict between "Judaism" and "Christianity" (between "church" and "synagogue") evident elsewhere in the Roman world is traceable in Galilee. As indicated in the previous section, a "formative" rabbinic Judaism was taking shape during the second and third centuries, eventually centered and institutionalized in the rabbinic academies in Sepphoris and Tiberias. Difficult to discern in our sources, however, is anything that could be identified as a separate Christian religion in Galilee, until late antiquity, that is. Meanwhile, life in the towns and villages of Galilee would appear to have continued according to indigenous Galilean traditions, presumably under increasing influence from the rabbinic circles. As in earlier periods, it is rare that we hear of the ordinary people, and only when the usual political economic structural conflict erupts in a popular insurrection.

It should be evident by now that it is inappropriate to speak of rabbinic Judaism as already developed in Galilee in the first several generations after the destruction of the Jerusalem Temple. The rabbinic "academies" were not even established in Galilee until after the Bar Kokhba Revolt and by their own testimony the rabbis had little influence among the people for a century thereafter. The rabbis, moreover, did not yet concern themselves with, nor did they have any role in local courts and assemblies (see further chapter 10). Social-economic-religious affairs in the village and town communities of Galilee were apparently conducted according to local customs and traditions. "Formative Judaism" had not yet developed identifiable social forms among the populace in Galilee.

The synagogue buildings unearthed in Galilee provide vivid illustrations of the lack of decisive rabbinic involvement in town and village affairs through late antiquity. In the third century and accelerating into Byzantine times, villages and towns with sufficient resources, or perhaps with some sufficiently well-off civic leaders or wealthy benefactors, constructed public buildings for meetings of their local assemblies (*knesset/synagōgē;* see chapter 10). Synagogue-building decor mixes typical Jewish motifs such as the ark and the menorah with fertility and magic symbols, Syrian sun-eagles, and zodiacs covering the floors. Such decor serves as a reminder that it is difficult to make distinctions in popular culture according to modern essentialist categories such as "Jewish," "pagan," and "Christian." The Mishnah lacks any focused, systematic treatment of the synagogue, and has only scattered references to readings and liturgies in local assemblies.[47] The rabbis did not seek or achieve effective control of the synagogues until later centuries.[48]

The extent to which a nascent rabbinic Judaism had become established in the cities may be a matter of definition and interpretation. Literary and archaeological evidence for the ethnic background and cultural orientation of the inhabitants of Diocaesarea and Tiberias is somewhat confusing. The mixed evidence suggests, among other things, that essentialist interpretive categories are probably inappropriate to the historical realities. One fourth-century Christian writer, Eusebius (*Mart. Pal.* 8.1) says that "all the inhabitants" of "the large city" Diocaesarea were *ioudaioi.* Another, Epiphanius (*Pan.* 30.11.9–10), asserts broadly that no "Hellene, Samaritan, or Christian lived among" the Jews in Diocaesarea and Tiberias. Yet Eusebius also assumes the presence of Roman officials. Recent archaeological discoveries at Sepphoris, moreover, include a Dionysiac mosaic in the banquet hall of a large villa from the mid-third century, Roman sarcophagi, and pagan Greek statues, supplementing evidence of the dominant Roman political culture already evident from the theater.[49] That the gods Zeus and Hygeia are depicted on the coins of Tiberias means that the authorities there thought them suitable symbols for the city. A rabbinic tradition has Rabbi Jonathan living next to a Roman in the late third century (*y. B. Bat.* 2.11.7b). Ethnically, culturally, religiously, the dominant cities in Galilee must have been mixed into late Roman times.[50] Given the rise of the patriarchate and increasing influence of the rabbinic academies, it seems likely that the Jewish population and culture were becoming consolidated in the midst of cities still dominated politically by Roman administration. The presence of bronze figurines and hundreds of disc lamps decorated with pagan symbols in Jewish residential areas,[51] however, suggests that the culture of these well-to-do Jewish residents of the city was not conformed to the Torah or the Mishnah.

Neither archaeological nor textual evidence suggests that there was any (religious) community self-consciously identifying itself as "Christianity" over against (rabbinic) "Judaism" in Galilee — conceivably even until after the time of Constantine. In the Sayings Source, "Q," used by both Matthew and Luke and by scholarly consensus now located in Galilee sometime before the great revolt, Jesus condemns the Pharisees and scribes and utters a prophetic lament over the ruling house of Jerusalem (Luke/Q 11:39–52, 13:34–35), but he does not attack "Judaism" or "Israel." In fact, the concluding saying of "Q" has the disciples as the representatives of the twelve tribes of Israel, "establishing justice for" (not "judging") the people. Even more clearly the Gospel of Mark, increasingly located in Galilee by interpreters and dated around the time of the great revolt, is more elaborate in portraying Jesus' ministry as the renewal of Israel, in the tradition of Moses and Elijah. In Mark also, Jesus condemns the Temple and the high-priestly rulers and the scribes and Pharisees, but not "Judaism." Insofar as we are uncertain what the proto-rabbinic council at Yavneh accomplished (see above), the interpretation of the Gospel of Matthew as the "Christian" response lacks a clearly delineated foil. Recent interpretation of Matthew discerns no decisive break with the Israelite-Jewish tradition. Thus, if the Gospel of Matthew were to be located in Galilee sometime toward the end of the first century, it also attests a community of Jesus followers who had not yet come to think of themselves as the "Christian" *church* over against the "Jewish" *synagogue*.[52] There may well have been communities with some special attachment to Jesus of Nazareth in late first-century Galilee. Assuming that early "Christian" literature such as the Synoptic Sayings Source and the Gospel of Mark represent or reflect such communities, however, they saw themselves as engaged in the renewal of Israel, not in establishing a religion separate from "Judaism."

The Book of Acts, of course, imposes its own grand scheme on the development of early "Christianity," bringing what must have been a variety of communities with some attachment to Jesus into one movement supposedly led by Peter and the apostles and radiating out from its supposed original center in Jerusalem. Given this Lucan historiography, the sudden reference to "the church" in Galilee as well as Judea and Samaria should pose no problem of interpretation; the author of Acts (Luke) is simply aware of communities in Galilee which he has not forced into his scheme by previous reference.

Indeed, much of the debate regarding the presence of "Christianity" or "Jewish Christianity" in Palestine in general and Galilee in particular following the great revolt turns out to be due to the imposition of the broad general constructs of "Christianity" and "Judaism" onto texts and events. In earlier studies of the relations between the two "religions," as the one rivaled the other in a period of general crisis following the destruction of the Temple, much was made of a supposed rabbinic ban against "Jewish Christians" and the supposed promulgation of the "blessing against heretics."[53] The former, however, was aimed not at expelling but at bringing someone back into acceptance of rabbinic authority. The "blessing against heretics" (*minim*), moreover, was directed very generally against all sorts of dissidents or "heresy" and not specifically against the followers of

Jesus, although one or two rabbinic passages may well refer to such.[54] Thus the "ban" and the "blessing against heretics" in rabbinic literature do not provide evidence of some branch of "(Jewish) Christianity" in Galilee that was understood as a religion different from "Judaism."

Evidence for anything that could be called "Christianity" in Galilee is virtually nonexistent prior to the time of Constantine. In attendance at the Council of Nicaea in 325 were bishops from churches in cities around the perimeter of Galilee, such as Paneas, Ptolemais, Maximianopolis/Legio, Scythopolis, and Gadara, as well as from other largely Gentile/pagan cities such as Caesarea, Aelia Capitolina/Jerusalem, Ascalon, and Gaza. None appear from Galilee.[55] Similarly, Eusebius lists among the Martyrs of Palestine people from Scythopolis, Gadara, Caesarea, Gaza, Jamnia, and Caesarea, but none from any location in Galilee.[56] Communities with some attachment to Jesus would thus appear to have been inconspicuous and/or to have made no significant break with their Israelite heritage — or to have simply disappeared.

Beyond the borders of Galilee, however, within the first generation of the fourth century, what had been a despised and persecuted religious movement suddenly became the officially sanctioned established religion of the whole empire. That development had political-economic as well as cultural consequences for Galilee insofar as Galilee and the rest of Judea became the Christian "Holy Land." There had been a few pilgrims before. Now they came in increasing numbers, with the attendant influx of money into the area. The imperial court, moreover, sponsored the "development" of special holy places and construction of lavish shrines as well as pilgrim churches at specially significant sites. Among these were the villages of Nazareth and Capernaum in Galilee. A leading figure in the construction of these new churches at holy places was the wealthy Jewish convert Joseph, who received the imperial blessing on his enterprises.

It would appear, therefore, that what was emerging as Christianity and rabbinic Judaism had not yet taken root in any major way among the villages and towns of second- and even third-century Galilee. As for earlier centuries, little or no literary evidence is available for the life of Galilean villagers, and archaeologists have only begun to focus on village life. It is thus not yet clear the extent to which Galileans may have shared in the empire-wide economic crisis of the third century and the sharper class struggle between cities and villages, as the latter began to assert themselves.[57] The new imperial demands for forced labor (*angariae*) and what amounted to new taxes (the *annona*) mentioned above brought added burdens particularly on the Galilean peasantry. Although the fourth century has been seen as a time of economic recovery and social stability in the eastern empire generally, there is also evidence of overtaxation, peasant abandonment of the land, and increased concentration of land in the hands of wealthy families in fourth-century Palestine.[58] It is likely that the influx of pilgrims and money attendant on the imperial establishment of Christianity also disrupted traditional social-economic life in Galilee, particularly at certain "holy" sites such as Nazareth and Capernaum.

In 351 or 352 large numbers of Galileans engaged in a widespread revolt under Gallus, nephew of Constantius and vice emperor in the East. The revolt apparently centered in the area around Sepphoris, where rebels seized arms from the Roman fortress, but included villages of Upper Galilee as well, judging from archaeological evidence.[59] In the earliest pagan source for the revolt, "the Jews raised up Patricius in some sort of kingdom" (Aurelius Victor, *Liber de Caesaribus* 42.9–12). Literary references to the burning of many villages and punitive measures against Diocaesarea by the Roman army are paralleled by evidence of abandonment of villages and destruction in mid-fourth-century Sepphoris (Diocaesarea) found in recent archaeological excavations.[60] The "Gallus Revolt" in late antiquity indicates that, after nearly three centuries of direct Roman rule, the Galilean people had not lost their independent spirit. As Sisera and the Canaanite kings had discovered in battle against the early Israelites inspired by the prophetess Deborah, and the Jerusalem general Josephus had discovered in his attempt to control the descendants of those Israelites in 66 C.E., the people of Galilee were still capable of resisting outside rulers. To paraphrase the Judean historian: "Never did the people lack courage, not the country people." Although it probably cannot be proven from historical evidence, it seems likely that the continuing independence of the Galileans was rooted in their continuing cultivation of popular Israelite traditions such as Mosaic covenantal ideals of justice and stories of resistance such as the Song of Deborah and the narratives of Elijah and Elisha.

◆ *Part 2* ◆

THE RULERS OF GALILEE IN ROMAN TIMES

Chapter 5

ROMAN IMPERIAL RULE
AND GALILEE

⚜

*Apologists for overseas American interests have insisted on American inno-
cence, doing good, fighting for freedom. . . . Yet for citizens of nineteenth-
century Britain and France, empire was a major topic of unembarrassed
cultural attention.*

— EDWARD SAID

*The only refuge, then, left to you is divine assistance. But even this is ranged
on the side of the Romans, for, without God's aid, so vast an empire could
never have been built up.*

— AGRIPPA II

Galilee and Galileans are usually hidden from history.[1] Under the Hasmoneans and Herod, Jerusalem was the dominant political-economic-
religious center of affairs. Until mid-first century C.E., the Romans always
controlled Galilee through client-rulers based in Jerusalem or Sepphoris or
Tiberias. Direct Roman rule did not play a role in Galilee until the death of
Agrippa I in 44 C.E. Even then, Rome's relations with Palestine or "Judea"
focused on Jerusalem. Galilee was either remote from the main arena of
affairs further south, or was the first principal stop for Roman troops on a
mission of retaliatory reconquest.

Greek and Roman writers thus focus on the political history taking place
in relations between Rome and the Judean client-rulers and other prominent Judeans. Such writers also use the terms "Judea" and "Judeans" in
a way determined by the political geography, which often leaves it unclear whether Galilee is included. This makes Josephus's accounts all the
more important as our principal source for the otherwise hidden events in
Galilee in the early Roman period. In his extensive and self-glorifying or
self-justifying accounts of his own activities in Galilee during the great war
between the Judeans and the Romans, Josephus has provided a substantial
amount of information on relations between Rome and Galilee as well as
on Galilee itself.

In addition to being hidden from history, Galilee often bore the brunt of the spinoff effects of imperial politics. During the first few decades of Roman rule, Galilee repeatedly felt the effects of the prolonged Roman civil war, of periodic conflicts between rival Roman and Hasmonean factions, and of the predatory practices of ambitious Roman politicians. The centuries-long struggle of the Romans against the Parthian empire to the east, however, had implications for Roman rule of Galilee that stretched into late antiquity.

Roman domination of Galilee proceeds in three stages that are also, in effect, different (but somewhat overlapping) policies of imperial rule: the initial period of conquest and consolidation of Roman control; domination through client-rulers; and the establishment of direct Roman rule in Palestine, which took the form of the urbanization of administration, at least in Lower Galilee.

The Roman Conquest from Pompey to Herod

As the Romans moved into direct control of the eastern Mediterranean and Asia Minor in the first century B.C.E., much of what happened to Galilee was a direct or indirect effect of the grand designs of empire, the career of some Roman general, or international politics. Closely related were the effects on Galilee of Roman determination of affairs in greater Judea. The initial conquest by the Romans was almost accidental and incidental. Their treatment of Galilee was determined by how they handled the Hasmonean regime in Jerusalem, with no separate arrangement for Galilee until after Herod's death.

Ironically enough, the Roman empire's expansion was partly due to generals seeking greater power and glory. For distinguished and ambitious Romans attempting to make their historic mark in the late republic, it was hardly enough merely to crush slave revolts. That was worth only the secondary honor of an "ovation."[2] Naval campaigns against pirates were worthy only of praetorian commanders, and the slaughter of fellow Romans brought no true glory. Moreover, the ambitious were after fortune as well as fame, and the standards steadily escalated with every new major conquest. Since appointment as a consul to deal with a particular area of the empire was usually limited to two years, finally, the ambitious general had to make his mark — and his "take" — expeditiously. The effects on conquered peoples, in this case the Galileans, can be seen in each one of the "distinguished" Roman generals on whom we have some information.[3]

The initial Roman "conquest" of greater Judea, including Galilee, was the indirect, almost accidental, result of Pompey's broader implementation of Roman imperial designs. Prior to being sent to the East, Pompey had engaged primarily in battles of Roman legions against Roman legions. Now he had the opportunity for true glory and great wealth. It seems unlikely that his activities in the East were driven simply by the bankers and publicans who thrived on the security of already pacified provinces. In the end, the principal beneficiaries of Pompey's campaigns were the Roman treasury, which more than doubled as a result, and the officers of his legions, who divided an extensive booty (nearly 100 million denarii apart from Pompey's own take).[4] The logic of imperial control dictated his conquests and arrangements. In the annexation of Syria, for example, the need to control piracy was probably a factor. Far more important, however, was the threat of a militarily effective Parthian empire just beyond the Euphrates River. Moreover, the local kings competing for power and territory in the political power vacuum left by the collapse of the Seleucid empire required a firm imperial hand. That is the context of Pompey's incursion into Judea, which lay outside his explicit mandate from the Roman Senate.

The Hasmonean temple-state was one of those warring expansionist regimes — only now it was divided against itself in a dynastic conflict as well. Both sides appealed to Pompey once he moved into Syria. There might well have been no military confrontation at all except for the precipitous action by Aristobulus in occupying the strategic fortress of Alexandreion, and the resistance of a sizable faction of priests when Pompey approached Jerusalem. Pompey thereupon laid siege to Jerusalem and the Temple in which the priests were fortified, eventually storming and violating the Temple precincts. More directly pertinent to Galilee, the Roman general removed the Hellenistic cities and their territories from Jerusalem's control and laid the whole land still subject to the Hasmonean regime under tribute (*B.J.* 1.153–56; *Ant.* 14.73–76; Cassius Dio 37.16.5; cf. Strabo, *Geogr.* 16.2.40, p. 762). Pompey had thus not implemented a planned "conquest" of Judea, although he was surely politically pleased to have "liberated" the Hellenistic cities of Palestine from the unstable Hasmonean regime. Nor — except for the siege of Jerusalem and the seizure of spoil from the Temple later paraded in Pompey's triumphal procession in Rome — had the country actually been conquered by the sword. That remained for Pompey's successors.

Gabinius was sent to the newly designated province of Syria with a three-year consular command, 57–55, during the height of Pompey's and Crassus's power in Rome and Caesar's campaigns in Gaul and Britain. Recent Arab raids supplied the pretext, and Syria provided a prospect of profitable ventures. First the Hasmonean pretender Alexander and then his father Aristobulus escaped from Roman captivity and, in leading rebellions against High Priest Hyrcanus (who had been *re*-installed by Pompey), raised sizable armies and reoccupied fortresses. Gabinius's campaigns to defeat these rebellions meant, finally, a Roman military conquest of Judean territory (*Ant.* 14.82–102; *B.J.* 1.160–78). These events also revealed considerable residual resistance to Roman domination. While most of the battles took place in Judea proper, Galilee was more directly affected in three connections. The last major battle, with huge losses among the rebels, took place at Mount Tabor in southern Galilee. Gabinius rebuilt many damaged or ruined Hellenistic cities, including Scythopolis just to the south of Galilee and Gamala to the east. Also, Gabinius decentralized the government of Palestine into five districts headed by councils (*synhedria*), the one in Galilee centered in Sepphoris (*Ant.* 14.91; *B.J.* 1.170). It is doubtful that this administrative reorganization lasted very long. After the insurrections were suppressed, says Josephus, Gabinius "reorganized the government" (*politeia*) in accordance with the wishes of Antipater, the Idumean strongman increasingly dominating Palestinian affairs under the authority of the Roman-backed high priest Hyrcanus.

Crassus, who came to Syria next (54–53 C.E.), to win glory against the Parthian threat, plundered the wealth of the Temple that Pompey had left, 2,000 talents worth (*Ant.* 14.105; *B.J.* 1.179). His disastrous defeat by the Parthians across the Euphrates surely contributed to the anti-Roman (and pro-Parthian?) inclination among Judeans aware of political affairs.[5] Rallying the Roman forces, Cassius secured Syria and advanced into Palestine, bringing disaster for Galileans. "He fell upon Tarichaeae, which he quickly took, and made slaves of some thirty thousand men" (*Ant.* 14.120; *B.J.* 1.180). Even assuming that Josephus exaggerates the figures and that many of those killed were partisans of Aristobulus, there was nevertheless a direct impact on Galileans in terms of enslavement and the usual devastation wrought by warring armies in the surrounding villages and towns.[6]

Following Julius Caesar's assassination ten years later, Cassius took command of the army in Syria, as the great empire-wide Roman "civil war" erupted. He imposed an extraordinarily heavy tribute on the cities in the area, demanding the huge sum of 700 talents of silver from greater Judea alone. The young Herod, having been appointed military governor of Galilee by his father Antipater, expeditiously squeezed a 100–talent allotment out of Galilee in time to meet Cassius's deadline. The Galileans thereby avoided the enslavement visited upon the Judeans in the towns of Emmaus, Gophna, Lydda, and Thamna for being too slow in payment of the levy (*Ant.* 14.271–76; *B.J.* 1.218–21). Cassius's attempt to control affairs in Syria by dividing it into smaller principalities disrupted the overall political-economic order, if Galilee is any example. Marion, the tyrant of Tyre, in a bid to assert Tyrian control probably of Upper Galilee, held three strongholds for a time before Herod drove him out again (*B.J.* 1.238–39; *Ant.* 14.297–98).

The Roman experiment with the Hasmonean regime might belong under the topic of client-rulers were it not so completely mixed up with Roman politics, from the rivalry of Pompey and Caesar to the conflict between Anthony and Augustus and the "civil war" that implicated the whole empire. The prevailing arrangement kept the cooperative Hyrcanus in the high priesthood, with the Idumean strongman, Antipater, gaining dominance in the administration of greater Judea and in mediation with rival Roman politicians and imperial contingencies. Repeatedly, however, the rival Hasmoneans themselves would initiate a rebellion or some Roman politician would use them as surrogates in attempts to gain advantage in this area of the East. Finally, as rival Roman forces focused increasingly on fighting each other, the Parthians made their move into Syria and Palestine, installing Antigonus, the remaining son of the rival Hasmonean Aristobulus, as their client-ruler in Jerusalem. In response to this Parthian move the Roman Senate finally designated the ambitious and effective strongman Herod, son of Antipater, as their client-king in greater Judea. It was precisely because of the turmoil, even civil war, between both rival Hasmonean factions and rival Roman factions that client-rulership was ineffective and the period of Roman conquest was prolonged in Palestine.

The effects of these events on Galilee are not difficult to discern. Far from being effectively "pacified" in the two decades following Pompey's incursion, the area was increasingly stirred up as one foreign military campaign after another moved through the area. Major battles that left thousands slaughtered or enslaved were fought both in the south, at Tabor, and at Tarichaeae, along the Sea of Galilee. Continuing chaos and hardship generally would have been the principal result of the repeated Roman depredations in Galilee. It seems likely that some of the rival Hasmoneans' success was due to a combination of anti-Roman, anti-Hyrcanus/Antipater, and anti-Herod sentiments among the Galileans as well as among prominent circles of Judeans, who repeatedly mounted delegations to the Romans in protest (*Ant.* 14.41, 302, 324, 327; *B.J.* 1.243, 245). It also seems likely that the increasing chaos generated by the Romans' repeated attempts to control the area would have contributed to the positive response experienced by Antigonus and the Parthians. Thus it is not surprising that once the Romans designated Herod as their "king" to control affairs in Palestine, he found it necessary to suppress sustained resistance in Galilee, not from Hasmonean officers or "gentry," who simply went over to Herod, but from the more popular circles who had borne the brunt of Roman-sponsored turmoil for over twenty years.

Roman Domination through Client-Rulers

One frequently encounters the misapprehension that Galilee at the time of Jesus was not just controlled by Roman power but occupied by Roman troops. It is assumed that when Matthew's Jesus says "if anyone forces you to go one mile, go also the second mile" (5:41) he refers to frequently encountered Roman soldiers who could require the "natives" to carry their military gear for a (Roman) mile. It is also assumed that the centurion in Capernaum whose slave Jesus healed was a Roman officer, and therefore a Gentile (Matt. 8:5–13 ‖ Luke 7:1–10; cf. John 4:46–53). Or, perhaps because the Roman governors based in Caesarea stationed troops along the walls of the Jerusalem Temple during the Passover festival, it is assumed that Roman soldiers were ubiquitous in Palestine.

Rome, however, did not run its empire by means of occupying troops. It had more — and less — subtle ways of deploying military violence. The "forceful suasion" of Roman military power functioned through the perceptions of the subject peoples. The Romans simply terrorized peoples into submission and, they hoped, submissiveness through the ruthless devastation of the land and towns, slaughter and enslavement of the people (as illustrated by the treatment of Galilee mentioned just above), and crucifixion of people along the roadways or in public places. The Roman legions were not (until much later) stationed evenly along the frontiers as occupying troops to defend the borders. Rather, they were deployed as a mobile striking force.[7] Accordingly, the legions were concentrated at certain sensitive points as a striking force directed at threats of two sorts. The primary threat was of "native revolts" within the territories already conquered by Rome. Particularly with the Parthian empire to the East, there was also the threat of invasion from beyond the frontiers of the empire. As we have just noted, during the empire-wide Roman "civil war" the Parthians had proven a serious threat precisely in Palestine, where they succeeded temporarily in placing their own client-ruler in power. The Romans thus had a sizable military force in Syria just to the north, but none in greater Judea under Herod and none stationed in Galilee until nearly mid-first century C.E.

With regard to native peoples, as the Romans knew from prior experience elsewhere in the empire, there was often a delay of more than a generation between initial conquest and the outbreak of serious revolt, once the full impact of imperial control and taxation made itself felt. In conquered areas that were already adequately "civilized," that is, organized into self-governing Greek cities that controlled the surrounding countryside, the Romans could simply annex the territory as a province, with a Roman proconsul or governor to provide general oversight and supervision. If the conquered area was still comprised largely of villages and towns or temple-communities under a local dynast, temple-state, or king, then Rome preferred to rule indirectly, through client-rulers. Rome made precisely this distinction within Palestine, placing the Hellenistic cities in the province of Syria, while keeping Judea, Galilee, and the other districts that had been ruled by the Hasmonean dynasty in Jerusalem under client-rulers. Rome kept Galilee as a whole subject to client-rulers for a century after the initial conquest, and eastern Galilee around the lake remained under Agrippa II nearly to the end of the first century C.E.

The Romans benefited considerably by ruling through client-states, with regard to both the control of newly subjected peoples and outside threats to the security of the empire. Client-rulers themselves could be intimidated and kept in line by the threat of punitive action by the Roman legions concentrated at crucial points, such as northern Syria.[8] Then, in turn, the client-kings or tetrarchs would check attacks against provincial territories and keep their own people under control as well. So long as Herod ruled with an iron fist, Rome felt no need to assign troops to greater Judea. After the widespread revolts in Galilee and Perea as well as Judea following Herod's death, they did station several auxiliary units in greater Judea in case of local disturbances.[9] These units were composed partly of local militia based in Caesarea and Sebaste (see below).

The basic arrangement of client-rulership developed on the basis of patron-client relations in Rome itself, in which the patron offered *beneficia* in return for "services" performed by the client.[10] The sons and potential heirs of client-rulers, of course, were brought up and "educated" in Rome. Although the client-rulers were accorded the status of "friends" of the Roman people and/or emperor, implying services rendered with no suggestion of subservience, virtually no area of authority was left as the client's own prerogative. Rule of territories such as Judea and Galilee through clients, however, was unstable, and required constant surveillance and management by Rome. The same Herod who kept tight control on his territories became acutely paranoid about his own sons, leading to turmoil in the succession. When Herod's son Antipas, who took over rule of Galilee and Perea, became enamored of his brother's wife Herodias, he offended his fellow client-ruler, the Nabatean king Aretas, with whose daughter he had earlier cemented an appropriate diplomatic marriage. The affronts led to military conflict, as Aretas finally attacked and defeated Antipas's forces, requiring Rome itself to restore the imperial order. Three short years after all of Herod's old territories had been placed again under the rule of another Herodian, Agrippa I, he died and different arrangements again were made for the various districts. In the widespread revolt in 66, Agrippa II quickly lost control of the limited area of eastern Galilee assigned to him little more than a decade earlier.

Not surprisingly, Rome appears to have shifted policy frequently, even during the first half of the first century C.E. Under Augustus a considerable portion of the empire as a whole was still controlled through client-rulers. The shift of "Judea" (including Samaria and Idumea) to provincial status in 6 C.E. may have been due to the particular factor of dissatisfaction with Herod's son Archelaus. Yet, after Augustus shifted Judea-Samaria to provincial status, Tiberius extended the policy elsewhere in the East. Gaius then reversed the annexationist policy, appointing as client-"king" the same Agrippa I whom Tiberius had imprisoned. Claudius apparently attempted to stabilize affairs with the extension of Agrippa's realm, then reverted to the provincial arrangement. Nero, however, made a divided arrangement even within the tiny territory of Galilee when he gave the toparchies of Tiberias and Tarichaeae to Agrippa II in 54. Such frequent changes in rulers and administrations would hardly have had a stabilizing effect on life in

Galilee. Considering how little control, direct or indirect, remained in Galilee by the summer of 66, one should not make too much of the lack of indications of overt resistance or active revolt under Antipas, Agrippa I, Roman governors, and Agrippa II before 66.

During the periods of conquest and client-kingship, the Romans reestablished the fundamental tributary political-economic system traditional in the ancient Near East, with Rome now as the ultimate beneficiary. As under previous empires, this meant at least a double level of rule and taxation for greater Judea. Ultimate political control belonged to Rome, with local order maintained by the client-rulers. Rome claimed its tribute, but taxation also provided a handsome level of revenue for the client-rulers. In the initial Roman incursion, Pompey had "laid both the countryside and Jerusalem under tribute" (*B.J.* 1.154; *Ant.* 14.74),[11] an action reinforced by Gabinius (Cassius Dio 39.56.6). As indicated in the decrees of Julius Caesar, this was to be paid directly (at Sidon), bypassing the infamous *publicani*, and amounted to 25 percent of the crop every other year (excepting sabbatical years; *Ant.* 14.202–3).[12] In addition, however, the subject populace, which included the Galileans, were also "to pay tithes to Hyrcanus and his sons, just as they paid to their forefathers." Herod undoubtedly extracted substantial revenues from his subjects, given his massive building projects and his lavish munificence to imperial figures and Hellenistic cities. Herod's take from his whole realm (presumably not including "income" from his private or "royal" estates) was 900 talents annually. Antipas's revenue from Galilee and Perea alone was 200 talents (*Ant.* 17.318–20; *B.J.* 2.93–97). These revenues simply were understood to go with the territory under the Roman arrangement, a guaranteed annual income for the client-rulers, as it were.

What is not completely clear, however, is whether the high-priestly regime subordinate to Herod continued to claim the traditional "tithes" guaranteed to Hyrcanus II and his sons in the original arrangement cited above. Obviously some income remained to sustain the elaborate Temple establishment. A related question particular to Galilee is whether, once Galilee was assigned to Antipas, Galileans continued to pay tithes and temple dues, as the Judeans still directly under the high-priestly regime would presumably have done.

The interrelated accounts of how Agrippa I became king and of Gaius's attempt to place his statue in the Jerusalem Temple illustrate several points about the Roman imperial domination of Galilee through client-rulers: (1) how the appointment of client-rulers was rooted in patron-client relations at the highest level in Rome rather than in the situation in Galilee; (2) how arbitrary Roman imperial rule could be, with rulers' personal whims having major implications for a subject people; (3) the fundamental political-economic structure through which Galilee was ruled; and (4) the economic dependence of both the Romans and the client regimes on the agricultural produce of the peasantry taken as tribute and taxes.

The future King Agrippa I (after his paranoid grandfather executed his father, Aristobulus) was sent to Rome for his education. He thus grew up in the inner circle of imperial princes, including Claudius, who eventually became emperor, and Drusus, Tiberias's only son (*Ant.* 18.143–46, 165). After what could only be called a "checkered" career, including a stint as *agoranomos* (supply/finance officer) in Tiberias under his uncle and brother-in-law Antipas and a conspicuous trail of debts, he made a comeback at the imperial court in Rome at age 45, becoming close to the 23-year-old Gaius (*Ant.* 18.147–68). When Gaius became emperor shortly thereafter, he appointed Agrippa king in Chalcis and, after Agrippa subverted his uncle and brother-in-law Antipas, gave him Galilee and Perea (*Ant.* 18.228–38, 240–55). When Agrippa heard of Gaius's order to place a bust of himself in the Jerusalem Temple, he intervened with Gaius (*Ant.* 18.289–301).

Meanwhile "out East" in Galilee, Gaius's orders for a Roman army to proceed through Palestine to install his statue in the Temple had evoked massive popular protests, many of the peasants having left the fields unsown (see further chapters 3 and 6). Josephus portrays a telling scene of the officers running the client-"kingdom" for Agrippa huddled with Petronius, the Roman governor of Syria instructed to implement Gaius's orders (*Ant.* 18.262–78; *B.J.* 2.185–203). Their common concern was that, with the ground remaining unsown, implementation of the emperor's order would result in "a harvest of banditry": the demand for tribute and taxes would go unmet, the people themselves would be desperate, and a Roman crackdown would not resolve but simply exacerbate the problem. This unusual situation reveals that ordinarily the mere threat of Roman military retaliation was sufficient to ensure the payment of tribute and taxes. Its near breakdown in this unique crisis illustrates the fundamental political-economic relationship among Rome, client-rulers, and Galileans.

Because Rome ruled through client-regimes, there would have been very little direct contact between Galileans and Romans — that is, aside from the techniques of "forceful suasion" applied in the period of initial conquest and again in punitive reaction to the revolts after Herod's death. Only in Sepphoris, which became the seat of direct Roman administration of western Galilee after Agrippa I died in 44 C.E., would more direct contact have developed and become regularized.

There can be no question, however, that the people knew who their imperial masters were. In addition to the cumulative social-economic impact of multiple levels of taxation, Roman political culture had a direct (as well as indirect) and lasting cultural effect on Galilee. This also was largely mediated through the client-rulers, primarily in their extensive and sometimes grandiose Roman(-Hellenistic)–style building programs, which advertised the glory and power of Rome. Herod was renowned for his massive building projects, including the completely rebuilt cities of Sebaste and Caesarea, pagan temples here and there (but outside of Judea or Galilee), and the major "public" buildings such as theaters, amphitheaters, and monuments. Yet Herod appears to have done no major building in Galilee (unless some new archaeological discovery indicates otherwise). Herod's building with the greatest, though distant, effect on Galileans would have been the complete rebuilding of the Jerusalem Temple on a most grandiose scale (see chapter 6). That Herod left Galilee unadorned means that his son Antipas's rebuilding of Sepphoris and foundation of a whole new city, Tiberias, all within two decades, would have had a sudden and dramatic impact on Galilee in the early first century C.E. (see chapter 7). The "urbanization" of Galilee begun under Antipas reached full flower under direct Roman rule in the second century, with a fuller array of institutions and façades of Roman political culture.

The emphasis on the emperor, particularly on the worship or service of Caesar as divine, appears to have been particularly onerous to Galileans as well as Judeans. The impact of the "emperor cult" has not previously received the attention it warrants for the history of Palestine for a variety of reasons. One obvious reason is that the ubiquity, pervasiveness, and effectiveness of the emperor cult in the urban public life of antiquity was not recognized until recently. Emperor worship was thought to lack emotional depth and genuine religious experience. It was dismissed as a politically expedient expression of allegiance largely confined to the Eastern urban elite. The second reason (perhaps also an explanation for the first) is that historians of religion were still influenced by the Christian understanding of religion as personal faith. Finally, since the Jews were assumed to be uninvolved with the emperor cult, it seemed unimportant, except for the apparently isolated incident of Gaius's attempt to have his image placed in the Jerusalem Temple and Herod's erection of temples to Caesar diplomatically *outside* the districts of Judea Galilee.

If the emperor cult was utterly absent in Judea and Galilee and innocuous elsewhere in Herod's realm, however, then major protest incidents and movements in Judea cry out for explanation (and the widespread popular resistance to Gaius's pretentious plan is isolated from its historical context). As Herod lay dying, the students of two famous sages dared to chop down the golden Roman eagle from atop the gate of the Temple (*B.J.* 1.648–55; *Ant.* 17.149–67). Herod was so furious that he had them burned alive. When Rome imposed direct rule in Judea ten years later, what Josephus calls the "fourth philosophy" led by Judas of Galilee and Saddok the Pharisee advocated refusal to pay the Roman tribute out of their fervent belief that God was their only "lord and master" (*Ant.* 18.4–10, 23–24). Again some years later, when Pilate was about to send troops into Jerusalem with their army standards, masses of Judeans rushed to Caesarea and appealed to Pilate to slaughter them rather than desecrate the holy city (*B.J.* 2.169–

74).[13] Something must have aggravated the populace to account for such major protests and resistance movements in the face of the predictable consequences of Herodian or Roman repression. Precisely those incidents and movements suggest how important the political cultural focus on the divine Caesar had become in Judea and Galilee.

A broader approach, with more sophisticated appreciation of the importance of the immediate urban environment and its imagery for the predominantly public life of antiquity, has resulted in much fuller appreciation of the centrality of the emperor cult, beginning early in Augustus's reign.[14] It started in the East, where the emperor was directly connected with indigenous myths of heroes and gods and a cult of the emperor already familiar from earlier Hellenistic empires. By the time Augustus died, nearly every Roman city in Italy and the western provinces had several cults linked with the imperial house. Mutual competition among the cities meant that hundreds of them set up altars and temples to Augustus. Sacrificial processions linked with parades, public meals, and lavish games were held in honor of the emperor. Even more, because the central public spaces of the cities were built or rebuilt with temples, movements, and symbols focusing on the emperor (and/or Rome, an imperial family member, or an imperial accomplishment) and because the coins they handled bore the imperial image, the people lived with constant reminders of the imperial presence and power. As the historian Nicolaus of Damascus, a contemporary of Augustus, declared: "The whole of humanity turns to the *Sebastos* ('August One') filled with reverence. Cities and provincial councils honor him with temples and sacrifices, for this is his due. In this way do they give thanks to him everywhere for his benevolence."[15]

Nicolaus's patron was Herod, king of Judea. Herod, says Josephus, "stood next after Agrippa (Augustus's close friend and presumed successor) in Caesar's affection," and "left no suitable spot within his realm destitute of some mark of homage to Caesar" (*B.J.* 1.400, 407). Not only did Herod orient the construction of the non-Judean part of his realm toward Rome and Caesar, thus setting the Judeans and Galileans within a broader "landscape" featuring the imperial presence, he also built "Rome" and the imperial presence into the rebuilt Jerusalem Temple and its daily ritual. Then his sons who took over in Galilee and Gaulanitis just to the east built the imperial presence into their urban foundations as well.

Just as the new Roman foundations in Greece, such as Corinth, were cities oriented westward toward Rome,[16] so the kingdom Herod constructed was oriented toward Rome and Caesar. This was dramatically embodied and symbolized in his rebuilding of Strato's Tower as "Caesarea." "In a circle round the harbor there was a continuous line of dwellings constructed of the most polished stone, and in their midst was a mound on which there stood a temple of Caesar, visible a great way off to those sailing into the harbor, which had a statue of *Roma* and also one of

Caesar" (*Ant.* 15.339). In a second major urban foundation, Herod built the new city of Sebaste ("August") on the site of the old Samaria, at the center of which he erected a huge temple to Augustus (*Ant.* 15.296–98; *B.J.* 1.403). He also constructed another temple to Caesar, of white marble, near Paneion, near the source of the Jordan River (*Ant.* 15.364; *B.J.* 1.404; later Caesarea Philippi, *B.J.* 2.168) — to complete only the list of major projects.

Herod's reconstruction of the Temple in Jerusalem was so massive that it took nearly eighty years to complete (*Ant.* 20.219). Besides the major disruption of the city for some years, one could imagine that the resulting Roman-Hellenistic "wonder of the world" probably changed the face and feel of the traditionally sacred center of the Judean temple-community. Herod had a golden eagle (symbolizing Rome) enshrined over the great gate of the Temple (*Ant.* 17.151). Moreover, just as Caesar was linked with traditional gods and heroes elsewhere in the East, so in the Jerusalem Temple, the priests "offered sacrifice twice daily for Caesar and the Roman people" (*B.J.* 2.197; cf. *c. Ap.* 2.77: "perpetual sacrifices for the emperors and the people of Rome"). Just how important those sacrifices were in symbolic political religion is indicated by Josephus's comment that the priests' withholding it in the summer of 66 c.e. "laid the foundation of the war against Romans" (*B.J.* 2.409).

While these constructions affected the Galileans indirectly as well, Herod's son Antipas finally brought the imperial "presence" into Galilee itself. His newly founded second capital was dedicated to the emperor Tiberius and stood as an immediate visible reminder to Galileans of the imperial ruling power (*Ant.* 18.36–38; to be discussed in chapter 7). Just across the Jordan River from Capernaum at the northern end of the Sea of Galilee, moreover, Antipas's brother and fellow Roman client-ruler Philip raised the village of Bethsaida into the city of Julias, named after the emperor's daughter (*Ant.* 18.28). He also built, as his own new capital at the headwaters of the Jordan just to the north, another "Caesarea" (Philippi).

Galileans and their neighbors as well as Judeans were thus living in a landscape with constant reminders of the emperor's power and glory, if not divinity. Leaders of the "fourth philosophy" in Judea such as Judas of Galilee and Saddok the Pharisee were simply the most vocal (or the ones Josephus chose to cite) in articulating the feeling of distress among the people that they now had a foreign "lord and master" in addition to their one true master, the God of Israel. The Roman impact on Galilee and Judea was cultural-religious as well as political-economic, and it focused on the lordship of Caesar in a way that conflicted in a particularly poignant way with traditional Israelite loyalties.

In contrast with their counterparts in the West, client-rulers in the East generally have been described as "sufficiently sophisticated to understand the full potential of Roman military power in the abstract" and as enjoying "secure political control over their subjects."[17] Both of these characterizations are surely true of Herod. His successors, however, do not appear to have been all that securely in control. More important, their Judean and Galilean subjects were not "sufficiently sophisticated" with regard to Roman military power. As mentioned, Rome's chosen means of controlling of subject peoples, by "forceful suasion," could function only through the perceptions and motivations of their subject peoples. To put it more bluntly, Rome's attempts to terrorize its subjects through devastation, slaughter, crucifixion, and enslavement would work only if the subject peoples were sufficiently cowed that they were dutifully submissive. Galileans and Judeans, like the peoples of northern Europe, had numerous occasions to become "educated" by repeated Roman reprisals against their intransigence and insurrections.[18] Galileans experienced repeated Roman military attacks in the period of initial conquest, as Gabinius moved through the area against rebellious Hasmonean pretenders and Cassius decimated and enslaved Tarichaeae. As noted in chapter 3, however, they then still mounted extensive and repeated resistance to Herod's conquest with the aid of Roman troops from 40–37 B.C.E. Little more than a generation later the Galileans again, at least in the area around Sepphoris, rose in rebellion at the death of Rome's client Herod, and again experienced the direct application of Rome's "forceful suasion." From the Roman point of view, the slaughter of people, devastation of towns and countryside, and enslavement of able-bodied survivors after the rebellions in 4 B.C.E. and the widespread revolt in 66 C.E. were all pointed attempts finally to terrorize the populace into submission.

Direct Roman Rule and Urbanization

Rome had always favored the formation of self-governing cities with surrounding territory under their control as the means of organizing and administering its provinces. As client-ruler, Antipas had paved the way for the final step in the "urbanization" of the Roman domination of Galilee.

The way in which the Romans reconquered Galilee provides a vivid illustration of how Rome depended on the cities as bases from which the countryside could be controlled. Sepphoris and the powerful elite of Tiberias remained loyal to Rome during the revolt. As soon as the requisite force was assembled, the Romans advanced to secure Sepphoris as a base of operations. In fortified towns such as Gischala or Jotapata they destroyed the fortifications; in villages where serious resistance was offered, such as Japha, they wrought terrible slaughter. At Tiberias the elite arranged a capitulation of the city, while the rebels fled to Tarichaeae. When both towns were taken, Vespasian made a clear distinction between the residents of the towns and the "outsiders" from the countryside. Assuming that we can trust Josephus's account on the matter, the bulk of the (tens of) thousands executed on the spot or sold into slavery were villagers. As under the client regimes, so under direct Roman rule, the *pax Romana* in Lower Galilee worked through the cities.

The great revolt and the Roman reconquest became a major turning point in Rome's treatment of Palestine. The Temple, along with much of the city of Jerusalem, was destroyed. Rome made the whole area into the province of Judea headed by a governor of praetorian rank, and by 120 C.E. of consular rank, with two legions at his disposal. The parts of Galilee not still under Agrippa II were included, and Agrippa II's territory was as well when he died. Surely as significant as the inclusion of the whole area in one province of higher rank was the policy of urbanization. It is thus likely that Sepphoris attained full municipal status sometime in the late first century. Under Hadrian, it was transformed into Diocaesarea, completing its change from the administrative city of a client-ruler to a provincial Roman city. The "urbanization" of eastern Lower Galilee soon followed. No longer simply the head of a toparchy subject to Agrippa II, Tiberias began minting its own coins as a sign of its status. All of Lower Galilee was now subject to these two cities (fuller discussion of the cities in chapter 7). The villages of Upper Galilee, however, remained the administrative district of Tetracomia, outside of any city territory, a factor that would clearly have affected continued regional variation within Galilee. By late antiquity, nearly every area of Palestine except Upper Galilee and the Golan was included in some city established by Roman fiat.

A series of developments in second-century Galilee of major, indeed foundational, importance for the subsequent development of rabbinic Judaism were the indirect product of Roman treatment of Judea. When the Roman armies finally reconquered Jerusalem in 70 C.E., they destroyed the Temple and dispersed what personnel remained of the temple-state apparatus, settling many scribes and sages in Yavneh and many priests in Gophna.[19] Sixty-five years later, the Roman reconquest of the country in suppression of the Bar Kokhba Revolt brought even greater devastation of the land, a punitive dislocation of large segments of the people, as well as repressive measures against Jews and Jewish traditions. These punitive measures touched off a series of developments in which the nascent rabbinic academies moved to Galilee and eventually established prominent centers in Sepphoris and Tiberias (see further chapters 4 and 7).

Following the massive and sustained revolt of 66–70, the Romans committed a much larger military force to maintain order in the expanded province of Judea. The Tenth Legion, along with nearly as many troops in auxiliary units, was stationed in Judea after 70, and from 120 (even before the Bar Kokhba Revolt in Judea proper) until the beginning of the fourth century two legions and 25,000 more auxiliary troops were based in the province. In contrast with the situation under the client-rulers, the Roman military was now more of a presence, particularly on the frontier of Galilee, but also in Galilee itself.[20] The city of Legio was established in the Great Plain, just to the south of Galilee, as the base of the new legion sent to Palestine. The presence of the Sixth Legion at Legio and the Tenth in Judea should also be seen in the context of the aggressively "imperialistic" Roman policy that continued in the East. Even after the disappointing results of Trajan's war against the Parthian empire to the east in 114–117, a succession of Roman emperors pursued military campaigns into Mesopotamia. In the 190s Septimius Severus formed two new provinces across the Euphrates River and created two new legions to hold them intact.[21] A heavy military presence in the province of Judea was clearly integral to Rome's wider imperial concerns.

Although not extensive, there was now also a regular Roman military within Galilee as well as on its frontiers. Sepphoris had always been a fortress city, and now a Roman garrison occupied the fortress, as indicated in the famous story of their having been ready to put out a fire on the Sabbath.[22] A Roman military fortress was also established on a hill overlooking Tiberias.[23] Although it is likely that there was less of a military presence in Galilee than in Judea, particularly following the Bar Kokhba Revolt, which apparently did not involve Galilee, rabbinic literature does complain about unwelcome incursions of soldiers into domestic scenes ("sampling" the wine) and especially about the forced labor that the military could require on an ad hoc basis.[24] It is difficult to determine whether popular Galilean attitudes toward Roman administration, taxation, and cultural incursions became modulated following the reconquest in 67 C.E. and the imposition of direct Roman rule in the rest of Galilee. If rabbinic texts of the late second and third centuries are any indication, a serious level of resentment and hostility remained.[25]

The presence of the army in general and Hadrian's visit to the area in 130 in particular were stimuli to the major expansion of the system of Roman roads in the province of Judea. A road from Legio to Diocaesarea was built for the imperial visit, and thereafter other major roads were constructed, completing a network that included Tiberias and Ptolemais as well.[26] The construction and maintenance of Roman roads became one among other tasks and occasions for which the Romans demanded *angariae* of the people, whether labor or the use of draft animals.

The emphasis on "urbanization" and the expanded "development" of roads and other Roman forms of civilization indicate that there would have been no diminished demand for tribute and taxes. Urban administration replaced that of the Roman client-rulers such as Antipas and the Agrippas. Moreover, at least partially replacing the dues formerly paid to the Temple and priests in Jerusalem was the yearly payment of two drachmae to the *fiscus iudaicus* for rebuilding the temple of Jupiter Capitolinus that Vespasian imposed on all Jews everywhere (Josephus, *B.J.* 7.218; Cassius Dio 66.7.2). Although there happens to be no evidence for how this affected Jews in

Palestine, presumably they, no less than diaspora Jews, were required to pay.[27]

Beyond the collection of taxes, which was delegated to the urban officials, Roman administration was lax and remote at best, with most matters left to the cities of Diocaesarea and Tiberias, under whose jurisdiction most of Galilee was now located. Some sort of Roman administrators must have been responsible for the network of villages in Upper Galilee, the Tetracomia. The Roman governor, of course, almost always remained in Caesarea with its culture and amenities.[28]

In sum, Roman domination of Palestine illustrates how the Romans gave little thought to anything other than the control and taxation of subject peoples, including those who just happened to be in the way of broader objectives, such as the Galileans. Insofar as they continued the basic political-economic structure of the ancient Near East in Galilee, the Romans were simply one more imperial force to rule and tax Galilee, following the Assyrians, Persians, Ptolemies, and Seleucids. Roman conquest of Galilee, however, brought three major new developments that changed the course of life and history in the area.

First, as was their practice in newly conquered areas not previously "urbanized," the Romans established indirect rule through client-regimes. Second, although Herod the Great apparently continued to administer and tax the district, his son Antipas not only used Galilee as an economic base but established a residential court there. His rebuilding of Sepphoris and foundation of the new capital of Tiberias was thus the beginning of the process of urbanization that was later consolidated under direct Roman rule. The Roman imposition of client-rulers and the evolution of the "royal" cities into Roman cities, however, left no opportunity for the development of an indigenous Galilean body as a voice that could represent Galilean interests. Because the traditional apparatus of the temple-state in Jerusalem included not only the reigning high-priestly families but also scribes whose traditional role was to apply the revered "laws of the Judeans," delegations of Judeans repeatedly journeyed to the dominant Roman consul or to the emperor to plead their case against certain rulers or arrangements. No such traditional regional aristocracy or local center of power had a chance to develop. Hence no political mechanism existed from or through which Galileans, of whatever station in life, could have pleaded their case in a similar way.[29] Popular insurrections and a peasant strike are the only expressions of which we have evidence. As noted in chapter 3 above, even in the massive insurrection of 66–67, resistance to Roman rule was regional and focused primarily on the cities where Roman or Herodian administration was based, that is, Sepphoris and Tiberias.

The third major development was the indirect result of the Roman destruction of the Jerusalem Temple and temple-state in 70 c.e. and their devastation of Judea and dislocation of Judeans in suppressing the Bar Kokhba revolt in 132–135. Those reconquests of Jerusalem and Judea by Roman armies initiated a chain of events whereby the priestly and scribal leadership in Judea began to consolidate what became rabbinic Judaism and then moved their residence and centers of activity north into Galilee during the second century.

Chapter 6

JERUSALEM AND GALILEE

❧

The religion administered by the aristocracy is always the religion of the aristocracy, not that of the peasantry which tends to remain quite distinct.

— JOHN KAUTSKY

Fear the Lord and honor the priest,
and give him his portion, as you have been commanded:
the first fruits, the guilt offering,
the gift of the shoulders,
the sacrifice of sanctification,
and the first fruits of the holy things.

— JESUS BEN SIRA

Missionaries of "great traditions," whether the tradition be religious or po-litical, commonly find themselves in a poignant dilemma when they attempt to carry the message to the peasantry. If the message and its bearers are accepted at all, they are assimilated into an existing set of meanings, sym-bols, and practices which frequently do great violence to the message as understood by its high priests in the capital city.

— JAMES C. SCOTT

In the absence of these integrating factors, the contours of non-elite beliefs are likely to diverge more strikingly from elite beliefs and the variety of beliefs among non-elites is also likely to be greater.

— JAMES C. SCOTT

Jerusalem was a holy city. The Temple was *the* sacred space in which ancient Jews served God in elaborate ceremonies, including three major pilgrimage festivals, as well as the daily communal sacrifices and offerings and occasional individual sacrifices and offerings. Because the Temple was so extremely holy and intercourse with the divine so fraught with danger as well as mystery, it was necessary to have set apart a sacred priest-hood, headed by the high priest, to serve before the altar and in the sacred precincts. The will of God was known through the sacred Teaching revealed to Moses, the Torah, of which the priests constituted the divinely sanctioned teachers. Toward the end of the second Temple, moreover, emerged the different Jewish "sects" of Pharisees, Sadducees, and Essenes, each with its distinctive interpretation of the Torah and theology.

That, of course, is the construction of ancient "Judaism" into which most of us have been socialized by scholarly training as well as religious education. The problem is not that this picture is wrong, but that it is incomplete, *and* so deeply rooted in our consciousness as to block from our view other dimensions of Temple, high priesthood, Torah, and Pharisees.

Three major qualifications are necessary to this standard understanding of ancient "Judaism" as "religion." (1) What moderns distinguish as a separate dimension of life was embedded with and inseparable from the fundamental social forms of life in ancient Palestine. (2) Religious formation and expression operated at more than one level, that of family and local village community being at least as important as that of the Jerusalem Temple for the vast majority of people, who lived in outlying towns and villages. (3) These two levels often operated with a certain degree of conflict.

The Temple and high priesthood were the central and dominating political-economic institutions of ancient Judea, their religious dimension inseparable from their political-economic function. The Torah served, in effect, as the constitution and law-code of the temple-state centered in Jerusalem. The Pharisees and other scribes/sages served a mediating political-economic-religious function in that Judean temple-state, as we shall see below. Two brief passages from Josephus suffice to illustrate how we must proceed in order to understand the temple-state of ancient Judea:

> The priests are entrusted with the special charge of [the community], and the whole administration of the state [*politeias*] resembles some sacred ceremony.
> (*c. Ap.* 2.188)

> Whoever was master of [the fortifications guarding the city and temple] had the whole nation in his power, for sacrifices could not be made without (controlling) these places, and it was impossible for any of the Judeans to forego offering these. (*Ant.* 15.248)

Discussion of local village and town religious formations and expressions will be one of the principal concerns of the chapters in part 3. This chapter will focus primarily on the temple-state based in Jerusalem and its relations with and impact on Galilee. It bears repeating that the political-economic and religious dimensions of Temple, priesthood, Torah, and so on, are inseparable. The discussion below will on occasion highlight the political and/or economic dimensions precisely because it is important to remind ourselves just how integral they were to the ways in which Temple, high priesthood, Torah, or Pharisees operated in ancient Judea.

As delineated in part 1, Galilee was under direct rule by the temple-state and Herodian regime in Jerusalem for only 100 years, after being under separate imperial jurisdiction from Jerusalem and Judea for eight centuries. The principal questions, therefore, are the ways in which Jerusalem rule affected life in Galilee and the ways in which Galilean life may have adjusted to Jerusalem institutions and influences.

The Foundation and Basic Structures of Second-Temple Institutions

While Galilee was not directly subject to the jurisdiction of the Jerusalem Temple and high priesthood at the time of Jesus, it had been subject to Jerusalem for the 100 years before Jesus was born. That the climactic events of Jesus' ministry focused on the Temple is surely rooted in Galilean experience under Jerusalem rule. Moreover, while the Temple had been destroyed by the Romans long before rabbinic Judaism took form in Galilee, its formative document, the Mishnah, is dominated by rulings and discussions concerning temple affairs, the priests, and the constituent sacred times, ceremonies, tithes, and offerings. For the rabbis, the Temple represented the normative and ideal order of reality. However removed it was geographically and however remote it was temporally, the Temple and the temple-state apparatus had profound effects on life in Galilee.

From its original conception and constitution, the second Temple was an integral institution of imperial order in which the religious, political, and economic dimensions were inseparable. The Persians' policy of imperial rule was at least selectively to restore the local-regional-ethnic social forms such as temples and law-codes, which often were integrally connected insofar as priesthoods and temples were the guardians of the laws.[1] Thus, when the Persians restored the Judean ruling class that had been taken into exile by the Babylonians a half-century earlier, they sponsored the rebuilding of a temple for "the god who is in Jerusalem" (Ezra 1:3). The scribe Ezra cites the founding imperial decree:

> Thus says King Cyrus of Persia: The Lord, the God of heaven, has given me all the kingdoms of the earth, and he has charged me to build him a house at Jerusalem in Judah.... Let the cost be paid from the royal treasury. Moreover, let the gold and silver vessels of the house of God, which Nebuchadnezzar took out of the temple in Jerusalem and brought to Babylon, be restored and brought back to the temple in Jerusalem. (Ezra 1:2; 6:4–5)

Headed by the repatriated Judean ruling class, that temple then became the central political-economic-religious institution of the province of Judea. In their position as client-rulers, the priestly families that quickly established their preeminence in Jerusalem were the heads of state in charge of a tributary economy centered in the house of God to which the people brought their tithes and offerings.

> We obligate ourselves to bring the first fruits of our soil and the first fruits of all fruit of every tree, year by year, to the house of our God, to the priests who minister in the house of our God.... And the priest, the descendant of Aaron, shall be with the Levites when the Levites receive the tithes;... and bring up the tithes... to the chambers of the storehouse.
>
> (Neh. 10:32–39; 12:44)

All was focused as thanksgiving and service to God, done at the command of God (in the Torah), and understood as a whole system of fertility and productivity centered in the Temple.

> Will anyone rob God?... Bring the full tithe into the storehouse, so that there may be food in my house, and thus put me to the test, says the Lord of hosts; see if I will not open the windows of heaven for you and pour down for you an overflowing blessing. (Mic. 3.10)

Indigenous Judean laws and traditions (Ezra's lawbook; Nehemiah 8) were compiled under Persian imperial sponsorship as a legitimating and regulating "constitution" and political-economic-religious law-code for the Jerusalem temple-state.

Lest it is not clear from the preceding biblical references, the biblical books of Ezra and Nehemiah also make clear that the Judean temple-community thus established was, like the rest of the ancient Near East, a society structurally divided between the wealthy and powerful and the peasantry who supported them, in this case partly through the tithes and offerings. Although the reestablished law-codes may have included provisions for debt-easement and other mitigation of severe economic exploitation, the problems of debts and debt-slavery had become severe soon after the founding of the second Temple and reestablishment of the Judean ruling class.

> Now there was a great outcry of the people against their Judean kin.... "We are having to pledge our fields, our vineyards, and our houses in order to get grain during the famine."... "We are having to borrow on our fields and vineyards to pay the king's tax. Now our flesh is the same as that of our kindred; our children are the same as their children; and yet we are forcing our sons and daughters to be slaves, and some of our daughters have been ravished; we are powerless, and our fields and vineyards now belong to others." (Neh. 5:1–5)

Although Nehemiah brought charges against "the nobles and officials" and effected a cancellation of debts and restoration of land, the fundamental (religiously legitimated) political-economic structure remained unchanged, with a subsistence peasantry under the authority of the priestly aristocracy in Jerusalem.

The fundamental structure of the temple-state sponsored originally by the Persian regime persisted under the Hellenistic regimes of the Ptolemies and Seleucids and was reestablished by the Romans after the interlude of Judean independence and expansion under the Hasmoneans. By Hellenistic times the Aaronide priesthood had established themselves securely at the center of the temple-state. The professional scribe Ben Sira provides what must be the classic articulation of the ideology of the high priesthood at the center of the Judean temple-state.

> How glorious he was, surrounded by the people, as he came out of the house of the curtain. Like the morning star among the clouds, like the sun shining on the temple of the Most High. When he received the portions from the hands of the priests, as he stood by the hearth of the altar. All the sons of Aaron in their splendor held the Lord's offering in their hands before the whole congregation of Israel.... Then the sons of Aaron shouted ... as a reminder before the Most High. Then all the people together quickly fell to the ground on their faces to worship the Lord, the Almighty, God Most High. (Sir. 50:5–7, 12–13, 16–17)

The political-economic-religious structure of the temple-community of Judea in second-temple times was a series of concentric circles of status in degrees of holiness. At the very center was the high priest, surrounded by the other members of the high-priestly families. The other, ordinary priestly families also served cultic and other functions and derived some of their economic subsistence from tithes and offerings. Around these more central circles of priests were the ordinary people of Judea (representing and represented as Israel), whose tithes and offerings constituted the economic basis of the whole. Scribes and sages, whether priestly or lay, served certain functions of the temple-state headed by the priestly aristocracy, and artisans supplied the various needs (for vessels and garments, and so on) of the priests and temple services.[2]

The Expansion of Temple-State and Temple

The structures of the temple-state had become so thoroughly entrenched in Jerusalem and Judea that, after Judas the Maccabee led a popular rebellion against the Seleucid armies, his brothers Jonathan and Simon took over the apparatus of state and negotiated themselves into the position of high priest. As sketched in chapter 2, the Seleucid regime's weakness, compounded by rival claimants to the imperial throne, enabled the Hasmoneans to establish the independence of the Jerusalem temple-state from imperial rule for the first time in its history. The continuing decline of Seleucid power in Palestine and Syria, moreover, created a political vacuum in which the Hasmoneans could take control of most of Palestine, including Galilee. Thus within two generations, the temple-state had expanded its territory from a tiny area in the immediate vicinity of Jerusalem itself, with a population that would hardly have exceeded 100,000, to nearly all of Palestine, with a highly diverse population of nearly one million. As the Hasmoneans expanded their control over additional territories, so the apparatus of the temple-state expanded in Jerusalem. Moreover, after the Romans placed Herod in control, in addition to establishing a separate royal administration, he not only expanded the priestly aristocracy but also rebuilt the Temple in grand scale. Jerusalem and the Temple underwent dramatic expansion precisely while Galilee was under Hasmonean and Herodian rule.

A telling indication of the growing power and wealth of the temple-state is the expansion of Jerusalem evident from archaeological explorations. The Western Hill, which had lain in ruins since the Babylonian conquest, was apparently resettled and rebuilt under the Hasmoneans, becoming the Upper City in which the priestly and Herodian elite resided in luxurious mansions. The expansion of Jerusalem probably began under the Hasmoneans, who built themselves a palace on a high spot that commanded an overlook into the inner court of the Temple, as well as a palace-resort for relaxation in Jericho. Continuing under Herod, the building of palaces and mansions in the Upper City reached its climax in the first century c.e. At least some of the families he appointed to the high priesthood established elaborate residences, as we know from Josephus's account of the attack on the mansion of Ananias during the initial stages of the revolt in 66 (*B.J.* 2.426). From the archaeologist who headed the excavation of the Western Hill, we have the picture in general that

> the individual dwelling units were extensive, and inner courtyards lent them the character of luxury villas. These homes were richly ornamented with frescoes, stucco work, and mosaic floors, and were equipped with complex bathing facilities, as well as containing the luxury goods and artistic objects which signify a high standard of living. This, then, was an upper class quarter, where the noble families of Jerusalem lived, with the High Priest at their head. Here they built their homes in accordance with the dominant fashion of the Hellenistic-Roman period.[3]

Amid the ruins were also found the handles of numerous storage jars stamped in archaizing Hebrew script with *Yehud* = "Judah" or "Jerusalem," that is, jars that served some official function, probably for taxes in kind for the royal and/or temple treasury.[4] The presence of these "official" storage jars in the elite residential area enables us to discern how what historical sociologists have called a "redistributive" or "tributary" political economy may have worked in the case of the Judean temple-state. Wine paid as tithes or taxes to the (high) priesthood in the Temple were "redistributed" directly to the principal wealthy and powerful officers of the temple-state. Also in the ruins were remains of large storage jars apparently of wine from Rhodes and other Greek islands and, from the Herodian period, fragments of similar wine jars with Latin inscriptions, as well as fine ware of rare beauty. Such finds indicate that the Jerusalem elite not only commanded the finest luxury goods of the Hellenistic-Roman world, but were also imbibing foreign wines.

By far the most remarkable of the expansions in Jerusalem in the late second-temple period was of the temple complex — indeed, it was one of the most remarkable buildings of Roman antiquity. While Herod the Great became world-renowned in his own time because of his massive building projects, his greatest cultural and architectural achievement was the rebuilding of the temple complex in Jerusalem.[5] The Hasmoneans had already expanded the area around the Temple, which remained in traditional Near Eastern style. Herod's Temple was far more of a departure from Judean tradition. The sheer size as well as the style of the edifice made a grand political-religious statement. As a Roman client-ruler eager to advertise his own magnificence, Herod had the Temple transformed in impressive Hellenistic-Roman style. The scale of the construction (which took nearly eighty years) was truly astounding. It was twice the size of the new Forum built by Trajan in Rome. Only in archaic Egypt were there temples of corresponding size. Herod's Royal Portico, across the south end of the complex, was itself the size of a medium-sized medieval cathedral, with white marble Corinthian columns. The front façade of the sanctuary itself within the overall temple complex was 150 feet high. That the temple complex comprised fully one-sixth of Jerusalem indicates how it dominated the city both physically and politically-economically. While the Upper City now contained the magnificent mansions of the priestly aristocracy as well as the Herodian elite, the Temple as the political-economic as well as religious center of the expanded temple-state was still *the* dominating institution in Jerusalem.

A central portion of the overall complex was used for cultic purposes. In physical layout as well as hierarchical sanctity, this sacred space was organized into a series of rectangular enclosures, moving from the court of women as antechamber before the main enclosure, to the court of (ordinary male) Israelites, within which was the court of priests containing the altar for burnt sacrifices, within which was the 150-foot-high inner sanctum containing the first chamber and the Holy of Holies, into which only the high priest entered once a year on the Day of Atonement. The vast outer "Court of the Gentiles" provided a wide-open public space, enclosed by the walls and porticoes, in which the civic life of the city and pilgrims from beyond was centered. Given the Temple's sacred political-economic function, the complex presumably provided storage facilities for the grain, wine, oil, and wood that were brought to the Temple as dues to the priests. Perhaps there were also facilities where the hides of sacrificial animals could be processed. More certain is that a sacred space was provided in which the wealth of the elite families could be securely held on deposit.

We should note, at least in passing, the economic cost of this expansion of Jerusalem in general and the rebuilding of the Temple in particular. Jerusalem was clearly thriving economically as well as culturally under the Hasmoneans and Herod. The expansion depended, of course, on the peasant producers of Palestine. The building of mansions for the elite and Herod's massive construction projects such as the temple platform, royal porticoes, and sanctuary obviously provided extensive opportunity for employment for those forced off the land by war or debts. A measure of the huge portion of the economy of Judea constituted simply by the construction of the Temple is Josephus's report that with its completion just before the great revolt, 18,000 were suddenly out of work, prompting the Jerusalemites to obtain King Agrippa's permission to use temple funds to set the workers busy again, paving the city with white stone (*Ant.* 20.219–22). Accompanying Jerusalem's growth as a political-economic-religious center of power, of course, was a growing division between the wealthy ruling class ensconced in their upper city mansions and Herodian or temple/chief–priestly positions, on the one hand, and the mass of Judeans, Idumeans, Samaritans, and Galileans whose produce in taxes and tithes provided the economic base for the whole, on the other.

Before moving to how the Hasmonean and Herodian regimes administered Galilee and their impact on the Galileans, we should note the increasing discontent and resistance to the ruling institutions in Jerusalem and their incumbents among the Judeans from late Hasmonean through Herodian times. There were apparently dissident voices from the very outset of the (re-)founding of the temple-state in Jerusalem, as indicated in late prophetic texts such as "Third" Isaiah, "Deutero" Zechariah, Haggai, and Malachi. Moreover, tensions had mounted during the domination by the Hellenistic empires until the Maccabean Revolt erupted against the Hellenistic Reform and repression of the traditional Mosaic covenantal way of life.

Concurrent with Hasmonean consolidation of expansion of power, however, was the emergence of strong and sustained opposition to the regime. The Pharisees, whose "traditions" or legal rulings had become part of the state law under the early Hasmoneans, came into conflict apparently first with John Hyrcanus and particularly with Alexander Janneus (*Ant.* 13.288–98, 401–8). Indeed, "the Judean populace revolted against him," and "as he stood beside the altar and was about to sacrifice, they pelted him with citrons" (*B.J.* 1.88; *Ant.* 13.372). The conflict escalated into virtual civil war, with Alexander killing thousands of his opponents, including 800 crucified before their wives and children in the midst of the city, and thousands fleeing Judea to escape the repression (*Ant* 13.379–83). Whether we see them originating in reaction to the Hasmoneans or to Herod, the community that produced the Dead Sea Scrolls was one of clearly dissident priests and scribes who utterly condemned the incumbent "Wicked Priest" and withdrew to the wilderness until such time as a legitimate and Torah-true priestly government could be restored in the Jerusalem Temple.

Despite Herod's extensive construction of military fortresses and other security measures, the steady opposition to his rule erupted in acts of protest and violent insurrection at the end of his reign (*Ant.* 17.149–67, 200–218, 271–85; *B.J.* 1.648–55; 2.55–75). For example, two sages inspired their students to cut down the golden Roman eagle from atop one of the gates of the Temple (*B.J.* 1.648–55; *Ant.* 17.149–67).[6] As soon as Herod died, the Jerusalem crowd clamored for relief from tyranny. And in Judea itself as well as in Perea and Galilee, widespread popular rebellions acclaimed their leaders as kings, obviously over against the king who had been ruling in Jerusalem.[7] Popular dissidence and even scribal attacks against high-priestly rule continued in Judea throughout the first century C.E. leading up to the great revolt.[8] Although most popular protests appear to have focused primarily on Roman (mis-)rule, the Roman-appointed high-priestly officers were usually implicated as well. By mid-first century certain high-priestly figures were actively engaged in predatory behavior against the people and ordinary priests, on the one hand, and the Sicarii or "daggermen" had begun their clandestine attacks against prominent high-priestly collaborators with Roman rule, on the other (*B.J.* 2.254–57; *Ant.* 20.181, 186–87, 205–10).[9]

One factor in the steadily disintegrating authority of the temple-state in late second-temple times was the lack of legitimacy of the high-priestly incumbents. The early Hasmonean high priests could counterbalance their non-Zadokite priestly origins with their status as popular heroes in the struggle for Judea's independence from foreign imperial rule. Beginning at least with Alexander Janneus, legitimacy of Hasmonean rule among the people declined. Herod more seriously undermined the legitimacy of the high priesthood, at least in Palestine. After the upstart Hasmoneans replaced the traditional Zadokite Oniads in the office, it had again become hereditary. After eliminating the last of the Hasmoneans, however, Herod appointed his own men to the high-priestly office and replaced them when it suited his purposes—which was "against the law," says Josephus, since, except for the action of the hated Antiochus Epiphanes, high priests were not deposed once they assumed office (*Ant.* 15.40). He even brought in men from abroad, from priestly families in Egypt or Babylon.[10] Not surprisingly, one of the principal cries of the Jerusalem crowd after the death of Herod was for the removal of the high priest appointed by Herod and the installation of someone "more lawful and pure" (*Ant.* 17.207–8; *B.J.* 2.7). The families of the men Herod appointed thus came to constitute a dramatically expanded priestly aristocracy that attempted to rule Judea under the Roman governors in the first century C.E. As the legacy of the hated Herod, the frequently changing appointees of the Roman governors, themselves remote from the people in their upper city mansions, these high priests lacked legitimacy among the people. Moreover, as fit the very structure of the imperial situation, in virtually every major overt conflict that erupted between the people and the Romans, far from representing the Judean people's interests, the high-priestly aristocracy collaborated with the Roman authorities on whom their positions depended.[11] When the great revolt finally erupted in the summer of 66 c.e., the high priests, along with the Roman troops, were the principal targets of the Jerusalem insurgents, including numbers of the ordinary priests.

Jerusalem Administration and Taxation of Galilee

Ancient rulers used military installations to maintain control of the people(s) as well as to defend their frontiers. It seems likely that they were also used in the collection and storage of taxes in kind, which in turn supported their economic maintenance. When the early Israelites clamored for a king "like other nations," Yahweh instructed Samuel to warn them that a king "will take your sons and appoint them to his chariots and to be his horsemen, ... and he will appoint for himself commanders of thousands and commanders of fifties.... He will take one tenth of your grain and of your vineyards and give it to his officers and his courtiers" (1 Sam. 8:11–12, 15). The best known biblical illustration is surely Solomon. He used "forced labor" to build not only the original Temple in Jerusalem and his own palace (twice the size), but to construct storage-cities, chariot-cities, cavalry-cities, and other fortresses throughout his realm (1 Kings 9:15–19; cf. 5:13–16). These included the major installations at Hazor to the north and Megiddo to the south of Galilee.

Although no Roman legions were stationed regularly in Galilee until well after the time of Jesus, there was clearly a military presence in the area in the first century b.c.e. Both rabbinic and archaeological indications confirm Josephus's numerous references to military fortresses and garrisons that Jerusalem rulers established in Galilee. According to recently developed critical reading of the Mishnah, "the old castra of Sepphoris, the fortress of Gush Halav, [and] old Yodpat" (*m. 'Arak.* 9:6) refer to installations of the Hasmoneans and/or Herod, which were already "old" to the rabbis of the late second century c.e.[12] The unusually large numbers of Hasmonean coins (particularly those of Alexander Janneus) found, for example, at Gush Halav, suggest a Hasmonean military presence at one of those very locations.[13] Josephus's accounts of Herod retaking three fortresses that had been captured by Marion, whom Cassius had installed as ruler of Tyre (*Ant.* 14.297–98; *B.J.* 1.238), indicate that the Hasmoneans had established fortresses and garrisons in Upper Galilee.[14] Another Josephus account suggests that Gischala (=Gush Halav) was already fortified before John of Gischala built up the walls during the revolt of 66–67 and Titus ordered their destruction (*Vita* 71; *B.J.* 2.590; 4.117).

Josephus also reports that Herod "posted garrisons throughout Galilee" shortly after reasserting control of the area once he was appointed military governor under his father Antipater (*B.J.* 1.210). Just how much those were needed to maintain control in Galilee was repeatedly evident not so much from the rival armies criss-crossing Galilee periodically during the next decade as by the persistent resistance the Galileans mounted to Herod's rule when he moved to conquer the realm to which the Roman Senate had appointed him. Josephus's accounts of Herod's repeated attempts to "pacify" the district give further indications of fortresses that had been established apparently by the Hasmoneans and were likely restored by the security-minded Herod. Although the "city" of Sepphoris was surely the major installation, including a major depot of supplies as well as a relatively large fortress, there were clearly other, probably smaller fortresses, some of them in towns against which Herod took punitive measures against local hostility to his rule (*Ant.* 14.413, 433; *B.J.* 1.304, 316). Presumably Herod and probably Antipas and other rulers of Galilee maintained a series of fortresses and storage depots around the area.

Sepphoris, of course, would have been the major fortress as well as the central administrative center in Galilee for Herod as for the Hasmoneans. Whether the *basileion* established there by Herod was a royal "palace" or not, it was definitely a military arsenal and major storage depot, presumably for taxes taken in kind from the surrounding area of Lower Galilee (*Ant.* 17.271; *B.J.* 2.56). Yet even the sizable fortress and garrison at Sepphoris did not provide sufficient security in Lower Galilee for Herod, who also established a military colony in the western Great Plain along the frontier of Galilee. That the function of the foundation of Gaba was a military check against Galilee seems evident from its location and from Josephus's indication that it was called "the city of cavalry" because Herod settled cavalry there (*B.J.* 3.36; *Ant.* 15.294). The settlement clearly continued its military function through mid-first century C.E., for "the inhabitants of Gaba" served as auxiliary troops for the Roman army in quelling the revolt in Galilee in 66–67 (*Vita* 115).

These Hasmonean and Herodian fortresses in Galilee cannot be explained away as primarily for defense against foreign attack.[15] The Hasmoneans were themselves expanding their territory, and even after the height of Alexander Janneus's expansion, his wife and successor Alexandra Salome maintained a large army, which does not indicate a defensive strategy. The Romans were not yet pushing directly into the area. It appears rather that the Hasmoneans, in Galilee as elsewhere, established fortresses and garrisons as a means of controlling recently subjected peoples who had not yet been assimilated under the Jerusalem rule and accustomed to living "according to the laws of the Judeans."[16] Herod, of course, was the Romans' own man. It is abundantly clear that his principal concern was his own internal security.

Presumably the Hasmoneans and later Herod would have appointed their own clients and protégés as administrative officers in Galilee. It is conceivable that those officers could have included native Galileans. On the other hand, it may be significant that Josephus and other sources make no mention of Galileans in such capacities. That stands in dramatic contrast with the Idumeans in the south. The base from which Herod rose to become king of (greater) Judea illustrates the contrast. After John Hyrcanus conquered Idumea, his son Alexander Janneus appointed Antipas, head of a wealthy, prominent, and powerful family of the Idumean nation (*ethnos*), as military governor (*strategos*) of Idumea. His son Antipater then became the real governing force behind the high priest Hyrcanus II (*Ant.* 14.8–10, 121, 403; *B.J.* 1.123) and gave his son Herod a start by appointing him military governor in Galilee. As he secured his own hold on power in Jerusalem and Palestine, Herod in turn appointed Costobar, the scion of the Idumea family, as his military governor (*Ant.* 15.253, 264). There appears to be a consistent pattern here. The Hasmoneans and later Herod controlled Idumea by establishing close alliances with the most prominent and powerful Idumean families among a people still characterized by a certain tribal structure (cf. *B.J.* 4.230–33, 516). Simultaneously, they brought those prominent Idumeans into high places in their regimes.

We hear of nothing that corresponds to this in the Hasmonean or Herodian government of Galilee. Probably no corresponding tribal structure remained in Galilean society. Having been under foreign administration under Seleucids, Ptolemies, Persians, Assyrians, and somewhat similarly even under the Israelite kingship based in Samaria, Galilee consisted mainly of villages and administrative towns. Thus neither powerful tribal heads nor an indigenous aristocracy corresponding to Jerusalem or Samaria had developed there. That situation would most likely have remained the same under the Hasmoneans and Herod. Given the prevailing structure of power relations, it is difficult to discern how Galileans could have risen to prominence under the Hasmoneans or Herod. The "gentry" that Josephus mentions in connection with Herod's conquest of Galilee must have been Hasmonean officers who had become powerful figures in Galilee and, aware that their future lay with Herod rather than a Hasmonean rival, went over to his side (*Ant.* 14.395). Such holders of power (*dynatoi*), however, were not exactly popular among the Galilean people. The latter simply drowned those partisans of Herod in the lake (*Ant.* 14.450).

Ancient rulers expected revenues from their subjects. Solomon, for example, set up an elaborate system of twelve administrative districts, each of which provided annual revenues equal to the regime's needs for one month (1 Kings 4:7–19). Multiple layers of rulers meant multiple layers of taxation. During the period in which Galilee was under Jerusalem rule, the Romans imposed themselves as a second and Herod as a third layer of rulers. Consideration of the tithes and offerings expected by the Jerusalem

Temple and priesthood must thus take into account the multiple demands for tribute and taxation once Herod took power, a situation that may have continued into the first century C.E.

Under the Hasmoneans, Galilee was subject only to one layer of rulers, the high-priestly regime in Jerusalem. Although the Hasmoneans may have instituted additional forms of taxation, they presumably extended the traditional Judean system of tithes and offerings sanctioned in the Torah and other sacred books to the annexed territories such as Galilee. As indicated in the biblical passages cited at the beginning of the chapter (Mal. 3:10; Neh. 10:32–39), these taxes were understood as obligations owed to God who was specially present in the Jerusalem Temple and whose representatives and mediators were the priests, particularly the high priest.

The sacred "tax structure" of the Jerusalem temple-state was apparently a combination of earlier systems in the history of Israel and Judah, principally the Deuteronomic and the Levitical or priestly systems (Deut. 14:22–29; Num. 18:21–32; cf. Lev. 27:30; Neh. 10:32–39; Tob. 1:6–8; Jub. 32:10–15). It seems likely that Josephus's summary of priestly revenues in *Ant.* 4:68–75, 205, 240, represents the situation in his own, late second-temple period, which has been called a "fourteen tithe system."[17] In addition to the tithes, much smaller amounts were due in the form of "first fruits" of nearly all products and the *terumah* or heave offering. At least in late second-temple times a yearly half-shekel temple tax for all adult males was added. Also part of the priestly revenues, of course, were the priestly share of the many kinds of sacrifices and offerings, which included the extremely valuable hides of the animals.[18]

When the Romans laid greater Judea under tribute, they confirmed the Hasmoneans in their position and sanctioned the continued payment of taxes to the high-priestly government in Jerusalem (as noted in chapter 2). Roman imposition of Herod as king then created a third layer of taxes. Herod's rule in Palestine was "efficient," to say the least. Given his ambitious building projects, renowned munificence to imperial figures and Hellenistic cities, and lavish palaces as well as network of fortresses, he had to utilize every possible source of revenue to the maximum without ruining his economic base. While we lack details of his tax system, the general effect on the various districts of his realm is clear. Far from dismantling the administrative and sacrificial apparatus of the Temple, Herod expanded it. This growth included expansion of the priestly aristocracy at the apex of the temple system through a series of appointments to the high-priestly office. By the end of his rule, there were four (instead of one) principal extended high-priestly families in Jerusalem, from whom the high priest and other temple officers were appointed in the next several decades. As noted above, the mansions uncovered by archaeologists in the Upper City give material evidence of their lavish lifestyle. The presence of these powerful aristocratic families at the apex of the temple system, along with the remarkable reconstruction of the temple complex itself by Herod, is evidence enough that the revenues supporting the Temple and priesthood were maintained under Herod and continued once Judea came under direct Roman rule.

Early second-temple texts make clear that annual collection of first fruits, heave offerings, and tithes were all brought to central storage facilities in the Temple (Mal. 3:10; Neh. 10:35–38; both cited above, and Neh. 13:5, 12–13; 2 Chron. 31:5–12). There temple officers took charge of storage and distribution to the priests and Levites. While "all Judah" or "the people of Israel and Judah" are said to bring the first fruits, tithes, and so on, to the Temple, participation was not strictly voluntary. The priests and Levites apparently went to "collect the tithes in all our rural towns" (Neh. 10:37–38; cf. Num. 18:26; Josephus, *Ant.* 20.181, 206). The presence of priests and Levites at the threshing floors would not have been incompatible with the people themselves taking the produce to the Temple. As can be seen in the discussion of pilgrimage below, particularly once the territory tributary to the Temple and priesthood had expanded beyond the immediate surroundings of Jerusalem, it would have been physically impossible for all of the people to bring produce at the same time. While administration of the first fruits and tithes was clearly centralized in the Temple, much of it even stored there, administration could have included local collection-distribution, that is, certain villages regularly supplying a certain priestly course.

That tithes and other temple or priestly revenues were centrally administered does not necessarily mean that the high priest or the high-priestly regime could determine the distribution or the purpose for which revenues were used. Josephus's reports of strong-armed gangs sent by high-priestly families to forcibly expropriate tithes from the threshing floors suggest that the distribution of regularly gathered tithes was not under their unilateral control, hence their extraordinary means (*Ant.* 20.181, 206). That, however, was at mid-first century C.E., when the high priesthood had lost much of its power as well as authority (see further below). The decrees of Caesar quoted by Josephus clearly understand the tithes as having been paid to the Hasmonean high priests — "they shall also pay tithes to Hyrcanus and his sons, just as they paid to their forefathers" (*Ant* 14.194, 203) — as if they then determined the disposition of the revenues. It seems likely that the Hasmoneans, having created a far more extensive and complex community tributary to the temple-state, also consolidated control of its revenues, including the tithes. Certain late rabbinic references to Johanan the High Priest setting aside the confession of the tithes and instituting "pairs" of state-appointed tithe collectors could well reflect just such a development under John Hyrcanus (*m. Ma'aś. Š.* 5:15; *m. Soṭa* 9:10; *y. Ma'aś. Š.* 5.56d; *y. Soṭa* 9.24a).[19]

The degree to which the Hasmonean rulers would simply have utilized revenues from tithes for state purposes such as maintaining a sizable army (not provided for in the second-temple scriptures) depends to a considerable extent on whether they also utilized a parallel secular form of taxation. It is conceivable that when the early Hasmoneans freed themselves of paying tribute to the Seleucid regime, they continued to collect some level of secular revenues.[20] They certainly took over the royal estates in the Great Plain and "the king's mountain country" in Judea-Samaria (*Ant.* 14.207). The half-shekel tax for the Temple expected from all adult male Israelites was apparently a late development, not explicitly stated in biblical texts, instituted probably in either Hasmonean or Roman times.[21] These other sources of income combined with tithes and/or other dues received from an expanded population would have generated a dramatic increase in revenue over the tiny original temple-community of Judea prior to the Hasmonean expansion. A diversion of tithes supposedly for support of the priests in general to other purposes of state could well have been one of the key issues over which thousands actively opposed Alexander Janneus in the early first century B.C.E. The scribal-sapiential authors of the Psalms of Solomon accuse the Hasmoneans of having stolen from the temple treasury (Pss. Sol. 8:11).

While it seems clear that Galileans were expected to pay tithes and/or other dues for the priests and Temple under the Hasmoneans (and Herod), there is little evidence for the degree and manner in which such revenues were taken and the degree to which Galileans complied with Jerusalem's demands or expectations.[22] A section in Julius Caesar's political-economic decrees reestablishing Hyrcanus II's "rights and privileges" indicates that parts of Galilee that had been and were now again under Hasmonean control rendered dues of some sort to the regime. "As for the places, lands, and farms, the fruits of which the kings of Syria and Phoenicia, as allies of the Romans, were permitted to enjoy by their gifts, these the Senate decrees that the ethnarch Hyrcanus and the Judeans shall have" (*Ant.* 14.209). The preceding context ("that the ancient rights which the Judeans and their high priests and priests had in relations to each other"; *Ant.* 14.208) suggests that those dues were tithes and other "religious" obligations.

If Galileans had been expected to render up tithes and other priestly or temple dues since the Hasmonean takeover it becomes easier to understand Josephus's comment about his fellow priests' behavior in Galilee when they were sent by the provisional high-priestly government in Jerusalem to take control of Galilee. "My fellow-envoys, having amassed a large quantity of goods/money from the tithes which they accepted as their priestly due, decided to return home ... [but] I declined to accept from those who brought them the tithes which were due to me as a priest" (*Vita* 63, 80). Assuming that compliance was not by coercion, at least some Galileans here delivered tithes to priests on the scene. Payment of tithes for priests was thus familiar in Galilee. Beyond that, we do not know how rigorously tithes and other dues had been requested or demanded in Galilee or the degree to which Galileans had complied. A few generations after the destruction of the Temple, at least in rabbinic circles, Galileans, by contrast with Judeans, had a reputation for being unfamiliar with "heave offerings belonging to the [temple] chamber" and "things devoted to the priests" (*m. Ned.* 2:4).[23] Without making any claims for their value as evidence of historical events and fully aware that they may reflect later polemics, we should also take note of the later rabbinic accounts of letters supposedly written by Gamaliel and then Simeon ben Gamaliel and Yohanan ben Zakkai to the Galileans (and to people of the south — Idumeans?) complaining about their extreme tardiness with removal of tithes and sacred produce, thus hindering the confession (Deut. 26:13; *t. Sanh.* 2.2; *y. Sanh.* 1.18d; *y. Ma'aśa. Š.* 5.56b; *b. Sanh.* 11b).

What can be made of such meager evidence for Galilean payment of tithes and other dues to priests and Temple? The historical changes in political-economic-religious jurisdiction over Galilee may be the key to what can be credible speculation at best. Surely the Hasmonean regime would have taxed the territories they annexed. The "laws of the Judeans" in accordance with which they governed newly acquired lands such as Idumea and Galilee, which seem to have had connotations of overall (political-economic-religious) polity, included demands of first fruits, heave offerings, first and second tithes, and other dues to priests and Temple. Thus it seems likely that the Hasmoneans would have actively collected these and/or "secular" revenues. This was a standard way of utilizing officers and garrisons and royal fortresses such as the Hasmoneans stationed in such towns as Sepphoris, Jotapata, and Gischala.

Having become accustomed to receiving such revenues from Galilee under the Hasmoneans, explicitly reinforced by Roman decrees at the very end of the Hasmonean regime, the Jerusalem Temple and (high) priesthood very likely continued to receive a certain level of tithes and offerings from Galileans under Herod. Presumably the high priesthood was still in a position to exert its authority over Galilee. Herod's own taxation, of course, may well have, in effect, stood in competition for the produce of the overburdened peasantry, probably increasing the usual peasant resistance to parting with its produce. After Herod's death and the assignment of Galilee to Antipas, however, the Jerusalem priestly aristocracy based in the Temple would likely have faced greater difficulties asserting their authority in Galilee. Their move to assert control over Galilee after the outbreak of the revolt in 66 C.E. indicates that they still claimed jurisdiction. In the seventy years intervening since they held official, recognized, direct jurisdiction, however, Galileans would likely have lapsed in their payment of tithes and other priestly and temple dues. Antipas and his successors were in a far better position to extract the taxes he demanded. By 66 C.E., on the one hand, many Galileans were still willing to give tithes to Josephus and his priestly colleagues sent by the priestly council in Jerusalem. On the other hand, Galileans in general had perhaps long since earned a reputation of ignorance and even resistance to the tithes and other dues that is reflected in later rabbinic literature.

Galileans and the Temple

Despite their reputation for laxity with regard to priestly and temple dues, Galileans have been claimed as loyal to the Temple in the first century C.E. This claim is based on the assumption that they regularly attended the pilgrimage festivals in Jerusalem.[24] Given their distance from Jerusalem and their divergent historical experiences in the centuries prior to the Hasmonean annexation of Galilee, however, it is likely that the frequency and tone of Galilean participation in the great festivals was appreciably different from that of Judeans.

"Three times a year all your males shall appear before the Lord your God...at the festival of unleavened bread, at the festival of weeks, and at the festival of booths. They shall not appear before the Lord empty-handed" (Deut. 16:16; cf. Exod. 23:17). Fantastic estimates have been made of the numbers of pilgrims crowding into Jerusalem on the basis of ancient sources: "Countless multitudes from countless cities come...at every feast" (Philo, *Spec. Leg.* 1.69): nearly 3 million if we trusted Josephus (*B.J.* 6.423–26), 12 million according to a rabbinic source (*t. Pesaḥ.* 4:3). Modern scholarly estimates of 100,000 to 125,000, however, may still be too high.[25] Calculations are based on a combination of sources, by multiplying the density of the crowd that could be packed into the temple courtyard by the three separate groups into which the crowd entered the courtyard (according to *m. Pesaḥ.* 5:5) by the ten individuals that Josephus claims shared each passover sacrifice (*B.J.* 6.423). The density of the crowd would appear overestimated and Josephus does not say that only one representative per passover fellowship group was allowed into the courtyard.

Far more realistic is the suggestion that "at each of these feasts, tens of thousands of pilgrims from Judaea, Galilee, and the Diaspora went up to the Temple."[26] Such "quantitative" conclusions appear warranted from the "qualitative" comments about participation in pilgrimage festivals in a number of ancient sources. The biblical command to appear three times a year was apparently considered among those with no "measure" (*m. Pe'a* 1:1), the emphasis falling on the obligations entailed when one did make a pilgrimage to one of the festivals. "Tobit," who claims to be super-scrupulous about taking all the required first fruits, tithes, and other dues to the Temple, apparently went "often," but not every year. Legendary portrayals of distinguished sages and those careful in observance of the Torah do not envisage them mounting a pilgrimage thrice-yearly. Josephus says that when the Roman army marched toward Jerusalem to crush the revolt in the summer of 66, they found the whole town of Lydda "gone up to Jerusalem for the Feast of Tabernacles" (*B.J.* 2.515). Obviously that was an unusual circumstance. The festival, celebrated in the middle of a fortress-like compound, may have appeared very compelling for such Judeans as the Roman army advanced, burning villages in its path (*B.J.* 2.514). There is no indication that such full participation was the usual practice. It would appear rather that many, including Judeans, would have gone to Jerusalem once in their lifetime, others once every several years.[27]

On the basis of this general picture of pilgrimage festivals we can project Galilean participation. Of the "tens of thousands" that made the journey bringing their sacrifices and/or tithes, first fruits and other offerings, most would have been Judeans from the towns and villages only a day's journey or less away from the city. For Galileans a journey of at least three days was required, plus a stay of several days in or around Jerusalem and the return. Judeans, moreover, had a several-hundred-year-old tradition of such festivals, whereas Galileans had come under Jerusalem Temple rule and the "laws of the Judeans" only in late Hasmonean times. Thus it seems likely that if Judeans came to Jerusalem at festival times by the thousands, Galileans would have come only by the hundreds. This estimate accords with Josephus's account of festivals at times of turmoil to which extraordinary numbers would have been attracted. When Herod died and Archelaus presumed to take charge just prior to Passover in 4 B.C.E., Josephus makes no mention of people from beyond Judea as part of "a vast crowd" (*laos apeiros*) that streamed in from the countryside (*chōra; B.J.* 2.10; cf. *Ant.* 17.214: "and even from abroad," but no mention of other districts in Palestine). After Archelaus turned his troops loose on the sacrificers and the Romans mobilized to suppress the imminent rebellion, "indignation drew the people in crowds to the capital" at Pentecost seven weeks later. "A countless multitude flocked in from Galilee, from Idumaea, from Jericho, and from Peraea beyond the Jordan, but it was the native population of Judaea itself which, both in numbers and ardour, was pre-eminent" (*B.J.* 2.43; *Ant.* 17.254). Besides the clear distinction made between the Judeans and the peoples from other districts, it is clear that the vast majority of the people flooding into the city for Pentecost and protest were from Judea itself. It is noteworthy, moreover, that only when a political crisis of extreme proportions develops are Galileans and others from outlying districts mentioned as coming in significant numbers to a festival.

The paucity of direct evidence for pilgrimage from Galilee throws into question previous claims of the "great devotion of Galileans in general to the Temple."[28] The report of "the Galileans whose blood Pilate had mingled with their sacrifices" in Luke 13:1 suggests that indeed some Galileans did journey to Jerusalem to make sacrifices. The legend about the 12-year-old Jesus in the Temple, including the opening comment that "every year his parents went to Jerusalem for Passover" in Luke 2:41–51, however, probably reflects a Lucan agenda rather than Galilean practices. Josephus's accounts about the flare-up of conflict between Judeans and Samaritans under the Roman governor Cumanus at mid-first century C.E. assume that "it was the custom of the Galileans at the time of a festival to pass through the Samaritan territory on their way to the holy city" (*Ant.* 20.118; *B.J.* 2.232; cf. Tacitus, *Ann.* 12.54).[29] It seems clear that the numbers involved were in the scores or hundreds, not the tens of thousands (which would have been a nightmare for the maintenance of public order as well as for sheer logistics of movement). Again Josephus distinguishes between Galileans and Judeans, and the focus falls on the Judeans' conflict with the Samaritans, which was touched off by the murder of (a) Galilean(s). Although not appreciable in volume or frequency, there was some Galilean pilgrimage to Jerusalem for the major festivals, probably mainly Passover.[30]

Nearly every one of these limited references to pilgrimage festivals, including the handful of references to Galileans involved, indicates that they were charged with (potential) political conflict. Pilate mingled Galileans' blood with their sacrifices and Judeans led by brigand heroes attacked Samaritan villages in retaliation for the murder of one or more Galilean pilgrims when the Roman governor did not act to restore justice (*B.J.* 2.232–38; *Ant.* 20.118–24). Especially poignant at festival times was the conflict between Roman domination and the people's yearning for freedom under their true, divine "king." This dimension came to a head particularly at the Passover festival, which celebrated Israel's deliverance from earlier foreign domination, the enslavement to the pharaoh in Egypt. To maintain strict control of affairs during Passover, the Roman governors stationed a cohort of troops on the porticoes of the Temple — which, of course, would have heightened the tensions (*B.J.* 2.224–27; *Ant.* 20.106–12).[31]

The acute tensions with Roman rule, however, were not the only dimension of conflict that heightened at festival times. Since the festivals centered on the sacrifices and offerings brought to the priests in the Temple, with the "high priest(s)" presiding, the people's attention was focused on the symbolic heads of the temple-community, families whom Herod had installed in their high positions and who occupied the high priesthood itself as Roman appointees. An ambivalent attitude of the people would have corresponded to the ambiguous position of the high-priestly families who were both their ostensible representatives to the true, divine king (and the beneficiaries of their offerings) and yet client-rulers beholden to the Romans.

This dimension of the conflict focused on the festivals can be illustrated from events in 4 B.C.E. and again in 66 C.E. In the Jerusalem crowd's agitation (in the temple courtyard) just prior to the Passover festival shortly after Herod died, the people clamored for Archelaus to remove from office Herod's favorites and install a high priest "more in accordance with the law and purity" (*Ant.* 17.206–7; *B.J.* 2.4–7). Seventy years later, at the outset of the great revolt in Jerusalem itself, the people attacked the mansions of the high priests as well as the priestly aristocracy themselves (*B.J.* 2.422–41). The level of Galileans' devotion to the Temple remains unclear. Pilgrimage to Passover or other festivals in Jerusalem, however, would have brought Galileans into heightened expressions both of popular ambivalence about the priestly aristocracy and of popular opposition to Roman rule.

The Laws of the Judeans (Torah) in Galilee

The history of Galilee sketched in chapters 1–3, along with the structure of political-economic-religious relations between Jerusalem and Galilee just above, should provide an appropriate historical framework for reconceptualizing the issue of the Torah in Galilee in late second-temple times. Discussions of the presence and role of the Torah/Law in Galilee require greater precision with regard to particular historical circumstances as well as to what we mean by Torah.[32]

First, more critical attention must be given to the different terms used in our sources, what those terms may refer to, and whether different terms refer to the same or somewhat different things. For example, Josephus frequently uses *nomoi tōn ioudaiōn* and also *nomima (tōn ioudaiōn)*.[33] Are those terms both consistent and synonymous, or must we determine somewhat different meanings from different contexts? Does either term refer primarily to the five books of Moses (Genesis, Exodus, Leviticus, Numbers, Deuteronomy), or to something wider that included (the contents of) the books of Moses? Were the "laws of the Judeans" thought of as oral or written or both?

Second, our focus is on a period well prior to the time when the rabbis were studying Torah and articulating halakhic rulings at Usha or Sepphoris or Tiberias. Presumably some version of the Torah or Laws of Moses were composed in Judea or Babylon and in use in Judea by late fifth century B.C.E. (i.e., by shortly after the missions of Ezra and Nehemiah). Assuming the particular formulation of the "laws of Moses" is not due to Josephus (or his source, Nicolaus of Damascus), such a scripturė was recognized as state law in Judea under the early Hasmoneans (*Ant.* 13.296–97). There is no evidence to indicate that these "laws of Moses" would have been used in Galilee prior to the Hasmonean annexation. But Josephus reports that following the Hasmonean takeover of Idumea and Galilee, the Hasmonean regime allowed the inhabitants to remain in their land if they agreed to live according to the "laws of the Judeans." We could reasonably surmise that these "laws of the Judeans" included at least the "laws of Moses" even if they comprised other traditions as well. What we cannot discern with much precision is whether that requirement had basically a political sense, that is, to live under the polity of the Judeans, under the temple-state, or a more comprehensive implication of conforming local Galilean life to the customs and traditions of the Judeans. Examination of the issue in chapter 2 led to the conclusion that whatever was meant in the requirement of living according to the "laws of the Judeans," the effect would have been closer to the acceptance of the polity of the temple-state. One factor leading to that conclusion is that there was no social or political mechanism by means of which the Galileans could have been thoroughly resocialized according to Jerusalem-sponsored laws and traditions.

The standard distinction that anthropologists make between the "great tradition" and the "little tradition" among traditional peoples may help us conceptualize the relationship that would have developed between the "laws of the Judeans" and the Galileans during the period of Jerusalem rule in Galilee.[34] In many societies the cultural traditions of a people bifurcate into an official tradition cultivated by formally educated priests or scribes often associated with the aristocracy or rulers, perhaps in written as well as oral form, on the one hand, and the popular tradition cultivated in families and villages in oral form, on the other. While the ostensible "contents" of the two parallel traditions can be the same or similar, interpretation and application is according to the respective social interests. Moreover, there is regular interaction between "great" and "little" traditions, the former repeatedly taking up into the official version and the latter often influencing certain reformulations in the popular tradition.

In Judea the rural population that remained on the land when the Babylonians deported the Jerusalem ruling class would have continued to cultivate their own Israelite and Judahite traditions. It seems unlikely that Judean villagers would have had much of a role in the establishment of the temple-state, including the promulgation and periodic reading of the Mosaic Law composed by priests and scribes and established as the state law. Many particular stories and laws in the latter, of course, would have overlapped with the popular traditions of ordinary Judeans. Yet there would also have been differences. For example, the sections of the Mosaic Law dealing with tithes and sacrifices to be brought to the Levites and priests in the Temple were promulgated in the interests of maintaining the temple-state apparatus. Nevertheless, over a period of generations and centuries, the Judean peasantry would have had plenty of opportunity to adjust to the officially promulgated Torah/Laws of the Judeans and to develop what became customary practices such as rendering tithes and offerings to the Temple and priesthood.

In Galilee, if at least a substantial portion of the inhabitants were descendants of Israelites, as argued in chapter 2, they would presumably have continued their Israelite traditions after the elite of the kingdom of Israel were deported by the Assyrians. In contrast with the Judean peasantry, however, the Galileans lived directly under foreign imperial administrators, without a native (priestly) aristocracy that cultivated an official tradition parallel to their own popular tradition. Their own popular Israelite tradition, moreover, may have been all the more self-consciously cultivated as a way of maintaining their own identity over against the foreign culture of the imperial administrators, although some influences may well have come from interaction with their Persian or Hellenistic overlords. That Galileans had customs different from those of the Judeans in certain areas, such as marriage and weights and measures, emerges explicitly at points in the Mishnah.[35] The most dramatic difference with the Judean peasantry, however, was the Judeans' centuries of interaction with and adjustment to the official Jerusalem tradition, whereas the Galileans came under the latter only with the Hasmonean takeover. If the Galileans were not descendants of Israelites, of course, then the problem of "resocialization" would have been far more difficult, since there would have been much less in common between their popular tradition and the official Jerusalem tradition.

How the official Jerusalem "laws of the Judeans" would then have affected the Galileans and how the Galileans would have interacted with or reacted to the "laws of the Judeans" would have depended on a number of interrelated factors. Among these are: (a) the differences between the popular Galilean and the official Jerusalem traditions (both rooted in Israelite traditions) that had developed over centuries of divergent historical experiences under imperial rule; (b) the ways the Jerusalem laws and traditions were pressed upon Galilean village life under the Hasmonean and Herodian regimes; and (c) the ways in which the Galileans responded. We have so little evidence for the Torah or "laws of the Judeans" in Galilee in late second-temple times that it is impossible to pursue this path of analysis with any intensity or precision. We can, however, take two steps toward further elucidation on the issue. (1) By reviewing the structure and history of the Jerusalem temple-state during the time it governed Galilee, it may be possible to discern whether and by what mechanism the Torah or the "laws of the Judeans" may have been pressed upon the Galileans (stated another way: by what mechanism the Galileans would have been resocialized into the Torah). (2) Keeping the interrelated factors delineated just above in mind, we can examine particular incidents that bring to the fore behavior that may have been rooted in Israelite and/or official Jerusalem traditions.

The Role of the Pharisees under the Later Hasmoneans and Herod

Limited but mutually confirming evidence indicates that the political-economic-religious role of the Pharisees (along with others) in late second-temple times was rooted in their social-political location as what sociologists call "retainers" of the high-priestly regime. Critically analyzed statements attributed to late second-temple sages in early rabbinic literature (Mishnah and Tosefta) indicate their concerns about ritual purity, tithes and other food laws, sabbath and festival observances, but nothing about their social position or role.[36] Josephus's accounts of the Pharisees under the Hasmoneans, however, portray the Pharisees as cultivators and interpreters of the "laws of Moses" and their own legal rulings, or "traditions of the elders," which had apparently been included as part of state law prior to their break with the high priest John Hyrcanus and again after their restoration to positions of influence by Alexandra Salome (*Ant.* 13.295–98, 408–9). That is, the Pharisees were legal-policy experts at court striving for influence with the Hasmoneans. Although they must have suffered a serious demotion under Herod, who brought in his own high officers and court retainers, the Pharisees continued to struggle for influence in the government (*B.J.* 1.571; *Ant.* 17.41–45). At the outbreak of the great revolt, they were still involved at the center of the temple-state politics, meeting in councils, making decisions, and forming delegations with key members of the priestly aristocracy (*Vita* 20–21, 197–98). The Gospel of John and, somewhat similarly, the Gospel of Matthew give a similar picture of the Pharisees as centrally involved in the politics of the temple-state, apparently working for as well as with the high-priestly councils (John 7:32–48; 11:46–47, 57). Thus the Pharisees appear to have functioned as the representatives of the priestly ruling circles in Jerusalem throughout the late second-temple period.[37]

Given the repeated representation of the Pharisees in the Gospels of Mark, Matthew, and Luke as harassing Jesus of Nazareth regarding matters of the sabbath, purity, marriage, and so on, and Jesus' sharp rejoinders and attacks, we should obviously probe the possibility that the Pharisees, as retainers of the temple-state concerned with interpretation and application of the state laws, were active in Galilee as well as at court in Jerusalem. The editorial statement in Luke 5:17 that "the Pharisees and teachers of the law...had come from every village of Galilee and Judea and from Jerusalem" must be discounted as a Lucan construction with no historical value. Mark (followed by Matthew), while presenting them as basically the representatives of the high-priestly regime in Jerusalem (with Herodian operatives plotting to capture Jesus; 3:6; 12:13–17) has the Pharisees active primarily in Galilee. Their "presence" in Galilee could possibly be explained (away) as due to a combination of two literary patterns: their function as the challengers in the "pronouncement" stories Mark has used (2:16–17, 18–20, 23–28; 7:5–13; 8:11–12), and their function (as agents of the Jerusalem authorities) in the overall plot of the Gospel (3:6; 7:1; 12:13). These pronouncement stories and plot lines thus offer little direct evidence that the Pharisees were active in Galilee as representatives of Jerusalem. On the other hand, they would have no credibility in either function unless they did, historically, on occasion at least, appear outside of their focus of operations in Jerusalem. Most suggestive is the condemnation of the Pharisees in Luke 11:43 and the parallel warning against them in Mark 12:38–39 for desiring the "seats of honor at assemblies (and banquets) and "respectful greetings in the (town) squares" (*agorai*).

Assuming then that the Pharisees were at least somewhat as numerous as Josephus claims — several thousand strong — and that only the leading Pharisees would have played a role directly in the court and high councils (as Josephus suggests in his account of the revolt), then most of these cultivators of legal traditions would have been active beyond the precincts of the Temple and metropolis of Jerusalem. Josephus's account of the delegation sent to displace him in command of Galilee toward the beginning of the revolt sketches a revealing picture of how the Pharisees worked in delegation from the priestly ruling circles in Jerusalem to implement particular items of state policy or strategy. Thus it seems warranted to conclude that Pharisees did function on a regular basis as representatives of Jerusalem's concerns in the towns and villages. With the expansion of the territory governed from Jerusalem after the Hasmonean annexation of Galilee and other districts, the regime would have needed such "retainers" all the more to represent their policies and interests in the outlying towns and villages. It seems credible that the Pharisees would have been known in Galilee as representatives of Jerusalem interests, even if not with the frequency and seeming ubiquitous presence portrayed in Mark.

Review of the history of Hasmonean and Herodian rule suggests that if the Pharisees or other "retainers" were active in Galilee pressing the "laws of the Judeans" upon the inhabitants (i.e., active in more than some presumably ordinary administrative capacity representing Jerusalem's interests), their activities would likely have been concentrated during two periods in particular: under Alexandra Salome and again once Herod had become entrenched in power.[38]

For the first generation after the Hasmonean annexation of Galilee in 104 B.C.E., Alexander Janneus was intensively engaged in wars of expansion and sharp conflicts with his own people, including apparently the Pharisees. The latter, moreover, had been pushed out of their previous positions of influence and their extrascriptural rulings rescinded as state law by John Hyrcanus. Thus only with the cessation of civil strife and their own restoration to influence under Alexandra Salome would they have been in a position to develop and implement a program of instruction in the official Mosaic laws, if they had been so inclined.

After only a decade came a whole generation of even greater chaos in Palestine, as Hasmonean battled Hasmonean for supremacy and Roman armies criss-crossed Palestine. Under Herod the Pharisees were, in effect, demoted from the center of power in Jerusalem. Yet precisely because of their loss of influence on the rulers, they may have sought consolation in greater influence over the people themselves — perhaps most in places removed from the center of Herod's regime. After Herod's death, of course, the Jerusalem Temple and high priesthood presumably no longer had any direct political authority over Galilee, although high-priestly officers in Jerusalem may have sought to continue their influence in Galilee.

While this line of reasoning is speculative, it would make better sense of the synoptic Gospel traditions such as the pronouncement stories and the woes against the (scribes and) Pharisees if we posit some activity of (scribes and) Pharisees in Galilee for a period of time prior to Jesus' ministry. It is also interesting that as soon as the Romans or a Herodian ruler no longer had de facto control over Galilee, the Jerusalem high-priestly regime sent its Pharisaic and priestly delegations to attempt to take control of the area (Josephus and his companions, then the delegation of four, a high priest and three Pharisees).

It must be acknowledged candidly that there is no direct evidence for Pharisees' presence in Galilee under the Hasmoneans and Herod. Yet it does seem likely that the Pharisees or other representatives of the Temple and high priests in Jerusalem would have been active there. Their activity in Galilee as representatives of Jerusalem Temple interests could have continued even after Antipas held political jurisdiction in Galilee, particularly if an active religious-economic relationship had become solidified between at least some Galileans and the Temple. Whatever the level and form of activity and influence by Pharisees or other representatives of Jerusalem interests in Galilee under Hasmoneans and Herod, it would have been sharply reduced once Jerusalem no longer had direct political jurisdiction.[39]

Galilean Incidents Rooted in Israelite or Jerusalem Tradition

Several particular persons and incidents have been cited in previous studies as evidence of Galilean loyalty to the Torah.[40] Neither of the two individual persons, however, would appear to provide much by way of an indication of observance of the Torah in Galilean society. Judas the Galilean, founder of what Josephus calls the "fourth philosophy," known as "the Galilean" because he was *from* Galilee, was operative in Judea opposing the tribute when the Romans imposed direct rule there (Galilee still being under a client-ruler). It would be unwarranted to extrapolate from this "teacher's" ideology to the views of Galileans generally just because he had come *from* Galilee at some point.[41] Eleazar, "a Jew who came from Galilee and who had a reputation for being extremely strict when it came to the ancestral laws" was, like the Jewish merchant Ananias, operating even farther afield from Galilee, in the royal court of Adiabene (*Ant.* 20.34–48). Here is a case of personal religious-ethical devotion among highly mobile wealthy figures sojourning in the courts of Eastern client-kings. Most of the incidents are in situations of extreme crisis, hence are not good illustrations of how normal social intercourse would have been guided by the popular or the official traditions. A critical review of the accounts of these incidents (mainly from Josephus's *Life*) may leave us with less evidence for the Torah in Galilee, but a clearer sense of the sharply conflictual social relations in that district.

The burning of Antipas's palace in 66 C.E. has been understood as motivated by Galilean concern for the Torah. Josephus claims to have arrived in Tiberias with orders from the Jerusalem *koinon* "to press for the demolition of the palace...which contained representations of animals...forbidden by the laws" (*Vita* 65–66). Capellus and the other wealthy and powerful "first men" of the city seemed no more concerned about violations of the laws than Antipas and their predecessors had been when Tiberias was built over graves and the decorations installed forty or fifty years previously. A coalition of Galileans and poor Tiberians led by Jesus son of Sapphias, however, burned and looted the palace before Josephus could carry out the instructions from Jerusalem. There is no indication that Jesus and the Galileans were motivated by devotion to the laws concerning images. In fact, Josephus claims they were simply after spoil — despite his admission that he himself ended up with the spoil. The Galileans and poor Tiberians were far more likely acting out of resentment at the luxury of the "king's palace" built and supported by (the fruits of) their own labor (cf. Luke 7:25). This incident offers no evidence about Galilean commitment to "the laws" on the basis of which the Jerusalem *koinon* had ordered a demolition of Antipas's palace. It rather indicates basic motives among the Galileans, which may well have been long-since shaped according to fundamental principles of covenantal justice. And it indicates that the aristocratic priestly representative of Jerusalem's concerns about "the laws" negotiated with the corresponding elite of Tiberias rather than seek alliance with the Galilean peasants and Tiberias lower class.

John of Gischala *supplied oil to the Judeans in Caesarea Philippi* some time after the outbreak of the great revolt in 66 (*B.J.* 2.591–93; *Vita* 74). The incident does suggest that those Judeans resident in Caesarea Philippi, like Josephus, recognized olives grown and pressed in Upper Galilee as satisfying purity requirements (*ta nomima, Vita* 74). This in turn may imply a ruling based on some concept of an approved *eretz Israel* delineated already in mid-first century C.E. by some recognized authorities, perhaps in Jerusalem (cf. *Ant.* 12.120; *m. 'Abod. Zar.* 2:6). It indicates nothing, however, about the use of the Torah or the recognition of those rulings in Galilee itself. We can no more accept Josephus's attribution of motives to actors in his accounts, in this case profiteering rather than piety by his archrival for control of Galilee, than we can project the opposite motives. The more reliable of his accounts in this case (*Vita* 74) suggests that the initiative came from Caesarea Philippi, not from John or others in Upper Galilee. Finally, the prohibition of gentile oil that may have motivated those Jews in Caesarea Philippi does not seem to have been part of the Law of Moses or other Judean scripture (although it may have been part of what Josephus calls the "laws/rulings of the Judeans"). The literature that attests the custom of avoiding gentile foodstuffs is late and was not included in the Jewish canon, when it was established (i.e., Jth. 10:5; 12:1–4; Tob. 1:10–11).[42]

The widespread *protest against the attempt to place Gaius's statue in the Temple* came to a head in Galilee (at least according to Josephus's accounts, *Ant.* 18.261–88; *B.J.* 2.184–203; cf. Philo, *Leg.* 188–249; Tacitus, *Hist.* 5.9). At least some Galileans must have been involved, although they cannot be distinguished within Josephus's general term, *hoi ioudaioi*. Both Josephus and Philo feature the Jews' readiness to die rather than allow such a violation of "the law(s)." Their accounts, however, are (understandably) heavy with apologetic rhetoric. Almost certainly the motives of whatever Galileans peasants became caught up in the "strike" (leaving the crops unplanted) would not have been as clearly formulated and focused as portrayed by the Alexandrian Jewish theologian and the Flavian Jewish historian. It seems more plausible historically that the peasant participants were distressed at the reports of mass movement of Roman and auxiliary troops through the countryside. In a situation already made somewhat uncertain by the recent Rome-imposed change of rulers in Galilee, the Galileans involved may have seized upon the symbol of (the statue of) the Roman emperor being paraded into their land, which crystallized long-standing grievances and resentments. Insofar as the statue's presence in their land (like the images on the Roman army standards earlier in Judean territory) would have been a violation of one of the basic "commandments of God" (borrowing a phrase from Mark 7:9–13), which was deeply rooted in the Galilean popular tradition as well as the official Torah, both of which were developments of the original Israelite Mosaic covenantal laws. While Josephus's and Philo's accounts of this incident provide a clear sense of Jewish apologetics over one of the most blatant cases of Roman imperial arrogance, they reveal little about the influence of the Torah (as distinct from the common Israelite covenantal tradition) in Galilee.

Josephus resisted a *demand that two renegade royal officials* (of Agrippa II) *be circumcised* as a condition of remaining in Galilee during the revolt in 66–67 (*Vita* 112–13, 149). In an apparent doublet, he writes initially that "the Judeans" demanded that the officers be circumcised as a condition of remaining among them, then later that "the crowd" insisted that they should conform to "the customs" (*ethē*) of those with whom they had sought refuge.[43] Circumcision, of course, was a general Israelite custom that would have had deep roots in Galilee prior to the arrival of the Torah as the law and/or scripture of the temple-state. Also deeply rooted in Galilee would have been the observance of the Sabbath, as part of the original Mosaic covenant between Israel and God. Thus when Josephus dismissed his soldiers for the Sabbath in Tarichaeae (*Vita* 159), it is not an indication of Galilean observance of official Torah.

The picture of *Jesus son of Sapphias*, the magistrate and leader of the popular faction in Tiberias, *taking in his hands the laws of Moses*, which he accused Josephus of betraying, clearly suggests that the scriptures or laws of the temple-state were indeed known in Galilee (*Vita* 134–35). It is more difficult than usual to sift through the rhetoric in this account. Why would Josephus have one of his archenemies in Galilee refer to him here as "your commander in chief"? As is clear from his own accounts, most of the feuding groups in Galilee in 66–67 did not recognize Josephus as their commander. That raises doubts about the intended tone of the adjoining phrase "the patriarchal laws." Is Josephus portraying Jesus as mocking him and his supposed agenda which (as Josephus himself unabashedly indicates) most groups saw through? Assuming that Jesus did take "the laws of Moses in his hand," the incident indicates that one copy of a Torah scroll, however costly, was present in a town the size of Tarichaeae.[44] We can imagine that, either in Josephus's strategic pose as representative of the Jerusalem council or for people who had been incorporated into the Judean temple-community prior to the Roman conquest, "the laws of Moses" could well have served as a symbol of independence of Roman rule. Other aspects of Josephus's account of this incident are also puzzling, however. Besides virtually admitting the double game he has been playing, he couches his own defense not in terms of loyalty to the laws of Moses, but in terms of his intent to use the spoil taken from the baggage train of the wife of the king's overseer to build fortifications for Tarichaeae (*Vita* 141–42). This suggests that concern for the defense of the "laws of Moses" was not a burning issue either for the Tarichaeans or for his readers.

Josephus's accounts of these incidents in Galilee have been used as evidence for the observance of Torah in Galilee. Indeed, the one story may well indicate that a Torah scroll was present in a large town. That same story, however, suggests that defense of the Torah was not a major issue, at least compared with security of the town against Roman reconquest. Some of the accounts in fact give no indication of Galilean attitudes or practices, but of those in Jerusalem or Caesarea Philippi. Others attest the continuing importance of basic covenantal traditions common to Israel in general. Those traditions would presumably have been deeply rooted in Galilee prior to the introduction of the "laws of the Judeans" or the Torah as the law or scripture of the temple-state.

Temple and Torah among Galileans

As to how Galileans responded to the Hasmonean takeover we can only speculate. Were they greeted as liberators from the Hellenistic rule of the Seleucids? Seleucid control of the area had been disintegrating for some time, and the Itureans would have displaced the Seleucid regime before the Hasmoneans drove them back. Assuming that the Galileans were descendants of Israelites, there may have been some (initial) identification with Judeans and Jerusalemites as fellow-Israelites and a certain receptivity to Jerusalem tradition or "laws of the Judeans" as having a common heritage with their own popular tradition. We can easily imagine Galilean identification and cooperation with Judeans and even Jerusalem institutions over against the Roman conquerors. Galileans and Judeans fought parallel battles, even if not common battles, against Roman reconquest. For the only case in which Galileans are reported to have made common cause with Judeans, resisting the installation of Gaius's statue in the Temple, however, it is difficult to know just how much to discount Josephus's standard apologetic rhetoric. Galileans clearly resisted Herod and erupted in revolt at his death in a movement parallel to Judean and Perean popular insurrections. A generation earlier it seems likely, but we have no clear evidence, that many Galileans favored the final rival Hasmonean pretender Antigonus and the Parthians over Hyrcanus II, Herod, and the Romans. It is thus unwarranted to extrapolate from that possibility to a presumption of a favorable earlier Galilean response to the Hasmoneans.

Given the criticism of and resistance to the Hasmoneans in Judea itself, it would also seem unwarranted to posit any sustained favorable reaction to their new rulers by Galileans in the early first century B.C.E. Galileans may well have seen the Temple and high-priestly regime in Jerusalem as remote and the "laws of the Judeans" as odd versions of Israelite traditions, imposed from the Jerusalem that their ancestors had rejected, according to their own Israelite traditions. If they already considered themselves members of the Israelite covenant with God, then how would they have viewed a new act of circumcision to bring them into a superimposed "Israel" centered in and dominated by Jerusalem, to which they now had to render up tithes? As discussed above, it is difficult to discern when (and why) any program of pressing official traditions and Judean laws upon Galilean villagers could have been mounted, except perhaps under Alexandra Salome by the Pharisees. With his obsession with his own fame and his relations with Jews in the diaspora, Herod is unlikely to have pressed the cultivation of Judean traditions in Galilee.

Indeed, it is difficult to discern ways in which the principal institutions of the Judean temple-state, the Temple and the Torah, could have established deep roots in Galilee. Our critical review of the limited evidence in fact suggests there is little to indicate that either one established a defining importance for life in Galilee during the time of Jerusalem rule. Temple and Torah were clearly what has been called the "redemptive media" for priests and Pharisees and others in Jerusalem and may also have established resonance among Judean villagers over a period of centuries. Several of the incidents in Galilee portrayed by Josephus indicate that fundamental principles of the Israelite covenantal heritage had defining significance that came to the fore in historical crises such as the revolt in 66–67. In those same incidents, however, the Galileans stood in conflict with representatives of the Jerusalem Temple authorities (or the Herodians in one case), or they were involved in fundamental social conflicts in which the Jerusalem authorities or their representatives were "caught in the middle," given the structure of the imperial situation. As explored in chapter 3, it is abundantly clear in Josephus's accounts of his attempts to take control of Galilee in 66 C.E. (either explicitly or via our critical reading) that the inhabitants of Galilean towns and villages were suspicious of the motives and agenda of representatives of the Jerusalem priestly government.

The Galileans, of course, were not alone in their suspicions of Jerusalem rulers. More than once they took action parallel with that of Judean and/or Perean and Idumean peasants against those rulers. The priestly-scribal community at Qumran also opposed the high-priestly rulers in Jerusalem. Moreover, although (apparently in contrast with Galileans) the Qumranites cultivated the Judean scriptures, intensively so, they based their community on somewhat the same Israelite traditions as did the Galileans: the Mosaic covenant.

Chapter 7

THE CITIES AND ROYAL RULE
IN GALILEE

✧

*Colonial conquest produced, if anything, a much sharper cleavage between
the little tradition and elite culture.*

—JAMES C. SCOTT

*Wealth is accumulated by aristocrats in aristocratic empires not to be saved
or invested but to be displayed.*

—JOHN KAUTSKY

In addressing a Hellenistic-Roman audience oriented to the Mediterranean Sea and the intercity trade and cosmopolitan culture it made
possible, the Jewish apologist Josephus had some explaining to do when it
came to the cities, the very locus of civilized life in antiquity: "Well, ours is
not a maritime country; neither commerce nor the intercourse which it pro-
motes with the outside world has any attraction for us. Our cities are built
inland, remote from the sea; and we devote ourselves to the cultivation of
the productive country with which we are blessed" (*c. Ap.* 1.60). Presumably he had more than just Jerusalem in mind in using the plural. In any
case, he points to the principal orientation and function of Sepphoris and
Tiberias in Galilee as well as Jerusalem, that is, administration directed to
the "cultivation" of the agricultural countryside, which provided the economic base of the Herodian and high-priestly rulers who lived, with their
governing apparatus and supporting cast of artisans and servants, in the
"capital" cities.

Under Herodian and Roman rule, Galilee underwent dramatic changes
with regard to cities. When the Hasmoneans and then Herod took over,
the area was surrounded by several cities, but within Galilee itself were
only a few fortress towns, the most prominent of which was Sepphoris.
Suddenly, in the first quarter of the first century, Sepphoris was rebuilt and
the completely new city of Tiberias founded in eastern Lower Galilee by
Herod's son Antipas. A century later, these two cities were more completely

Romanized and all of Lower Galilee placed under their jurisdiction as the Romans "urbanized" nearly all of Palestine.

Recent constructions of a highly urbanized Lower Galilee, in excitement over new archaeological excavations, are basically synchronic treatments, drawing evidence from across several centuries into a composite picture. Interpretations of archaeological finds also continue to rely heavily on essentialist dichotomies, such as "Jewish" and "pagan" (or "Hellenistic"), derived from earlier ancient Jewish and biblical studies. There is also a tendency to believe that the presence of a few key Hellenistic-Roman urban buildings or artifacts means the presence of a more complete Hellenistic-Roman urban ethos.[1]

While drawing on recent archaeological reports as well as literary sources, our approach must be more historically precise, more critically comprehensive in terms of the dominant imperial system, and more relational in terms of the political-economic power relations between cities and villages.

The Circle of the Cities

Historically "the circle of the peoples" could well have referred to the ring of cities that surrounded the area. From earliest times, Tyre had been the principal power immediately to the northwest, with Hazor to the northeast and Megiddo and Beth Shean in the Great Plain to the south. The northern tribes of early Israel had to contend with other cities as well: "Zebulun did not drive out the rulers of Kitron or of Nahalol....Asher did not drive out the rulers of Acco or of Achzib....Naphtali did not drive out the rulers of Beth-shemesh or of Beth-anath, but lived among the Canaanites, the rulers of the land" (Judg. 1:30–33). Megiddo continued as an important fortified administrative city under the Solomonic and Assyrian empires, and Tyre was always a dominant force, whether independent or part of an imperial network of cities. Encirclement by cities as the centers of both political-military power and ruling-class culture was nothing new to Galilee in Hellenistic-Roman times.

The city that surely had the most influence on Galilee prior to the first century C.E. was Jerusalem, from which David and Solomon ruled the area in the tenth century and the Hasmoneans and then Herod ruled during the first century B.C.E. (as explored in the previous chapter). In the intervening centuries, after the fall of Samaria to the Assyrians, Galilee was apparently ruled from Dor or Megiddo or perhaps Acco as regional imperial centers of power. Particularly important for possible influences on the area were the Hellenistic cities that continued into Roman times and the new foundations by Roman client-rulers that bordered directly on Galilee.

In their general policy of founding new cities or refounding old ones by superimposing Greek forms onto older towns, the Hellenistic imperial regimes established several cities that dominated the areas immediately adjacent to Galilee. Most important of these were Ptolemais, the refounded Acco on the Mediterranean coast immediately to the west, and Scythopolis, the Hellenistic refounding of the old Beth Shean immediately to the south, along with the city of Tyre, which continued to dominate the territory to the northwest. Later, in the early Roman period, Herod's son Philip "made improvements at Panaeas, situated at the headwaters of the Jordan, and called it Caesarea [Philippi]; he further granted to the village Bethsaida on the Sea of Galilee... the rank of a city and named it after Julia, the daughter of Caesar [Augustus]" (*Ant.* 18.28). Although none of these cities influenced Galilee much directly, Ptolemais, Scythopolis, and Tyre played major roles in the history of Galilee.

Ptolemais (Acco) was important for Galilee primarily as a base of military operations for rulers striving or vying for control of the area. As the next principal city along the Mediterranean coast south of Tyre, it was the natural gateway south into Samaria and Judea as well as east into Galilee and the Great Plain, which had traditionally held special economic importance to rulers as royal land. The Ptolemaic regime and then the Seleucids maintained a strong military fortress there. Following a pattern established by the Seleucids, the Romans, time after time, launched their military expeditions into Palestine from Ptolemais, striking first into Galilee, then south into Judea (e.g., *B.J.* 2.66–71, 184–87, 499ff.).

Particularly for the Ptolemies, but for the subsequent imperial regimes as well, strong military installations at towns such as Ptolemais were important for their economic exploitation of the subject areas.[2] Ptolemais probably served as the key depot through which the imperial officers shipped goods and revenues they had taken. That does not imply "commercial links" between Ptolemais and the Galilean interior, with "lively movement of people in both directions," however, on an early modern mercantilist economic model.[3] Transfers of goods were "managed" by state officials or contractors in the Hellenistic empires, and trade was primarily for consumption by the wealthy and powerful. On the other hand, simply because Galilee was adjacent to Ptolemais-Acco and its territory, there would have been cultural contacts and the usual skirmishes along the frontier. The houses in Chabulon, a Galilean village on the frontier of Ptolemais, were "built in the style of those in Tyre, Sidon, and Berytus" (which the Roman general Cestius burned even though he admired their beauty; *B.J.* 2.503–4). At times of turmoil and weakened political control in Galilee, bands of brigands raided along the frontier of Syria or Ptolemais, as we know from the band murdered by the brash young Herod and, over 100 years later, the sizable band led by the brigand-chief Jesus, who confronted Josephus at Sepphoris (*B.J.* 1.204; *Ant.* 14.159; *Vita* 105).

Scythopolis (Beth Shean), south of Galilee at the eastern end of the Great Plain, was also primarily of military significance for Galilee, although it

also exhibits an intriguing mixture of peoples and cultures in close proximity to Galilee. In 67 C.E. it served as a base from which Galilee could be
watched and kept in check by a small contingent of troops as well as a staging area from which eastern Galilee could be reconquered by a whole army
(*Vita* 120; *B.J.* 2.412, 446). It is conceivable that its name derives from
the colony of Scythian troops settled there by the Ptolemies.[4] If that were
true, it would make the cultural mixture in the city all the more interesting.
The official god of Scythopolis was Dionysus, who was also the principal
deity of the Ptolemies who founded the city, and excavations there turned
up a temple of Dionysus.[5] Underneath the dominance of Hellenistic political and cultural forms, however, appears the persistence of the old name
of Beth Shean, leading some to speculate that, in contrast to the more persistent conflicts in Caesarea, the unusually large population of Judeans in
Scythopolis had established a certain symbiosis with the dominant gentile
population and culture.[6]

That its Judean inhabitants had developed a strong loyalty to the city
is suggested by Josephus's intriguing report that, amid the armed conflicts
between Jews and Gentiles in the other Palestinian cities in 66 C.E., "the Judeans" of Scythopolis stood together with their fellow inhabitants against
outside attacks by other Judeans. That report is all the more striking because of the parallel history of Scythopolis with other Hellenistic cities
in Palestine in the first century B.C.E. After being taken over by the Hasmoneans, who ordinarily forced the "Greek" population of the cities they
conquered into exile, it was rebuilt and restored to its "legitimate citizens"
by Pompey and Gabinius forty-some years later (*B.J.* 1.66, 156–57, 166;
Ant. 13.280, 355, 396–97; 14.75, 88). Perhaps in Scythopolis the pendulum had not swung so far each way as Josephus and modern scholars
suggest, with "Greeks" continuing under the Hasmoneans and Judeans
continuing in the city after its "restoration" by the Romans, and a common
culture or toleration of different cultures worked out.[7] This Greek-Judean
cultural mixture and symbiosis remains largely speculation, however. If
such a symbiosis had developed before, it did not keep the Scythopoli-
tans from betraying, then massacring the Judeans resident among them
as tensions erupted in violent conflict in the summer of 66 (*B.J.* 2.466–
68; *Vita* 26). Nothing in our sources, finally, suggests that Scythopolis was
exerting significant economic pressure or cultural influence on Galilee just
to the north. Since the Roman "restoration" of the independence of the
Hellenistic cities after 63 B.C.E., Scythopolis had been politically part of
the province of Syria and independent of Hasmonean or Herodian rule of
Samaria and Galilee.

Tyre, on the other hand, had a consistent impact on the villages of Upper Galilee, particularly along the frontier. The prophet Ezekiel provides
an extensive paean of praise to Tyre, "merchant of the peoples on many
coastlands," elaborating on how "by your great wisdom in trade you have

increased your wealth" (Ezek. 27:3–28:5). Because the transport of heavy agricultural goods at any distance was prohibitively costly in the ancient economy, however, Tyre, with its limited arable land along the narrow coastline, was always pressing into the immediate hinterland for agricultural resources, despite its lucrative trading network. Luke clearly indicates the relationship with northern Palestine: "Tyre and Sidon...depended on the king's [Agrippa I] country for food" (Acts 12:20). The Hasmoneans had established a series of fortresses along the northwestern frontier with Tyre to maintain their own dominance of the area. It was those fortresses that Marion, the "tyrant" of Tyre, captured when he invaded Galilee in the Roman and provincial political turmoil from which Herod emerged as king (*B.J.* 1.238; *Ant* 14.297).

Tyre's drive to extract more agricultural produce from the interior provides the context in which we can understand the periodic conflicts along the Upper Galilean frontier. Because of Josephus's own experience in Galilee, our literary sources are concentrated around the events of 66–67. Kedasa, a Tyrian village, was one of the places supposedly raided by parties of "Judeans" in retaliation for attacks on Judean in Caesarea (*B.J.* 2.459). This "strong inland village of the Tyrians" (i.e., apparently fortified) was then the staging area for Titus's assault on the fortified Upper Galilean village of Gischala. In that context, however, we learn that Kedasa had always been "at feud and strife with Galileans" (*B.J.* 4.105). There is no reason to believe that this long-standing conflict between Kedasa and the Upper Galileans was an ethnic and/or religious one, however, as suggested by Josephus's inclusion of the raid on Kedasa in 66 in his catalogue of reprisals by "Judeans" for the attacks in Caesarea. It is far more convincingly interpreted as due to Tyre's "dependence for food" on villages in the interior, some of which it controlled and others of which it could pressure. That large numbers of fugitives from Tyrian territory joined forces with Upper Galileans during the social unrest in 66–67, as noted in chapter 3, further confirms the political-economic basis of the persistent conflict between Tyre's fortified outpost at Kedasa and the villagers of Upper Galilee.

Preliminary interpretation of archaeological excavations at the villages of Meiron and Khirbet Shema' has led recently to the suggestion that Upper Galilee was economically oriented toward Tyre, with villagers making a "conscious decision" to market their produce at Tyre rather than at the more accessible Ptolemais or with "their brethren" in Tiberias.[8] This hypothesis presupposes a market model inappropriate to ancient economic life, and has not taken into account the historical political-economic relations sketched just above. More problematically, it depends almost exclusively on the finds of coins that have not been placed in an overall interpretative context of the function and significance of coins in village life and the comparative distribution of Tyrian coins in the Eastern Mediterranean generally. Tyre, of course, was perhaps *the* major supplier of money throughout the Levant for centuries. A coin hoard found at Magdala in Lower Galilee displays the same dominance of Tyrian coins as the finds in the villages of Upper Galilee.[9] Given the comparative coin finds elsewhere, it seems doubtful that we can even infer special Tyrian influence in Upper Galilee on the basis of coins, let alone extensive trade and economic orientation.[10]

Simply on the basis of proximity and regular political-economic conflict, we can discern Tyrian influence on Upper Galilee. That influence, however, may have been more indirect, mediated through centuries of Tyrian dominance of its hinterland, rather than direct influence of the cosmopolitan trading center itself oriented toward the Mediterranean. Along the frontier in particular, where dominance had shifted from time to time among Hasmoneans, Tyrians, and Herodians, we would expect life in Galilean and Tyrian villages to have been rather similar culturally. Archaeologists find that ceramic forms "point to a cultural affinity to the north and to western Gaulanitis"[11] as well, again culture shared with other villages rather than with an urban metropolis.

This brief survey of cities on the periphery of Galilee indicates that there was little direct contact between them and Galileans, and probably little direct cultural influence. Their principal importance for Galilean life was in providing bases for military control of and invasions into the Galilean interior (Ptolemais and Scythopolis) and in the political-economic pressure placed on frontier areas of Galilee (Ptolemais and especially Tyre). Far more varied cultural influence and political-economic impact was wielded by the two cities that were founded and/or came to prominence in Lower Galilee in the first century C.E.

Sepphoris: "The Ornament of All Galilee"

The city of Sepphoris was built on a hill that rises steeply 350 feet (115 m) above the surrounding plain. It was known primarily as a military fortress in late second-temple times, and was strategically located in the middle of western Lower Galilee.

> Sepphoris was the strongest,...greatest city of Galilee, in an exceptionally strong position in the territory, ready to keep guard on the whole people.
> (*B.J.* 2.511, 3.34)

> Situated in the heart of Galilee, [the city] was in a position, without any difficulty, had she been so inclined, to make a bold stand against the Romans.
> (*Vita* 346)

Topped by a citadel (*akropolis, Vita* 376), Sepphoris was still famous in rabbinic literature as a fortress (e.g., *m. 'Arak.* 9.6), and centuries later the crusaders built a fort on the site of the ancient citadel. Any discussion of

Sepphoris must thus take into account its function as an administrative city. Moreover, since the rulers using Sepphoris as their fortified administrative base changed frequently during late Hellenistic and early Roman periods, and rulers determined the cultural ethos of the city, we must also attend to those changes in regime.

Settled already during the Assyrian and Persian periods, Sepphoris almost certainly served as an administrative town for the Hellenistic empires of the Ptolemies and Seleucids.[12] Clearly the Hasmonean high-priestly regime in Jerusalem inherited it as an already defensible fortress, as indicated in Josephus's report of Ptolemy Lathyrus's unsuccessful attack shortly after Alexander Janneus became king–high priest (*Ant.* 13.338). Sepphoris would have been a Greek-speaking Hellenistic town prior to the Hasmonean takeover, and presumably the Hasmoneans would not have replaced all the Hellenistic inhabitants with Judeans. It may be significant that Greek words referring to titles of officials and administrative functions were found in Hebrew from the Hasmonean period.[13] The Hasmonean regime was otherwise characterized by increasing Hellenistic influence, particularly under Alexander Janneus. These Greek terms for administrative officers and functions in Hebrew letters may indicate that despite Hebrew being the official administrative language of the city Hellenistic administrative patterns and culture continued during Jerusalem rule in Galilee. The Hasmoneans presumably placed their own trusted officers in charge of the administration in Sepphoris, and these would have formed the aristocracy dominant in Galilee for the next two generations. While the Hasmoneans established garrisoned fortresses elsewhere in Galilee (*Ant.* 14.413–14; *B.J.* 1.303), Sepphoris was clearly their principal administrative town in the district. Thus, when the Roman general Gabinius divided the realm into five districts headed by aristocratic councils (*synhedria*) in 57 B.C.E., he centered the northernmost one — Galilee — at Sepphoris (*B.J.* 1.170; *Ant.* 14.91).

The weakening Hasmonean regime governed Galilee from Sepphoris only two generations before Herod took over Sepphoris as his principal fortified administrative town in Galilee (*Ant.* 14.413–14). Presumably he systematically rooted out any remaining Hasmonean loyalists in Galilee as he did elsewhere. Presumably also Herod's administration in Sepphoris would have had much less direct connection with the Temple and high priesthood than the Hasmonean regime. Given his general practices of sponsoring Roman-Hellenistic–style buildings and monuments, it seems unlikely that Herod would have fostered Judean religious-political forms, representatives of the Temple's interests, or Judean culture in Sepphoris. That a royal palace and armory were there at the end of Herod's reign (attacked by the rebels in 4 B.C.E., *Ant.* 17.271) indicates that the ethos of Herodian Sepphoris would have been that of a provincial royal administrative town.

After the Romans "burned the town and enslaved its inhabitants" in 4 B.C.E. in retaliation for the insurrection in the area (*B.J.* 2.68; *Ant.* 17.289), the new Roman client-ruler Antipas "fortified Sepphoris to be the ornament [*proschema*] of all Galilee and called it Autokratoris" ("Imperial" or "Capital" City; *Ant.* 18.27). However extensive Antipas's rebuilding may have been,[14] it marks the beginning of Sepphoris as a Roman provincial city.[15] In a significant break with Hasmonean and Herodian times, Sepphoris and Galilee were no longer directly under Jerusalem rule after Herod's death. Antipas, a Roman client-ruler who had been raised in Rome (*Ant.* 17.20), would have established a Roman-style capital at Sepphoris both to tout his own position and to advertise the rule of his imperial patrons. The theater unearthed by a series of archaeological digs at Sepphoris, which may have been built by Antipas himself, is a prime example of the Roman political-cultural style.[16] Even if the Roman burning of the town and enslavement of the inhabitants in 4 B.C.E. was not extensive, there would have been a break in continuity of the population when Antipas brought in his own people to staff his administration and court, including "the archives and bank" (*Vita* 38).[17]

While Antipas moved his own capital and court to Tiberias around 18 C.E., Sepphoris regained its position as the capital of Galilee following the brief reign of Agrippa I, 39–44 C.E., again becoming the locus of the state archives and bank. Continuing as the seat of the imperial administration in western Galilee another generation later, Sepphoris remained faithful to its political-cultural character and function in the imperial structure of things during the popular insurrections of 66–67, ironically hiring local brigand bands for protection until the legions of "the masters" (*pros tous despotas*, *Vita* 346) could regain control of the area.

After the revolt and the Roman reconquest of Galilee in 66–67, Sepphoris would have been even more dominated by Roman administrative and probably military presence.[18] Indeed, this would appear to be the time that the city's culture became more fully Romanized. It is still unclear whether the theater dates from the time of Antipas or the late first or second century. Clear, however, is that around 130, under Hadrian, the city was reconstituted as Diocaesarea ("City of Zeus-Caesar"), with a Capitoline temple and, presumably, an even more completely Romanized administration.[19] A second Roman legion assigned to maintain order in Palestine was located at Legio in the Great Plain just to the south. A network of Roman roads was built connecting the growing city with the other major cities of the region such as Acco and, of course, Legio. An aqueduct joined the theater, among typical Roman urban institutions, and the city's coins displayed an image of a temple to Zeus-Jupiter as well as the title of the reconstituted city, Diocaesarea. Symbolic of the Roman-Hellenistic cultural ethos now dominant in the city is the beautiful and elaborate Dionysus mosaic recently discovered on the floor of the triclinium of a Roman mansion near the theater.[20]

Assuming that numbers of Judeans lived in the recently excavated western domestic area of the city, they also were well assimilated into the dominant culture, judging from the pagan figurines and disc lamps found in the houses there.[21]

In the excitement over recent archaeological finds at Sepphoris, some rather grand, but problematic and conflicting, claims have been made regarding the cultural character of first-century Sepphoris. In reaction against earlier representation of Galilee as almost exclusively rural, as if no cities existed in the district, come claims that Lower Galilee was heavily urbanized.[22] Symbolic of this synchronic construction of a cosmopolitan atmosphere in Lower Galilee are rather high population estimates. Characterization of the Sepphoris reconstructed by Antipas as a "Roman urban overlay" would be consonant with that cosmopolitan construct.[23] The claim that virtually all of the inhabitants of Sepphoris in the first century were Jewish, however, seems to stand in conflict with the hypothesis of such an "overlay," as does the characterization of Sepphoris as "Galilean urban culture."[24]

The understandable excitement that attended the recent excavations at Sepphoris and other sites, along with a synchronic synthetic approach, has led to inflated pictures of the "urbanization" and population of Lower Galilee. Symptomatic of the excitement are the estimates of the population in the cities and large towns of Lower Galilee, which run to 30,000 for Sepphoris, somewhat less for Tiberias and Magdala, and even 12,000 to 15,000 for Capernaum.[25] Studies focused specifically on population in antiquity and how to estimate it are far more cautious. A survey of population in the Late Roman–Byzantine period, one of maximum density, concludes that Diocaesarea (Sepphoris) and Tiberias in Galilee were medium-sized cities, 60 and 40 hectares, respectively, compared with Caesarea at 95 or Aelia Capitolina (previously Jerusalem) at 120.[26] If the density of the Galilean cities was more comparable to that of Pompeii, at 125 to 156 per hectare, than that of Ostia, at 435,[27] then the population of Sepphoris or Tiberias at their maximum size in late antiquity would have been half of the recent estimates. The population of Sepphoris would have been correspondingly less in the first century just after Antipas began building up the city and before the influx of population into second-century Diocaesarea (see below).[28] Initial explorations in calculating the carrying capacity of the land in Galilee, moreover, suggest that a population of 24,000 in Sepphoris alone would have required nearly the entire agricultural produce of the area governed by the city.[29] Since the peasant producers also received their subsistence from that produce, it stands to reason that the population of Sepphoris was considerably less than that.

The concept of a "Roman urban overlay" would at first glance appear to be appropriate to what Antipas would have done in making Sepphoris into a suitable capital for a Roman client-ruler. One might argue that Herod the Great had already begun the process of imposing on indigenous Judean culture the major Roman institutions and symbols, such as "baths, hippodromes, theatres, amphitheatres or circuses, odeons, nymphaea, figured wall paintings, statues, triumphal monuments, and temples."[30] Aside from the severe problems in the conceptualization of this "overlay" with regard to Jewish Palestine in particular,[31] there are serious questions regarding the extent to which such a "Roman overlay" had been put in place in Sepphoris by early in the first century. The rebuilt Sepphoris, as the fortified capital of a client-ruler, would likely have expressed Roman imperial dominance. Yet archaeologists have still to find most of the principal "symbols" of the "Roman urban overlay" in Sepphoris itself. All that we can say at present is that the major Roman institutions built elsewhere in Herodian Palestine provide a pattern into which Sepphoris fits. In the course of the second century, of course, with the transformation of Sepphoris into Diocaesarea, the "Roman urban overlay" was probably more fully articulated.

That first-century Sepphoris was not completely Romanized does not mean that it was therefore "Jewish." The claim that "virtually all of the inhabitants of Sepphoris in the first century C.E. were Jewish"[32] simply does not take into account the ways in which the frequently changing rulers would have determined the character of the city. Numbers of Judeans had surely become well established in the previously Hellenistic fortress town of Sepphoris during the two generations of Hasmonean rule. Under Herod more Judeans probably came to the city along with Hellenized officers of non-Judean extraction typically in the service of Herod. Despite the Roman damage to the city in 4 B.C.E., there would likely have been some continuity, at least, from Herod's administration to that of his son Antipas, with yet other Judeans likely have been among those seeking opportunities in the latter's service.

Whatever the numbers and cultural influence of Judeans in first-century Sepphoris, however, they either could not or did not bring the city around to a pro-Jerusalem or pro-rebel stance during the great revolt in 66–67. Sepphoris spurned the leadership of the provisional high-priestly government generally, not just that of its "general," Josephus. The latter's complaint that the Sepphorites, in their steadfast loyalty to Rome, sent no assistance to the defense of the Temple "which was common to us all" must be discounted as an expression of a Jerusalem priest himself implicated in the revolt (*Vita* 348). His further complaint that the Sepphorites promised the (re-)conquering Roman general Vespasian support against their own "compatriots" (*homophulon*) is part of his portrait of himself as the ideal "Judean" general opposing the future Roman emperor (*B.J.* 3.32). Nevertheless, these complaints of Josephus, which contrast the Sepphorites with the Judeans, indicate the extent to which Sepphoris was a "Roman" city in its cultural orientation as well as pro-Roman in the revolt.[33] More significantly, perhaps, Josephus's accounts indicate the degree to which the principal lines of division on major issues were not between Jews and Gentiles/Romans but between rulers and ruled. Shifting from essentialist to more relational concepts may facilitate a more adequate comprehension of the historical dynamics of such situations in Roman Palestine. That is, the percentage of the population of Judean ethnic extraction probably matters less than the role played by the most prominent Judean and other Sepphorites in the prevailing pattern of imperial political-economic relations.[34]

While it is difficult to gauge the numbers and influence of Judeans in Sepphoris in the first century C.E., there would appear to have been a significant increase in the Jewish presence during the second century C.E. Prominent Jerusalem families of sages-scribes and/or priests had settled in the coastal plain near Yavneh following the destruction of Jerusalem and the Temple in 70. There is general agreement that some of those families relocated to Galilee after 135, with early rabbinic "academies" located in western Galilee at Usha and then Sepphoris, toward the end of the second century.[35] The influx of former Jerusalemites at this time may well have included certain priestly families, although the priestly "course" (*mishmar*) of Yedaiah cannot be located in Sepphoris until the third or fourth century.[36] Archaeologists believe that major signs of expansion in the western domestic area of the city indicate an influx of many new people during the second century. The several bronze figurines and numerous lamps decorated with pagan symbols suggest many pagan residents and/or a high degree of Hellenization among the Jewish residents, presumably those of the upper class.[37] In the course of the second century, therefore, as an increasing number of sages, priests, and others from the south settled in Sepphoris, their culture and traditions would have coexisted and mingled with the Roman-Hellenistic culture already well established in the city. In sum, while there is little concrete evidence for Judean presence and culture in Sepphoris in the first century, after the city was more fully Romanized as Diocaesarea in the second century, there are more reliable indications that increasing numbers of sages and others from the south settled in the city and shared in its increasingly mixed culture. It must have been precisely in the context of that mixed culture of Diocaesarea that Judah the Prince presided over the compilation of the Mishnah around 200 C.E.

To characterize Sepphoris as a center of "Galilean urban culture," finally, seems inappropriate, especially for the first century.[38] If anything, Sepphoris would appear to have entailed an imposition of outside political culture upon indigenous Galilean society. Josephus, our principal source for Galilee in the first century, reports repeatedly that "the Galileans," the people from the villages and towns, stood over against Sepphoris (see further below). The elites that dominated Sepphoris under successive regimes using the fortress city would presumably have brought their own Hellenistic, Judean-Jerusalemite, and Roman cultural forms with them. If a strong

Judean presence survived the Roman destruction and Antipas's rebuilding of the city after 4 B.C.E., there may well have been a mixture of these cultures by the first century C.E. But the structure of political-economic-cultural relations under the Roman empire makes it difficult to see how Galilean culture might have been appropriated by the ruling fortress city. From at least the time of Antipas's rebuilding of the fortress city as his "ornament," the major institutions such as the theater embodied Roman culture. Perhaps by late antiquity there may be more archaeological and literary evidence of interaction between the urban culture developed in Sepphoris and the traditional culture of the Galileans.[39] In the first century C.E., however, Sepphoris must have been dominated by an urban political culture superimposed upon the Galilean towns and villages.

From this survey it is evident that Sepphoris was always an administrative fortress city. That meant, however, that the rulers using it or based there determined its political-cultural ethos and, insofar as the regimes changed frequently, that ethos would also have shifted somewhat from the Hellenistic culture of the Ptolemies and Seleucids to the Judean culture of the Hasmoneans to the Roman-Hellenism of Herod, which was intensified under Antipas and subsequent Roman administrations. None of those rulers and political cultures, of course, were of the same people and same precise cultural heritage as the Galilean populace (although the Judeans came closest, with common Israelite heritage). Hence Sepphoris would always have been somewhat alien culturally as well as dominating politically-economically vis-à-vis the Galileans.

Tiberias: "Founded in the Best Region of Galilee on the Lake"

It could not be clearer that in its very foundation Tiberias was a royal-administrative city artificially imposed on the Galilean countryside. As befitted a ruler attempting to manifest the cultural style of Roman client-kingship, Antipas founded a new capital city in tribute to the new emperor, his new patron.[40]

> The Tetrarch Herod, inasmuch as he had gained a high place among the friends of Tiberius, had a city built, named after him Tiberias, which he established in the best region of Galilee on Lake Gennesaritis. There is a hot spring not far from it in a village called Ammathus. The new settlers were a promiscuous rabble, no small contingent being Galilean, with such as were drafted from territory subject to him and brought forcibly to the new foundation. Some of these were magistrates. Herod accepted as participants even poor men who were brought to join the others from any and all places of origin. It was a question whether some were even free beyond cavil. These latter he often and in large bodies liberated and benefitted (imposing the condition that they should not quit the city), by equipping houses at his own

expense and adding new gifts of land. For he knew that this settlement was contrary to the law and tradition of the Judeans because Tiberias was built on the site of tombs that had been obliterated, of which there were many there. And our law declares that such settlers are unclean for seven days.

(*Ant.* 18.36–38)

Josephus's account must reflect the "raised eyebrows" among properly cultured and propertied Greeks and Hellenized Jews that Antipas had been so crass in the "selection" of the inhabitants for his foundation. This was clearly a client-ruler at work, seeking to implement an imperial Roman cultural script, but incapable of pursuing the cultural ideal in the appropriate style, and insensitive to the sensitivities of Judean (and likely also Galilean) traditions. In his attempts to control the volatile situation in Galilee at the outbreak of the revolt in 66–67, Josephus had several serious struggles with the grandchildren of the Galilean "riff-raff" who had been the original settlers in Tiberias. Thus, while he knows Tiberias only too well, we must be especially wary of his snide and/or self-serving rhetoric.

One may be particularly suspicious of the gratuitous slam at "those in office," considering Josephus's own sharp conflicts with Tiberias officials in 66–67, one of whom was his archrival Justus, a high-ranking intellectual retainer of Agrippa II. By no means should we conclude that the royal officers originally stationed in Tiberias were drawn from among Antipas's Galilean subjects. In fact it is clear in the account that only some of the original inhabitants were Galilean. As we shall see, the most prominent figures in Tiberias bear Greek or Latin names, suggesting that they were well-Hellenized Herodian clients, and not representatives of the indigenous people. Nevertheless, apparently some of the new "Tiberians" were Galilean. The reference to coercion suggests that perhaps villagers in the area were simply forced from their villages displaced by the foundation of Tiberias and included as inhabitants of the new city. Probably they continued as cultivators of some of the fields in the surrounding area. Some settlers are said explicitly to have received new donations of land around the city. The close collaboration of the Tiberian party of the poor with nearby "Galileans" in 66–67 suggests that some Tiberians had maintained contacts with nearby villagers.

The comment about Tiberias having been built partly on the site of a cemetery, hence in violation of the law and tradition of the Judeans, does testify to Antipas's lack of concern for Judean laws, but it is not an indication of Galilean religious sensitivities. It is rather the expression of a Jerusalem priest to readers who were primarily well-educated Judean elite who survived the great revolt (and who share his disdain for the Herodian Antipas).

We may also have to be cautious about jumping to conclusions on the basis of other Josephus references to Tiberias in terms of the standard Greek terminology for institutions and officers of a city. Judging from the way in which Roman imperial officials addressed their formal correspondence, the government of a Greek *polis* would have consisted of magistrate(s), council, and citizen-body (*archon[tes], boulē, dēmos*).[41] Influence and actual power, moreover, gradually came to be held by the *dekaprōtoi*, the "ten principal men," within the council or citizen assembly. On first glance, Tiberias seems to fit precisely this picture, as Josephus summons "the council of Tiberians and the principals of the people" (*ten Tiberieon boulen kai tous protous tou demou*), and later attends a meeting at which the *archōn* Jesus presides (*Vita* 64, 271, 278, 296, 300, 381). However, it would have been highly unusual in Roman times for the magistrate to have been so revolutionary as was Jesus, the *archōn* of Tiberias (see further chapter 12). Moreover, the confident scholarly assertion that "there was a *boulē* of six-hundred" in Tiberias is based on an account in which Josephus has typically exaggerated the numbers (how many fishing boats would he have had to commandeer from the Tarichaeans in order to transport the 2,600 Tiberians he supposedly arrested up to the town of Tarichaeae? *B.J.* 2.641). Perhaps we should not lay too much stock in the standard terminology used by Josephus with regard to Tiberias, although the political structure of Tiberias is more likely to have resembled a Hellenistic city than did that of Jerusalem, for which Josephus uses some of the same terminology.[42]

There are a number of other indications that Tiberias was not a typical Hellenistic city, but a royal administrative city. A proper Greek city had its own territory (*chōra*) under its own political-economic control. Yet like Tarichaeae, Tiberias was merely the center of a toparchy of Agrippa II's kingdom just after mid-first century (*B.J.* 2.252),[43] hence held no such jurisdiction over its own *chōra* (despite what *autōn tēn chōran* [*Vita* 155] would suggest if taken at face value). A Hellenistic city would have had its own coinage dated according to the era of the city. Yet coins from Tiberias are Antipas's coins dated by the year of his rule. Not until Trajan did Tiberias mint its own coinage dated by the city's era.[44] Tiberias clearly had a stadium where large assemblies could be held; there Josephus had some tense confrontations with the Tiberians, and Vespasian ordered refugees captured in Tarichaeae either executed or enslaved, after reasserting Roman control in 67 (*B.J.* 2.618; 3.539; *Vita* 92, 331). Yet important political assemblies were held (also) in the *proseuchē*, "a huge building capable of accommodating a large crowd" (*Vita* 277). The name "prayer(house)," as used in diaspora Jewish communities, suggests this must have been the meeting place of a *synagōgē*, that is, congregation or assembly (see further chapter 10). Josephus's description, however, makes it appear much larger than the later Galilean synagogue buildings uncovered by archaeologists. The most important building in Tiberias must have been the royal palace, which was lavishly decorated and furnished in a Hellenistic style that observed no scruples about Judean or Galilean religious sensitivities (*Vita* 65).

Under Antipas and under Agrippa I as well, the royal court and administration would have dominated the city's life. The very names mentioned by Josephus indicate that those who were the wealthy and powerful "leading men" of Tiberias had themselves been, or were descended from, prominent members of Antipas's or Agrippa's administration (Julius Capellus; Herod son of Miarus, Herod son of Gamalus, Compsus son of Compsus, the latter's brother Crispus who had been prefect under Agrippa I,[45] Pistus, and his son Justus; *Vita* 32–36). Antipas's nephew, later Agrippa I, of course, had served as *agoranomos* ("commissary" or supply-officer; *Ant.* 18.149; cf. 14.261). That the loss of its prominence as the capital of Galilee, with "the archives and the royal bank" transferred back to Sepphoris (when Nero split Tiberias and Tarichaeae from the rest of Galilee and assigned them to Agrippa II in 54 C.E.) was such a sore point twelve years later indicates the degree to which the life of the city was oriented around its royal administrative function.

Although Tiberias was, like Sepphoris, basically an administrative city, its inhabitants and character must have been more diverse and complex. The language of administration was likely Greek. There were apparently hundreds of "Greeks" living in the city. Justus of Tiberias, Josephus's archrival, had aspirations toward a sophisticated Greek literary culture, later becoming secretary-historian to Agrippa II. Yet those Greeks comprised only a small percentage of the population, and were apparently resented by other Tiberians to the point of being massacred during the revolt (*Vita* 67). Hence Tiberias was not exactly a thriving center of "Greek" Hellenistic culture and influence (did all those settlers brought in from Antipas's territory learn Greek as a second language?) during Jesus' ministry and the rise of the early Christian movements.

Tiberias is less likely to have had a substantial contingent of Judeans than Sepphoris, since it lacked the latter's history as an administrative city under the Jerusalem high-priestly government during which Jerusalemites and other Judeans might have settled there. The *proseuchē* would almost certainly not have been a particularly Judean building, but a "Tiberian" one — if we take its name seriously, perhaps even built as an alternative to the Jerusalem temple as a place of "prayer."[46] Antipas clearly built Tiberias with no attention to how its site or the style of his own palace would stand in the view of attentive Jerusalem priests or Pharisees (such as the Jerusalem council who delegated Josephus two generations later). It is unclear what the mechanism would have been for Jerusalem officials to have influenced affairs in Tiberias prior to their delegation of Josephus and others in 66–67. Given their Herodian and/or Latin names, it should not be surprising that "the leading men" of the city staunchly resisted the instruction of the Jerusalem government in late 66 to destroy the royal palace with its animal representations in a style prohibited by "the laws" (*Vita* 65). Neither Hasmonean nor Herodian rulers had observed the prohibitions against such representations (e.g., *Ant.* 12.230; 14.34; 19.357), and one would not expect their officers and associates to have been concerned. In this case the royal palace represented the principal heritage of the city whose very foundation had been centered around it.

It is noteworthy that many of "the poor" in Tiberias must have been Galilean, surely giving it more links with Galilean culture than Sepphoris had. Nevertheless, as Josephus reports in no uncertain terms, "the Galileans" were as hostile to the upper strata of Tiberias as they were to Sepphoris generally (*Vita* 381–89). Except for the unusual circumstances of the revolt in 66–67, the Romanized/Hellenized powerful and wealthy families dominated the city's life and ran the royal administration of Galilee, and Antipas brought them in at the founding of the city. Thus in its cultural orientation the city was predominantly neither "Greek" nor "Judean" nor Galilean, even though the majority of the populace was likely of Galilean extraction and many of the "Herodian" elite likely of Judean background. It was rather, as the factionalism and virtual class war of 66–67 indicate, an uneasy composite of disparate elements dominated by those wielding power in the royal administration.

Tiberias was presumably dominated less by the (previous) royal administrative apparatus after the revolt, and particularly after the Romans finally phased out Agrippa II toward the end of the first century. Thereafter the city appears to have become more Roman politically and culturally. Once the city began minting its own coins, they used images such as the Capitoline temple and a Victory.[47] Tiberias even began building a temple to Hadrian in the early second century (Epiphanius, *Adv. Haer.* 136), and displayed images of Zeus and Hygeia on its coins.[48] Judeans appear not to have moved into prominence in Tiberias as quickly as they did in Sepphoris following the Bar Kokhba Revolt.[49] Early in the third century, however, Judah the Prince is found appealing to Rome to grant Tiberias the high status of *colonia*, and the patriarchate finally moved the base of its own operation there. Thereafter Tiberias became the principal center of rabbinic Judaism in Palestine for the next several centuries. A highly important rabbinic academy was established there, and the Jerusalem Talmud was probably compiled in Tiberias. Thus at Tiberias, as at Sepphoris/Diocaesarea, while the early presence of Judeans is not clear, after the city was more fully Romanized in the course of the second century, increasing numbers of Jews settled in the city and contributed to its increasingly complex cultural ethos.

Little archaeological exploration of ancient Tiberias has been completed as yet.[50] The city apparently had no wall until the beginning of the third century. Of the first-century city, a gate to the south flanked by two columns mounted on pedestals has been discovered, along with streets leading to the original area of buildings. The substantial intervening open space between the gate and the buildings suggests a city founded with room to expand its population. This would confirm the suggestion above that Sepphoris and Tiberias were originally less populous than at their peak in late antiquity. Underneath the fourth-century synagogue building found at Hammath, which was apparently incorporated by Tiberias as it grew, was a building with Corinthian and Doric features, perhaps a gymnasium.

The Cities and Herodian "Royal" Rule in Galilee

In their very origin and function, Sepphoris and Tiberias were in but not of Galilee. They were set over Galilean society as the institutions by which it was controlled and taxed and, as long as they were royal administrative cities, by which the ruler's position and fame were manifested in the context of Roman imperial rule.

The previous emphasis on these cities as centers of Hellenistic culture and its influence reverberating into Galilee has not taken adequately into account the extent to which the cultural ethos of such small and recently rebuilt or founded cities would have been dominated by their political role in the Roman imperial system. That is, so long as the "Ethnarch" Antipas and "King" Agrippa I had their court and government in Sepphoris and/or Tiberias, these cities were dominated by the pretensions of these Romanized and Romanizing client-rulers. Once the Romans imposed direct rule, and especially as they came to depend more generally upon the cities for administration of their surrounding areas, fuller currents of general Roman Hellenistic culture likely became more prominent.[51] But those currents would have mixed with the indigenous and/or previous cultural components. In any case, the degree of the Roman client-ruler's dominance would have been the key.

We can appreciate the manner in which Antipas and Agrippa I would have set the tone from a few stories of their behavior as Roman client-kings competing for status and influence (and income) in the eastern regions of the empire. The "queen" at Antipas's court was for some time an Arabian princess, daughter of Aretas, king of Arabia. As a dutiful client-ruler, Antipas did his part cementing ties with rulers on the eastern frontiers of the empire. He and other client-rulers also apparently visited each others' courts periodically; clearly such competitive hospitality was one of the motives for the competitive founding of cities and building of ornate palaces. During one such stopover on his way to Rome, Antipas intrigued a marriage with his half-brother Herod's wife, Herodias, the daughter of another brother and sister of the future Agrippa I. Having alienated his Arabian wife and her father Aretas, Antipas now found his whole army destroyed by the Arab king's troops. That turn of events, however, brought the Roman governor and his troops marching through Judea on their way to vindicate the Roman-appointed Tetrarch's honor and authority (*Ant.* 18.109–15, 120–22).

When the new emperor Gaius appointed her brother Agrippa as "king" over the tetrarchies of Philip and Lysanius, the jealous Herodias, envision-ing "the spectacle of his royal visits in the customary regalia before the multitudes," piqued her Tetrarch husband's ambition for a correspond-ing promotion to royal rank. We can imagine the impact such continual competition for honor and position had on life in Sepphoris and Tibe-rias. In fact, the competition between the two cities was merely a reflection of that competition among the client-rulers for rank and prestige in the imperial ethos.

An incident from the short reign of Agrippa I illustrates the direct im-pact of the courtly culture of the Roman client-kings on Tiberias. Although Agrippa seldom visited Tiberias himself, preferring to live first at Rome and then apparently at Caesarea, while dabbling in Jerusalem high-priestly poli-tics, he hosted a great conclave of Near Eastern kings at his Galilean capital (*Ant.* 19.338). The conclave of Roman clients involved two sets of broth-ers and several cases of intermarriage among petty monarchs all raised and educated at Rome and then elevated to kingships along the eastern fron-tier of the empire.[52] This must have been the greatest and most elaborate of all the comings and goings of Eastern royalty in what must have been remembered by the leading Sepphoreans and Tiberians as the glory days of their respective cities.

What supported all this royal culture, of course, was the political-economic administration of the subject territories. Whether in the rebuild-ing or founding of the capital cities in the first place or in the continuing collection of revenues to support the rulers in the appropriate style, the royal administration set up first in Sepphoris and then in Tiberias per-formed the governing functions necessary to extract the 200 talents revenue that Antipas had been assigned by Caesar (*Ant* 17.318–19; note the un-abashedly economic way in which the award of client-rulerships was understood in ancient empires).

One event in particular, or rather Josephus's and Philo's reports thereof, allows us to see the role of the administrative city of a Roman client-ruler in relation to the subject people and in the context of the overarching network of indirect imperial rule.[53] Angered over the Jewish rejection of his claim to divinity, the emperor Gaius (Caligula) ordered Petronius, the legate of Syria, to proceed with a large military force through Judea to Jerusalem in order to erect a bust of the emperor in the Temple. Having en-countered extensive (but apparently) pacifist resistance upon his arrival in Ptolemais, Petronius proceeded to Tiberias, seat of the recently appointed king Agrippa I's court, for further negotiations amid a spreading peasant strike now threatening the next harvest (and hence the Roman revenues from Palestine).

> At this juncture Aristobulus, the brother of King Agrippa, together with Hel-cias the Elder ["Prefect and Friend of the King," *Ant.* 19.353] and other most

> powerful members of the (ruling) house and the principal men [*hoi prōtoi*] appeared before Petronius and appealed to him not to incite [the people] to desperation, but to write to Gaius...that there would be a harvest of banditry, because the requirement of the tribute could not be met....[Agreeing to do this, Petronius] requested those in authority [*hoi en telei*] to attend to agricultural matters and to conciliate the people with optimistic propaganda.
> (*Ant.* 18.273–84; cf. *B.J.* 2.193, 199)

We glimpse here the role of the city and its officials in the overall structure of imperial rule through client-kings such as Agrippa I and Antipas. While Agrippa I himself was still living in Rome, his highest-ranking courtiers — his brother and his prefect, and others — were in charge of affairs in his kingdom, which included other districts besides Galilee, but which was governed from his capital city, Tiberias. Also included in the summit meeting with the Roman governor of Syria about how to handle the peasant strike, however, were the *prōtoi*, presumably the leading men of Tiberias, the officials who ordinarily administered the realm on behalf of Agrippa and his courtiers. The story of Herod Antipas's birthday party in Mark 6:17–29 portrays basically the same structure of the Roman client-government: in attendance at the birthday banquet were "his nobles [*hoi megistanes autou*] and the military officers and the principal men of Galilee" (6:21).[54]

That is, the client-ruler and the Herodian "nobles" and highest ranking officers, such as the prefect, would have resided in and thus dominated the capital, Sepphoris, until around 18 C.E. and then Tiberias at least until around 44 C.E. The "principal men" of the city would have been identical with the "royal" administrators in Sepphoris and/or Tiberias, the chief officers of institutions such as "the royal bank and archives" that gave the city its importance and political-economic *raison d'être*. Those officers would have been in charge of tax collection from and pacification of the people of Galilee, as indicated at the end of the account just cited ("those in authority"). Because of just these political-economic functions of the city and its officers, compounded by the alien provenance and cultural style of the latter as non-Galileans, however, Galileans sharply resented Sepphoris and Tiberias. The people may have been pacified following the incident with Gaius's statue, perhaps because Gaius died before his order could be implemented. But they were sharply hostile to (the ruling elite of) both cities in 66–67, as Josephus bears repeated witness.

Impact of the Herodian Cities and the Reaction of the Galileans

This historical survey of literary and archaeological evidence for Sepphoris and Tiberias indicates that first-century Galilee cannot be constructed in terms of a *Jewish* rural ethos that came under cultural influence to a greater or lesser extent from basically *Hellenistic* cities. Nor is it historically appropriate to claim that Galilee became "urbanized," either in the sense that large proportions of the inhabitants were brought into the ethos of city as opposed to rural life or in the sense that Galilee had become the *chōra* (i.e., land + villages + peasants) belonging to Sepphoris and Tiberias. This latter step may have been taken in the second century or later, as Roman imperial policy moved away from reliance on client-rulers and toward reliance on the cities for control and tax collection in areas not previously "urbanized." In either case, a Hellenistic *polis* with its *chōra* or a Near Eastern royal- or temple-city and its territory (such as Jerusalem and Judea), city and countryside are correlates, the latter providing the economic base of the former, the former ruling the latter. As we have seen, moreover, in Galilee the cultural influences were mixed and the cultural-political forms were hybrids, the "Hellenistic" phase in Sepphoris preceding "Judean" rule and its influence, and both Herodian cities dominated by Romanizing native "royal" culture.

It has long been understood that cities in the ancient Hellenistic and Roman empires were "parasitic" on the surrounding villages. This has been reaffirmed in a recent programmatic study:[55] "The task of extracting the surplus resources of the provinces was handled by the cities." The constructive functions of the city, such as social, legal, and religious amenities and craft production,

> have to be set against its fundamentally exploitative role: it was the city which as the agent of the central government supervised the taxation system, adding its own burdens on the rural population in the form of financial demands and personal labour services. It was the city to which the flow of rural rents was directed, in its function as the base and consumption center of the large landowners. There was no radical readjustment of the priorities of the urban elites away from the traditional goals of conspicuous consumption, social status, and political honour toward profitable investment.

With a minor adjustment to the form of tetrarchy or kingship and its courtiers and officers (corresponding to "large landowners" elsewhere in the empire), this generalization is directly applicable to the political-economic-cultural relationship between the cities of Sepphoris and Tiberias and Galilean villagers. Although the statement just cited was couched in primarily economic terms, the political-economic and cultural dimensions of the impact of city on villagers cannot ultimately separated. Because the ethnic-cultural background and orientation of the urban elite were often different from that of the villagers and because the intensity of the urban exploitation of its economic base varied, we may need to focus analytically on the cultural or the economic dimension in certain circumstances.

Considering that the only economic base of Antipas's tetrarchy was the "surplus" agricultural product of the Galilean and Perean villagers and townspeople, his massive building projects would have required intensified exploitation of that base. "Economic growth" and cultural-political "development" by the governing elite meant intensified economic pressure on the producers. The rebuilding of Sepphoris would have been costly; the founding of Tiberias would have at least sustained and more likely escalated the pressure on the people.[56] It is pertinent to recall that, centuries earlier when King Solomon had problems funding similar development projects (the construction of the Temple and royal palaces in Jerusalem), he ceded twenty towns in Galilee to Hiram of Tyre (1 Kings 9:10–13). Land and peasant labor were the only resources Solomon or the Herodian rulers had to support their grand building projects as well as the on-going expenses of court and administration.

An interrelated way in which the impact of the cities was intensified under Antipas was simply the building of Tiberias as a second major city in the limited area of Lower Galilee. The resulting ratio of surrounding territory to city proper may be roughly the same as for Scythopolis or Ptolemais or Joppa. The impact of the initial foundation by an alien Herodian king and his Hellenistic-Roman royal administration, however, would have been most dramatic on the generation during which it happened (i.e., that of Jesus and his followers), who remembered only the administrative town of Sepphoris, an outpost for Herodian, Hasmonean, or Hellenistic regimes, which were themselves based in a distant city. Once Tiberias was built there was, within a day's walk of every village in Lower Galilee, a city in which lived their rulers and tax collectors. Thus, in both these interrelated ways of intensified economic demands and of the doubling of the *presence* of cities, Antipas's founding of Tiberias soon after the rebuilding of Sepphoris must have had a major impact on life in Lower Galilee.

We may be better able to appreciate how the cultural impact of the ruling city(ies) compounded the political-economic impact on the Galileans by comparison with the relations between Jerusalem and Judea. Not only were the high-priestly rulers in Jerusalem of the same ethnic lineage[57] as the Judean peasantry they ruled, but (despite the Herodian undermining) the form of Jerusalem's rule, the Temple and high priesthood, still retained a certain legitimacy among the Judeans that only centuries of tradition could establish. There had also been centuries of interaction between the official Jerusalem-based tradition (the "laws of the Judeans"), through which the society was governed, and popular Judean tradition, and both were rooted in the same pre-exilic Judahite-Israelite tradition. Moreover, there was a divinely legitimated ethnic-cultic link between the Judean people and the ruling city, Jerusalem, in the (lower) priests who lived in villages but served several weeks a year in the Temple, particularly at the principal festivals celebrated there. Notwithstanding the structural and ad hoc conflicts that also characterized relations between the Jerusalem rulers and the Judean people, the links that bound them were unusual in the context of the Roman empire for their extent and sanctity.

As should be clear from the history outlined in the first few chapters and the sketch of the history of Sepphoris just above, the rulers of Galilee and their officers based in the cities were, to a greater or lesser degree, alien to Galilee. Thus the culture they brought with them into the cities would have been not only that of the ruling elite but different in tradition from that of the Galilean villagers. Galileans would thus have been exposed to a mixture of cultural influences for centuries prior to the time of Jesus or Antipas. Under Ptolemaic and Seleucid rule, they would have been exposed to Hellenistic culture, particularly to Greek as the language of administration. The Hasmoneans surely brought Jerusalem-based cultural forms with them when they took over Sepphoris as the administrative city, although we cannot be sure that they replaced Greek with either Aramaic or Hebrew as the administrative/official language. When Herod replaced the last Hasmoneans two generations later, Hellenistic culture may have had a resurgence, although Judean culture would have continued. Herod had left the high-priestly apparatus in place, albeit with vastly reduced power, and it would presumably have attempted to continue its own influence in towns such as Sepphoris. One has the sense that during the time prior to Antipas, the cultural influences from Sepphoris would have been slow and steady, but never aggressive or programmatic, first Hellenistic and then Jerusalemite-Judean, under the Hasmoneans and Herod.

When Sepphoris became the seat of the royal court of Antipas, however, and particularly when Antipas then founded Tiberias as his new capital, the Roman political-cultural influence intensified. Antipas apparently had little interest in Judean cultural forms. As sketched above, the new style of both cities was decisively more Hellenistic, but in the amalgamated form of a Romanized Near Eastern royal culture. That this is the way it struck both Galilean common people and prominent Jerusalemites can be seen from our principal literary sources, the Gospel of Mark (Herod as "king" and particularly his birthday banquet in Mark 6) and Josephus (the reports of Tiberias and particularly of the royal palace).

Having noted that the Roman-Hellenistic cultural impact intensified under Antipas, however, we should be cautious about how we imagine this happening in two respects: the ways in which Galileans had contact with the cities, and their response or stance toward the cities. Judeans (and apparently even Galileans) were expected to go to Jerusalem periodically, to bring tithes and offerings, and to attend the great festivals such as Passover. Yet there would have been no corresponding occasions for Galileans to have visited Sepphoris or Tiberias. We should not imagine Galileans as having entered one of the cities every so often to sell their produce, that is, projecting a modern market economy back onto ancient Palestine. What little "surplus" the people produced was taken by officials from the city in the form of taxes (and, increasingly, interest or perhaps even rent). As was the custom in most traditional agrarian societies, officials went to the village threshing floors, where they took Caesar's and Herod's cuts off the top at harvest time.

Nor should we imagine that people from the surrounding area "flocked to Sepphoris" to attend "events and spectacles" in the theater, or ran into Tiberias for some entertainment in the stadium.[58] There was apparently less "hustle and bustle" than we might imagine in Roman provincial theaters, which were used only infrequently (five to twenty-five times a year).[59] That use, moreover, would have been integral to the imperial Hellenistic ethos fostered by the Herodians in cities such as Caesarea and Sepphoris, but alien to the Galileans. Theaters were closely related to the city political administration, providing the meeting place of the assembly. When needed, they could also be used for the rulers' special purposes such as the "demonstration effect" of a public political trial of dissidents who had dared to demonstrate against their native ruler's collaboration with Roman domination (*Ant.* 17.155–67). They were further used for Roman imperial celebrations and other religious ceremonies. The stadium in Tiberias would have had similar functions, alien to the Galileans. One suspects that the tradition-minded ("conservative") Galilean peasantry of the first century, like the rabbis later, identified the theater as "Roman" and otherwise alien and hostile.[60] Both the theater in Sepphoris and the stadium in Tiberias were probably built primarily for Antipas's self-promotion directed to the outside world of other client-rulers and his own administration, not for the entertainment of native Galileans.[61] But they would have been useful for internally directed political cultural events as well.

Of course, villagers might have been called into the city for a court appearance, but that would hardly have been a visit they enjoyed. One has the sense that villagers' contacts with the city were minimal during the first century just as they were in the next century or two reflected in early rabbinic literature: "The impact of a city on its territory was, according to the rabbis, negligible. Tax collection was the city's only important function. The provision of security, a market for goods, or a coinage to facilitate exchange had comparatively little effect on its villages."[62]

That Galilean villagers would have had little direct interaction with the city fits the picture Josephus gives, in no uncertain terms, of Galilean hostility to Sepphoris and (the dominant elite of) Tiberias. This hostility cannot be explained as due simply to the Sepphoreans deciding to remain loyal to Rome in the summer of 66, as it might appear in the speech Josephus places in the mouth of his archrival Justus of Tiberias, in order to paint him as a revolutionary agitator (*Vita* 39).[63] Another passage may be more representative: "The Galileans, seizing this opportunity, too good to be missed, of venting their hatred on one of the cities which they detested, rushed forward, with the intention of exterminating the population" (*Vita* 375).

Allowing for his usual hyperbole, what Josephus portrays here is a long-pent-up resentment against Sepphoris that must have been deeply rooted in the generations of control and taxation from the city. Moreover, despite the Galileans' occasional collaboration with the working-class faction in Tiberias, "they had the same detestation for the Tiberians as for the inhabitants of Sepphoris" (*Vita* 384). Since, in the course of his accounts of affairs and events in Galilee in 66–67, Josephus provides several illustrations of how this Galilean detestation of the cities was manifested, we appear to have no choice but to trust him on this point.

The general impact of the cities on the Galilean populace in the first two-thirds of the first century was such as to have evoked an unusual degree of hostility. It is tempting to find a correlation between that popular resentment and the intensification of the economic and cultural impact of the cities by the very foundation of Tiberias in the middle of Antipas's reign. Galileans expressed their hostility to the royal administrative cities in their midst in both actions and words. "Galileans" eagerly joined the party of sailors and the destitute from Tiberias itself in burning and looting the royal palace in 66 (*Vita* 66). In the Synoptic Sayings Source "Q" Jesus makes a pointed contrast between the popular prophet John and the Herodian rulers: "What then did you go out to see? Someone dressed in soft robes? Look, those who put on fine clothing and live in luxury are in royal palaces" (Luke 7:25). In part 3 we will explore further the situation of the Galilean villagers and the movements they mounted occasionally in resistance to "those who lived in luxury."

Patriarch, Rabbis, Cities, and Galilee in Late Antiquity

After the unprecedented rebuilding and founding of cities in Galilee in the first century, we must wait over a century before much evidence, archaeological or literary, emerges for developments in Diocaesarea and Tiberias in the course of the third century. This may not be by accident. The late first and particularly the second century must have been times of extreme social disruption and turmoil for all of Palestine, particularly Judea, but also Galilee, partly because of the Roman devastation of Judea. As noted in chapter 4, following the destruction of Jerusalem and the Temple in 70 many prominent wealthy, priestly, and/or scribal families relocated in the coastal plain around Yavneh, Lydda, and Joppa. Some of those families and others then emigrated to Galilee in the aftermath of the Bar Kokhba Revolt of 132–135. The rabbis established academies on the western frontier of Galilee at Usha and Beth Shearim before eventually locating in Sepphoris and Tiberias by around 200. As noted above, recent archaeological explorations at Sepphoris, moreover, have found evidence of an influx of people into the western residential section during this same period. Also around

200, with his base at Sepphoris, Judah the Prince emerged with considerable social power and influence, and within the next generation or two the rabbis were apparently claiming a share of such social influence. Both of these interrelated developments came at a propitious time in the Roman empire. Included in the broader Severan dynasty's policy of encouraging local customs in the east was a rapprochement between leaders of Jewish communities in Palestine, such as Judah Ha-nasi, and the Roman imperial government.[64]

What seems to have happened in the two cities of Galilee during the course of the third century is that a new social infrastructure emerged. It was apparently not officially recognized by the Romans, but was nonetheless important in the development of social and cultural affairs, both in the cities themselves and in relations between the cities and villages. Most societies have some sort of informal infrastructure parallel to or underneath the official institutions, often intertwined with the latter, particularly at the top of the social pyramid. This is often the case in an imperial or colonial situation where certain indigenous social forms are left intact, such as village communities or the priestly apparatus of a temple-community (e.g., Jerusalem). The history of Judea and Galilee under Roman domination and devastation offers a fascinating case of a mutation of the indigenous social forms into a historically unique new social infrastructure based in the cities of Galilee, but wielding ever increasing influence in Jewry throughout the Roman empire and beyond.

Social institutions and events in Judea came together with social institutions and events in Galilee in this historically creative response to Roman disruption and devastation. When the Romans destroyed Jerusalem and the Temple in 70, many of the priestly and scribal families who had staffed the traditional governance of Judean society regrouped in order to continue their role as guardians of the social-religious traditions of the people. When the Romans again devastated Judea sixty years later, they relocated, eventually in Sepphoris and Tiberias. Meanwhile in Galilee, there was a vacuum of social-political leadership for the society as a whole based in the capital cities. Historically there had been nothing in the district corresponding to the Jerusalem Temple and priesthood in Judea which, over several centuries, had been established as the religious-political-economic "head" of the body-politic. The ethos of the cities in Galilee had always been somewhat alien to the rest of the society, from the Hellenistic origins of Sepphoris through the somewhat Hellenized administration of the Hasmoneans to the Romanized ethos of the Herodians. As illustrated by events in 66–67 (see chapter 3) there was no central body or leadership to speak for Galileans as a whole, only local leadership (such as John of Gischala or Jesus *archōn* of Tiberias). With the cities becoming increasingly Romanized in the early second century, the cultural-political gulf between city and village would only seem to have widened. Yet (as argued above, chapters 1–2) the Galileans appear to have shared the Israelite heritage with the Jerusalem-Judean priesthood and sages and had been subject to the Judean temple-state for a century. Many of the residents of Diocaesarea and Tiberias, moreover, would have been of Judean background. There would appear to have been a possibility of some confluence of interests between a traditionalist Judean-Israelite scribal-priestly elite and a traditionalist Galilean-Israelite peasantry, along with the Judeans already resident in the cities.

In terms of the official structure imposed by the empire, Rome treated Galilee like any other part of the eastern empire.[65] Once the whole of Lower Galilee was placed under the jurisdiction of the two cities, for example, the urban officers were responsible for controlling and taxing their territories on behalf of Rome. While there are few rabbinic references to the official civic government bodies,[66] the cooperative relationship is articulated in the standard imperial ideology inscribed on coins: "Diocaesarea the Holy City, City of Shelter, Autonomous, Loyal, Friendship and Alliance between the Holy Council and the Senate of the Roman People."[67] A story in the Jerusalem Talmud refers to *bouleteri* and *pagani* as two leading groups in Sepphoris (*y. Šabb.* 12.3.13c; *y. Hor.* 3.48c), presumably the city's council members and the wealthy landowners (from within the city or from outside?).[68] At least some members of the city council, ordinarily members of the most prominent and wealthy families who attained distinguished rank, would have been Jewish.[69]

As already outlined in chapter 4, beginning with Judah the Prince around 200, a "patriarchate" emerged with considerable informal political-economic-religious power, based initially in Diocaesarea, then moving to Tiberias in mid-third century. By mid- to late fourth century, the operations of the patriarchate were more formally incorporated into the imperial system.[70] Key to understanding the emergence and functioning of the patriarchate, however, is what the *nasi* did *not* do in the third century, that is, collect taxes on behalf of Rome, which remained in the hands of the formally recognized city officials. What might look like the patriarch's collection of special taxes for construction of a wall in Tiberias involved an appeal to his authority regarding obligation for a city tax.[71]

In fact we have little or no evidence of the patriarchs' relations with the cities other than their location first in Sepphoris and later in Tiberias. What is clear from the various references to their activities and relationships, however, is that the patriarchate was the center of an elaborate network of patron-client relations that came to operate in effect as an unofficial political-economic-religious government in Galilee.[72] The patriarchs' own power depended, first of all, on imperial patronage. Wealthy families in Diocaesarea and Tiberias then vied for favor, ingratiating themselves with the *nasi* through such means as study of Torah or bonds of marriage. Judah and his successors, having acquired the authority to make certain appointments to various instructional, judicial, or other communal posts, rewarded favorites with positions with substantial benefits. The patriarchs thus formed an effective pattern of patronage with the wealthy and powerful Jews first in Diocaesarea and then in Tiberias. Because the patriarch was so powerful, he would be consulted on matters such as city taxes (the case in Tiberias), and his advice on such matters may have carried a good deal of weight in people's actual behavior. The patriarchs, while not empowered to collect taxes for official purposes, engaged in some serious "fundraising" for their own purposes. In the course of the third century they even began to use their own unofficial enforcers, in effect, a private police force. Such blatant use of power, however, must have contributed to the sharp criticism that the rabbis (and presumably others) leveled against them later in the century.[73] Ironically, it was after the patriarchate had lost a good deal of respect among rabbis and people that the now Christianized imperial court recognized it more formally later in the fourth century.

During the course of the third century the rabbis moved into prominent roles in the network of influence built up by the patriarchs, and later apparently in effect replaced the patriarchate with their own authority. As sketched in chapter 4, by the end of the second century the rabbinic movement was centered in Sepphoris. Early in the third century its center of gravity shifted to Tiberias, which was eventually recognized as a center of Jewish authority by Jewish communities from Rome to Babylon. A number of prominent rabbis in the third century were themselves Babylonians. Like the patriarchs, the rabbis had no officially sanctioned authority during late Roman times to enforce their decisions on religious matters, let alone on social-economic matters. During the course of the third century, however, apparently under the patriarch's influence, they broadened their appeal, partly by laying less emphasis on purity regulations. The patriarchs appointed some rabbis to communal posts and eventually began to share power of communal appointments with a "court" (*bet din*), likely the patriarch's own inner circle, but including rabbis in increasingly influential ways. From mid-third century rabbinic polemics begin to castigate the wealthy judicial appointees for incompetence as well as the patriarch himself for making such appointments. Apparently even as rabbinic respect for the patriarchate declined, the rabbis themselves were consolidating their own influence in the network of patronage and communal appointments, while themselves avoiding the kind of abuses for which they were criticizing the patriarchs.[74]

As we move into late antiquity, the role of the cities in Galilee thus becomes more complex than in earlier centuries. After a certain power vacuum and fluidity in the societal infrastructure between the ruling cities and the towns and villages in the second century, there emerged a new infrastructure with its own dynamics. First the patriarchs and then the rabbis generated networks of patronage centered among the prominent wealthy urban families but extending their influence into villages and towns by means of certain communal appointments. Like the official governments, these unofficial, informal networks were based in the cities. Non-Israelites could and probably did largely ignore the emerging infrastructure. In Galilee itself as well as beyond, however, this infrastructure may have become as important and influential in social life as the official civic and imperial institutions.

The emerging network of rabbinic influence also apparently served to mediate between the Galilean populace and the Roman authorities in late Roman times. For example, as the new "taxation" of the *annona* and the *angariae* became intolerably burdensome, the rabbis complained to the authorities, although some of the patriarchs' attempts at raising funds were clearly competing for limited popular resources. As the patriarchate and rabbinic circles began to wield influence over Galilean villages parallel to the Roman administration based in the city, moreover, they helped to maintain the social order important to Rome, but in ways rooted in the Israelite traditions indigenous to Galilean local communities.

Part 3

GALILEAN VILLAGE COMMUNITIES

Chapter 8

VILLAGE AND FAMILY

⁓❦⁓

The little tradition's latent dissent may also derive from the fact that its social base, the peasant community is both historically and functionally prior to cities and to the great tradition.... It is not possible to imagine a non-cultivating elite without a subordinate producing class by which it is sustained.

—JAMES C. SCOTT

When Adam delved and Eve span,
Who was then the gentleman?

—OLD ENGLISH SONG

Galilee, like Judea proper, was a traditional agrarian society. The vast majority of people were peasants living in villages of varying sizes farming the land or, near the lake, supplementing farming with fishing. As noted in chapter 6, Josephus carefully distinguishes his people's life from that of other peoples of the ancient Mediterranean world, such as the Greeks and Phoenicians: "Ours is not a maritime country;...we devote ourselves to the cultivation of the productive country with which we are blessed" (*Ap.* 1.60). Galilee in particular makes a striking contrast to the commercial cities of Tyre, Sidon, and Ptolemais on the coast.

> The land is everywhere so rich in soil and pasturage and produces such variety of trees, that even the most indolent are tempted by these facilities to devote themselves to agriculture. In fact, every inch of the soil has been cultivated by the inhabitants; there is not a parcel of waste land. The towns too are thickly distributed and the multitude of the villages everywhere, thanks to the fertility of the soil, are densely populated, so that the smallest of them contains above fifteen thousand inhabitants. Galilee...is entirely under cultivation and produces crops from one end to the other. (*B.J.* 3.42–44)

The exaggeration is obvious. Some of the land was untillable and by Josephus's count the population would have been well over 3 million. The basic point, however, is that Galilee was clearly agrarian. With the livelihood of the people so completely dependent on the productivity of the soil, little

189

wonder that their principal fear was drought. A whole tractate in the Mishnah, *Ta'anit*, was devoted to fasting and other measures designed to avert such a catastrophe.

In a traditional agrarian society such as that in Galilee, the most fundamental social form was the family or household, the basic unit of production and consumption as well as of reproduction. Families or households lived together in villages and towns of varying sizes, these local communities comprising the basic social-political form in which the people (of Israel) was embodied. That cities were built, rebuilt, and expanded in Lower Galilee does not mean that the villages disappeared. Indeed, productive families and villages provided the economic base of "urbanization." Until recently, evidence for life in the villages has been extremely limited, partly because nearly all of our sources stem from the cities and express the viewpoint of the literate elite who ordinarily resided there. In the last two decades, however, information about villages and village life, while still limited and fragmentary, is increasingly available from new archaeological surveys and from social historical analysis of literary sources.[1]

Villages across the Landscape

In order to appreciate the concrete reality of the scores of villages in Galilee it is necessary to note names and sites identifiable from literary sources and/or archaeological explorations. Because of his own intensive activities there in 66–67 c.e., Josephus should be a good source for Galilean villages and towns. At one point he says that "there are two hundred and four cities and villages in Galilee" (*Vita* 235). In this count Josephus is probably not exaggerating. Although only Sepphoris and Tiberias really qualified as cities,[2] Josephus may be working from official lists, and recent surface surveys have identified roughly the same number of settlements inhabited in late second-temple times. Thus, "the multitude of villages" must have been situated at close proximity across the landscape. Josephus mentions by name a number of villages in every area of Galilee. In southwestern Galilee, within three to five miles of Sepphoris ("surrounded by numerous villages," *Vita* 346), were Japha, "the largest village of Galilee," very close to Nazareth (*Vita* 230, 270; *B.J.* 3.289–306), Simonias and Besara (*Vita* 115, 118–19), Asochis (*Vita* 207, 233, 384), Rumah and Garis (*B.J.* 3.233; *Vita* 395, 412; but cf. *B.J.* 3.129). Further north, not far from Jotapata, were the smaller villages of Cana, Chabulon, Sogane, and Saba (*Vita* 86, 213–14, 227, 234, 265–66; *B.J.* 3.229). The large village of Gabara/Gabaroth is also surrounded by other "villages and country towns" (*komai kai polichnai; B.J.* 3.132; *Vita* 229–43), and Josephus claims to have fortified Bersabe and Selame, just to the east, as well as Jotapata itself, still in "lower Galilee" (*B.J.* 2.573, 3.39; *Vita* 188). In "upper Galilee" were numerous villages, including Baca to the west, Thella to the east, as well as the large village of Gischala, and the villages that Josephus claims to have fortified, Meroth, Jamneth, Sepph, and Acchabare (*Vita* 71; *B.J.* 3.39–40; 2.585, 590, and so on; 4:84, *polichne*; 2.573; *Vita* 187–88). Along the lake were Capernaum, Arbela, and other villages near Tarichaeae, and Bethmaus, Adamah, and other villages near Tiberias (*Vita* 188, 403, 310; *B.J.* 2.598; *Vita* 64, 129, 321–22). Finally, coming full circle, swinging southwest into the interior, were Itabyrion (Tabor), Dabaritta, and Xaloth (*Vita* 188, 126, 318, 227; *B.J.* 4.54, 2.595, 3.39).

Archaeological surveys have identified a number of those same villages along with many other settlements from this period.[3] The sites of numerous villages have been identified in Upper Galilee near Gischala: Gush Halav itself, Meiron,[4] Khirbet Shema' only a kilometer away, Khirbet Qeiyuma, Sasa, Ein es-Sumai, Farod, Kefar Hananiah, Qadesh, Nabratein, Dalton, 'Alma, 'Akbara, Beer Sheva, and Qatsyon. In the area north of Sepphoris, around Yodfat/Jotapata, are the sites of thirty-one villages, including some names that indicate continuity from settlements in ancient times, such as Sha'b (Saba?) and Kabul (Chabulon), Arav, Khirbet Qana ("Cana of Galilee"), with Kaukab and Khirbet Shifat being near the ruins of Yodfat (Jotapata). In the area south of Sepphoris, in the Nazareth mountains or further south and east, the sites of nineteen villages have been found.[5] Then further east and south a few more have been located, such as Umm el-Amad, and Arbel and Tabor, both sites of several military engagements, according to ancient sources. With fifty village sites located in the wider area surrounding Sepphoris alone, Josephus's figure of 204 cities and villages for Galilee as a whole may not be that much of an exaggeration.

Moreover, a number of these villages mentioned by Josephus and/or discovered in archaeological investigations were apparently identical with, and in continuity with, villages mentioned at various points in Hebrew biblical narratives. Japha would appear to be identical with Japhia, the village of Zebulun mentioned in Joshua 19:12. Chabulon is clearly in the same area as the twenty villages called Chabul which Solomon had ceded to Hiram of Tyre to help pay for the building of the Jerusalem temple (1 Kings 9:10–13).

Villages varied considerably in size, as we might expect, and perhaps in type of settlement. It seems highly doubtful that different terms used in rabbinic sources indicate either a reliable difference in size or in type of settlement, particularly its relation to an administrative city. Even though the Hebrew term *kefar* meant "little village," a village so labeled might have increased in size. The term *'ir*, by far the most frequent (well over 100 occurrences in the Mishnah), undergoes an evolution of meaning parallel to the Latin term *villa*.[6] It would appear to be used for villages generally, settlements of different sizes, and types of "ownership." Mishnaic references to a man selling an *'ir* or an *'ir* passing from several "owners" to one should not be interpreted by means of a few archaeological sites further south in

Judea to suggest that *'ir* refers mainly to settlements that are parts of large estates. Nor can we determine that an *'ir* or an *ayarah* or a *qiryah* was juridically subordinate to a city or other administrative entity in some special way.[7] The relationship of settlements to cities, rulers, and/or "owners" is more appropriately considered in the context of the political economy of Galilee, in the next chapter. Settlements referred to with terms such as *'ir* in the Mishnah and with *kōmē* in Greek sources were clearly settlements of varying sizes and perhaps types.

Galilean villages varied in terms of location, shape, and style as well as size.[8] Generally lacking in the villages was the "rationalized" planning that one finds in cities founded in the Hellenistic period.[9] Several were built in protected locations on the top of defensible hills, and some were fortified with walls, for example, Gischala, Jotapata, and Japha (*m. 'Arak.* 9:6; *B.J.* 3.289–306). In other cases, the outer walls and roofs of the houses or courtyards formed a protective barrier for the village; but even a tiny village of three courtyards with only a few houses each might also have a wall (*m. 'Arak.* 9:6). Larger villages and towns were often apparently unprotected by anything more than the clustering of the buildings.

Both archaeological excavations and Mishnah texts indicate that the dwelling space or "house," where a family of five or six lived, generally consisted of a small room or two (3+ x 4+ m, with 5 x 5 m being "large"; *m. B. Bat.* 4:4; *m. 'Erub.* 9:1, 4). An individual family and its room(s) generally shared a courtyard with other families and their room(s), and shared use of installations such as oven, cistern, and millstone in the common courtyard. Several such complexes of courtyards and rooms would open into a passageway or alley in larger villages or towns. Construction was usually crude, of undressed basalt stones without mortar. One can gain a sense of the living conditions as well as collective responsibilities in such villages from several of the case laws in the Mishnah tractate *Baba Batra*. For example:

> Everyone [who dwells within a courtyard] is compelled to share in building a gate-house and a door for the courtyard....Not all courtyards are such that need a gate-house. Everyone [who dwells within a town] is compelled to share in building a wall for the town and double doors and a bolt....Not every town is such that it needs a wall....If [a man] has acquired a habitation therein he forthwith counts as one of the men of the town. (*m. B. Bat.* 1:5)

The Mishnah tractate *'Erubin* also indicates that the families of a courtyard or along the whole alleyway could form an association or partnership (an *'erub* or *shittuf*) in which they shared food supply and gained freer movement around their shared living area on sabbaths (e.g., *m. 'Erub.* 6:8, 7:6).

Settlements ranged in size from tiny villages of a few score to relatively

large towns of several thousand. Estimates of population, both for individual settlements and for Galilee as a whole, have almost certainly been
on the high side.[10] The figure of 160 to 200 persons per acre used in calculations seems too high for the density of settlement in the villages and
towns. If we retreat to a more realistic figure of between 40 and 60 persons per acre,[11] then the average village sites of seven to twelve acres in
Upper Galilee would have housed roughly 300 to 700 people each.[12] The
vast majority of villages, however, occupying two to five acres, would have
had fewer than 300 people each.[13]

Nazareth, Capernaum, Meiron

Intense interest focuses on Nazareth and Capernaum because Jesus ostensibly grew up in the one and his ministry centered in the other.
Reconstruction of a realistic picture of these villages has been complicated
and confused because both sites became the center of the development of
Christian pilgrimage and "tourism" in late antiquity. It has been difficult
to sort though the resultant literary and architectural accretions.[14] Yet because of the intense religious interest in these villages, more information is
available for them than for others. Moreover, because of those accretions,
it is necessary to attend to the historical differences at the sites, from one
period to another.

Settlement at Nazareth, a few miles south of Sepphoris, may date from
at least the Middle Bronze Age. It must have been among the villages of
ancient Israel, judging from pottery fragments found at the site.[15] It was
expanded or refounded during the Hellenistic period.[16] Until it became popular for Christian pilgrims to visit from the fourth century on, Nazareth
was an inauspicious agricultural community of under 500 people somewhat
off the main route. The much larger village of Japha a mile and a half to the
southwest, and on the main route, was much more prominent. Yet because
Nazareth was so close to the ruling city of Sepphoris, its people were likely
directly affected by events focusing there, such as the insurrection led by
Judas son of Hezekiah in 4 B.C.E., the Roman retaliatory destruction and
enslavement, and the rebuilding of the city by Antipas.

Capernaum[17] was situated just to the west of where the Jordan River
enters the Sea of Galilee from the north. Hence it lay near the border between Galilee and the Golan, just opposite the village of Bethsaida, which
Herod Philip transformed into the city of Julias in the early first century
C.E. Although the site of Capernaum was inhabited earlier (thirteenth century B.C.E.), excavators believe that the village was refounded in Hellenistic
times. Located near a border crossing, it housed a garrison of "royal"
troops under Antipas (cf. Matt. 8:11 ‖ Luke 7:1), and perhaps a detachment of Roman soldiers from the second century on. Underneath a second-
or third-century Roman bathhouse[18] excavators have found remains of a

similar building from the first century, although its precise function has not been established with clarity.

Inflated recent estimates of the size and population of Capernaum created the misleading impression that the western shore of the Sea of Galilee was virtually "urbanized" in Roman times.[19] More critical analysis indicates that Capernaum was, rather, a largish village of 1,000 or more inhabitants.[20] One section of the "village of Nahum" appears, more than other Galilean villages, to have been laid out systematically in blocks 40 meters square, each with three or four of the usual one-story multifamily houses with individual rooms opening onto common courtyards. Directly under an octagonal church building dating from Byzantine times was found a large room (7 x 6.5 m) apparently used for meetings, possibly worship, as early as the late first century C.E. This has traditionally been identified as "St. Peter's house." Like the octagonal church, however, the beautiful white synagogue building must be dated late, fourth or fifth century.[21] Probably Capernaum did not become a major pilgrimage site until the fourth century.[22] While fishing surely accounted for some of the economic activity and sustenance of the villagers, Capernaum appears to have been basically an agricultural community. We can only surmise that transit trade would also have figured in the local economy, although that seems more likely for a border town than for other Galilean villages.[23]

Meiron and Gischala/Gush Halav and smaller nearby villages were located in the rugged hills of Upper Galilee, more remote from the centers of power and the interregional trade routes such as passed through Capernaum and near Nazareth. Meiron later became famous as a popular Jewish pilgrimage site, just as Capernaum attracted Christian pilgrims, gaining a prominence it did not have in Roman times. The bulk of the findings from the recent "regional" archaeological explorations of these villages pertain to the "Middle" and "Late Roman" periods (135–450), leaving interpretation of earlier artifacts heavily dependent on literary sources for Gush Halav and the surrounding villages.[24]

Meiron was apparently inhabited at least by Hellenistic times, while Gush Halav and Nabratein had been well-established settlements for centuries, from the Early Bronze Age through earlier Israelite times, as well as during the Persian and Hellenistic periods.[25] At least in late antiquity both Gush Halav and Meiron appear to have been larger than the other villages in the area, which averaged between seven and twelve acres in area, or around 500 in population. Gush Halav (and not Meiron) was evidently fortified and garrisoned as a military and/or administrative outpost during Hasmonean and Herodian times.[26] Thus, while these villages were some distance from the center(s) of power in Galilee, the villagers would have felt the administrative-military presence. One reason for the military presence was that these villages were along the frontier with the territory of Tyre. A passing comment by Josephus indicates the implications for Gush Halav,

Meiron, and other villages: "Kadasa, a strong inland village of the Tyrians [presumably a Tyrian fortress and garrison] was always at strife and war with the Galileans" (*B.J.* 4.104). Josephus's earlier accounts of Marion, the "tyrant" of Tyre who took three fortresses in Galilee before being driven back by the young Herod (*B.J.* 1.238–39; *Ant.* 14.297–99), provide a window onto what must have been a recurrent struggle between outside rulers for control of these villages.

It is highly unlikely that Meiron, Gush Halav, and nearby villages specialized primarily in production of olive oil, as suggested by recent archaeological interpreters.[27] The oil of Meiron and other Upper Galilean villages was legendary for its quality (but not necessarily its quantity) in rabbinic literature. Like other Galilean villages, they produced grain as well, including the "surplus" that their rulers siphoned off in taxes. Josephus himself had designs on the imperial "stores of grain" in the Upper Galilean villages in 66–67 C.E.

Other observations by archaeologists about Meiron or Gush Halav also seem questionable. While there was likely more direct Roman influence on all of Galilee following the two revolts, the limited evidence of one "planned insula laid out over Stratum II [early Roman] remains" does not appear to suggest "an attempt to lay out the framework of a town plan on the model of a Roman grid."[28] It is unclear what the archaeological evidence is for the claim that the population was growing during the Early and Middle Roman periods or that during the Middle Roman period (135–250 C.E.) there was a sizable influx of population from Judea. Such an immigration of numbers of new settlers, particularly those of higher status as Judeans and priestly families, would presumably have been disruptive of the traditional village social order. The archaeological findings do indicate that a nascent social stratification had emerged by late Roman times (250–365). The "Patrician house" and "Lintel house" at Meiron are larger than others and fine-wares were found in them.[29] Also from this period are the basilical synagogue building at Meiron and the synagogues in nearby villages, the construction of which presupposes the possession or mobilization of considerable economic resources.

Household and Family in Galilean Villages and Towns

Insofar as most Galilean families lived on the edge of subsistence, one might say that the purpose of production was simple year-to-year survival. Difficult as simple survival may have been, however, the lives of Galilean peasants involved other dimensions as well, cultural, historical, biological. The family was the basic social unit, of production and consumption, of reproduction and socialization, of personal identity and membership in a wider community. And because, in an agrarian society, families could not survive without land on which they have at least some rights, the two went together. Thus, the purpose of both production and reproduction was to perpetuate the family on its land. Other social institutions and customs also served this purpose. Perpetuation of the family on its land required heirs as successors. Inheritance was vested in patriliny. Marriage produced heirs. And marriages were formed according to a strategy of keeping the inheritance of land within certain boundaries. In the maintenance of generational continuity, the family household carried out a number of political, economic, and religious functions.

The most basic social form in Galilee as elsewhere in the ancient eastern Mediterranean world was thus the patriarchal family.[30] Not only most social relations, but identity as well was determined by one's place in a multigenerational family, which in turn belonged integrally to a village or town. This has implications for how we focus our investigation. Just as what modern Westerners think of as religion was embedded with the basic forms of political-economic life, so what we think of as individual persons were embedded in corporate social forms. This can be seen perhaps most vividly in the case of a woman: she was part of either the family headed by her father or the family headed by her husband; there was virtually no other possibility (as we shall explore further below). Similarly, although the eldest son became the head of a family, his identity and roles were embedded in that family, and he was responsible both to ancestors and to descendants. Since the transgenerational family was the basic unit of identity as well as the fundamental social form, it is thus inappropriate — as well as impossible, given the lack of evidence — to focus on individual life, as modern Western intellectuals tend to do. Our focus must be at least as wide as the family household, in terms of which rights, roles, and relations were defined. Moreover, since the transgenerational household was the basic social form and the basis of participation in wider community, pressures on and disintegration of the patriarchal family were the pressure points at which the wider social order would begin to break down.

That the family/household was the basic social-economic form of Israelite society can be seen in its very foundational tradition, the Mosaic covenant. The basic covenantal principles of social policy governing relations between God and the society and social-economic relations within the society, in form addressed to the male heads of households, focus on the matters of most importance for social life: relations between generations within the family, the sanctity of human life, the sanctity of (patriarchal) marriage, the inviolability of movable property, dealings with other heads of household, and the inalienability of the members of households and the principal instruments of economic viability (ox and ass) as well as the house (or whole estate) itself (Exod. 20:12–17). Of those six principles of social policy governing relations within the society, all but (perhaps) "thou shall not murder" protect the continuing viability of the family/household. Unless the prohibition of coveting the "house" was understood in a comprehensive sense (the entire family holdings of land, animals, and other belongings), then none of these covenantal principles actually mention the family land itself. However, that is probably because it was understood as inalienable as the family inheritance, with God as the true landowner (see Leviticus 25, esp. 25:23).

We cannot move very far into a discussion of the implication of Israelite traditions for family life in Galilean towns and villages, however, without considering the orientation of our literary sources. We have virtually no sources from the Galilean villagers themselves, except for what can be deduced from archaeological explorations. The principal literary sources for family and community affairs in Galilee or in Judaism inclusive of Galilee, moreover, the Torah and rabbinic literature, express the interests and concerns of Jerusalem-based priestly and scribal classes or of rabbinic circles still oriented toward the now-idealized Temple, at least into tannaitic times.[31]

Once we attempt more precise historical and sociological analysis of Galilee, however, it becomes problematic to use the miscellaneous legal materials of Deuteronomy 18–25, for example, as source for life in Galilee in the first century. The Deuteronomic legal code is presumed to have taken shape toward the end of the Davidic monarchy in Judah and (perhaps) to have become state law under Josiah at the end of the seventh century B.C.E. Once incorporated into the Torah, it would appear to have functioned as part of the Judean state law before long into second-temple times. In Judean village communities, therefore, the Deuteronomic code may well have effectively displaced or at least overlaid earlier laws and customs, such as those reflected in the covenant code of Exodus 21–23. Galilee, however, had been independent of the monarchic or second-temple state in Jerusalem from before the time of the "Deuteronomic reform" of the seventh century, coming back under Jerusalem control only at the end of the second-temple period (as noted above). Quite aside from not knowing much of anything about Galilean life under the Assyrian, Persian, and Hellenistic empires, we have little indication of the degree or way in which the Deuteronomic code may have come to affect Galilean village interaction. If the Torah, including the Deuteronomic code, was being observed as state law in Galilee under the Hasmoneans and Herod, then would it have just begun having an effect on Galilee similar to its effect on Judea several centuries earlier? And what would that effect have been?

Weber, one of whose special areas of attention was the law, noted that the Deuteronomic code accorded the father of the family a good deal less authority than did the original covenantal code. This was apparently part of a general design in the Deuteronomic legislation to reduce the power of local kinship and local authority in the interest of enhancing the centralized authority of the monarchy. Extended kinship connections and family authority were weakened. The central authority still depended on the local village elders to administer justice, but reduced their political functions as the monarchy (and later the temple-state) extended its political control into local community life.[32] Even the laws regarding sexual relations (e.g., adultery and rape) in Deuteronomy 18–25 can be understood as weakening local solidarity and authority, particularly those other than the basic marital bond that could be the basis of a loyalty alternative to the monarchy/temple-state. If the Deuteronomic code functioned as "state law" in the temple-state, then how is it useful as a source? For Galilee, apparently not as a window onto customs (except at historical points prior to its codification many centuries before), since Deuteronomy had exercised an effect in Galilee only since the Hasmonean takeover in 104 b.c.e. But if it was part of the "laws of the Judeans" that the Hasmoneans brought to Galilee, then it may have had the effect in Galilee in the first century that it had in Judea centuries before, reinforcing certain Israelite traditions indigenous to Galilee and shaping family and village life according to the concerns of the Jerusalem-based Hasmonean and Herodian state.

An interrelated factor that should be considered is that the dominant institutions of a society, in the case of Judea the Temple and priesthood, affect the local institutions such as family, especially over a sustained period of time. The temple-community, with priestly rank and prerogatives figuring prominently at the center of the society, including the male-only participants in certain cultic activities, could have made Judean and rabbinic family life more androcentric than Galilean family life, in which the Temple and priesthood would have dominated less intensively and for a far shorter period of time.[33] Similarly, since the monarchy that adopted Deuteronomic legislation and the later temple-state did not impact the Galilean peasantry so strongly for so long, is it possible that the old clan solidarity persisted in Galilee, perhaps as one of the ways in which Galileans could maintain their cultural solidarity over against a succession of foreign imperial regimes?

The problems with rabbinic literature as sources for Galilean village life are similar. The Mishnah, by and large, attests the situation after the destruction of Jerusalem and the Temple. As noted above, only certain types of material in the Mishnah, such as case laws, may be viable reflections of social life in Galilee.[34] Besides the idealizing orientation of its promulgators, the sages whose opinions are cited indicate explicitly that there is a discrepancy between their rulings and popular practices. Nevertheless, it may be possible to make extrapolations from rabbinic rulings and opinions if we allow for the difference in social location and cultural background.[35] Most directly useful, of course, are cases in which they refer to local folklore or customs. With these qualifications in mind, pending a fuller critical "ethnography" of Galilean life in antiquity, we can make a few observations focused on the gendered roles and relationships key to the reproduction of the family so central to traditional agrarian life in Galilee.[36]

To maintain the family on its land as a viable economic unit, biblical law-codes stipulate patrilineal inheritance by primogeniture, the first-born son inheriting twice as much as any brothers (Deut. 21:17). In the absence of a son, then the daughter would inherit, followed by the brother and father's brother (Num. 27:8–11). It seems likely that this custom pertained in Galilee, considering the circumstances and motives indicated at the opening of Jesus' parable of "the Prodigal Son" (Luke 15:11–32). The traditional Israelite *mishpahah* (clan) was normally endogamous, in order to preserve Israel's system of land tenure (Num. 36:1–12; cf. 27:1–11). Similar concerns to preserve the families of particular villages on their ancestral land would presumably have been expressed in customs regulating or influencing marriage patterns. Marriages among families and villages, of course, would have helped cement relations within and across villages.

Women's sexuality, or more broadly, their fecundity, was the principal resource for families' reproduction. Because the social structure was patriarchal, authority over this precious resource was vested in the fathers/husbands of the families. Both the young woman's potential fruitfulness and the authority of the father can be seen in a rabbinic "parable":

> an unripe fig, a ripening fig, and a fully ripe fig. "An unripe fig" — while she is yet a child [under twelve]. "A ripening fig" — refers to the days of her pubescence. In both her father has the right to anything she finds and to [the products of] her labor and to annul her vows. "A fully ripe fig" — after she has become mature [twelve and a half], her father no longer has dominion over her. (*m. Nid.* 5:7; cf. *m. Ketub.* 4:4.)

That the father represents the family, including the girl, is seen in rulings regarding seduction or rape: the penalties for damage, pain, and shame are paid to the father and are assessed according to his social standing (*m. Ketub.* 3:4–7). The value placed on the full potential fertility of the young woman can be seen in the different price of the marriage contract for a virgin (200 zuz) compared with that for a widow (100 zuz).

Despite the value placed on the potential fertility (sexuality) of the daughter, which was placed in no uncertain terms under the power of her father, she was of less value than a son (Sir. 22:3, 42:9–14). Although there was likely less of a discrepancy among the villagers than among sages and later rabbis, the ruling of the latter that a father was liable for the maintenance of a son but not that of a daughter (*m. Ketub.* 4:6) likely reflects traditional patriarchal values common in the heritage of Israel. And when it came to sending out a family member to help pay off debts — given the value placed on preserving the family on its land over the "rights" of an individual — a daughter would become the debt-slave, not the son in whom the continuity of the family was vested (*m. Ketub.* 3:8). The father's control over the minor daughter, finally, included the power to arrange her marriage — that is if he did so before she "came of age" at twelve and a half.

A young woman passed from the control of her father to that of her husband. The patriarchal family's, as represented by the husband's, vested interest in the potential of her fertility to reproduce the family took precedence over any competing interest, including her own. Thus the wife's sexuality is, in effect, the husband's private preserve, instrumental to the perpetuation of his family (by his paternity), and subject to his exclusive use and authority. On the other hand, as seen in rabbinic rulings governing the marriage contract, the wife had certain customary rights in the marriage, such as the return of the value of her "dowry" from her husband's (family's) estate in the case of divorce or widowhood, the maintenance of her sons and daughters from their father's estate if she predeceased him, and her own maintenance as a widow so long as she remained in his house (*m. Ketub.* 4.7–12).[37] All resources and their use, however, fell under the final authority of the male head of household. Even whatever inheritance the woman brought into the marriage with her, its use or produce came under his control (*m. Ketub.* 6:1).[38]

According to the Mishnah, the basic division of labor was inside-outside, within the house for her, outside in the fields and interaction with other heads of household for him. He raised the crops, she prepared the food. He brought materials, she processed them and made the clothing.

> These are the kinds of labor which a woman performs for her husband: she grinds flour, bakes bread, does laundry, prepares meals, feeds her child, makes the bed, works in wool.... And how much work does she do for him? The weight of five *selas* or warp must she spin for him in Judea (which is ten *selas* weight in Galilee), or the weight of ten *selas* of woof in Judea (which are twenty *selas* in Galilee). (*m. Ketub.* 5.5, 9; see also *m. Ned.* 7:8)

The division of labor according to specific gender roles, however, was probably not as clear among Galilean peasant families as it was in the rabbis' schematic formulations, even if the latter had some relation to common practices. The customs governing mutual expectations and obligations of husband and wife in the different regions of Galilee, moreover, were likely expressed less in terms of his proprietary rights and her obligations than apparent in rabbinic rulings. At harvest time, for example, all able-bodied adults and children in the family would likely have worked together in the fields, just as families within the village would help each other. Men as well as women, moreover, were involved in such matters as the production of textiles.[39] Productive labor and home (household/family) constituted a closely knit fabric, with no rigid separation of roles.[40]

That there was far less division of labor according to gender and generation among Galilean villagers than among higher-class families is an important reminder not to make too much of the supposedly gender-correlated division between domestic and public life.[41] With more than one family living off of central courtyards, where they shared common ovens and other facilities, it is difficult to find a clear division between private and shared space in Galilean villages. One might argue that much of village-household life was simultaneously public and domestic. The living space of the house was also a work-space for "domestic" production such as crafts and textiles. The family as a domestic unit across gender and generational lines worked together in their ancestral family's fields "in public," particularly at harvest time. Some work for the support of the households, moreover, was done at facilities apparently common to the whole village, such as threshing floors, olive and wine presses, and sites for tanning animal hides situated sufficiently distant from the houses presumably because of the attendant odors. In addition to such common facilities, it is clear from early rabbinic literature that families/households shared the use of (borrowed back and forth) such items as grinding and cooking implements (*m. Šeb.* 5:9; *m. Git.* 5:9).[42] The gendered division of labor was not highly developed in Galilean villages and reciprocal social relations persisted among families in the very structure of daily and yearly local social-economic life.

Since the patriarchal family was the fundamental social form in Galilee and other traditional agrarian societies, we should attend to the potential breakdown of the family as a major factor in social distress and conflict. Families/households had limited resources. As in most peasant societies, the living was barely subsistence for most. Households were economically marginal and susceptible to any disruption in the annual agricultural cycle. In the historical chapters as well as the structural treatments of relations between the Galileans and their rulers above, we have noted several sorts of disruptions that could have a major effect on the economic and social viability of peasant families, from suddenly disruptive military expeditions through their territory to the steady escalation of economic pressure in the form of new demands from additional layers of rulers. Interestingly enough, it is precisely in times of such disruptions, for which we have evidence in Josephus, that overt social conflict erupted in Galilee, whether escalating banditry, peasant strikes, or widespread peasant revolt. In the chapters that follow we can explore successively the economic, political, and cultural dimensions of family/village life, with a look at the few popular movements for which we have evidence in the final chapter.

Chapter 9

GALILEAN VILLAGE ECONOMY AND THE POLITICAL-ECONOMIC STRUCTURE OF ROMAN PALESTINE

❧

How can one become wise who handles the plow?

— JESUS BEN SIRA

While the peasant produces and consumes, the aristocrat does not produce and yet consumes — and generally consumes far more than the peasant.

— JOHN KAUTSKY

The economic life of ancient Galilee, like that of antiquity generally, has often been constructed according to a "market" economy based largely on modern European experience.[1] The fundamental assumption is that of "private property," particularly important with regard to the land, which was supposedly held by "owners" as "private land," including "large estates." Economic life then supposedly proceeded through exchange, to create a "thriving commercial life" involving "wider economic growth" with "better marketing facilities" in which "merchants" and even "small but successful businesses" engaged in "exploiting the larger markets."[2]

On the assumption of a market economy, the principal question with regard to Galilee comes down to whether the local village economy was caught up in the larger market economy and/or was a market economy itself. One approach equivocates: even though the peasants may have "lacked interest in the purely commercial aspects of running a farm," they were "open to the uncertainties of the markets" in which the "more wealthy landowners" had the advantage.[3] Nevertheless, "what was really distinctive about their class was their non-involvement in the larger commercial life of the area."[4]

Another approach projects the market economy not only onto the wider area but directly into the local village economy. Thus, although "Galilee, like Palestine in general, was not primarily commercial," there were "large-scale trade patterns between Galilee and surrounding areas." In particular, "the desire to buy...luxury goods (and the need 'to earn coin to pay Roman taxes')...impelled Galileans to use the bigger city markets on their borders....In return the Galilean farmer could rely on a market for his oil."[5] Even the "internal economy" of the Galilean village, however, was basically a market.[6] "The village markets" were the "main centers for exchange" in which food was "the commodity sold most often," for which "bringing in the produce for sale" was "a complex and expensive business" that involved the hiring of ass-drivers. Also "the villages themselves [were] the centers of production" by craftsmen who had "permanent shops" in the marketplaces and formed "guilds of wool-weavers, bakers," and so on. There were also "service industries" employing moneychangers and scribes. "This was a monetary economy" and "monetarization went very deep: loans, like payments on divorce, were certainly computed and probably paid in coin." Thus "commerce depended heavily on the activities of moneychangers" who worked "once a week in the smallest villages." Since they were used "for loans and sales," scribes also wrote in the marketplaces. Services such as those of barbers, prostitutes, and doctors, finally, were available in the local marketplace.

Rather than assume the modern market-economy model and then "discover" data in our literary and archaeological sources that illustrate it for ancient Galilee,[7] it would make more historical sense to reason dialectically back and forth between an economic model derived from studies of traditional agrarian societies and the literary and other evidence available for ancient Galilee.[8] The rich series of case laws largely from early rabbinic literature (Mishnah and Tosefta) may be used to construct a picture of village economics in circumstances that will not have changed that much from late second-temple times.[9] It makes sense to examine in particular those tractates that deal with the production and consumption of food, including taxation and festivals, and those that deal with disputes that arise primarily in the production process (that is, in the first, second, and fourth divisions: "Seeds" [or Agriculture, *Zera'im*], "Set Feasts" [or Appointed Times, *Mo'ed*], and "Damages" [*Neziqin*]).

The Household and Village Economy

As in any traditional agrarian society, among any peasantry, food was the primary product. Not only was food produced primarily for local consumption, but for family or household consumption. This should be evident in the very origins of our word "economics" in *oikonomia*, "household management," which focused originally especially on the production of crops. The household (with its ox and/or ass) was the fundamental unit of production and consumption. Case laws in the Mishnah assume that most families produce most of their own needs, raising grapes for wine and olives for oil as well as grain, not that each farmer specializes in one crop and

then enters "the market" to trade for other staples. The assumption behind the laws on the location of threshing floors is that each farmer or
household threshes its own grain (*m. B. Bat.* 2:8). Indeed most of the civil
law in the Mishnah and Tosefta, especially in the tractates of the division
concerning "Damages" (*Neziqin*), concerns behavior of and relations between ordinary "heads of households" and/or what they are responsible
for (e.g., oxen) while engaged in the processes of raising crops and maintaining a household. There was very little specialization and division of
labor, even according to gender-specific tasks. What division there was lay
largely within the family insofar (for example) as women may have done
relatively more of the weaving and men more of the plowing (e.g., *m. Ketub.* 5:9, with the critical reading suggested in chapter 8). Families did their
own building and made their own clothing, although there were apparently
specialists in weaving and carpentry, especially in larger towns. Archaeological field surveys have found only minor variation in the size of individual
plots. This relative uniformity in families' holdings suggests a limited economic stratification among villagers (no extremely wealthy villagers) and a
relative uniformity of land use.[10]

The interactions and transactions between households and/or individuals which corresponded to such production primarily for local/familial use
were thus not those of monetarized exchange, but primarily those that arise
in the production process: borrowing and lending of produce or animals or
labor, hiring of temporary help, leasing of land, compensating for damages done by draft animals to crops or humans, finding lost objects, and
building-maintenance problems of shared courtyards and adjacent houses.
A few illustrative citations may help sketch the picture.

> The four primary causes of injury are the ox and the pit and the crop-
> destroying beast, and the outbreak of fire. (*m. B. Qam.* 1:1)

> If a man stacked his sheaves in his fellows' field without permission and the
> cattle of the owner of the field consumed them, the owner of the field is not
> culpable. (*m. B. Qam.* 6:3)

> A man may say to his fellow, "Help me to weed and I will help thee to
> weed"...but he may not say "Help me to weed and I will help thee to
> hoe..." (*m. B. Meṣ.* 5:10).

> It is usury when a man lends two seahs of wheat for three. (*m. B. Meṣ.* 5:1;
> note the loan in kind, and compare the 50 percent interest on grain here
> with the 25 percent on grain and 100 percent on oil in the parable of the
> "dishonest steward" in Luke 16:1–7)

> The creditor may not dwell without charge in the debtor's courtyard or hire
> it from him at a reduced rate, since that counts as usury. (*m. B. Meṣ.* 5:2)

The owner may lend his tenants wheat to be repaid in kind, if it is for sowing, but not if it is for food. (*m. B. Meṣ.* 5:8)

If a man hired an ass to drive it through hill country....If a man hired a heifer to plough....If a man hired laborers...(then what are they entitled to eat and what must he provide; *m. B. Meṣ.* 6:2–3; 7:1–8).

If a man borrowed a cow....If a man took a cow in exchange for an ass....If a man leased a field...(*m. B. Meṣ.* 8:1–4; 9:1–10)

If a house and an upper room belonging to two persons fell down...
(*m. B. Meṣ.* 10:1–3)

If two jointholders would make a partition in a courtyard...(*m. B. Bat.* 1:1)

None may dig a cistern near his fellow's cistern...(*m. B. Bat.* 2:1)

Title by usucaption (several years' use) to houses, cisterns,...dovecots,... olive presses, irrigated fields...(*m. B. Bat.* 3:1–5)

As seen through the laws generated with regard to village economic affairs, the economic life of a village involved a great variety of interactions among persons, households, and/or their animals, fields, and houses. The focus of economic activity was clearly the production of food, household by household, but involved a number of potential interactions of assistance, borrowing, and contingencies. Housing maintenance was another principal concern clearly involving close interaction with other households.

Although they would not have been major aspects of the village economy, there clearly were some production for exchange and some exchange relations. The production of pottery, for example, depended on availability of the right kind of clay. Hence pottery would have been produced at sites where appropriate clay was at hand, and not in every town or village. Archaeological evidence suggests that a distinctive style of pottery became widespread in Galilee and even the Golan in the second century, although the amount of a particular kind of pottery found in a given locality varied with the distance from the site of production because of the high cost of overland transport. Much of the pottery used in Galilee and even in the Golan was apparently produced at two villages, Kefar Shikhin, adjacent to Sepphoris, and Kefar Hananyah, centrally located between Lower and Upper Galilee.[11]

Because of the special contingencies inherent in the production of pottery, of course, we cannot generalize from its distribution pattern to a general "trading network." In fact, archaeological evidence does not tell us whether the distribution of special products such as pottery was by "marketing" or "ordered" directly from producers by those in need of them or perhaps was "managed" somehow by the government. Mishnaic rulings about liability between two "pot-sellers" and pots broken by a cow in a courtyard suggest that the selling, if not the production, of pots was local and small-scale (*m. B. Qam.* 3:4, 5:2). Archaeological evidence that the amount of pottery from Kefar Hananyah found in various sites varied inversely by the distance from the site of production would seem to work decisively against the hypothesis of Sepphoris and Tiberias serving as central markets for Galilee. Rabbinic references indicate that the potters themselves sold their own wares directly to the buyers.[12] The "peddlars" active in Galilee were apparently not the means by which basic products such as pottery were "marketed," but they carried specialized lightweight items such as cosmetics and spinning goods to women in outlying settlements.[13]

Most clothing would have been made within the household, although there was some specialized weaving and dyeing, apparently in villages (*t. B. Meṣ.* 11.24). It is difficult to judge from the law whether the local tanneries belonged to households specializing in that activity or were shared village installations (25 meters from, and to the east of each village) where each household did its tanning (*m. B. Bat.* 2:9). The village of Amki in western Galilee was known for the shoes made there (*m. Kelim* 26:1). In any case, except for such items as pottery or metal objects, it seems likely that most things needed in a village or household were locally made.

Shopkeepers there were, but apparently little of what was produced, bartered, bought and sold, and consumed or used passed through their hands. The placement and operation of their shops had to yield to the rights and "quality of life" of other householders (e.g., *m. B. Bat.* 2:3). International trade routes passed through Galilee. But the transit trade was primarily in luxury goods for the benefit of the ruling elite of the imperial cities, with some probably destined for the elite of Sepphoris and Tiberias as well. This transit trade had little or no relation to the village economy. Even small- or medium-scale merchants or middlemen seldom appear in the Mishnaic rulings (e.g., *m. B. Meṣ.* 4:11; *m. B. Bat.* 5:8). Judging from early rabbinic laws, moreover, the economy appears far from monetarized. Most "deposits" appear to have been goods, not money, and, whether goods or money, were left with fellow villagers, although money was occasionally left with moneychangers (possibly in large towns only; *m. B. Meṣ.* 3:4–12). The local economy was apparently not heavily monetarized. For example, nearly all leasing of fields was for a percentage or an amount of the crop, with rental for money clearly being an exception (*m. B. Meṣ.* 9:1–7).

Little information is (yet) available regarding any specialization of agricultural production in Galilee.[14] Much has been made of a supposedly large volume of export of olive oil from Upper Galilee into Syria and beyond on the basis of Josephus's report of John of Gischala's entrepreneurial activity (*B.J.* 2.590–92).[15] It is hardly appropriate, however, to make such a generalization on the basis of a sharply polemical account of what were special circumstances. In the parallel but very different account (*Vita* 74–75) Josephus writes that John was supplying pure oil only to the Judeans of Caesarea Philippi who had been confined to the city amid the turmoil of the revolt of 66–67. Upper Galilee may well have produced more oil than needed for local consumption. Archaeological finds in one area of the lower Golan suggests that villagers there may have produced oil in abundance but not much wine, apparently being involved in a certain amount of "trade" for essentials.[16] It is also possible that such specialization was done at the behest of rulers or holders of large estates. In any case, whatever its olive production, Upper Galilee also produced a "surplus" of the principal staple, grain, for there were storage depots of imperial grain in the villages (*Vita* 71).

That last bit of information Josephus supplies, however, points to what was the major factor in the Galilean or any traditional agrarian or peasant economy: the economic demands made by the rulers and/or landlords. This is precisely what we may obscure or miss completely when we impose a market model onto such a traditional agrarian economy.[17] Hence this is what we must explore, despite the fragmentary evidence available, if we want to understand the economic circumstances of Galilean villagers.

Political Economic Relations and Land Tenure

The Question of Large Estates

In a traditional agrarian society, the economy depends primarily on production from the land. In order to maintain their positions of power and privilege, the nonproductive aristocracy and/or rulers had to organize production in such a way that they could extract a "surplus" from the labor of the producers (over and above what was necessary for the subsistence living of the producers themselves). In "classical" Greece and Rome, much of the production was done by slaves. In the late Roman republic and early empire, wealthy and powerful Romans had gained huge estates or *latifundia*, which were farmed by tenants or slaves (thousands of whom had been taken from Galilee in the series of Roman conquests and reconquests, as noted in chapters 2 and 3). There is no evidence, however, that any appreciable amount of production in Galilee was done by slaves. The other principal means by which the elite of ancient agrarian societies extracted economic production from the producers was taxation or rent in various forms. Tribute, tithes, taxes, rents, interest on debts — all involved certain claims on the produce of the land (and the labor of the producers).[18] These claims were the major factor determining the lives of villagers in ancient Galilee or Judea. Thus, in order to understand the relations of the Galilean peasants to the land they worked, we must set aside our assumptions about private property and (an industrialized) capitalist economy and recognize the fundamental structure, the basic political-economic(-religious) relations of an ancient society such as that in Palestine.

The Israelite clans and tribes may have begun as a free peasantry, independent of the overlords or rulers to which peasants are ordinarily subjected. Even then, however, the people did not themselves "own" the land individually. As elsewhere in the ancient Near East, the land belonged to the god(s) and was used by the people who then owed certain "offerings" or "rents" to their "lord." Biblical texts (perhaps somewhat idealizing) understood the land as occupied, used, and held in trust as an inalienable inheritance, by the particular lineages of the people, which in turn were broken down into families. This can be seen in the division and assignment of land to the people in Joshua 14–19, where many of the village names are also names of lineages or clans (see Joshua 19 for the tribes of Zebulun, Issachar, Asher, and Naphtali in Galilee). This understanding of the land as God's grant held in trust by lineages and families is also vividly expressed in the priestly statement of the Israelite covenantal mechanisms designed to maintain the people on their family inheritance of land in Leviticus 25.

Since at least Solomon, however, Israel was ruled by a monarchy or high priesthood/temple (or foreign imperial regime) which, as regent for God (or by virtue of conquest), laid claim to the land, its produce, and thus apparently also (the labor of) its inhabitants. Thus Solomon not only claimed a certain percentage of the produce of the land and people to support the lavish lifestyle of his court in Jerusalem, but he also imposed a levy of "forced labor" on Israelites, as well as his Canaanite subjects, in order to build the temple, his palaces, fortresses, and storehouses (1 Kings 4–5). The extent of the ruler's power over land and people is illustrated by the way in which Solomon solved his "balance of payments" with Hiram, king of Tyre, who had supplied "technical assistance" as well as materials for Solomon's massive building projects such as the Temple: Solomon simply ceded to Hiram "twenty towns in the land of Galilee," peasants included.

This political-economic(-religious) system then resulted in certain variations on the peasants' precise relationship to their lord(s) and land. Samuel's warning to the Israelites about "the ways" of the king for which they were clamoring (1 Sam. 8:11–18) provides a window onto how the system worked in particular concrete relations. Some of the land was claimed directly by the ruler — originally probably land of the Canaanite city-states or petty kings conquered by David — and this "royal land" was worked by peasants who had little or no "rights" of their own vis-à-vis the ruler. Next, the ruler could expropriate land ("the best of your fields and vineyards and olive orchards") from his subjects. Like the "royal land," this could then be assigned to his courtiers and officers as the source of their income. Anthropologists and economic historians would call this "prebendal domain."

The peasants on such land, however, would not necessarily be displaced but could become subject, at least temporarily and with regard to a percentage of (the fruits of) their labor, to a royal family member or officer, remaining ultimately subject to the king. Finally, the vast majority of the peasantry, remaining on their traditional family inheritance, was subject to the tithes or taxes taken by the ruler (such as grain, wine, and flocks) who used this produce to support his court, bureaucracy, and army. The dynamics of the system were such that even these peasants who retained traditional rights to the land could fall under the power and further exploitation of the royal officer in their area when they experienced repeatedly bad harvests (and/or high taxes) and fell heavily into debt to the regional officer in charge of the royal storage facilities.

This system remained in force from Solomon through second-temple times and was continued by the Romans even after the destruction of the Jerusalem temple.[19] The story of Naboth's vineyard attests the expropriation of traditional family inheritances by Ahab and Jezebel in the kingdom of Israel (1 Kings 19). The "reform" Nehemiah carried out indicates that, based on their privileges as rulers of the second-temple Judea, certain powerful priestly families brought ordinary Judeans under their power through the debt mechanism (Neh. 5:1–10). Certain areas remained "royal land" from David through the various empires and continued under the Hasmoneans, Herod, and the Romans. An additional possibility, or a variation on the system, may have been introduced by Alexander the Great and his successor Hellenistic rulers who founded several cities around the perimeter of Galilee. It is still unclear whether peasants and villages on the land (*chōra*) of a city resembled peasants and villages on royal land or perhaps had moved in the direction of the essentially private property that had emerged in Greece and Rome and been imposed at some point in the Hellenistic or Roman period.

The question is, then, which of the variations of these overlapping claims on the land and peasant labor and produce were operative in Galilee in late second-temple times, and what other claims on the land and producers' labor had been imposed in the course of Hasmonean, Herodian, and Roman rule in Galilee?[20] The older debate, in somewhat vague terms, about whether Galilee was dominated by "large estates" or "large (absentee) land-owners" can appropriately be shifted to more precise terms. The most likely possibilities, other than freeholders subject to claims by various rulers, would appear to be royal estates (including land granted to royal officers) worked by tenants, city land worked by peasants whose status was somewhat unclear, and land and peasants over which powerful figures (such as prominent priests, Herodian families, or royal officers) had gained control, perhaps through the debt mechanism.[21]

Were Parts of Galilee Royal Estates?

That so much royal land or royal estates can be documented in Judea and Samaria and the Great Plain and east of the Sea of Galilee (Batanea, Gaulanitis, and Trachonitis) but not in Galilee is surely a reliable indicator that very little Galilean territory had become royal land.[22] Without pretending to make a complete survey of the many royal estates in Palestine, we can examine evidence that sheds light on the situation in Galilee.

With regard to large tracts of royal land, the positive evidence for Judea and the Great Plain and the negative evidence for Galilee are explainable historically: royal land was ordinarily taken over by one regime from another — Herod from the Hasmoneans from the Seleucids from the Ptolemies from the Persians, and so on — and virtually the whole Great Plain and the large tracts of royal land around Jericho and in the coastal plain in Judea had been royal land for centuries. Galilee had nothing corresponding to those rich and productive agricultural lands that had traditionally been directly under royal control.

Historical reasons would also explain why, at the end of the second-temple period, royal estates were most extensive in Judea proper. The royal land around Jericho consisted primarily of an extensive (eleven miles long), world-famous balsam plantation (Strabo, *Geogr.* 16.2.41). Since balsam grew only here in the Jordan valley and in Egypt and the dates were among the finest in the world, this plantation must have been highly profitable as well. The Hasmoneans, who built a winter palace nearby, probably took the plantation over from the Seleucids, whose predecessors the Ptolemies must have taken it over from the Persian regime (Theophrastus, *Historia Plantarum* 9.6.1–4, who uses the Persian loan-word *paradeisoi*). After the Roman general Mark Anthony gave them to Cleopatra, Herod leased them and later apparently took full control, since Archelaus, his son and successor in Judea, rebuilt the royal palace at Jericho and extended the palm groves around Archelais, which then passed to Herod's sister Salome, who bequeathed them to the empress Livia (*B.J.* 1.361–62; *Ant.* 15.96, 17.340, 18.31). In the coastal plain, the land around Lydda was ceded to the Hasmoneans by the Seleucid Demetrius I and the Romans confirmed Hasmonean possession (1 Macc. 11:34; *Ant.* 14.204). After Hasmonean conquest and temporary Roman "liberation," Azotus and Yavneh and the surrounding lands were possessed by Herod, who bequeathed them to Salome, who passed Yavneh on to Livia (*Ant.* 17.321, 18.31; cf. 18:158).

The Great Plain (of Esdraelon) just to the south of Galilee had also traditionally been royal land, apparently since conquered by David. It was intensively exploited by the Ptolemies' extraordinarily efficient royal administration in the third century. The Hasmonean high priests also treated it as royal land and Julius Caesar confirmed Hyrcanus II in the same rights as his forefathers had possessed over "the villages of the Great Plain" (*Ant.*

14.207). Herod founded a colony of cavalrymen at Gaba, toward the western end, for security purposes (*Ant.* 15.294; *B.J.* 3.36; cf. *Vita* 115). In 6 C.E., when the Romans deposed Archelaus, Herod's successor in Judea and Samaria, they "leased out" (*apodōsomenos*) his "house" or "property" (*Ant.* 17.355, 18.2). Yet at the outset of the great revolt in 66–67 we find the villages in the western Great Plain still part of the royal land, "large quantities of grain belonging to Queen Berenice (sister of Agrippa II) having been collected from the neighboring villages and stored in Besara" (*Vita* 118–19). These villages apparently had a different, more direct and complete (economic) subjection to a ruler than did the nearby villages of Galilee from one of which (Dabaritta) the brash young men plundered the baggage train of Ptolemy, the royal finance officer (or his wife; *B.J.* 2.595; *Vita* 126). After the Bar Kokhba Revolt, if not before, the Great Plain was used as an economic base for the military camp of the Sixth Roman Legion at Legio.[23]

After John Hyrcanus's conquests of Gerizim and Samaria, the Hasmonean regime, succeeded by Herod, took over certain extensive lands in Samaria. Herod established the military colony of Sebaste with a generous grant of productive land (*B.J.* 1.403; *Ant.* 15.296–98). Herod apparently had much of the rest of Samarian land at his disposal as well. This land he used to support his principal ministers and courtiers, such as Ptolemy, "the most honored" of his inner circle (and eventually his executor), who possessed the village of Arous, which has been identified with the site of the modern village of Haris, south of Shechem (*B.J.* 1.667; 3.14, 69; *Ant.* 17.289). Archaeological explorations have found just to the west of Haris/Arous distinctive evidence of other large estates such as at the village of Qawarat Bene Hassan, near which are ancient towers and storehouses still known by the Arabs as the "Citadel of Herod" (*Qal'at Firdus*) and "the ruin of Herod" (*Hirbet Firdusi*). The same archaeological explorations found that the extensive series of towers in western Samaria were apparently used in agriculture and fit a pattern of managed land use.[24] These might well be further royal estates dating from Ptolemaic or Hasmonean times. Finally, in Samaria and perhaps northern Judea as well, because of its associations with the Hasmoneans in Talmudic literature, the "king's mountain country" (*har ha-melek*) would appear to have contained royal estates. In any case, the Hasmoneans and Herod added extensive territory (and villages) to the royal land from which they extracted revenues themselves or used as grants of land-with-peasants to support their high officials and family members.[25] Whether from literary sources or archaeological explorations, however, we find nothing in Galilee similar to these royal estates taken over or established by the Hasmoneans or Herod in Samaria.

Once Caesar Augustus gave him the territories to the east of Galilee and Gaulanitis (*Ant* 15.343–48; *B.J.* 1.398–99), Herod established a military colony of 3,000 Idumeans in Trachonitis to help restrain the brigands in the area (*Ant* 16.284–85). He further settled a military colony of Babylonian Jews in Batanaea, originally free of taxation and, even when taxed by Herod's successors, still having their "freedom" in the sense that the villagers were not totally subjected to the ruler in the same way as villagers on royal land (*Ant.* 17.23–25). Josephus mentions each of these foundations because they were unique instances. Hence we should not imagine that any similar removal of population or colonization took place in Galilee under Herod. The case of the Babylonian Jews in Batanaea, however, helps make clear the distinction between these and other ordinary subjects of the rulers, who retain a certain "freedom," and people on royal land, who lack certain traditional political and economic rights.

The foundation of Tiberias by Antipas might appear to indicate that this area of Galilee generally was royal land insofar as some settlers were forcibly brought to the new foundation and some were "not clearly free" (trusting Josephus's report, *Ant.* 18.37). It is possible that some of the settlers were former royal peasants; there were royal estates in Perea subject to Antipas. But there is no indication that prior to Antipas Galilee had been royal land, and it seems unlikely that its status changed with its assignment to him. Moreover, whatever the unfree status of some of the settlers, Antipas both freed them and gave them land (*Ant.* 18.38).

Under Antipas's successors, the Agrippas, there is evidence of royal land given as prebendal domain[26] to high royal officials, continuing the pattern familiar from Solomon to Herod (e.g., the village of Ptolemy, Herod's finance minister, "friend," and executor, *B.J.* 2.69; *Ant.* 17.289). When he arrived in Galilee in 66, Josephus found "Crispus, formerly prefect under the great king [Agrippa I] absent on his estates beyond the Jordan" (*Vita* 33). Also, Philip son of Jacimus, Agrippa II's prefect and military commander, had villages assigned to him near the fortress-town Gamala, villages clearly different from his native village in Batanaea (*Vita* 47; *Ant.* 17.29–30). That in both cases these lands/villages assigned to royal officers are "beyond the Jordan" in Gaulanitis, however, leads one to believe that Antipas and his successors did not (or could not) use Galilean lands/villages as royal land for the support of high officials.

After the Roman reconquest of Palestine in 67–70, Galilee as a whole was apparently not taken as imperial land, as explained in chapter 4. Recent scholarly inclination is to read Josephus's report that Vespasian instructed his Roman officers to "dispose of [*apodōsthai*] all the land of the Judeans" as "his own country" (*chōra*) (*B.J.* 7.216–17) as referring only to the land of the insurrectionaries.[27] It would thus appear likely that some, but by no means all the Galilean *chōra* was confiscated as royal land. Some early rabbinic texts refer to people who had to lease their ancestral holdings from foreigners. Certain *midrashim*, moreover, provide evidence that the unprecedented figures of the *matziqim*, "harassers," who are either Roman officers or (absentee) Roman aristocrats, were levying exactions or in other ways controlling land and people. Apparently, however, the land could be recovered by the original possessors or their successors.²⁸ Moreover, early rabbinic literature does not reflect the closer supervision by a representative of the Roman governor one would expect if considerable Galilean land had been operated as imperial estates.²⁹ Mishnaic rulings assume that households farming their own family inheritance was the usual situation in the second century. However, the indications that some Galilean territory was taken as royal land after the great revolt only points up all the more the paucity of evidence of royal estates in Galilee prior to the revolt.

The question of "large land–owners" can be reconsidered in connection with land possessed or controlled directly by the Judean royal and/or priestly state. As noted in the cases of Herod's sister Salome and his minister Ptolemy and the later Herodian prefects Crispus and Philip son of Jacimus, one of the principal dispositions of royal land was as economic support for the officers and family members of the ruler. It seems likely that to a considerable extent the evidence for "large land–owners" coincides with that for just this disposition of royal land. Given the particular political-economic structure of ancient Palestine, those who were wealthy and powerful occupied particular positions in that system. In fact, virtually the only way to become wealthy was by holding some position of political(-religious) power. The people or families who held — and were able to enjoy the income from — large tracts of land and the villagers' labor that went with it were either royal family members or high royal officials or Jerusalem priests, usually of high-priestly families.

We can see how the system worked when Herod took over from the Hasmoneans. He simply killed the Hasmonean family and officers, expropriated their land and property, and then granted his own family members and high-ranking officers various estates (*B.J.* 1.358; *Ant.* 15.5–6, 17.305–7). It seems likely that, after he murdered the last Hasmonean high priest, he would also have provided the new high priests he brought from Babylon and Egypt with estates near Jerusalem. After Herod died and his son Archelaus was deposed in Judea, the Romans apparently allowed both a number of Herodians other than the ones who became ethnarchs or kings (and presumably the four principal high-priestly families as well) to retain their estates as the continuing basis of their wealth and power. Some of them — for example, Saul and Costobar, who like some of the high priests had their own private "goon squads" — were active in trying to suppress the revolt in the summer of 66 and then fled Jerusalem (*B.J.* 2.418; *Ant.* 20.214). That other such "nobles" were so consistently under attack by the Zealots proper, peasants-turned-brigands from northwest Judea, may indicate that these Herodians held land precisely in that area (*B.J.* 4.140–41, and so on).³⁰

The phenomenon of "large land–owners" is thus a function of the fundamental political-economic structure outlined above, and many of the "estates" were held in grant from the ruler in Jerusalem. Most of the evidence for such "landowners" and estates, however, locates them not in Galilee but in Judea, Samaria, the coastal plain, the Great Plain, or the *har ha-melek* — again what we would expect considering that they are so closely tied in with the royal land, which was concentrated in those areas.[31] Even much of the rabbinic evidence for large estates controlled by certain early rabbis themselves pertains to Judea, not Galilee; for example, Gamaliel II, Tarfon, and Eleazar ben Harsum held large estates (*m. B. Meṣd.* 5:8; *t. Ketub.* 5.1; *y. Taʻan.* 4.69a; *b. Yoma* 35b). As noted just above, even Herodian officers who lived in the capital city of Galilee, such as Crispus in Tiberias, had their estates not in Galilee itself, but across the Jordan in Gaulanitis (*Vita* 33). The only case of such an estate to have been located supposedly in Galilee, that of Beth Anath known from the Zenon papyri in the Ptolemaic period, is placed there not by the literary or archaeological evidence itself, but by modern scholarly interpretation.[32] Alternative reading of the evidence now places Beth Anath in Samaria to the east of Caesarea.[33] It may well be that, during the course of the intensive economic pressures on the Galilean peasantry in the first century C.E., Herodian officers or rulers attained control of lands particularly in Lower Galilee (the estate of a "king" [Agrippa II?] in Shikhin, *t. Šabb.* 13[14].9). Certainly some of the most prominent rabbis of the third century are portrayed as having extensive fields between Sepphoris and Tiberias.[34] At the beginning of the first century C.E., however, there is no evidence for "royal estates" in Galilee.

Were Parts of Galilee Land that Belonged to a City?

It is most unlikely that any sections of Lower Galilee were transformed into the land (*chōra*) of a city on the pattern of independent Hellenistic cities such as Tyre as long as the Romans kept the Herodian rulers in place. We read frequently of "the *chōra*/villages of Tyre" (e.g., *B.J.* 2.588) and of "the villages of Gadara and Hippos," cities in the Decapolis across the lake (*Vita* 42; cf. "the villages of Caesarea Philippi," Mark 8:27). We may presume that the villages on "the land of Scythopolis" (*B.J.* 4.453) just south of Galilee were subordinated to that city in a similar way. Although cities were established around the periphery of Galilee, however, there were none in Galilee itself until Antipas. Sepphoris had been simply an administrative town under the Hasmoneans and Herod. Sepphoris was rebuilt and Tiberias built by Antipas as capital cities from which to rule his tetrarchy or "kingdom," not founded as independent Hellenistic *poleis*.[35] Although he once uses the phrase "their *chōra*" when writing about the Tiberians, Josephus never refers to areas of Galilee as "the *chōra* of" Tiberias or Sepphoris or Gabara. It is always "the villages around Tiberias" or "all the villages and countrytowns around" Gabara or "Sepphoris having many villages around it" (*Vita* 129, 346; *B.J.* 3.132). Thus the villages in Lower Galilee were subject to the jurisdiction of the tetrarch or "king" such as Antipas or the Agrippas who ruled from the cities of Sepphoris or Tiberias, but they were not made into the *chōra* of a city.[36] The situation in the generations just after the Roman reconquest of Galilee in 67 is not clear. Eventually nearly all villages in Galilee would have come under the jurisdiction of one of the cities in accordance with the policy of the later empire.[37] But Galilean villages were not part of the *chōra* of a city in late second-temple (early Roman) times.

Land Controlled by Royal Officers or Priests

Probably only the highest royal officials and/or special family members and a few key high-priestly families received grants of land or estates. The Hasmoneans, Herod, and Herod's successors most likely supported their other officers and courtiers out of their general revenues. Powerful people, whether vested with estates from the ruler or not, however, were in a position to gain control over land and those who worked it. This worked primarily through the debt mechanism. State officials, including priestly officers of the temple-state, had access to resources.[38] Even commanding officers of garrisons along the frontier may have been in a strategic position, since they were likely in charge of tax collection and storage depots in the district under their oversight. Peasants in need, quickly exhausting the limited resources of their neighbors, sought loans from those with access to resources, for example, the wealthy and powerful. We can imagine that even middle-level officers in charge of a district or wealthy priestly families could gradually acquire control over lands and/or their produce by virtue of their access to resources by making loans to desperate peasants.[39] Certainly already wealthy and powerful figures could expand the land and labor they controlled by this means. One wonders just how the priestly family of Josephus himself came to have such extensive holdings of land near Jerusalem (*Vita* 422).

This more dynamic and contingent relationship among the peasant producer, the land, and the creditor-landlord would have developed in Galilee as well as in Judea. Under the Hasmoneans, then under Herod and his descendants Antipas and Agrippa, some officials would have been successful in gaining control of a certain amount of land and its produce by means of loans and the peasants' spiraling indebtedness. But they would not have been a "landed aristocracy" in the sense that they held independent ownership of land or in the sense that Alexander Janneus had granted his officers in charge of fortresses (e.g., at Sepphoris or Gischala or Jotapata) estates as their own land.[40] Nor would these landholders have been a *Galilean* aristocracy. Once Herod was appointed "king of the Judeans" by the Roman Senate, some of these Hasmonean "aristocrats" saw exactly where their self-interest lay and went over to Herod (*B.J.* 1.291; cf. 303; *Ant.* 14.395; cf. 413). Their exploitation of their political-economic position, however, and not simply their going over to Herod, is likely to have been the reason that these nobles (*dynatoi*) were drowned in the lake by the Galileans (*B.J.* 1.326; *Ant.* 14.450).

From several parables in the synoptic Gospel tradition it seems clear that Galileans were familiar with just such a relationship between creditor and debtor, including the predatory, usurious practices of the creditors (royal officers).[41] In the parable of the unmerciful servant (Matt. 18:23–33), the creditor is explicitly a royal "servant" or officer. "The unjust steward" parable (Luke 16:1–13), besides attesting the standard "manager" (*oikonomos*) in charge, indicates how severe were the "going rates" of interest: 25 percent on grain and 100 percent on oil. The parable of the talents/pounds, in different versions in Matt. 25:14–30 and Luke 19:11–27, hence probably in the Synoptic Sayings Source "Q" (now usually placed in Galilee) is even a transparent allusion to Antipas and his royal officials (note especially their "reward" in Luke's version).[42] Josephus's account of the insurrection led by the popular king Judas son of Hezekiah at the death of Herod in 4 B.C.E. provides further evidence of this economic relationship among producers, land, and creditor-royal officer in Galilee: "Judas got together a large number of desperate men (cf. "those who were indebted..."; 1 Sam. 22:2) at Sepphoris in Galilee and made an assault on the royal palace...and made off with all the goods/property [*chrēmata*] which had been seized there" (*Ant.* 17.271). That same relationship can be discerned behind "the mansion of Jesus, which was a great castle, imposing as a citadel" in Gabara (*Vita* 246). As the third principal "city" of Galilee, and, like Sepphoris and Tiberias, the object of sharp hostility among the Galileans (*Vita* 82, 123–25, 203; cf. Josephus's differentiation of Gabara from Galilee, *Vita* 240), Gabara must have been an administrative town. One suspects that Jesus and/or his father had been a royal officer under Agrippa I and/or Antipas and, like the Herodians in Judea, left to his wealth when the Romans took over direct rule in the area.

The Impact of Rulers' Overlapping Claims on the People's Traditional Rights

There is thus no evidence that large sections of Galilee were either royal land or city land in late second-temple times. The principal way in which a few wealthy and powerful figures would have come into control of a large amount of land, with tenant producers, would have been by using their official positions or wealth to exploit the increasing indebtedness of desperate peasants. This survey of the other principal patterns of peasants' relation to the land and their rulers' demands suggests that Galilean villagers must have been primarily "free" peasants who, on the one hand, held certain traditional rights on the land, but who, on the other hand, owed taxes or tribute to their rulers. A semi-independent peasantry subject to taxes and tribute is the situation presupposed in stories such as Josephus's accounts of the royal and imperial officials worried about their "take" from the next harvest as the peasants sat protesting Gaius's order to place his bust in the temple. This is also the situation presupposed in the synoptic Gospel traditions that portray people in debt, that is, who are not simply sharecroppers but have land and crops on the basis of which they can borrow and which they can lose to their creditors. We have then to examine the various claims on the produce of the Galilean peasantry in order to understand their difficult economic position.

Imperial regimes always claimed tribute from subject peoples, a large part of the purpose of imperial conquest and government. The tightly organized Ptolemaic imperial administration that controlled Palestine during the third century B.C.E. engaged in intensive economic exploitation of the land and people, as evident in the Zenon papyri.[43] As the successor Seleucid regime weakened during the second century and was replaced by the Itureans and finally by the Hasmonean high priesthood in Galilee, we can assume that the peasantry became free of imperial tribute — as it was replaced by Iturean and Hasmonean claims. The Romans, however, reinstituted the tribute and, during the first decades of their rule of Palestine, periodically imposed special levies of taxes in addition. The young Herod, recently appointed as the commander of Galilee, vigorously enforced the special levy there by Cassius, collecting the huge sum of 100 talents (*B.J.* 1.220; *Ant.* 14.274). Julius Caesar regularized the tribute to the amount of one-quarter of the crop every second year, except for the sabbatical year. In addition there was a "head tax" (the same as the *laographia?*) of one denarius yearly (Appian, *Syr.* 50.8, *phoros tōn sōmatōn*).[44] The Roman client-rulers, that is, the high-priestly regime in Judea and Antipas or Agrippa II alongside the Roman administrators in Galilee during the first century C.E., were responsible for collection of the tribute. In the early summer of 66 C.E. we find the high-priestly officers busily collecting the tribute, seriously in arrears, from Judean villages (*B.J.* 2.404–5). The Romans considered the nonpayment of the tribute tantamount to rebellion. Thus, except for a generation or two just before and after the Hasmonean regime took over, Galilean villagers were subject to payment of imperial tribute, amounting to 12.5 percent a year under the Romans. "The imperial grain stored in the villages of upper Galilee," raided by John of Gischala at the beginning of the revolt in 66, is evidence of the concrete reality of the Roman tribute in Galilee (*Vita* 71).[45]

The Hasmonean high-priestly regime almost certain subjected the Galileans to taxation at the same time as it brought them under the "laws of the Judeans." Those laws stipulated a complicated system of tithes and offerings to priests and temple. The sum of the various dues expected has been

estimated as constituting over 20 percent of the crops.[46] Nothing in any of
our sources leads us to believe that the temple authorities or other priests
canceled or reduced any of these dues during Roman times. The high priests
and regular priests remained in place and indeed the temple-cult of sacrifices and offerings was gloriously expanded under Herod. Thus we would
expect that under Herod Galileans were still expected to pay tithes and offerings to the priests and Temple. The only matter that remains somewhat
unclear is whether the high priests in Jerusalem had any means of enforc-
ing their claims while Galilee was under separate political jurisdiction under
Antipas, Roman governors, and the Agrippas. The facts that Josephus's colleagues sent with him to Galilee in 66 so easily "amassed a large amount
of property [money?] from the tithes which they accepted as their priestly
due" and that Josephus also was offered tithes suggest that Galileans were
still accustomed to paying such dues (*Vita* 63, 80; see further chapter 6
above).

The heavy Herodian taxation came on top of these two claims to the
Galileans' produce. Herod's expenditures were obviously enormous (as outlined in chapter 6). In addition to the usual lavish Hellenistic royal court
and bureaucracy to be supported, Herod engaged in extensive building
projects: fortresses all around the country and new urban foundations and
pagan temples, as well as the rebuilding of the Jerusalem temple. He made
numerous gifts on a grand scale both to imperial figures and to Hellenistic
cities. Some of the resources he needed to meet these huge expenses were
derived from the extensive royal estates, including the highly profitable balsam plantation near Jericho. But most of his revenues were derived from
the "rich crops of the *chōra*" (*Ant* 15.109, 303). Herod's "income" from
all his territories amounted to over 900 talents annually toward the time of
his death (*Ant.* 17.317–21).[47] Such heavy taxation by a client-ruler continued under Antipas, whose revenue from Galilee and Perea was 200 talents
a year. The rebuilding of one city and the foundation of a completely new
one were ambitious projects for a ruler with such a limited revenue base.
It is conceivable that after Agrippa I (44 C.E.) the burden on Galileans in
the west relaxed somewhat. But from 54 on, the eastern districts came
under Agrippa II. That the towns of Tiberias and Tarichaeae "and their
toparchies" were to submit to Agrippa meant that Galilean villages in the
districts toward the lake would have paid taxes through the royal administration in those towns (*B.J.* 2.252; *Ant.* 20.159, mentioning "the villages"
around Julias in Perea, parallel to "the toparchies" in the earlier account).
The rivalry between Sepphoris and Tiberias over which city would serve
as capital and house "the royal bank and the archives," finally, provides
evidence that Antipas and subsequent rulers of Galilee (and Perea) had
systematically exploited their revenue base in the Galilean peasantry.

Given the general lack of attention it receives, we should focus pointedly
on what must have been a time of dramatic economic and social impact

on Galilean villages and households: the vast building projects mounted by Antipas. Within the first two decades of his reign he rebuilt Sepphoris and founded Tiberias, all on a very limited economic base, particularly by comparison with that of his father, Herod, who had more than four times the revenues from the *chōra* plus the extra revenues from extensive royal estates largely in the districts other than Galilee and Perea. Antipas's reign was indeed "long and peaceful" on the surface, but it would not have had a "stabilizing effect on the economy of Galilee."[48] The first part of his reign would have had a severely draining effect on the producers in villages and towns of Galilee and Perea, whose "surplus" product was virtually his only economic base.

Subjection to these heavy demands for tribute, tithes, and taxes by three different levels of rulers would almost certainly have affected the Galilean villagers' economic and social life adversely. Peasant plots were tradition-ally barely large enough to provide a subsistence living for a family of five or six as well as meet the dues imposed from above.[49] The peasant pro-ducers had first to meet the demands for taxes and then to live until the next harvest from what was left. Tithes, and apparently tribute and royal taxes as well, were taken right from the threshing floors. Conceivably over one-third of their crops may have been taken with the combination of the three different demands.[50] With insufficient food left to live on until the next harvest, many would have found it necessary to borrow. Both the synoptic Gospel tradition and early rabbinic literature provide numerous portrayals of people perpetually, even heavily, in debt. The viability of the peasants' tenure on traditional landholdings was thus seriously and steadily undermined by the imposition of heavy tax burdens. When desperate peas-ant households were forced heavily into debt, probably to the very officers who administered the system and/or controlled the royal or imperial stores of food, they or the produce of their fields would come increasingly under the control of their creditors. All indications are, from the structure of the situation in Galilee and from parables and other traditions in the synoptic Gospels that may reflect the dynamics of that situation, that a process of steady erosion of the people's position on their land accelerated during late second-temple (early Roman) times.[51]

The intense burdens placed on the peasant producers by the multiple layers of taxation compounded by the increasing indebtedness would have produced just the effects we discern in our literary sources: large numbers of people looking for day-labor and increasing numbers of people who had become tenants on others' estates. The parable in Matthew 20 and a whole series of laws in the Mishnah (*m. B. Meṣ.* 7, and so on) reflect the abun-dance of day-laborers. If other peasant societies are any indication, these were not simply the same as the landless "rural proletariat." They would have included many the size of whose plots were too small and/or the amount of whose debts were too large for them to make a living simply by farming their family lands. But the laborers almost certainly included people who had lost their inheritances as "the agrarian crisis" deepened in the mid-first century C.E., judging from the burgeoning bands of brigands in the frontier areas.[52]

Given the structure of economic affairs in Palestine, it seems more likely that people who were losing control of their own land would have become, in effect, tenants of someone else, probably their creditor, than that they would simply have left the land altogether. Some mishnaic rulings assume just such a phenomenon. We can hardly conclude from such passages that by the time the Mishnah was framed (ca. 200 C.E.) virtually all Galilean peasants had become tenants on large estates.[53] It would seem more appropriate to see the Mishnah as attesting a process that had been developing for several generations, perhaps accelerated in the aftermath of the revolt and Roman reconquest. While the Mishnah still assumes that a "head of household" on his own land is the normative case, a number of rulings in the tractate "Middle Gate" address various contingencies for a tenant (*hoker*) who leased a field for a prescribed amount in produce (*m. B. Meṣ.* 9.1–10). The *hoker* was not necessarily a poor tenant; the case of a lease for ten kors of wheat would have involved a field of nearly 25 acres (9:7).[54] But many a *hoker* was clearly a marginal tenant (e.g., 9:5). The Mishnah and Tosefta also mention a similar type of tenant (*soker*) who leases a field for an agreed rental in money (*t. Dem.* 6.2; cf. *m. B. Meṣ.* 9:6). Yet another type of tenant (*aris*) agreed to work in a field for a certain percentage of the harvest, from one-quarter to one-half of the crop (*m. Pe'a* 5:5).[55] The *aris* was clearly the most marginal and vulnerable of tenants:

> I shall plough, sow, weed, cut, and make a pile (of grain) before you, and you will then come and take half of the grain and straw. And for my work and expenses I shall take half. (*t. B. Meṣ.* 9.13)

> If two men have leased a field on a share-tenancy [*arisut*], each may give the other his portion of poor-man's tithe. (*m. Pe'a* 5:5)

All tenants, however, had to yield to the prior claims on the fruit of their labor: after the tenant harvested the crop, then came "the measurers, the diggers, the bailiffs (representing the landlord) and the town clerks" to collect their respective shares (*t. B. Meṣ.* 9.14). Poor tenants were in such a weak position that many had to borrow even the seed grain as well as draft animals. The ruling forbidding landlords to lend tenants grain for food indicates that landlords did indeed take advantage of their tenants in precisely that way (*m. B. Meṣ.* 5:8). Another ruling that landlords may not impose contracts without the consent of the tenants indicates that tenants were usually at the mercy of those who controlled the land (*m. B. Bat.* 10:4).

In sum, in late second-temple times the bulk of the peasants in Galilean villages would appear to have held traditional rights to ancestral land.

Although there may have been some large estates, most people do not appear to have been mere tenants working the land of absentee lords. Even "free" peasants, however, were under obligation to render up large percentages of their produce to their rulers. As the Romans first conquered the temple-state centered in Jerusalem and then placed Herodian client-kings in charge, Galilean producers were forced to meet the demands of three layers of rulers, the dues to temple and priests, tribute to Rome, and taxes for Herod, Antipas, and the Agrippas. Unable to meet these demands and still feed themselves, many peasants fell increasingly into debt. The downward spiral of indebtedness would have meant that many eventually either left their ancestral land or became tenants of their creditors. Literary sources from the late first century C.E., such as the Gospels, reflect the disintegration of the fundamental forms of social life that accompanied these economic burdens on the people.

Chapter 10

SYNAGOGUES:
THE VILLAGE ASSEMBLIES

❦

The peasants largely govern themselves within their villages, generally in accordance with immemorial custom, and there is little conflict between villages given the lack of communication between them. ... The peasantry requires little, if any, regulation, supervision, or intimidation beyond that necessary to extract from it a part of its product.

— JOHN KAUTSKY

We have been assuming for some time that what the Gospels refer to as *synagōgai*, "synagogues," were religious buildings. That assumption, enshrined in Jewish history books, Gospel commentaries, and reconstructions of Jesus' ministry, is solidly rooted in the standard modern presuppositions discussed at the outset: that rabbinic and New Testament literature are basically about religion, in particular about Judaism and a new "Christian" religion that broke away from it. Even though the abstract terms "the synagogue" and "the church" are often used in reference to these religions in general, the penchant for the buildings takes over in connection with the "synagogues" in which Jesus healed and taught and contemporary Jews prayed and learned the Law. The retrojection of modern European or American urban experience back into biblical times is most dramatic, perhaps, in the interpretation current not long ago that the Gospel of Matthew was written for a church in competition with "the synagogue down the street." The recent fascination with archaeological discoveries of ancient "synagogues" with richly symbolic mosaics on the floors and torah-shrines on the walls facing Jerusalem has powerfully reinforced the assumption that "synagogues" were religious buildings.

A closer look at those archaeological finds, however, indicates that there is little or no solid evidence for the existence of synagogues as religious buildings in Galilee before the third century C.E. Many of the excavated synagogue buildings date from even later, the fifth and sixth centuries. Not only that, but it is also difficult to find uses of the term *synagōgē* for a building in Jewish literature or inscriptions until well after the destruction of the Temple. Because the synagogue has been the central institution in Jewish life for thousands of years, the questions of its origin and the character are of considerable importance and attract lively scholarly debate. One begins to sense, however, that the assumptions and concepts with which we approach these questions are as problematic as the lack of evidence in second-temple times. We need to take another look, at our assumptions as well as at ancient texts and inscriptions, in order to discern what those synagogues were in Galilee in the times of Jesus and early rabbinic activity.

Synagogues as Community Assemblies

The very meaning of the Greek word *synagōgē* at the root of our "synagogue" suggests that more than a building was involved. The term means a gathering, a congregation, or an assembly. In the Septuagint, the Jewish Bible in Greek, the term is used to translate *edah* and sometimes *qahal*, the local or tribal assembly or the congregation of all Israel. The Mishnaic and Talmudic Hebrew term *knesset* also means an assembly, whether local or that of the people as a whole. Consistent with this is usage in inscriptions and literature (such as the first-century Jewish philosopher Philo of Alexandria) from the Mediterranean diaspora. *Synagōgē* refers to the assembly or congregation of people, while the term *proseuchē*, "prayer(-house)," is used for the building in which the congregation meets.[1]

It is clear from other texts that these congregations of Jews in the diaspora were clearly more than a worshipping group. They were social-ethnic, one might even say quasi-political, communities of Jews resident in a particular city attempting to run their own affairs insofar as the imperial and civic authorities would tolerate. Citing official documents, Josephus notes that such communities in Asia Minor, including Sardis,

> from earliest times...had an association of their own [*synodos idia*] in accordance with their native laws and their own place, in which they decide their affairs and controversies with one another.... Their laws and freedom restored to them, they may, in accordance with their accepted customs, come together and have a community life [*synagontai kai politeuontai*, where the connotation is almost "civil life"] and adjudicate suits among themselves, and at a place be given them.... They may gather together with their wives and children and offer their ancestral prayers and sacrifices to God.
>
> (*Ant.* 14.235, 260)

The religious activities are clearly only one dimension of this community, inseparable from the broader social-political aspects. Insofar as other documents indicate that they were gathering funds and/or sending funds to Jerusalem, they clearly had a significant economic dimension as well.[2]

If a *synagōgē* was the whole community including social-economic aspects, and not a specially religious building, in the Jewish diaspora, then we would expect that a *synagōgē* would be a social-economic as well as religious congregation even more clearly in Palestinian villages, each of which was a semi-autonomous community. Ironically, New Testament occurrences of *synagōgē* have been taken as evidence for the widespread presence of "synagogues" as religious buildings.[3] It is increasingly clear from critical examination of archaeological findings, however, that we cannot identify *buildings* to which the term *synagōgē* could have referred.

By contrast with the Greek-speaking diaspora, where inscriptions and literature attest "prayer-houses," there is precious little evidence, either archaeological or literary, for Jewish meetinghouses in Palestine prior to the third century C.E. Archaeologists claimed to have found "synagogues" at the massive Herodian royal fortresses of Masada and Herodium. More critical assessment of the evidence indicates that those rooms display no features "that would identify them as specifically Jewish, let alone as synagogues."[4] Moreover, it would be utterly unjustifiable to extrapolate from the use of rooms in Herodian royal fortresses to social patterns and institutions in Judean and Galilean towns and villages. What were claimed as "synagogue" buildings in the towns of Magdala and Gamla turned out to be private houses, and it is unclear what was found in either site that suggests that "the pious gathered (there) for prayer."[5] Recent critical reviews of archaeological finds thus conclude that "no building dating from the first century has so far been positively identified as a synagogue."[6]

The reports of Josephus thus provide the only evidence of meetinghouses (excluding the Temple) in or around Palestine prior to 70 C.E., and those are in Syrian Antioch, the coastal cities of Caesarea and Dora, and the royal city of Tiberias, founded around 20 by Antipas.

Amid the struggles for control of Tiberias during the political turmoil in 66–67, says Josephus, "all assembled in the prayer-house, a huge hall [*proseuchen, megiston oikēma*], capable of accommodating a large crowd" (*Vita* 54.277–80). The term *oikēma*, used here to define the *proseuchē* more closely, can be used in the sense of a (room in a) temple, but it can also refer to a workshop, a prison, a horse stable, or a brothel. So the function of this large "hall" must be determined from literary context. Although "all" were assembled there on the Sabbath (and broke off the meeting "at the sixth hour, at which it is our custom on the Sabbath to take our midday meal"), they were discussing political affairs, and were not gathered for worship or a religious meal. Whatever its other, religious functions may have been, the "prayer-house" in Tiberias was clearly being used here as a place for city-wide political assembly.

Josephus also uses the term *synagōgē* in reference to buildings in which Jews met in Dora, Caesarea, and Antioch. The phrase "in the place of the assembly" (*en tō tēs synagōgēs topō*) in one of those passages suggests that the usage of the term is now being extended from the congregation itself to the place of congregation (*Ant.* 19.305, cf. 300). In at least two of these accounts, the synagogue building is associated with religious rites, in Dora the comparison of the *synagōgē* with a shrine of Caesar (*Ant.* 19.305), and in Antioch the "religious ceremonies" that were highly attractive to Greeks as well as Jews (*B.J.* 7.44–45). In all three places, however, the *synagōgē* is a center for a community that clearly has a social-political as well as religious dimension, with "the twelve leading officers" (*dynatoi*) headed by John the tax collector in Caesarea (*B.J.* 2.287, 292), their long-recognized political rights and their own "magistrate" (*archōn*) in Antioch (*B.J.* 7.44, 47; cf. *c. Ap.* 2.39), and the references to their having been allowed heretofore to conduct their community life according to "the [ancestral] laws" (*B.J.* 2.289; *Ant.* 19.301, 304). Since all of these cases are from diaspora Jewish communities in Hellenistic cities on the nearer or farther fringes of Palestine, however, no conclusion can be drawn for the possible existence of "synagogue" buildings in Judean or Galilean villages and towns, as is usually recognized. It is noteworthy, however, that these three synagogue buildings-and-communities are not simply religious, but have social-political dimensions as well.

With no archaeological or literary evidence for synagogue buildings in Judean or Galilean towns and villages until the third century or later, it is difficult to justify the standard reading of *synagōgē* in the New Testament as a religious building. In fact a brief critical survey indicates that, with two or three exceptions, New Testament texts use *synagōgē* to refer to assemblies, usually local congregations, but sometimes (an assembly of) the whole people.[7]

Synagōgē always refers to an "assembly" in the few occurrences outside the synoptic Gospels and Acts (James 2:2; Rev. 2:9, 3:9; John 6:59, 18:20). Only in Luke 7:5 (a Lucan addition to Q) and Acts 18:7 does *synagōgē* clearly and unambiguously refer to a building. Most numerous in Acts are passages in which *synagōgē* clearly refers to an assembly exclusive of the place or building in which it gathered, such as 6:9, 9:2, 13:43 ("when the synagogue broke up"), 18:26, 22:19, 26:11. Otherwise the term refers primarily to assemblies, with possible connotation of location in a few instances, such as 13:14.

Most important as possible evidence for Galilee are synoptic Gospel passages, particularly Mark and "Q," the "Source" of the non-Markan discourses and sayings common to Matthew and Luke. Clearest are Mark 13:9 and Luke 12:11, where the parallelism with councils or rulers and authorities, and so on, indicates clearly that "synagogues" does not mean buildings but rather assemblies with political jurisdiction and authority to keep the peace and to discipline troublemakers. *Synagōgai*, along with *agorai* and *deipnoi*, in Mark 12:38–39 (par. Matt 23:6–7; Luke 20:45–46) and the Q parallel, Luke 11:43, also indicate not buildings, but public scenes and occasions, in which the scribes/Pharisees love "the best seats and salutations." In all other Markan references, whether particular (1:21, 23, 29;

3:1; 6:2) or general ("throughout all Galilee," 1:39), and in their Matthean or Lucan parallels, the *synagōgai* are local assemblies in which Jesus carries on his teaching and healing. Nothing in those passages suggests that buildings were involved. Even 200 or 300 years later, when there is evidence for actual public buildings in certain Galilean towns, they were apparently in those towns with sufficient population and/or productivity (or patrons) that they could afford to construct such a structure.[8]

It is thus clear from the synoptic Gospel tradition as our principal evidence that the *synagōgai* in Galilee were not buildings, but assemblies or congregations of people. The term *knesset* has the same reference in early rabbinic literature. In some cases *synagōgē* in the New Testament or *knesset* in the Mishnah refers to the assembly of (or representing) the whole people Israel. In a few passages in Luke-Acts and in Josephus's reports we are evidently seeing a transition usage in which, at least in Hellenistic situations, buildings in which the assemblies met are beginning to be referred to as *synagōgai* by association. But *synagōgē* and *knesset* both referred primarily to the local village or town assembly in first- and second-century Galilee.

The place where these assemblies met was apparently the village or town square prior to the construction of buildings for public assembly in late antiquity. Texts from the Mishnah and other early rabbinic literature indicate that the "town-square" (*r'hova shel 'ir*) was the location of the *ma'amadot*, prayers for fasting, trials, general assemblies, the bringing of first fruits, and prayers for rain.[9] This use of the village or town square as the place in which local assemblies and courts met during late second-temple and early rabbinic times appears similar to earlier times in ancient Judah when communal matters such as administration of justice, proclamations, assemblies, and social life generally took place in the open space or plaza inside the gate of a town or city (e.g., Jer. 5:1; Ezra 10:9; Neh. 8:1; Job 29:7; 2 Chron. 32:6).

Even when local Galilean communities began to construct buildings in the late third century C.E., the very architectural design they chose indicated that they were for purposes of assembly. Their functional design simply serves to confirm that the *synagōgē* or *knesset* was a local assembly or congregation. Both of the principal hypotheses about the architectural derivation of the "Galilean" type of synagogue building emphasize that the type of building was designed for a seated *assembly* and *congregational* participation. One hypothesis is that the early synagogue buildings were derived from the Hellenistic *ecclesiasteria* or *bouleteria*, that is, halls of assembly. These halls were arranged with stepped benches on three or four sides to facilitate free discussion among those assembled and hearing speeches delivered from the center of the hall. "The most important element was the *congregation*."[10] An alternative hypothesis is that the nearest parallel to the "Galilean" type of synagogue buildings was the partially roofed forecourt of Nabatean temples in the Hauran and elsewhere in southern Syria. These have two rows of stone benches along three walls, with columns in front of the benches, enabling the assembled people to witness and participate in the proceedings.[11]

The Synagogue as the Form of Local Governance and Social Cohesion

We must thus conclude that a synagogue in ancient Galilee was not a building, but an assembly or congregation of people in a local community, and that the assembly gathered not simply for religious ceremonies but to deal with any and all community affairs such as fundraising, public projects, or common prayer.[12] Almost certainly the local court was also a function of the local synagogue, as clearly assumed in the Mishnah (e.g., *m. Šeb.* 4:10) and possibly in the synoptic Gospel tradition as well (even if the *synagōgai* in Mark 13:11 and Luke 12:11 are higher level official courts, the village assemblies would also have constituted courts, locally). The conclusion seems almost unavoidable that, beyond the household or family, the synagogue was the principal social form of the local community in Galilee, providing governance as well as collective expression and group cohesion for the village or town. Examination of the fragmentary literary and inscriptional evidence, both Jewish rabbinic and comparative, will confirm this conclusion and further flesh out a provisional reconstruction of this form *(synagōgē/knesset)* of local community cohesion and governance. Such matters can be discerned particularly in the information we possess regarding officers or leaders of the assembly.

At the outset it would be well to remind ourselves of a few important aspects of ancient political-economic-religious relations that are very different from those in modern societies. First, local communities in the ancient Mediterranean and other traditional agrarian societies, while under imperial rule and often also oppressed by imperial client rulers, were subject to but not "administered" by central or regional governments.[13]

Second, towns and villages, while subject to kings, temples, and/or cities, remained semi-autonomous local communities with relatively continuous membership over the generations, communal relations and responsibilities, traditional social forms, and traditional ways and customs. Rulers such as the Herodians, the high priests in Jerusalem, or cities such as Tiberias or Sepphoris interfered very little in village affairs as long as the taxes or tribute were paid regularly. Early rabbinic sources simply *assume* local governance in the villages of Galilee, the people of an *'ir* (village/town) "being competent to control their own assembly, to regulate local barter or trade, and to determine wages for workers."[14]

Third, since religious affairs were not yet structurally differentiated from political-economic matters and village or town communities were not large or complex, much being structured by lineage and kinship relations, it is inherently unlikely that any distinctively religious social form(s) had evolved separate from the "civil" form(s). Scholars reading rabbinic texts with the assumption that the synagogue was a specially religious institution have difficulty determining whether certain passages refer to "the synagogue itself" or to other community affairs. The obvious solution to their confusion is to recognize that "local government is constantly identified in our sources with synagogue government."[15] Obviously that statement must be qualified for certain circumstances, such as the cities in Galilee that (later) may have had more than one assembly-with-building as well as diaspora cities in which Jews were an identifiable community within or beside the larger population. In such cases the municipal government would have been different from that of the synagogue. But even in cities outside Palestine that had municipal government, the synagogue was almost certainly the social-political form of the Jewish community itself, and not simply a religious association. In the smaller and more homogeneous Galilean villages and towns, in any case, one local assembly, with its officers, apparently dealt with the various aspects and contingencies of intracommunity life and with certain relations with higher jurisdictions beyond the local community.

Fourth, and closely related to, as well as implicit in the previous points, there would have been a persistent continuity of local social forms over the generations and centuries. Because most scholarly investigations of "the synagogue" have focused on religious buildings and on the synagogue religious service as an alternative to the Temple after its destruction in 70 C.E., much of the discussion has naturally focused on the "origin" of the synagogue. However, it is highly unlikely that the assemblies or congregations referred to as *synagōgai* in the Gospels or *knesset* in early rabbinic texts originated as new social forms only in the course of the first century C.E., for example, as "informal gatherings" gradually transformed under Pharisaic leadership or influence.[16] There may well have been rabbinic influence in the development of standardized patterns of synagogue activities in late antiquity. But town and village assemblies and local courts had traditional forms well before the first century C.E., forms that had developed without much influence from Jerusalem and/or the Pharisees.

The paucity of sources will not allow a highly precise reconstruction of the patterns, leadership, and activities of local assemblies, let alone the tracing of any development or change in such patterns. There would almost certainly have been considerable local variation in social forms and practices. But some tentative projections are possible through critical comparison of early rabbinic texts and Syrian inscriptions. We have become critical of how earlier generations of scholars read ideas and opinions of later rabbinic texts back into first-century Pharisaism or "normative Judaism." In dealing with the basic social patterns of village life, in which there is generally a high degree of continuity from century to century, the danger of "reading back" later evidence is appreciably less than in dealing with the rabbis and the earlier Pharisees, where the respective historical situations changed so dramatically from second-temple Judea to second/third-century Galilee. Nevertheless, the procedure to be followed here is first to discern social patterns and practices of second-century Galilee and of fourth-century Hauran, and only then to extrapolate critically backwards to first-century Galilee. Where a fragment of first-century evidence is available, it will be included with the discussion of the later period for comparative purposes.

We can discern the rabbis both reflecting on and adjusting to local patterns and customs in certain texts. For example:

> Cities encompassed by a wall...recite [Esther] on the 15th [of Adar]. Villages and large towns recite it on the 14th, save that villages [sometimes] recite it earlier on a day of assembly. (*m. Meg.* 1.1)

> A virgin should be married on a Wednesday and a widow on a Thursday, for in towns the court sits twice a week, on Mondays and on Thursdays; so that if the husband would lodge a virginity suit he may forthwith go in the morning to the court. (*m. Ketub.* 1:1)

Villages and towns held an assembly twice a week, Mondays and Thursdays, which were also the days on which courts were held if necessary and probably "market" days for selling and bartering as well. These also appear to have been the days on which the sacred traditions were recited. As in biblical times, fasts were also connected with public assemblies.[17]

Local leadership and administration were not complex, although more was involved than a single "ruler of the synagogue," as the mistranslation of a few New Testament texts might suggest. There was often more than one "synagogue-head" (*archisynagōgos* or *rosh ha-knesset*; Mark 5:22, 35–38; Acts 13:15). At first glance, there seems to be a bewildering variety of terms for local officers or administrators. Given the diversity of texts on which we are dependent, local and regional differences, and the broad range of time over which our sources are spread, some variation is to be expected. It does seem possible, however, to discern certain common patterns in local community leadership.

Some rabbinic texts refer to *parnasim* (the root means "assign") and/or *gabbaim* (the root means "collect," and the term is often translated "treasurers"). The principal function of both was the collection of goods for distribution to the local poor or vagrants (e.g., *m. Pe'a* 8:7; *m. Dem.* 3:1).[18] They may have operated singly, but were expected to act in twos and threes on some matters, such as collection and distribution of food for the poor. The local "treasurers" responsible for such collections were clearly different from the "tax collectors" (*mokšin*) sent out by the cities or Rome.[19] *Parnasim* also appear in Judean desert documents from Bar Kokhba times, certifying a man's ownership of an ox to prevent its confiscation, or leasing out land (possibly for the village).[20] Judging from patterns of local governance elsewhere in the Roman empire, these magistrates must have been "representative members of the local village court, acting as the leading members and the executive officers of the *bet din*."[21] They are frequently found in early rabbinic texts carrying out the orders of the local "house of judgment," as well as tending to matters of social welfare and public works.

In other early rabbinic texts, however, the orders of the court, along with certain other instructional or financial duties, were carried out by the *hazzan* (the minister or superintendent) of the assembly. For example, a *hazzan ha-knesset* administered the beating when such a penalty was ordered by the "house of judgment" (*m. Mak.* 3:12). The *hazzan* also appears to have been a leader or facilitator in religious ceremonies, although the evidence lies in texts of questionable applicability to Galilee. The *hazzan* is said to have "conducted the public liturgy in a large assembly in Alexandria by waving a scarf so the congregation would know when to say 'Amen.'"[22] The *hazzan*'s duties as master of ceremonies during assembly services appear to be portrayed in the "synagogue" scene in Luke 4, where the *hyperētēs* takes charge of scrolls and gives signals for certain speakers or responses (Luke 4:16–20). It is relevant to note in this connection that in Greek texts an officer called the *hyperētēs* is often (also) responsible for tax collection and enforcement of court rulings against debtors.[23]

Such references to these various local officers and their duties raise two interrelated questions. One question is the relationship between the *hazzan* or the *hyperētēs* in his religious functions and the *hazzan* or the *hyperētēs* in his financial or judicial duties. There is no reason whatever to posit two different local officials with the same name, one the superintendent of the "synagogue" (=religious building) and the other a secular officer of the community.[24] In traditional ancient agrarian societies, there was no differentiation between the religious and the political-economic dimensions of life. Even in Jewish diaspora communities outside Palestine, what appear as "synagogue" officials are also the leaders of the community.[25] The second and related question concerns the relationship or overlap between the *parnasim* and *gabbaim*, on the one hand, and the *hazzanim* or *rosh ha-knesset* (*archisynagōgoi*) on the other, along with other officers of local communities, such as the *archontes* (magistrates) or *presbyteroi* (elders). Again there is no reason to posit separate religious and political structures within the local community. It seems likely that variation in terminology simply reflects parallel terms for similar functions or officers such that in some cases the same people could be referred to with different terms depending on their function or role.

The Book of Judith, which likely reflects patterns of second-century B.C.E. Judea, provides an interesting illustration with the local officers of "Bethulia." When the Israelites find Achior, they bring him to the three *archontes* of the town, Uzziah, Chabris, and Charmis, who call together "all the elders of the town," whereupon all the young men and women run to the assembly (*ekklēsia*; 6:14–16). But subsequently in the narrative Chabris and Charmis are termed the "elders of the city" (8:10) and Uzziah appears to take a leading role, such that he and the other two are referred to as "Uzziah and the *archontes*" (8:35) and again as "Uzziah with the elders of the town, Chabris and Charmis" (10:6). But subsequently "the elders of the town" seems to refer to a larger group than the two or three (13:12, as in 6:14–16). Thus "the elders" seem to be a special, distinguished number (more than three) within the whole assembly, and the *archontes* three magistrates or special officers from among the elders, and Uzziah perhaps head of the assembly.

We can therefore hypothesize, by analogy, that the *parnasim* and/or *gabbaim* and/or *hazzanim* of tannaitic texts refer to certain functions or roles that might be termed generally *archontes* in Greek, and that such officers or administrators would likely be chosen from among the elders of a local community assembly, and that one or more of those officers might play the role of "head," *rosh ha-knesset* or *archisynagōgos*. It is clear from passing references in early rabbinic texts that the officers of local assemblies often acted in concert, in groups of two, three, or seven. The story of Susanna (like Judith, reflecting patterns in second-century Judea) provides a case of two "elders" from the people being appointed as "judges" — and finally themselves being overruled and executed by "the whole synagogue" (Sus. 5, 41, 60). Although we may be justifiably skeptical that he actually did what he claimed, Josephus's report about how he structured the government of Galilee in 66 almost certainly reflects the existing arrangement of local government in Galilee, with "seven men in each town to adjudicate upon petty disputes" (*B.J.* 2.570–71).

Comparative materials suggest a similar pattern in the villages and towns of Syria in late antiquity. An older survey primarily of inscriptional evidence is highly instructive. Earlier historians of antiquity were aware that "the religious cult of an ancient community played so important a part in the life of that community that there can have existed no sharp line of division between an official of the cult and an officer charged with ordinary municipal matters." Inscriptions indicate that high village officials were sometimes called *prōtokōmētēs* (village heads), sometimes *komarchoi* (village magistrates), and sometimes *strategoi* (officers); but apparently such terms designated the most important official in a village, so that where there was a *strategos* there was no *komarchos*. It has been stated that some village officials in Palestine or, more broadly, in Syria generally were called *komogrammateis* (village scribes). Except for the famous story about the younger sons of Herod threatening to make "village scribes" out of the older sons (*Ant.* 16.203), however, evidence for such officials comes only from Egypt.

Perhaps most interesting comparatively are the inscriptions concerning multiple officials named variously but all having similar functions, usually concerning finances and public works, often involving religious matters. In six different inscriptions from villages in which no higher officials appear, groups of between two and seven *pistoi* ("trustees") supervise the building of a temple or a house at common village expense. In inscriptions from other villages, groups of from two to four *pronoetai* (supervisors, administrators) have similar duties, and in one inscription two *pronoetai* worked in concert with two *pistoi* toward the construction of a "common house." In six other Syrian inscriptions, three or four or even thirteen *dioikētai* (administrators, managers), in one case explicitly designated as elected by the people of the village, supervise the erection of a gate or a building. Inscriptions frequently indicate other officials (as many as six in one place) called *epimelētai* (managers) supervising funds of the god or of the village or the water of a village. Since one inscription from one of those same sites also mentions a *prōtokōmētēs* (village head), the *epimelētai* were apparently not the highest officials of their villages (cf. the distinction between a *rosh ha-knesset* and a *hazzan* or several *gabbaim*). Even civic officials designated *episkopoi* (overseers; cf. the Christian usage "bishops") appear charged with building projects or supervision of the local market, analogous to *agoranomoi* (supply officers) elsewhere.[26]

There is a "striking similarity" between the pattern of village government in Syria to the east of Galilee, as revealed in these inscriptions, and that in Galilee, as reflected in early rabbinic texts.[27] Semi-autonomous villages apparently preserved indigenous social structures and customs inside a democratic framework, with the local officials responsible for supervising communal finances and public works such as common buildings, gates, water supply, as well as religious matters. The *parnasim* in rabbinic texts correspond, for example, to the *pronoetai* and other similar officials in Syrian villages.[28]

Judging from the similar patterns found in second-century Galilee and somewhat later in Hauran to the east, and the further parallels from earlier in Judea reflected in Judith and Susanna, there was a considerable persistence of local social forms across regions and centuries. It would seem reasonable, therefore, to extrapolate from evidence of local assembly officers and their responsibilities attested in both early rabbinic and comparative Syrian materials — with full allowance for changes in terminology and functions — in reconstructing a picture of local assemblies in first-century Galilee. Governance and cohesion of village and town communities were provided by local assemblies (and courts) operating more or less democratically with certain officials such as the *archisynagōgos* and *hyperētēs* mentioned in the synoptic Gospel tradition responsible for supervising communal finances, aid to the poor, public works, and religious matters. Through Josephus's emphasis on the religious dimension of Moses' "legislation" we can still clearly discern the "civil" dimension in the standard practice of assembly "to listen to the law" (*c. Ap.* 2.175; *Ant.* 16.43; cf. the sabbath "assemblies" in Acts 15:21).

Relations between Galilean Synagogues and Pharisees/Rabbis

How then would the Pharisees fit into this reconstructed picture of the Galilean synagogues as local village assemblies? To put it simply, they do not. The modern scholarly notion persists that the Pharisees, like their supposed successors the rabbis, were the leaders of the synagogues in Galilee.[29] Yet there is no evidence that the scribes and Pharisees and, until much later, the rabbis were even members, let alone leaders of local synagogues in Galilee.

Indeed the picture is very different if, as outlined above, the congregations and courts in Jewish villages and towns were the traditional forms of local government, the assemblies dealing with community concerns and religious expressions and the courts hearing local civil and criminal cases. In early rabbinic times neither the head(s) of the assembly nor the *hazzan* nor the *parnasim* nor the *gabbaim* would have been sages or scribes, but indigenous leadership from among the members of the community; and in the courts "their judges were not rabbis."[30] There is a concrete reason for this which we do not think of unless we attend to concrete social relations: if the assembly and court were the forms of local community governance, then one had to be a member of the local community in order to be part of the assembly. It is commonly hypothesized that, after moving to western Galilee after the Bar Kokhba Revolt in mid-second century, the rabbis lived in villages before concentrating in the cities of Galilee in the third century.[31] This indicates that the rabbis (and their supposed predecessors, the Pharisees) had no traditional base in the villages.

An early tannaitic tradition (*m. Soṭa* 9:15) indicates that in social status *hazzanim* ranked well below sages and schoolteachers, but above the other peasants (*am ha-aretz*). According to *Sipre Deut* (169, pp. 212–13), sons usually succeeded their fathers as *parnasim*, which points to their being from important local families, not (proto-)rabbis from outside. Far from being sages or rabbis (or earlier, scribes or Pharisees) the *gabbaim* knew enough about the latter's purity concerns not to touch anything if they entered the house of a *haver* (*m. Ḥag.* 3:6). Finally, if the courts were functions of the local assemblies, then they were neither controlled nor led by (proto-)rabbis. The rabbis, rather, complained of the local judges' ignorance of Torah and corrupt dealings (e.g., *Sipre Deut* 14, p. 24), and assumed that those serving as judges were basically prominent, well-off local figures (*MdRi Amalek* 4:60–70).

Far from having constituted the leadership of local assemblies and courts, the rabbis viewed association with the peasants (*amme ha-aretz*) as highly problematic: "Morning sleep and midday wine and children's talk and sitting in the assemblies of the peasants put a man out of the world" (*m. 'Abot* 3:11). This rabbinic disdain for the masses may help explain "the failure of the rabbis to mount any sort of outreach program to them."[32] In the second century as well as afterwards, the rabbis were themselves wealthy and associated with and dealt with questions important to wealthy landowners (*t. Šabb.* 2.5, 13.2; *t. 'Erub.* 1.2, 6.2; *t. Pesaḥ.* 10.12; *t. Sukk.* 1.9; *t. Ter.* 2.13).[33] The rabbis were apparently not scrambling to take over the local assemblies from within. Close studies of early rabbinic literature suggest that the rabbis were "an insular group which produced an insular literature." Indeed, the rabbis did not gain control of the synagogues until much later, perhaps the seventh century C.E., and never played any official role in the synagogues themselves.[34]

Given the early rabbis' own testimony that they were not leaders of local synagogues, it would seem difficult to argue that their supposed predecessors, the Pharisees, were. That "Pharisees and law-teachers.... had come from every village of Galilee and Judea and from Jerusalem" (Luke 5:17) is a generalizing statement by Luke, and cannot be taken at face value as an accurate sociological representation.[35] That the scribes and Pharisees expected the best seats in the assemblies and the best seats at banquets and respectful greetings in the town squares (Mark 12:38–39; Luke 11:43) would imply their leadership of the synagogues only if read according to the standard old conceptualization of "Judaism" as institutionalized in "synagogues" and led by Pharisees. On the other hand, if read on the assumption that most scribes and Pharisees were based in Jerusalem, as is generally accepted, then these passages suggest no more than that the scribes or Pharisees expected deference in the *agorai* and seats of honor at assemblies and feasts when they visited towns and villages, as we might expect from "retainers" of the Temple-based government in Jerusalem.[36]

Matthew's discourse against the Pharisees (Matthew 23), in particular, has been read as indicating that the scribes and Pharisees were the leaders of local "synagogues" contemporaneous with Matthew's post-70 "church."[37] If "Moses' seat" (23:2) was symbolic of authoritative interpretation of Torah, however, its locus was hardly diffuse and local, but centralized and official, in Jerusalem or later in Yavneh.[38] This reading of "Moses' seat" is confirmed by the way Matthew has framed the whole discourse at the end with the prophetic lament against Jerusalem (23:37–39):[39] the scribes' and Pharisees' activities, laying "heavy burdens" on the people, delivering legal rulings but neglecting justice, and building the tombs of the prophets, are understood as centered in and emanating from Jerusalem. Matthew has the Pharisees more explicitly based in Jerusalem and paired with the chief priests as the rulers (Matt. 15:1; 21:45; 27:62). The "broad phylacteries and long fringes" (23:5) are hardly characteristics of synagogues, but the ostentatious garb of the scribes and Pharisees who also expected deference from the locals when visiting feasts and assemblies.

Moreover, the "scourging in your assemblies and persecution from town to town" (23:34) brings immediately to mind the portrayal of Saul/Paul persecuting the followers of Jesus in the synagogues in Acts (9:1–3; 22:19; 26:11). But Saul was an official (supposedly) delegated from Jerusalem, not a leader of one of those synagogues.

Otherwise in the synoptic Gospels it is difficult to find passages that even link the scribes and Pharisees with synagogues. Mark 1:21–22 does not suggest that the scribes taught in the synagogues (although they well may have), but only that the people were familiar with the scribes' social function. The scribes or Pharisees are not even present in other passages mentioning synagogues, such as Mark 1:23–29, 39; and 6:1–6 (and par.). They are not mentioned in Mark 13:9–10 (and par.) where, if they had been leaders of local assemblies and courts, one might have expected their presence. Most important, however, in regard to recent work on synoptic traditions, in only one pronouncement story (Mark 3:1–6) of the ten in which Pharisees and/or scribes figure in Mark 1–10 do they appear at the local assembly watching and challenging Jesus. Most of the pronouncement stories involving the Pharisees and/or scribes concern Jesus' eating or healing activities, which have little or nothing to do with the synagogue (except insofar as some of the healings are portrayed as having occurred at local assemblies).[40] There is conflict aplenty between Jesus and the scribes and Pharisees, but it is not centered in or concerned with the synagogues.

Women and Men in Public Life

In an ironic sort of way, rabbinic sources may be useful as evidence for the relative roles and degree of participation of women and men in public life to the extent that we can imagine how village life may have differed from rabbinic prescriptions. Rabbinic literature represents women as secluded and excluded from public activities.[41] Inscriptions and other sources from diaspora Jewish communities lend a very different impression of the relative roles of women and men in public life.[42] Insofar as early rabbinic sources do not represent common practices in Galilee, as the rabbis themselves admit, it may be possible to establish a picture of popular practices by comparison and contrast. As noted in other connections in previous chapters, moreover, a similar difference must be taken into account when attempting to extrapolate from Jerusalem-based literary sources to life in Galilee, which came under direct control of Jerusalem only at the end of second-temple times.

As the temple-state was established in Jerusalem and the priesthood gained power in Judea, certain activities in public life were located exclusively in Jerusalem and certain prerogatives were concentrated in the hands of the priests. This meant that, in addition to their own semi-autonomous village affairs, Judean villagers were included in the larger religious-ethnic community headed by the Temple and high priesthood and staffed by the priests. Certain activities were thus not carried out primarily or only in Judean towns and villages. Moreover, insofar as the priesthood and the functions it served were exclusively male, generating a concern for the purity of the priesthood, women with their potential for pollution posed a threat to the performance of certain functions. The effect was to concentrate certain functions in priestly hands and to make the remaining local functions more into male prerogatives. The rabbis perpetuated this tendency to reduce the participation of women in public life. "The sages go far beyond Scripture in excusing women from many religious practices not directly connected with Sanctuary or Temple," particularly the practices that replaced the sacrificial cult after the destruction of the Temple.[43] The Mishnah exempts or excludes women from a number of obligations that remain incumbent on men. Several interrelated motives appear to have been involved.[44] For example, since women are understood to function primarily as the enablers of men, they must be released from religious obligations that might interfere with domestic chores. Since the requirement of cultic purity was understood to fall on (male) Israelites, priest and lay alike, women, who might be sources of pollution, had to be confined and their potential contact with men charged with religious obligations limited. Such concerns led to increasing restrictions on women's participation in public life.

As noted above, however, Galilee was under the direct jurisdiction of Jerusalem for only 100 years in late second-temple times and the people did not follow the sages' rulings and opinions, at least in early rabbinic times. Prior to the Hasmonean takeover villages had been directly under the administration of an imperial regime, with no institutional embodiment of a larger Galilean or Judean community that villages participated in, such as the temple cult in Jerusalem operated by the priesthood. Thus insofar as indigenous social-religious life was perpetuated in Galilean villages, it was cultivated in the villages themselves, perhaps even over against the imperial culture with which the villagers disidentified. After several hundred years of such independent village and household cultivation of the people's traditions prior to the Hasmonean annexation of Galilee, the Galilean villages would have become accustomed to conducting their public communal activities themselves, without a priesthood and without restrictions on women's participation beyond those indigenous to the patriarchal peasant family. It seems unlikely that priests and Pharisees would have affected local Galilean practices any more than the early rabbis, who explicitly mention their lack of influence in popular Galilean life. Thus we should assume that women participated relatively more in religious rites and obligations according to popular customs, by contrast with mishnaic concerns to restrict their public activities. Presumably the male heads of households constituted the local village or town assembly. Women and perhaps children, however, were included among those assembled. A local court would also have been all male. Yet even the rabbis, who would have been relatively more protective, hence restrictive, of women, allow a woman to be a witness in certain cases such as the husband's death or her own virginity at betrothal-marriage. It seems likely, therefore, that women would have been accorded relatively more respect and participation in village courts and assemblies.

It may be possible also to extrapolate to the situation in Galilean villages by comparison with diaspora Jewish evidence. For diaspora Jewish communities, there is no evidence to suggest that women were seated apart from men in synagogues. Critical reading of inscriptions and other evidence from diaspora Jewish communities, moreover, indicates that women frequently served as the principal officers of local congregations, such as *archisynagōgoi* or *presbyteroi*.[45] While women as leaders in Galilean village assemblies should not be ruled out, pending possible inscriptional evidence from archaeological explorations, this seems unlikely for traditional patriarchal village communities in Galilee. What seems highly likely, however, given the evidence from diaspora communities and the portrayal of young women as well as young men as running to the assembly in the Book of Judith, is that women participated actively in Galilean village assemblies.[46]

Chapter 11

DIVERSITY IN
GALILEAN VILLAGE CULTURE

❧

Compared with, say, the proletariat, the political culture of the peasantry is strongly influenced by factors which are not purely a consequence of its relationship to the means of production. To put it somewhat differently, the proletariat has to create its class subculture in a new environment while the peasantry, like traditional artisans, inherits a far greater residue of custom, community, and values which influences its behavior.

— JAMES C. SCOTT

Peasants do not generally share the religious and moral assumptions of the aristocracy; even where they formally have the same religion, the difference between the aristocracy's "great" and the peasants' "little" tradition can be far-reaching.

— JOHN KAUTSKY

Although limited in area, Galilee lacked coherence and unity both culturally and politically. In the survey of Galilean history above, this was most evident during the great revolt of 66–67. Most striking in Josephus's portrayal of the Galilee he attempted to control were the split between the villagers of Upper Galilee (particularly Gischala and Gabara) and those of Lower Galilee, and the hostility between the Lower Galilean villagers and (the ruling officers of) the cities of Sepphoris and Tiberias.

As noted above in other connections, there never developed in Galilee a sacred center with institutionalized political-economic-religious power relations with the towns and villages. Such a center might have served as a unifying force within Galilee over the years, as had the Jerusalem Temple in Judea and perhaps the temple on Mount Gerizim in Samaria. It might also have served as a rival to the temple-state in Jerusalem, somewhat as the temple on Mount Gerizim had done earlier in second-temple times — the most likely explanation for its destruction by the Hasmonean high priest John Hyrcanus. Also lacking in our sources is a hint of anything analogous to the cult of Cos in Idumea, an indigenous religion that persisted among

Idumeans for at least several generations underneath the official "laws of the Judeans." The persistence of a traditional tribal social structure along with an indigenous aristocracy among the Idumeans in connection with this cult of their god Cos illustrates how a people could maintain some semblance of ethnic-religious identity even after incorporation under the Jerusalem temple-state, despite the lack of political-economic-religious institutionalization in the form of a temple-community. The history of Galilee as a peasantry subject to a succession of imperial administrators, without an indigenous aristocracy or ruling class based in a cultic center such as the Jerusalem Temple or the Samaritan Mount Gerizim, suggests that its indigenous cultural traditions and social customs were cultivated basically at the popular level, which probably also meant considerable local variation.

Discussion of the diversity of Galilean culture has focused recently on "regionalism," as evidenced in the material culture of Upper Galilee and Lower Galilee.[1] For example, while Aramaic-Hebrew dominates inscriptions in Upper Galilee, bilingual Greek and Aramaic-Hebrew inscriptions are numerous in Lower Galilean sites. Certain ceramic types are found only in Upper Galilean villages. Such evidence becomes the basis of the hypothesis that a distinctive, isolated, regional "conservative" culture had been traditional in Upper Galilee, in contrast to the "great urban centers linked to the more pagan and hence Greek-speaking west, with its more cosmopolitan atmosphere" which in turn dominated towns such as Nazareth, Nain, Cana, and Capernaum.[2]

While this hypothesis is suggestive, the synchronic and socially synthetic approach behind it may obscure other factors and phenomena in Galilean village culture. Upper Galilee is judged to be solidly "Jewish," even "conservative," on the basis of material evidence which is almost all "middle and late Roman, largely third and fourth centuries C.E." The claim that Lower Galilee is more cosmopolitan and Roman-Hellenized, on the other hand, rests on arguments focused on Sepphoris-Nazareth in the first century or materials primarily from cities or large towns near cities, such as Hammat-Tiberias, Magdala, and Beth Shearim, the latter not even clearly considered part of Galilee in the first century. The comparison is thus between upland villages in late antiquity and lowland cities and towns mainly in the period of the initial impact of Roman-Hellenistic culture. This hypothesis of "regionalism" thus appears to collapse or preclude other possible factors in the diversity of Galilean village culture. As further archaeological explorations and historical analyses are carried out, it will be important to compare the villages in one region with the villages in another, then to consider the differential impact of the developing urban culture on the villages of different regions. Pending decisive additional evidence from such explorations, it is possible to consider some of the multiple factors involved in the apparently varied culture of Galilean villages, including the differences between city and village and historical developments that affected local culture.

Regional and Local Diversity

Even geographical and climatic differences within the relatively limited area may have strongly influenced Galilee's cultural diversity. Complicating Josephus's delineation of Upper and Lower Galilee, rabbinic legislation recognizes three distinct geographical-climatic regions within Galilee. In addition to the significant regional differences among Judea, Perea, and Galilee, there were three different climatic zones within Galilee. These determined the times at which crops would ripen, in turn affecting when the various tithes and sabbatical-year produce would be ready for removal: Upper Galilee (where sycamores do not grow), (western) Lower Galilee (where sycamores grow), and the valley, or the region around Tiberias and the lake (*m. Šeb.* 9:2). Variations in rainfall and growing season, as well as certain geographical characteristics, help determine the pattern of life in these different districts.[3]

Upper Galilee is more rugged, the mountains being higher, over 3,000 feet compared with under 2,000 feet in western Lower Galilee, and the east-west mountain ridges intersected by other faults with a southeast-northwest direction, producing a series of valleys, ridges, basins, and mountains. Communication was thus difficult, both within the area and from outside, particularly directly from the south (i.e., western Lower Galilee), hence the villages were more isolated.

Western Lower Galilee is dominated by a series of ridges separated by basins running roughly west to east, giving way to a series of plateaus oriented northwest-southeast which rise to the escarpment overlooking the huge basin around the lake.[4] Communication within those basins was easy, but more difficult north and south between them. It is worth noting that the main roads and trade routes connected the cities and large towns, but not many of the villages, which (especially in late second-temple times) were situated either on the ridge (south) or around the edges of the basins.

The region around the lake is dramatically different in climate, the lake itself lying below sea level and the area having far less rainfall than western or Upper Galilee. There are plains at the northern end (around Capernaum and Ginnesar) and the southern end of the lake, with more rugged terrain west of Tarichaeae/Magdala around Arbela, traditionally a stronghold of fugitives in times of social unrest.

Reinforcing the differences between the areas of Galilee that may have resulted from geographical and climatic conditions were certain political and historical factors. At the outset of the historical survey in chapter 1, we noted that the very name "Galilee" ("Circle") or "Galilee of the Peoples" may have referred to the frequently shifting political jurisdictions and conquests that the area had experienced even in the earliest times. Late second-temple times brought dramatic shifts in influence and control over the area. Ptolemaic and Seleucid regimes sponsored the foundation of cities such as Ptolemais, Scythopolis, Hippos, and Gadara in the immediately surrounding area. Then Galilee came briefly under Iturean control as the Seleucid empire declined, before the Hasmonean regime took over. The Romans restored the Hellenistic cities to their former position, leaving the Hasmonean regime ostensibly in control of Galilee. But before Rome finally imposed Herod on the area, in the course of the war between rival Hasmonean factions, Tyre, under the leadership of the "tyrant" Marion, invaded Galilee and took several "strongholds" there (*Ant.* 14.298; *B.J.* 1.238). It is clear that it makes no sense historically to think of Galilee as having had clearly defined boundaries, along with distinctive citizens and national culture, like a modern nation. Historians and political scientists have developed a concept appropriate to just such a situation: a frontier.[5]

In the case of Galilee the concept may be doubly applicable. The area as a whole was a frontier between the great empires in their historical struggles. More important for our recognition of the differences between different districts within Galilee, certain villages lay on the frontier with Ptolemais or with Scythopolis and the Great Plain or with Tyre. Villages in such a position were more subject to certain cultural influences and/or political conflicts than Galilean villages further to the interior. We have particular evidence of just such frontier situations in three cases.

Chabulon/Cabul ("which is not far from Ptolemais on the coast," *B.J.* 3.38) was originally part of the territory of the tribe of Asher, but became a pawn in Solomon's grandiose development projects of temple, palaces, and fortresses, having been (part of) the twenty villages ceded to Hiram of Tyre (Josh. 19:27; 1 Kings 9:11–13). Clearly Chabulon was vulnerable to influence and domination by the Phoenician city-states and later by the Hellenistic cities, particularly Ptolemais. More than once Chabulon and nearby villages had to bear the brunt of the initial assault in the conquest or reconquest of Galilee starting from Ptolemais. In 66 C.E. that included sacking and burning villages along the frontier as the Romans gathered their forces for full-scale warfare (*B.J.* 2.503–5; *Vita* 213–14). Of special interest here is Josephus's report that the Roman general Cestius, despite his admiration for Chabulon's beauty, burned "its houses built in the style of those at Tyre, Sidon, and Berytus" (*B.J.* 2.504). Chabulon had clearly been in a sphere of cultural influence from the coastal Hellenistic cities, as indicated by its houses apparently so distinctive by comparison with those elsewhere in Galilee.

It is difficult to imagine that there would have been a clear boundary, politically and culturally, along the Great Plain, from the west to the territory of Scythopolis in the east. Traditionally this would have been a frontier area between the clans/villages of Zebulun and Issachar and the Canaanite city-states (cf. the situation suggested by the story of the fight led by Deborah and Barak, Judges 4–5) and later the royal lands more completely subject to kings and emperors. Herod established a settlement of cavalry at Gaba, which still wielded influence at the western end in 66–67. Although Beth Shearim (=Besara) was evidently part of "rabbinic" Galilee, Judah the Prince having been buried there in the early third century C.E., its culture was strongly Hellenized, the majority of the burial inscriptions being in Greek. At the time of the revolt, however, Besara must have been part of the royal land, since the grain collected from the surrounding villages and stored there belonged to Queen Berenice (sister of Agrippa II; *Vita* 118–19), unless some special arrangement existed for storage in a village directly under Roman jurisdiction prior to the revolt. If Beth Shearim had not consistently been part of Galilee in terms of political-economic jurisdiction, it should make us hesitate about taking evidence from this site as valid for the culture of Galilee generally. Along the frontier of the Great Plain further to the east the brash "young men" of the village of Dabaritta had raided the baggage train of Agrippa's finance officer. Indeed, our historical survey of incidents in the revolt of 66–67 indicated that one of the few areas of recurrent resistance to the Romans was along the frontier of the Great Plain, particularly at Japha and Itabyrion (Mount Tabor), as well as Dabaritta (*B.J.* 3.289–306; 4.54–61). Would such resistance be rooted in these villages' historical experience of having to guard their independence jealously lest they too become more completely subject to the rulers, as were the villagers just across the frontier into the Great Plain?[6]

Gischala/Gush Halav and other villages of Upper Galilee lay along the frontier with Tyre. This appears to have been a region of persistent conflict. As noted in chapter 7, the rulers of the commercial city of Tyre would have had a continuing interest in controlling as large a territory as possible as an agricultural base for their city. The invasion led by Marion as the Hasmonean hold on Upper Galilee weakened is readily understandable in that connection. Particularly interesting is Josephus's comment that Cydasa/Kedasa, "a strong inland village of the Tyrians, had always been hostile and even at war with the Galileans" (*B.J.* 4.105). Centuries earlier Kedesh would have been one of the principal villages of Naphtali ("Galilean territory," *Ant.* 5.63). Somehow it had become separated from the other tribal clans and villages. How long it had belonged to Tyre is unclear; Josephus describes it as "between the land of Tyre and Galilee" (frontier) in Maccabean times (*Ant.* 13.154). Gush Halav and other northern Galilean villages must have held their own, however. They would likely have been the ones who attacked Kedasa at the outset of the revolt, if we can trust Josephus's report (*B.J.* 2.459). And they became the haven to which "fugitives from the villages in the *chōra* of Tyre" were fleeing just prior to the revolt, when, under John of Gischala, they formed a formidable force allied with the Gischalans (*B.J.* 2.588, 625). In the case of Gush Halav and perhaps nearby villages as well, repeated conflicts along the frontier with Tyre had apparently contributed to their strong self-reliance and fierce independence.

Another factor contributing to the diversity within Galilee was a certain mixture of peoples. It should be clear from the outline of the history of Galilee in the larger context of the history of Israel that the Galileans were not the same as the Judeans.[7] Yet some of the people living in Galilee must have been Judeans. In fact, a certain number of Judeans may have lived in Galilee prior to the Maccabean Revolt. Given the large number of *ioudaioi* in the near diaspora, in coastal cities, Syrian cities, and Alexandria, by that time, it would not be surprising if some had located in Galilee as well. If the account in 1 Maccabees 5 is not simply a fiction, there were Judeans along the frontier with Ptolemais (under attack by "all Galilee of the Gentiles" as well as the people of Ptolemais, Tyre, and Sidon) at the time of the Maccabean Revolt. Once the Hasmonean regime brought Galilee under Jerusalem rule, numbers of Judeans must have become resident in Galilee, in the military garrisons and/or as officers and representatives of the Jerusalem government. Moreover, given the other movement of peoples under Herod, it would not be surprising if at least some Judeans were relocated into Galilee. Then in the wake of the two major revolts and Roman devastation in Judea, even larger numbers of Judeans relocated in Galilee. The bulk of the Galilean population, however, while not Judean, would likely have been other descendants of former Israelites. While sharing certain common Israelite traditions with the Judeans, they would have had traditions of their own and distinctive versions of the shared Israelite traditions.[8]

Yet it is also inherently unlikely that all Galileans in late second-temple times were descendants of former Israelites. There had simply been too many conquests and shifts in rulers, with whatever minor movements of people those entailed. Thus at least some of those living in Galilee must have been non-Israelites, ethnically or in cultural heritage. Such is the situation presupposed in early rabbinic literature. Numerous rulings pertain to dealings between "Israelites" and "Gentiles." The prominence of those rulings cannot be explained away either as due to a sudden influx of Gentiles after 67 (there is no evidence for any but the "harassers," i.e., Roman officials or landlords) or as pertaining almost completely to interaction with Gentiles across the borders or in frontier areas.[9] Rabbinic case laws simply cover too many contingencies of interaction between "Israelites" and "Gentiles" which are clearly those within the same village. Land was shared or produce stored in a common place, presenting problems of separation of tithes (*t. Dem.* 6.14; *m. Makš.* 2:10). Within the same village, Israelites and Gentiles lived in adjacent houses or shared the same courtyard (*m. ʿErub.* 6:1), or perhaps even shared a house or oven (*t. Neg.* 6.4; *t. Ḥal.* 2.3). A great variety of cooperation between Israelite and gentile peasants took place on a regular basis: joint possession of fields or vineyards; watering an animal or putting out a fire; loans of animals, produce, or finances; a Gentile farming the land during the sabbatical year; even a woman lending a garment to a gentile friend.[10] This situation reflected in second-century rabbinic case laws cannot have developed suddenly. It is clear that "Gentiles" in some numbers must have been living side by side with "Israelites" in the villages of Galilee for generations. Indeed, it would help clarify what Josephus meant that the inhabitants of the area had been circumcised, as well as brought under "the laws of the Judeans" by the Hasmonean regime, if numbers of those inhabitants had not been descendants of former Israelites.[11]

The final factor in the considerable diversity that must have characterized Galilean villages from district to district, frontier to interior, background to background, was the persistence of local customs. Again the evidence comes from early rabbinic observations and rulings. As noted above, rabbinic observations ostensibly referring to late second-temple times mention, in contrast to what could be assumed about Judeans, that Galileans were ignorant with regard to heave-offerings and "things devoted to the priests" (m. Ned. 2:4). The rabbis also refer to variant customs and practices between Galilee and Judea (and the TransJordan) in several connections, such as the different measures and their equivalents (m. Ter. 10:8; m. Ketub. 5:9; m. Ḥul. 11:2), marriage customs (m. Ketub. 13:10), securing title through usucaption (m. B. Bat. 3:2), and observance of the sabbath and festivals (m. Pesaḥ. 4:5; m. Ḥul. 5:3). Differences in local customs depended upon the particular climate for and produce from agriculture, as much among the different regions of Galilee as between the different districts of Palestine, Judea, and Galilee (e.g., m. B. Qam. 10:9; m. Šeb. 9:2). More to the point here, however, are repeated statements in early rabbinic case laws that certain matters must be done according to local custom. "In any place where they are accustomed to put water in to wine, they may do so" is a qualification on rulings to the contrary (m. B. Meṣ. 4:11). With regard to whether hired laborers are to work early or late or how they are to be fed, "everything should follow local use" (7:1). Again with regard to contingencies in the leasing of fields, such as cutting the crops or plowing after reaping or sharing the straw as well as the grain, "everything should follow local use" (9:1). Local custom might even be allowed to prevail over (to override) "the Law," as well as over rabbinic rulings, as in the case of the guards of the crops being allowed to eat from them (7:8).

These recognitions in early rabbinic rulings merely point to and provide secure evidence for what we would expect in any traditional agrarian society such as Galilee, but particularly one in which there are other indications of geographical and other factors making for regional and local differences in the culture. Two illustrations from European history may provide useful comparisons. In the social-economic crisis that led to the Peasant War in southwest Germany in 1524–25, the Twelve Articles are only the most famous of numerous local or regional statements by the peasants of their traditional rights to the "common" woodlands, streams, and their own labor. Those traditional rights varied somewhat by locality. Second, what became codified as English Common Law through a long process of sifting and comparison by circuit judges sponsored by the royal court began with what was "common" among local and regional variations in traditional customs on matters of possession, usage, theft, and so on. The early rabbis in their own way both defer to and build on local customs. And those local customs were just that, time-honored ways of how things were done, differing from village to village, region to region, which were derived from generations or even centuries earlier.

Popular versus Elite Culture

Literacy

It has often been claimed that literacy in Hebrew (and/or Aramaic) was widespread in Galilee. A number of early rabbinic texts have been cited as evidence. But modern assumptions that learning and knowledge of culture entail literacy have been projected onto such rabbinic passages as well as ancient Galilee generally.[12] In recent years we have gained a much greater appreciation of cultures, both ancient and modern, that are primarily oral. In such societies, people who are illiterate nevertheless have a rich knowledge of their own cultural heritage. Even in cultures where writing has become dominant and the ability to hold much knowledge in memory has declined, people are still able to recite prayers, portions of religious liturgies, and popular and patriotic songs in particular. A closer look at some of the early rabbinic texts previously cited to attest general literacy reveals instead a populace with varying abilities to recite from memory certain key prayers, psalms, and rituals.

> Rabban Gamaliel says: a man should pray the Eighteen [Benedictions] every day. R. Joshua says: The substance of the Eighteen. R. Akiba says: If his prayer is fluent in his mouth he should pray the Eighteen, but if not, the substance of the Eighteen. (*m. Ber.* 4:3)

> Beforetime all that could recite [the prescribed words] recited them, and all that could not recite them rehearsed the words [after the priest]; but when these refrained from bringing [their first fruits] it was ordained that both they that could recite them and they that could not should rehearse the words [after the priest]. (*m. Bik.* 3:7)

> If a slave, a woman, or a minor recited [the Hallel] to him he must repeat after them what they say (and let it be a curse to him!)[13] If one that was of age recited it to him he responds only with "Hallelujah!" (*m. Sukk.* 3:10)

Recognizing that cultural knowledge and even being "learned" in a formal, intellectual way does not necessarily mean literacy, we may then explore the manner in which Galilean villagers may have cultivated and reproduced their culture. Some of the other early rabbinic texts that have been used to attest literacy and education generally can be seen to reflect the narrow circles of scholars who focused on formal learning of ritual and civil laws. Given the character of the tractate *'Abot*, with its recitation of the venerable chain of sages, the saying attributed to Judah ben Tema ("At five years old [one is fit] for the scripture, at ten years for the mishnah, at thirteen for the commandments") belongs in such a category (*m. 'Abot* 5:21, a passage missing in some manuscripts). Likewise, rulings about not reading by lamplight or observing children reading, when they are juxtaposed with a ruling about a scribe, do not appear to pertain to the general populace (*m. Šabb.* 1:3). The ruling about "teaching scripture" in relation to one's vows, in a context that indicates extreme scrupulosity about purity regulations, also appears to pertain to learned circles. Indeed, much if not most of what has been discussed with regard to cultural learning and knowledge in Galilee pertains only to the narrow circles of the rabbis and their students, and should not be included in a discussion of "Galilean village culture."[14]

However different it may have been from the formal learning of the rabbinic circles, Galilean villages most certainly cultivated their own culture. Many rabbinic texts assume that parents taught their children the sacred traditions of the people as well as key prayers and rituals. That is, the ordinary people would have learned orally, with fewer formal controls perhaps, the same or similar traditions that the learned elite would have learned orally, but with the controls available in a written text. In discussion of the Pharisees and the Torah in Galilee in chapter 6 we discussed the possible relations and differences between the popular traditions in Galilean villages and the Torah and other official traditions cultivated by Pharisees and, later, by the early rabbis. At this point it is important primarily to recognize that the villages had their own cultural traditions in oral form, whatever the lack of literacy and however ignorant the villagers were of the official culture.

Nor is it necessary to imagine special cultural institutions such as schools or synagogue buildings in order to understand how village culture was cultivated and celebrated. We need go no further than the typical celebrations of the life-cycle and rites of passage such as circumcisions, marriage feasts, special family feasts, and funerals to recognize how much of the essential and distinctive family and village culture would be carried and expressed. Our principal literary sources mention just such rituals and celebrations as integral to local life.[15] It is well to remember that Passover was not a distinctively Judean festival but presumably Galilean Israelite as well, and that whether or not it was celebrated in Jerusalem it was primarily a family festival.

Language

It is difficult in the extreme to interpret the fragmentary evidence available and draw conclusions for the use of languages in late second-temple Galilee.[16] Only the historical framing of the linguistic situation is clear. The Hebrew of the biblical traditions indicates that this Israelite version of Canaanite language was used in the time of kings and prophets and presumably thereafter. Under the Assyrian, Babylonian, and Persian empires, however, Aramaic was the official language of administration for centuries and became the *lingua franca* of the Near East. With Alexander the Great and his successors, Greek replaced Aramaic as the official language but did not completely replace Aramaic as a spoken and literary language. Many Greek-speaking Hellenistic cities were founded around Palestine in the Hellenistic and early Roman periods, including Ptolemais and Scythopolis on the frontiers of Galilee and, apparently, Tiberias and Sepphoris within the territory. The early rabbinic discussions, customs, and rulings of the Mishnah, on the other hand, were in Hebrew, apparently a Hebrew that had contacts with colloquial Hebrew still being spoken, while the retelling of biblical (hi)stories in the Targums was largely in Aramaic, again in a language with colloquial contacts.

The fragmentary evidence for language usage in Palestine in general and for Galilee in particular suggests a mixture and interaction between those three languages.[17] A number of people must have been at least bilingual, using Greek along with their Aramaic and/or Hebrew. But great care must be taken in interpreting and drawing conclusions from the fragmentary evidence available. Greek was apparently the official language of administration in Sepphoris under Herod and Antipas as under the Seleucid and Ptolemaic imperial administrations earlier (and in Tiberias, once it was founded). Yet we cannot conclude, on the basis of their supposed contact with Sepphoris, that most Galileans had become accustomed to speaking Greek by the first century C.E. At least some of the Herodian, priestly, and other Hellenizing elite in Jerusalem were sufficiently well trained in Greek letters that they could produce a thriving Jewish historiography in Greek (e.g., Eupolemus, Josephus; cf. Justus of Tiberias).[18] Yet Josephus himself admits to seeking help with his Greek in writing his histories. We can surely not simply extrapolate from the more cosmopolitan elite culture to Galilean or Judean towns and villages. Nor can we conclude that Hebrew, rather than Aramaic or Greek, was the religiously rooted language of the people because it predominates among the Dead Sea Scrolls found at Qumran and is used by the sages of formative "Judaism" in the Mishnah. This much does seem clear: language usage in Galilee is heavily interrelated with the fundamental social (political-economic-religious) division between the rulers and ruled, cities and villages, and the historical changes introduced by the rulers based in the cities.

Ostraca (graffiti scratched on potsherds) are likely to be better than official inscriptions as evidence for the language actually being used by the people. Burial inscriptions, however, because they were formalized and stilted, can be used only with caution and qualification. They must be carefully assessed with regard to their occasion or purpose, their geographical location, and any possible indication of the "social location" of their authors. For example, the predominantly Greek ossuary or tomb inscriptions found at Beth Shearim[19] might be claimed as evidence for the widespread usage of Greek in Galilee generally. Beth Shearim (Besara in Josephus), however, is located on the frontier with Ptolemais, hence under heavy general Hellenistic cultural influence. Moreover, these cemetery inscriptions date from early third century C.E., after Beth Shearim became a privileged burial spot (possibly because Rabbi Judah the Prince was buried there), and once reinterment in the land of Israel became popular for diaspora Jews, many of those buried there may not have been from Galilee.[20] Prior to 70 C.E., furthermore, Besara appears to have been an administrative town in the Great Plain (where the grain of Queen Berenice was stored), and not part of Galilee (*Vita* 118–19). Hence these inscriptions, in addition to being late, are hardly representative of Galileans generally, either in geographical or in class terms. Close attention should be paid to possible regional variations and to what particular pieces of evidence may indicate about actual linguistic usage. For example, the Greek inscriptions reveal little systematic knowledge of language, grammar, or literature.[21] But does this suggest common speech in everyday use, or a rather limited knowledge of a language that was not the writers' vernacular? We must remain prepared to change our assessment as new evidence and/or methods of assessment emerge.

Recent surveys of inscriptions from seventeen sites along the western shore of the lake and in southern Lower Galilee found about 40 percent attesting Greek, 40 percent attesting Hebrew, and more than 50 percent attesting Aramaic. Depending on the social locations and purposes of these inscriptions, they suggest that some people of Lower Galilee were bilingual, knowing some Greek as well as Aramaic and/or Hebrew. One is tempted to compare the situation reflected by the documents found in the Murabba'at and Nahal Hever caves in the Judean wilderness dating from just before the Bar Kokhba Revolt. Documents were found in both Greek and Aramaic, dealing with such matters as grain transactions, marriage contracts, and items needed for the celebration of the festival of booths. The letters are specially interesting, indicating that Simeon bar Kokhba, leader of the Judean revolt in 132–135 C.E., and his lieutenants communicated in Greek (along with both Aramaic and Hebrew) even as the Judeans were resisting outside political domination.[22] Not many may have been as fluent in Greek or literate as Simeon bar Kokhba and his correspondents, whose Greek is awkward (nothing compared with Josephus, who apologizes that even he is not skilled in Greek, at least for literary purposes). But, assuming a situation in Galilee similar to that in Judea, much of the population of Lower Galilee must been able to communicate a bit in Greek.

Aramaic (and/or Hebrew), however, may still have been predominant in the villages as a "first" language. Increasing numbers of burial inscriptions in Aramaic have come to light. Aramaic is the most frequently represented language in the survey of Lower Galilean sites. In Upper Galilee very few inscriptions have been found in Greek. Aramaic and/or Hebrew must have dominated far more than in Lower Galilee.[23] Most interesting perhaps is the prominence of Hebrew, apparently never completely supplanted by Aramaic or Greek. Analyses of such inscriptions have not yet clarified just how Hebrew was likely being used, whether primarily for prayers and other formal speech or for ordinary communication as well, and whether there is any clear factor of social location or function involved.[24] Rabbinic exhortations about the value of speaking Hebrew, on the other hand, indicate that it was certainly not as widely known as they would have liked. That the early rabbis had to allow "any language" to be used for the recitation of several common oaths, prayers, and benedictions indicates that Aramaic (or possibly Greek in some places) must have been the preferred or only language of many if not most (*m. Soṭa* 7:1; cf. *t. Giṭ.* 7(9).11 on different languages used in signing a document).

Two further sorts of evidence may shed light on language usage in Galilee in the early Roman period.[25] Increasingly sophisticated analyses of the history of the Hebrew language find a northern dialect ("Israelian Hebrew") with significant differences from the "Judahite Hebrew" that dominates in the Hebrew Bible. Not only is the northern dialect discernible in certain stories (e.g., of particular judges or Elijah–Elisha) and songs (e.g., Song of Deborah) that emanated originally from the north, but it seems clear that the same northern dialect has influenced and been continued in the Mishnah, which was given shape in Galilee. This northern Hebrew, moreover, has strong affinities with Aramaic. Such linguistic analysis suggests that mishnaic Hebrew grew out of the northern Hebrew that was still used in Galilee, where it was in regular interaction with Aramaic. Such extrapolation from literary texts parallels the inscriptional evidence for the continuing use of Hebrew alongside Aramaic (and Greek) in early Roman Galilee.

Yet another kind of literary evidence suggests both a continuity in the usage of Hebrew parallel to the use of Aramaic in Galilee from early to late Roman times and the likelihood that Aramaic was the more widespread colloquial language. Embedded in later rabbinic literature every so often is a traditional Aramaic proverb introduced by a phrase such as "that is what the people used to say."[26] The early rabbis offered regulations concerning the translation and interpretation of Torah readings from Hebrew into Aramaic (e.g., *m. Meg* 4:4, 6). There is no text suggesting that such translation was intended for common people who did not understand Hebrew.[27] Yet even if such translation and the Mishnaic regulations pertained primarily to the rabbis' own gatherings, they suggest that Aramaic must have been the common vernacular in which most people, including their own communities, would converse and comprehend. Inscriptional evidence suggests somewhat the same relationship between Hebrew and Aramaic, at least in the late Roman period.[28] For example, the bilingual inscription on the lintel of the synagogue building at 'Alma in Upper Galilee offers a blessing in Hebrew for local people and other places in Israel, then switches to Aramaic to identify the inscriber more personally: "I am Yose bar Levi the Levite, the artist who made [this]."

It is likely that both Hebrew and Aramaic made something of a comeback in late antiquity. Nevertheless this fragmentary literary and inscriptional evidence suggests that, as in late Roman times, so earlier, Hebrew may frequently have functioned as a formal and/or sacred language, while Aramaic was primarily a vernacular. Greek would have been familiar to a certain percentage of people in Lower Galilee, but the inscriptional evidence available is not sufficient to indicate that it had become the primary or only language in Galilean towns and villages.

Cities and Villages

Studies of traditional societies, ancient and modern, usually emphasize the differences between urban and rural culture. Some recent studies of Galilee, however, contend either that cosmopolitan culture spread quickly through the cities into the villages of Lower Galilee or that "there is evidence for a cultural continuum from city to country" once the first-century political divisions had healed.[29] Such contentions appear to be based on a serious underestimation of just how deeply rooted structurally and historically the political-economic tension was between ruling cities and the villages under their control. As argued in previous chapters, moreover, we should neither overestimate the degree of cosmopolitan culture even in the cities in the first century, nor imagine that what the Herodians had built in the first century had become mere empty shells by the end of the second. Nor is it possible to separate, except analytically, the cultural dimension from the political-economic dimensions.[30]

Although one cannot draw a line of mutual exclusion between the culture of Galilean villages and that of the cities, with their more obvious adaptation of Hellenistic-Roman forms, there is no literary or archaeological evidence for much influence of the latter on the former. As already noted in chapter 7, theaters such as that in Sepphoris likely involved certain alien religious forms as well as expressions of Roman imperial rule. Such theaters were normally used only five to twenty-five times a year. Use, moreover, was predominantly for political-cultural affairs of the city people. The theater in Sepphoris had a seating capacity of 5,000, that is, for roughly half of the adult population of Sepphoris itself. Thus it seems highly unlikely that people from the surrounding villages "flocked into Sepphoris" on occasions of supposed spectacles "to attend the theatre."[31]

It also seems highly unlikely that "every aspect of Greek bathing was adopted with enthusiasm" in Galilean villages.[32] Archaeological excavations have not found such baths in villages, and literary references to baths do not support such a claim. There were special baths at the "hot springs" in Tiberias which John of Gischala visited for his health (*Vita* 85; *B.J.* 2.614). Mishnaic references are to private "baths" that presuppose the considerable wealth of the owner of the estate or "village" (*m. B. Bat.* 4:6, 7; *m. Ned.* 5:3; *m. 'Abod. Zar.* 1:9). References to public baths do not appear to pertain to villages, and could even pertain to baths in cities outside of Galilee (e.g., *m. Me'il.* 5:4; *t. 'Abod. Zar.* 4.8). One may seriously doubt that it was the villagers for whom the rabbis ruled that "they may anoint or rub their stomach but not have themselves kneaded or scraped" (on the sabbath; *m. Šabb.* 22:6).[33]

The issue of the cities' cultural influence on the villages of Galilee should be formulated more precisely. Such influence would have been mediated through the structure of political-economic relations discussed in the previous chapters. Thus, for example, since most villagers produced most of what they consumed and consumed much of what they produced (that is, virtually all that was not taken by the cities in taxes and rents), villagers would not have made frequent trips into the cities to "market" their produce. Since local disputes were handled by local village courts, few peasants would have availed themselves of the city's "justice." Villagers' contact with the cities would thus appear to have been limited.

Equally important to consider is that the cities' influence depended on the popular reaction. While villagers may not have interacted with the cities often, they certainly had vivid images of what went on in high places. Certain synoptic Gospel passages provide windows onto those impressions, such as "fine clothing . . . in luxurious royal palaces," "great banquets," and rulers' birthday celebrations (Luke/Q 14:16–24; Mark 6:17–28). Villagers sometimes demonstrated their impressions more actively. When numbers of "Galileans" joined the riff-raff of Tiberias in the attack on the royal palace in Tiberias in 66 C.E. (*Vita* 64), cultural hostilities were probably tied up with political-economic resentment.

Diversity of Religious Heritage and Influences

The conclusion that seemed warranted by the fragmentary evidence for the cultural heritage of the Galilean people examined in chapters 1 and 2 was that, as descendants of the northern tribes of Israel, they must have continued Israelite traditions, such as the Song of Deborah, the Mosaic covenant, and stories of Elijah. Several of Josephus's accounts of incidents that had previously been claimed as evidence for Galilean observance of the Torah indicate rather that Galileans seemed to be acting on the basis of some Israelite traditions such as Sabbath observance and circumcision as a sign of the people's covenantal solidarity (chapter 6). Perhaps the most direct and extensive evidence of Galileans being rooted in Israelite traditions are the Jesus-traditions repeated in the Christian Gospels. There Jesus is implicitly and explicitly compared with Moses and Elijah (Mark 4–9), he declares the renewal of Israel underway (Luke/Q 13:28–29, 22:28–30), he presupposes and restates Mosaic covenantal teaching (Luke 6:20–49; cf. Matthew 5), and (apparently) stands opposed to specifically Jerusalem institutions such as the Temple and high priests on the basis of an alternative understanding of Israel. Fuller understanding of the Josephan and gospel representations of Israelite traditions among Galileans will require more thorough and careful further investigation. It does seem warranted, provisionally, however, to conclude that at least many Galileans in late second-temple times lived primarily out of some version of Israelite social-religious traditions.

Those Galilean Israelite religious traditions, however, probably cannot and should not be isolated from other religious traditions and practices and other influences on Galilean practices that varied from region to region. Most important historically from Hasmonean times into rabbinic times, of course, were Jerusalem/Judean institutions and influences. With the possible slackening during the first century C.E., when Galilee was no longer directly under Jerusalem jurisdiction, Judean influences steadily increased from the first century B.C.E. into late antiquity. The destruction of the Temple removed the ruling institution from which certain influences were exercised on Galilee. Yet that led numbers of Judeans, including the nascent rabbinic movement, to relocate in Galilee, where rabbinic "Judaism" was developed and consolidated. If certain "courses" of Judean priests settled in particular towns and villages, moreover, Judean religious traditions carried particularly by those priestly families would have become solidly rooted in Galilee by late antiquity.

Prior to and continuing "underneath" those Jerusalem/Judean influences, however, would have been other religious traditions and influences indigenous to Galilee or operating on its frontiers.[34] In fact, while we have little or no information about such religious practices and influences from Galilee itself, information on particular cults or temples from the immediately surrounding territories provide a sense of what the other strands and influences in Galilean religion may have been.

One example of a regional cult that persisted on the frontier of Galilee under Hasmonean and Herodian rule of Palestine was worship of the god (of) Carmel. According to Tacitus: "Between Judea and Syria lies Carmel: this is the name given to both the mountain and the divinity. The god has no image or temple — such is the rule handed down by the fathers; there is only an altar and the worship of the god" (Tacitus, *Hist.* 2.78.3).

So long as local gods were respectful of Rome, Romans were respectful as well as solicitous of local gods. Tacitus says that Vespasian sacrificed to Carmel, and received a highly positive oracle from the attending priest Basilides. There was continuity of worship of/on Carmel, both prior and subsequent to the imageless altar visited by Vespasian. A second-century C.E. inscription connects Carmel with the deity of Heliopolis (Baalbeck), and Pseudo-Scylax, in the mid-fourth century B.C.E., mentions that Carmel is a "mountain sacred to Zeus."[35] One can appropriately imagine the Carmel god's Semitic or Phoenician ancestor as *Ba'al Shemem* (*ba'al shamaiim* in biblical Hebrew) or Hadad, to whom there was an earlier inscription just northeast of Carmel, near Acco-Ptolemais.[36] One is also reminded of the famous contest between Elijah and the 450 prophets of Ba'al in 1 Kings 18. It is intriguing that worship at/of Carmel in the first century C.E. is imageless and focused on an altar without temple, particularly considering the indications by way of the Elijah legend that Israelites had used the site, at least at some time. Obviously, the form of religion at Carmel varied with or depended upon what people were using the site.

Within Galilee itself Mount Tabor was a traditional sacred site. It had been an important gathering point for the tribes of Zebulun and Issachar (where "they offered the right sacrifices," Deut. 33:19; and to which Deborah and Barak summoned those tribes to prepare for holy war against the Canaanite war chariots, Judg. 4:6). The mythic motifs that surround "[Mount] Tabor and [Mount] Hermon" praising Yahweh as the enthroned heavenly king in a royal psalm (Ps. 89:12) suggest that a Canaanite royal or fertility cult was being subsumed in the legitimation of the Davidic dynasty. Hosea's prophetic condemnation (5:1) indicates that later Israelite kings sponsored some sort of royal and/or fertility cult on Mount Tabor. Even prior to Alexander the Great, a "Zeus Atabyrios" crops up in the widely divergent sites of Crimea, Rhodes, and Sicily, perhaps stemming from whatever royal cult Hosea was condemning earlier.[37] The popular Israelite heritage of Mount Tabor was surely significant for later generations in Lower Galilee. That it was a defensible height, a refuge for a people under (potential) attack would have been an integral aspect of its religious importance for the peasantry in the area. It is at least suggestive that Galilean peasants in the area fled to Tabor when the Roman troops advanced to retake control in 67 C.E. — before some of them finally fled to another sacred fortress, that is, Jerusalem (*B.J.* 4.54–61). Tabor's special importance appears to continue into early rabbinic times, when it was a traditional place from which flares were sent up to signal the new year (*t. Roš Haš.* 2.2).

Two other traditional sacred sites along the frontiers of Galilee were the spring and cavern at the foot of the massive Mount Hermon and the site of Dan above another stream that comprised the headwaters of the Jordan

(Josephus, *Ant.* 5.178; 8.226; *B.J.* 4.3). As noted in chapter 6, Herod built a temple to Augustus at Paneion, which Herod Philip later made the site of his capital, Caesarea Philippi. The Deuteronomistic polemic against Dan as a legitimate religious center (Judg. 17–18; 1 Kings 12:29–30; 2 Kings 10:29) hides what must have been an important religious center for early Israelites in the far north. We have no way of knowing, however, whether the residents of Galilee in late second-temple times (when Galilee reached only as far north as Lake Huleh) would have had any continuing attachment to either of these sites.

A second/third–century temple to the "Holy Sky God," most likely the Syrian semitic Baal Shamin identified in Hellenistic-Roman times with Zeus-Jupiter, has been excavated in Kedesh, across the frontier in Tyrian territory. Above both the central eastern and northern doorways appears an eagle with outstretched wings, similar to those that appear over the doors of other temples of Baal Shamin in Syria.[38] Assuming that this temple is a Hellenistic-Roman "overlay" of earlier indigenous religion, then it is at least worth noting that one of the symbols found in Upper Galilean synagogue buildings contemporary with this temple is an eagle. This eagle symbol would appear to be an indication of the survival of local-regional religious customs and symbols that are not suppressed or replaced over generations of pressure from Jerusalem regimes or rabbinic circles for conformity to "dominant" religious canons.

There is perhaps no more vivid illustration of the mixture of cultural backgrounds and local variations in Galilee than the decor on the synagogue buildings of late antiquity.[39] The architectural type of building seems to vary as much by locality as by region. Some, but not the majority, had a fixed Torah-shrine. Others featured a complete zodiac centrally located on the floor mosaic. By far the most frequent motifs in the decor were geometric, animal, vegetable, fowl, and mythic-composite. But specific Judean motifs, particularly the menorah, are also well represented. Interestingly enough, it would be difficult to claim that distinctively Judean motifs dominate. Rather, as portrayed on their building for public gatherings, the Galileans chose a variety of geometric, animal, and mythic motifs as expressions of their indigenous culture.

The net effect of all these factors of regional and local differences in culture is just what we encountered in the historical survey above, particularly in Josephus's accounts of affairs in 66–67 C.E. Far from being a cultural and/or political unity, Galilee was fragmented into various regions and/or particular villages that insisted on autonomy and resisted outside control. The passion for autonomy became "manifest" perhaps only when the rulers ordinarily in place were temporarily unable to assert effective control, as happened in the summer of 66, and before that in 40–37 and 4 B.C.E. Yet they were undoubtedly "latent" all along, being mixed up with the hostility that "the Galileans" exhibited against Sepphoris and the ruling class in

Tiberias. Precisely because of the local and regional differences in Galilee, however, it was virtually impossible for a movement to spread throughout the area very effectively. We can examine further the localized resistance in connection with the few popular movements for which we have evidence in chapter 12.

Chapter 12

Bandits, Messiahs, and Urban Poor: Popular Unrest in Galilee

❧

The little tradition achieves historical visibility only at those moments when it becomes mobilized into dissident movements which pose a direct threat to the elites.

— James C. Scott

Epidemics of banditry . . . may reflect the disruption of an entire society, the rise of new classes and social structures, the resistance of entire communities or peoples against the destruction of its way of life.

— Eric Hobsbawm

Since Galilee was the matrix both of rabbinic Judaism and of the Jesus movements from which Christianity began, it would seem that the activities and concerns of Galileans would have been of unusual historical interest. That our textbooks have concentrated so exclusively on "the Jewish sects," Pharisees, Sadducees, and Essenes/Qumran, in treatment of the origins of Judaism and Christianity is a mark of how removed we have been from the concrete social world of ancient Palestine. These groups all together constituted a tiny fraction of the population of Palestine. They were all based in Jerusalem or the wilderness southeast of Jerusalem, even though some of the Pharisees may have represented Jerusalem's interests in Galilee from time to time. Moreover, they were all part of the ruling or literate scribal and priestly elite of Judea.

As mentioned in the introduction, however, there are good reasons for our having focused primarily on this narrow elite. In addition to modern scholarship's bias toward the politically and culturally dominant strata, virtually all literary sources for ancient societies were produced by the literate elite. The Christian Gospels, or at least the earlier stages in their production, are notable exceptions. Illiterate peasants, the vast majority of any society in antiquity, left no literature. We can know of their lives and concerns only when the literate, who were generally linked with their rulers, mention them. Since the literate elite tend to mention the peasants and urban poor only when they disrupt the established order of things, we get a highly distorted picture in two ways. We see only their outcries against oppression or other distress and an occasional movement to create a better life. And we see those only through the hostile eyes of a literate elite threatened by their disruptions.

If we want access to the Galilean people, therefore, we are virtually limited to the protests and movements they mounted and we are dependent almost entirely on Josephus for our fragments of information on such social unrest, even though we have some other data for the social-historical context. That Josephus was not only present in Galilee but actively "engaged" with some of those movements himself gives us at least a minimal reason for taking his accounts seriously. He is a hostile witness, however, who despises the popular leaders and movements he was attempting to control as a representative of the government in Jerusalem. Moreover, his principal concern is either a glorification of his own role as a great general in a war of monumental import (in *Jewish War*) or a self-serving defense of his own actions (*Life*).[1] The reader of Josephus's accounts, particularly of the ordinary people, must constantly sort through the arrogance and polemics.

Although some investigations have focused on popular movements in recent years, they have included movements from all districts of Palestine, primarily Judea, and have continued the standard assumption that the population generally was "Jewish." Focusing more particularly on unrest and movement in Galilee may involve appropriate shifts toward more precise conceptualization. The obvious case is the movement headed by the popularly acclaimed "king," Judas son of Hezekiah, which appears to have been informed by a long-standing *Israelite* tradition of popular kingship, which can be discerned only because there were parallel movements of the same type in both Judea and Perea. On the other hand, the only other sorts of unrest for which we have evidence, banditry and a faction of urban poor, are not distinctive to Galilee or Palestine generally, but have widely attested parallels in numerous preindustrial societies. In those cases the patterns and dynamics of political-economic relations may be important regardless of whether any distinctively Israelite or Galilean features appear.

Methods and concepts of the social sciences have proven useful as we complexify our approaches and conceptual apparatus to deal appropriately with the political-economic conflicts and social movements of the ancient world. Such methods must be adapted appropriately and critically, however, to the particular patterns and dynamics of each historical situation. In fact, the comparative studies of social historians such as Eric Hobsbawm appear to be more helpful with regard to ancient social banditry and the urban poor than the more rigorously "scientific" models of sociologists. Given the paucity of evidence, such comparative social history can perhaps do little more than make a few generalizations about typical characteristics of social phenomena that recur across several societies.[2]

With regard to banditry in particular one must attend to the social historical context, since banditry is an inherently unstable social form. One of Hobsbawm's principal points was that banditry is a prepolitical and "primitive" form of social protest. One of the things that ordinary social banditry lacks is a vision of a different social order that one might aspire to. Another of Hobsbawm's principal points is that social banditry sometimes but rarely escalates into wider peasant rebellion. If there is a situation of wider insurrection, then not only has the situation changed dramatically from that in which social banditry usually arises, but the character and role (and size) of brigand groups has changed. Thus if we want to appreciate the possible impact or role of social banditry in the origins of wider revolt, we cannot juxtapose incidences of ordinary social banditry in a noninsurrectionary situation and those of banditry in the midst of a wider rebellion.

Banditry, Endemic and Epidemic

Banditry in Galilee was concentrated in two periods of general social turmoil and weakened central political power, so far as we know. That Galilean banditry is attested only for mid-first century B.C.E. and toward the beginning of the great revolt in mid-first century C.E. may be due to the interests and experiences of our principal source, Josephus. He devotes a great deal of attention to the Hasmoneans' demise and Herod's rise, and he expands at great length on the Galilee he attempted to dominate in 66–67. Given the extent of the epidemic banditry he witnessed and exploited in the 60s C.E., it is likely that banditry was a recurrent social phenomenon in Galilee. That banditry became epidemic in Galilee during times of political power vacuum and general social turmoil fits the usual pattern of social banditry in traditional agrarian societies.

Discussion of banditry in Galilee as well as in Judea proper has been skewed by the question of whether Jewish Palestine in general and Galilee in particular were hotbeds of religiously motivated anti-Roman insurrectionary agitation. Debate crystallized around what has turned out to be a modern scholarly construct of "the Zealots," supposedly an extensive, organized, long-standing movement advocating violent rebellion against Roman rule.[3] The reasons that this extensive debate implicated Galilee as a supposedly insurrectionary ethos are several and are interwoven in the synthetic scholarly construct of "the Zealots." Josephus names Judas of Galilee as (co-)founder (with Saddok the Pharisee) of the "fourth philosophy," which was taken to be the origin of "the Zealots." Judas of Galilee was, further, identified with Judas the popularly acclaimed king active ten years earlier around Sepphoris, who was son of Hezekiah the Galilean brigand-chief murdered by the young Herod over half a century before. But in addition to that link with banditry, nearly all of Josephus's references to "bandits" (*lēstai*) were taken as references to "the Zealots," and since banditry was prominent in Galilee, particularly at the outset of the great revolt, Galilee was identified as a special hotbed of Zealotry.[4] Some have even gone so far as to take the term "Galileans" to mean rebels.

Closer analysis of our sources for the period has indicated that, although there was indeed widespread revolt in 4 B.C.E. as well as in 66–70 C.E., there was very little violent insurrectionary activity anywhere in Jewish Palestine in the interim. There was a good deal of social unrest, including periodic protests over particular abuses and some distinctive types of popular movements. But there is no evidence for any organized and long-standing "nationalist" or "resistance" movement such as that imagined in the Zealot movement.[5] The group actually called the Zealots did not even emerge until the middle of the Jewish revolt, apparently in Jerusalem during the winter of 67–68.[6] An important part of this new view of the diversity of groups, movements, and ad hoc protests in first-century Palestine is the recognition that *lēstai* is not just another term that Josephus used for "the Zealots," but in fact, in most cases, a term for what appears to be social banditry. If that is the case, then far from being "revolutionary," the *lēstai* were simply what Hobsbawm calls a prepolitical form of social protest against particular local conditions and injustices, and lacked a larger view of the whole society or a critique of the dominant social order.[7] As should have been evident from the large gang of brigands that sold its services to the staunchly pro-Roman city of Sepphoris in 66–67, banditry by no means implies anti-Roman insurrection.[8]

Partly if not largely to counter the view that Galilee was particularly revolutionary, the banditry there in the mid-first century, along with the whole resistance to Herod's conquest of the district, has been explained as the continuing struggles of the Hasmonean landed nobility.[9] Such an explanation, however, lacks evidence and historical credibility.

First, Josephus, our only source for these and related events, writes nothing that would suggest that either Hezekiah and company or the cave-dwelling brigands at Arbela were Hasmonean nobles. Second, the conception of a "native" "land-owning" nobility does not fit the historical situation of Galilee under the last of the Hasmoneans as the Romans were taking control in the eastern Mediterranean. Like other principalities in the ancient Near East, the Hasmonean regime had officers in command of fortresses and responsible for tax collection and other administrative duties. Moreover, the officers in charge of the fortresses in Galilee (e.g., Sepphoris, Jotapata, Gischala), as elsewhere in Palestine, may well have been clients or retainers of Aristobulus II (see *Ant.* 13.417; *B.J.* 1.117), whose son Antigonus continued the intermittent civil war against Hyrcanus II and Herod for twenty-five years. Hasmonean officers in charge of tax collection in regional centers likely came into control of additional agricultural resources through the credit-debt mechanism. Nor, because of the lack of evidence for royal estates in Galilee, can we completely rule out the possibility that a few high-ranking officers may have held grants of land during their tenure. Neither of those means of controlling land would have produced a landowning nobility, however, since the basis of their power and wealth was their office in the regime. It is thus difficult to imagine what sort of base they would have had in the countryside to be able to sustain a struggle against Hyrcanus II and Herod for years and decades.

Third, explaining both Hezekiah and his band and the Arbela brigands nearly ten years later as resistance to Hyrcanus II, Herod, and Roman rule entails an oversimplified reconstruction of events in Palestine between the initial Roman takeover in 63 B.C.E. and Herod's final consolidation of power by 37 B.C.E. Power struggles had been happening among rival Hasmonean factions for some time, prior to and utterly unrelated to Herod's elimination of Hezekiah and his brigands in Galilee in 47 B.C.E..[10] The struggle for control of Palestine between Antigonus and Herod, in connection with which the former obtained the backing of the Parthians and the latter was named "king" of the Jews by the Romans, did not begin until 40 B.C.E., long after the elimination of Hezekiah. Josephus says nothing that would suggest that the various battles Herod fought in Galilee between 39 and 37 B.C.E. all involve the same people, let alone that their "leaders, Hezekiah and the others, were aristocrats."[11] Indeed, far from suggesting the "cave-dwelling brigands" were the same as the "garrisons of Antigonus" who had fled Sepphoris, Josephus indicates that these are two different groups by his presentation of these two actions by Herod in immediate sequence in both accounts (B.J. 1.304; Ant. 14.413–15), and gives the impression that the brigands had been active in the area of Arbela for some time. There was apparently resistance to Herod's conquest of his kingdom at all levels of society, including the peasantry, as noted in chapter 2. Some of the former Hasmonean officers or nobles (dynatoi), of course, had prudently cast their lot with Herod (Ant. 14.450; B.J. 1.326); this must be what Josephus meant earlier that "all Galilee" had gone over to Herod (War 1.291; Ant. 14.395).

Fourth, and decisive against the Hasmonean nobility's explanation of the brigands, is Josephus's report that the relatives of the brigands killed by Herod in 47 appealed to Hyrcanus II for redress of grievances against Herod. They would hardly have appealed to the rival Hasmonean ruler whose regime they continued to resist after the defeat of their own patron, Aristobulus II.

Hezekiah and His Horde of Brigands (47 B.C.E.)

Josephus's accounts of Hezekiah and his band appear to be straightforward reports of brigand activity and its suppression.

> Herod,... discovering that Ezekias, a brigand-chief, at the head of a large horde, was ravaging the district on the Syrian frontier, caught him and put

him and many of the brigands to death. This welcome achievement was immensely admired by the Syrians. (*B.J.* 1.204)

The activities of Hezekiah and his horde can be easily understood as the product of fifteen years of social disruption and dislocation caused by the Roman conquest and reorganization of Palestine and the ensuing civil war in Palestine.[12] As Hobsbawm and others have pointed out, such conditions can produce widespread banditry, as peasants are driven off their land or their livelihood simply destroyed in the course of wars. Even ancient historians such as Cassius Dio were aware that precisely these conditions could result in *lēsteia:*

> Ever since war had been carried on continuously in many different places at once and many cities had been overthrown, while sentences hung over the heads of all the fugitives, and there was no freedom from fear for anyone anywhere, large numbers had turned to banditry. (Cassius Dio 36.20.2)

In mid-first century B.C.E. Galilee, however, the disruption by intermittent warfare was compounded by changes in rulers. In restoring the cities in Syria/Palestine to independence (Scythopolis and Gamala are in the list; *B.J.* 1.166; *Ant.* 14.88), the Romans reduced the territory subject to Hasmonean rule. This probably also meant that the villages in the surrounding areas came under the control of those cities, meaning either a change in rulers or displacement for peasants in villages along the frontiers. This picture is confirmed by the Roman decrees some fifteen years later (dated between 48 and 44 B.C.E.) restoring some of this border area to Hyrcanus's rule: "The kings of Syria and Phoenicia, as allies of the Romans," had been "permitted to enjoy the fruits of the places, lands and farms" formerly under Hasmonean control (*Ant.* 14.190–212, esp. 209).

Bandits often operate in frontier areas. That common factor is compounded in this case because the frontier areas were the location of the most sustained turmoil and dislocation. Hence it is highly credible that displaced or disrupted people would have formed brigand groups and would have been raiding the "Syrian" cities or territories to which they had been subjected. The circumstances of recent changes in the rulers who were demanding taxes amid the general turmoil may also help explain why they raided Syrian cities or their villages. The immediate cause of their displacement and malaise was subjection to or encroachments by the Syrian cities.

The general turmoil and shift of rulers also meant a relative vacuum in political power in the frontier areas, that is, another of the conditions in which banditry erupts and thrives.[13] It is highly unlikely, at least, that the Hasmonean regime, punished by the Romans and divided into two warring factions, had been able to exert effective control in outlying regions. The attempt by Herod's father, Hyrcanus's prime minister Antipater, to reassert control of Galilee by appointing his ambitious and strong-willed son commander (*strategos*) of the district is precisely what led to the crackdown on such brigand groups.

Josephus's second account of Herod's "murder" of Hezekiah and his brigands indicates that they had the sympathy and possibly the support of the Galileans in the area.

> The Syrians admired [Herod's] achievement... and sang his praises throughout their villages and cities, saying that he had given them peace and the secure enjoyment of their possessions.... [But] every day in the temple the mothers of the men who had been murdered by Herod kept begging the king and the people to have Herod brought to judgment in the Sanhedrin for what he had done. (*Ant.* 14.160, 168)

Syrians, particularly those with some property, would understandably have been delighted at Herod's killing the brigands. The appeal to the Hasmonean government in Jerusalem by the murdered men's mothers suggests that they and their sons alike enjoyed widespread support among the Galileans. That ordinary people would appeal to the king for redress of injustice, even against the abuses of his officers, is a typical occurrence, according to Hobsbawm.[14] In a traditional village context, and with the Hasmonean temple-state in Jerusalem so remote for Galileans in both the geographical and political sense, the mothers would not and could not have taken such a step without widespread support in their villages, where Herod — not the men he "murdered" — was considered the "outlaw." Moreover, that Herod "first posted garrisons throughout Galilee" before he went to Jerusalem to face charges (*B.J.* 1.210) suggests that his repressive actions had evoked a serious outcry there. Like many legendary social bandits, Hezekiah and his band were remembered in Galilee and beyond. It cannot have been by sheer coincidence that a son of Hezekiah emerged as a principal leader of the popular insurrection in Galilee after the death of the hated tyrant Herod.

The high-priestly officers in Jerusalem (*hoi en telei/hoi prōtoi tōn ioudaiōn, Ant.* 14.163, 165), increasingly anxious about the concentration of power in the hands of Antipater and his sons, must have taken the popular outcry over Herod's murder of Hezekiah's brigands as an occasion to attempt to clip Herod's wings. They complained that "Herod had killed Ezekias and many of this men in violation of our Law, which forbids us to slay a man, even an evildoer, unless he has first been condemned by the Synhedrion" (*Ant.* 14.167), forcing Hyrcanus to summon Herod to what turned into an abortive trial. Josephus's account, however, indicates two interesting things. Prior to Herod's action, the "leading men of the Judeans" had been either uninterested in or incapable of suppressing the brigands active along the Syrian frontiers. And there was no stabilized and legitimate definition of "law and order" for Galilee at the time, with who viewed whom as "outlaw" being a fluid relationship among the people, tradition, and rivals for power in Jerusalem.

Brigands in the Caves near Arbela (39–38 B.C.E.)

Nearly a decade later, as Herod proceeded to conquer the kingdom to which he had been appointed by the Roman Senate, he encountered widespread opposition, as noted in chapter 2. In addition to the remaining fortresses occupied by garrisons of Antigonus, the Parthian-backed last Hasmonean rival for power, he faced repeated resistance from the Galilean people. A distinctive part of that opposition which he took special pains to suppress was, near Arbela, just east of Tarichaeae/Magdala, "the brigands living in the caves, who were infesting a wide area and inflicting on the inhabitants evils no less than those of war" (*B.J.* 1.304). The struggles between rival Hasmonean factions and rival Roman rulers and the resultant turmoil that preceded the banditry of Hezekiah and his horde had simply continued unabated. Given the continuing displacement of people that such turmoil inevitably entailed, it would not be surprising if banditry had been a continuing phenomenon. More particularly, the renewed Roman civil war following the assassination of Julius Caesar in 44 B.C.E. spilled over into Palestine. Cassius's extraordinary levy of taxes, moreover, was rigorously collected from Galilee by Herod, still commander of the district (*B.J.* 1.220–21; *Ant.* 14.271–74). Furthermore, Galileans in the area around Tarichaeae were probably still reeling from Cassius's enslavement of several thousand people only a few years earlier (in 52–51 B.C.E.). Also continuing was the periodic shift in rulers, with no regime able to exert effective power over Galilee (or much of the rest of Palestine) for a prolonged period of time. Eastern Lower Galilee was not a frontier area, but many of the other conditions that foster banditry had been present there for some time.

So, apparently these brigands had holed up in the caves near Arbela. Both Josephus's account (they were "infesting a wide area"), even allowing for extreme exaggeration, and the seriousness with which Herod took them indicate that their numbers were sizable.[15] While we cannot trust an aristocratic author's account that they were inflicting horrible evils on the general populace, we cannot rule out raids on villagers, given the extreme circumstances of the time. Clear, however, is their common cause with other Galileans against their former military governor and now Rome-appointed king, Herod. Josephus takes great relish in telling the story of their defeat, embellishing both Herod's creative commando-like tactics and their passionate preference for suicide rather than tyranny. While the account of the latter may wax legendary (cf. the story of Taxo in the Assumption of Moses 9), it nevertheless gives expression to a typical feature of banditry.

With ropes he lowered [over the cliffs] the toughest of his men in large baskets until they reached the mouths of the caves; they then slaughtered the brigands and their families, and threw firebrands at those who resisted.

(B.J. 1.311)

An old man who had been caught inside one of the caves with his wife and seven children... stood at the entrance and cut down each of his sons as they came to the mouth of the cave, and then his wife. After throwing their dead bodies down the steep slope, he threw himself down too, thus submitting to death rather than slavery. (Ant. 14.429–30)

The Diversity of Banditry in 66–67 C.E.

Under the tight control and sharp repression of Herod's regime it would have been difficult for banditry or any other form of protest to emerge. For Antipas's reign in Galilee we simply have no information. By contrast, one of the dominant themes of Josephus's histories of "the Judeans" during the 40s, 50s, and 60s C.E. is the widespread occurrence and escalation of banditry — until it virtually flowed into the great revolt in the summer of 66. While most of the incidents he mentions were in Judea proper, it is highly likely that banditry was moving from endemic to epidemic in Galilee as well, given the extensive bandit forces on the scene in 66–67.

Behind the escalating banditry were again many of the conditions that typically produce banditry in traditional agrarian societies. Economic factors such as the severe drought in the late 40s and heavy taxation leading to increasing indebtedness undoubtedly played a role. Political factors such as insensitive Roman administrators and the declining legitimacy (and predatory behavior) of both high-priestly and Herodian authority also contributed to the instability. The inconsistency of Roman governors, alternating between sharp repression and inattention, only revealed how much support and "complicity" the bandits enjoyed among their friends and relatives in the villages.

In Galilee in particular the frequent shift in rulers and relative political power vacuum likely played a role again in the mid-first century C.E. as it had in the mid-first century B.C.E. Jurisdiction had shifted from Antipas to Agrippa I to Roman governors to a division of the district, with direct Roman rule in western (and Upper) Galilee but the Herodian client Agrippa II in eastern Lower Galilee. Economically the Galileans may have been under more pressure than the Judeans because of the continuation of Herodian rule, along with continuing expectations of tithes and offerings for the Jerusalem priesthood and temple, as well as the Roman tribute. The cost of Antipas's massive building projects earlier in the century may have pushed many peasant families to the very edge of economic viability on their ancestral lands, unable to survive an escalating spiral of indebtedness.

Even the Herodian rulers knew what might be the results of the peasants' inability, or unwillingness, to produce as usual: "There would be a harvest of banditry, because the requirement of tribute could not be met" (*Ant.* 18.274).

In such conditions banditry escalated to epidemic proportions in Galilee as well as in Judea during the years prior to the great revolt. Relatively speaking, the now sizable and multiplying brigand groups were far more important in Galilee than in Judea (with its diverse types of resistance) at the outset of the revolt. Escalating banditry flowed imperceptibly into, or became the form assumed by the gradually expanding insurrection in the district. Josephus's reports suggest that the sizable bands of brigands already in existence constituted one of the two types of resistance to the Romans' initial attempt to "pacify" Galilee in the summer of 66. As Sepphoris, the strongest city of Galilee, welcomed the Roman forces, "all the rebels and brigands fled to the mountain in the heart of Galilee" where they temporarily held off a whole Roman legion (*B.J.* 2.511). Clearly, as Josephus recounts, "the whole of Galilee had not yet revolted from Rome" (*Vita* 28). Ironically, the Romans' "scorched earth" practices expanded the very rebellion they were attempting to suppress by creating thousands of fugitives (e.g., *B.J.* 2.504–5, 3.60–63). Depending on how much credibility we find in Josephus's highly schematic and apologetic account, there may already have been fugitives aplenty after the Greek and Syrian cities' attacks against their "Judean" inhabitants and/or their tributary villages (*B.J.* 2.457–80). Many such fugitives would have joined or formed bands of brigands, particularly in northern Galilee and along the border with Ptolemais (*Vita* 77–78, 105). The fugitives expanding the ranks of brigand groups would not necessarily all have been "Galileans." Josephus claims that many of those mustered by his rival John of Gischala were "fugitives from the region [*chōra*] of Tyre and the villages in that neighborhood" (*B.J.* 2.587–88; cf. *Vita* 372).

Epidemic banditry that flows into rebellion, however, is not necessarily revolutionary. Nor could those large hordes of *lēstai* be understood any longer as "social banditry" in Hobsbawm's sense once the whole of Galilee slipped into virtual anarchy. Indeed, for the most part the numerous and sizable brigand bands in Galilee appear to have become pawns in the struggles between the different leaders and cities and factions in the months before the Romans reasserted their control. To the general picture of diversity in Galilee we must add the diversity of "banditry" in 66–67, particularly with regard to how such generally prepolitical social phenomenon can be manipulated by others or, in rare circumstances, contribute to a potentially revolutionary situation. Not to be included here, and not connected with *lēstai* by Josephus, are the raids or guerrilla actions of popular rebel forces, such as the plunder of Ptolemy's (wife's) baggage by the "young men" (*neaniskoi*) of Dabaritta (*Vita* 126–27; *B.J.* 2.595), which might be indistinguishable from banditry were they not in the context of a wider revolt.[16]

During the months at the end of 66 and beginning of 67 many of the brigand groups, including the largest "hordes," had become, in effect, mercenaries fighting for someone else's interests — in striking similarity to the bands of *hapiru* in the Amarna age, some of whom may have comprised some of the original "Israelites" in Galilee.[17] Sepphoris remained steadfastly loyal to Rome amid a sea of hostility from the Galilean villagers in the surrounding area, and resisted Josephus's attempts to assert Jerusalem's control. With an eye to their own security, the Sepphorites therefore offered a huge sum to the brigand-chief Jesus and his force of 800 to defend them (*Vita* 104–5). This unusually large force of brigands, active along the frontier of Ptolemais, must have included some of those fugitives created by the initial Roman strike into western Galilee in the summer of 66, as well as many from villages ruled and taxed from the royal administrative city of Sepphoris. With resources taken in that very taxation, they were hired as mercenaries to defend those who staffed the administration that taxed them. Josephus's claim to have outwitted Jesus appears to mask a certain accommodation to these mercenaries' prominence in the area of Sepphoris (*Vita* 106–11).[18] This "brigand-chief" with his 800 may or may not be the same as the "Galilean named Jesus" mentioned somewhat later as "staying in Jerusalem with a company of 600 men under arms" whom the provisional high-priestly government in Jerusalem sent as the bulk of the mercenary force supporting the Pharisaic delegation sent to replace Josephus in Galilee.

Josephus himself, who accused John of Gischala of being a mere brigand-chief (at least in the *War*), was surely the greatest manipulator of the brigand bands in Galilee. The real basis of the temporary power he wielded in Galilee was clearly his own mercenary force of several thousand, as noted in chapter 3. That is, in addition to the bodyguard of 600 picked men about his person, he boasts of "4,500 mercenaries" (*B.J.* 2.583). If he did not simply bring those mercenaries with him from Judea (which is possible), however, they must have been identical with the brigands he persuaded "the Galileans" to pay as mercenaries. He claims that his own mercenaries were not maintained by the Galilean towns that provided the (probably utterly fictional) huge army he supposedly commanded (*B.J.* 2.584). Yet his strikingly imprecise account of how he handles the prominent bands of brigands in Galilee invites suspicion.

> I also summoned the most stalwart of the brigands and, seeing that it would be impossible to disarm them, persuaded the people [*to plēthos*] to pay them as mercenaries, remarking that it was better to give them a small sum voluntarily than to submit to raids upon their property. I then bound them by oath not to enter the district [*chōra*, countryside] unless they were sent for

or their pay was in arrears, and dismissed them with injunctions to refrain from attacking the Romans or their neighbors. (*Vita* 77–78)

Given the social turmoil and anarchy, it is credible that "the multitude" of villagers and townspeople may well have been willing to be taxed to support mercenaries. But to what place and purpose were they dismissed? And from whom were they taking orders if not from Josephus? Thus one suspects that these "most stalwart of the brigands" may well have been the same as Josephus's own mercenaries and/or that they were the principal fighting force among "the Galileans" whose support he often depended upon.[19] Of course, even if our suspicions were true, Josephus was by no means in complete control of the sizable brigand element in Galilee (not counting those in league with John of Gischala) or he could not have credibly used the threat of "the brigands" in his manipulation of the likes of Justus of Tiberias and "the Galileans" generally (*Vita* 174–76, 206; cf. 145–48). Even if these brigands hired as mercenaries were not the same as Josephus's own mercenaries, however, the point remains that Josephus, apparently successfully, manipulated large numbers of brigands as well as Galilean townspeople for "his chief concern: the preservation of peace in Galilee" (*Vita* 78).

In at least one instance, in Upper Galilee, the escalating banditry appears not simply to have flowed into rebellion and not to have been simply manipulated for others' interests, but to have stimulated wider peasant revolt. Despite the extreme hostility of Josephus's references to his principal rival for control of Galilee, we can discern two key facets of the relationship between John, the brigands in the area, and the people of Gischala. Brigand bands, many of whom were "fugitives from the *chōra* of Tyre and its villages" (*B.J.* 2.588, 625; *Vita* 371–72), formed much of the nucleus of John's fighting force upon which he depended for his expanding influence in Galilee (e.g., *Vita* 94, 101, 233, 292, 301, 304). Whatever the degree to which John determined their activities, his agenda appears to have been "revolutionary," particularly by contrast to Josephus's concerns to hold things in check. The more revolutionary orientation of John and his allies appears dramatically in two incidents. As Josephus indicates clearly, John took the initiative to "seize the imperial grain stores in the villages of upper Galilee," a blatant act of revolt against Roman domination (*Vita* 71–73). When the Roman armies eventually marched into Galilee, in contrast to the capitulation of Tiberias and the self-serving surrender of Josephus at Jotapata, John and the forces of Gischala resisted as long as they could, and then headed for what they must have believed was the center of revolt and a more defensible fortress in Jerusalem (*B.J.* 4.98–120).

The second point, ironically, is well articulated by Josephus himself:

In Gischala, a small town in Galilee,...the inhabitants were inclined to peace, being mainly farmers [*georgoi*] whose whole attention was devoted to the prospects of the harvest. But they had been afflicted by the invasion of numerous gangs of brigands, from whom some members of the community had caught the contagion. (*B.J.* 4.84)

As Hobsbawm points out, although rare, this is exactly what can happen in certain circumstances. Given the previously oppressive conditions and the anarchic circumstances in mid-first-century Galilee, the influence of large numbers of brigands in the area very likely led peasants of Gischala into active rebellion. The attacks on Gischala from Tyre (and elsewhere) in mid-66 (*Vita* 43–44), of course, were likely a contributing factor both to the burgeoning brigand bands and to the politicization of the Gischalans. In contrast to Lower Galilee, in and around Gischala brigand groups and peasants joined in common rebellion against both Roman domination and the representative of Jerusalem rule.

"The Galileans," that is, the villagers and townspeople, were clearly potentially revolutionary.[20] That they were loyal to Josephus is his own self-serving apology. Their sharp hostility to the cities, Sepphoris and Tiberias, was deeply rooted in the history of Galilee (*Vita* 30, 97–100, 374–85). Josephus's own statements about how he checked the potential attacks by the Galileans against Sepphoris and the leading men of Tiberias are credible indications that they were ready to act on those deep-seated hostilities against their rulers, particularly in connection with the latter's continuing loyalty to Agrippa or the Romans. The revolutionary potential of the sizable brigand groups in Lower Galilee, however, was cut short by Sepphoris, Josephus, and perhaps others, who coopted them as mercenaries in the service of other interests.

The Popular Kingship of Judas Son of Hezekiah

At Sepphoris in Galilee, Judas, son of Ezekias (the brigand-chief who once overran the country and was suppressed by king Herod), having organized a sizable force, broke into the royal armories, armed his followers, and attacked the others who vied for power. (*B.J.* 2.56)

There was Judas, son of the brigand-chief Ezekias (who had been a man of great power and who had been captured by Herod only with great difficulty). This Judas, when he had organized at Sepphoris in Galilee a large number of desperate men, raided the palace. Taking all the weapons that were stored there, he armed all of this followers and made off with all the goods that had been seized there. He caused fear in everyone by plundering those he encountered in his craving for power and in his zealous pursuit of royal rank. (*Ant.* 17.271–72)[21]

If these parallel reports about Judas were completely isolated and unique we might suppose that Judas was simply an ambitious regional strongman opportunistically seizing the chaotic situation after Herod's death to set himself up as king in Sepphoris. Josephus, however, clearly understands Judas and his followers as a phenomenon parallel to at least two other movements. Moreover, quite distinctively in his accounts of these disturbances in Galilee, Perea, and Judea respectively, he uses the terminology of kingship. He has already described revolt and rebellion in Jerusalem and elsewhere in the wake of Herod's death. Now he focuses on disturbances in which Judas "aspired to royal rank" (*basileious timēs*) or "attacked the others who vied for power" (*dynasteia*). Simon "assumed the diadem" and "was proclaimed as king" by his followers, and Athronges "aspired to a kingship" and for some time "was called a king" (*B.J.* 2.56, 57, 61–62; *Ant.* 17.272, 273–74, 278–81). In the *Jewish War* (2.55), moreover, he even provides a topical introduction: the opportunity induced many "to become king." Just as he has on occasion described some figures as "prophets" and others as "brigands" and yet others as "a special species of brigands," so now he has something more particular in view than just another *stasis* or *apostasis*. Simply from Josephus's procedure as a historian we thus have reason to think that these are distinctive figures and movements and that some similarities exist among them.

The common characteristics of these three movements led by popularly acclaimed "kings" along with the highly similar features of Simon bar Giora during the great revolt and acclamation of Simeon bar Kokhba as "messiah" in the second revolt have led to the recognition of a distinctively Israelite social form of popular kingship rooted in ancient Israelite tradition. Israelite history and historical memory provided a vivid tradition of popular kingship, exemplified by Saul, David, Jeroboam, and Jehu, among others.[22] In each of its manifestations this tradition of popular kingship is revolutionary, the popularly acclaimed "king" heading a revolt against foreign domination and/or domestic oppression. This heritage of popular kingship is visible in the scriptural "great tradition" of the Deuteronomistic history, but it was surely carried also in the oral "little tradition" of Galilean and Judean villages and towns. Judas's movement, like those of Athronges and Simon, and so on, was evidently informed by this tradition of popular kingship, which may have revived among the people precisely because the Hasmonean and/or the Herodian kingship was illegitimate and oppressive.[23]

The reports about Judas son of Hezekiah, however, are much shorter than the others, hence provide much less by way of particulars. Thus we must proceed cautiously in comparison with the accounts of the other popular kings in constructing a picture of Judas. Josephus mentions that Athronges was a "mere shepherd" and Simon was a royal servant, meaning perhaps a lower-level officer or a peasant or sharecropper on one of the royal estates (*B.J.* 2.57, 60; *Ant.* 18.273, 278). Judas is identified only as "the son of Hezekiah the brigand-chief." There is no reason to think that Hezekiah was a Hasmonean noble, as noted above, hence there is no basis for believing that his son was attempting to revive Hasmonean king-ship.[24] Moreover, it is clear from Josephus's reports here and elsewhere that Judas son of Hezekiah was not the same as Judas of Galilee, who is iden-tified rather as a teacher (*sophistēs*) and one of the principal leaders of the "fourth philosophy" that agitated against the census in 6 C.E. when Judea came directly under Roman rule (*B.J.* 2.118). Thus there is no basis for scholarly speculation about a "messianic dynasty" continuing from Judas of Galilee in 6 C.E. to Menahem, a leader of the Sicarii in 66.[25] We cannot simply assume from the general parallel with Simon and Athronges that Ju-das son of Hezekiah also was a commoner, although that seems most likely. It is possible that, as the son of a famous brigand-chief, Judas was already recognized as a popular leader even before his "ambition for royal rank" in 4 B.C.E.

In the introductory generalization in the *War*, Josephus writes that these movements occurred in various places in the countryside, and his accounts of those headed by Simon and Athronges confirm our impression that they were based in the peasantry (*B.J.* 2.55, 57, 65; *Ant.* 17.273–85). Is Judas's movement an exception? The extremely cursory report in *B.J.* 2.56 has "in Sepphoris," while the somewhat longer *Ant.* 17.271 indicates more clearly that Judas "gathered together a large number" of men "around Sepphoris," in which he raided the royal palace and then "made off" back into the countryside from which they had come. That the Roman retaliation in-volved burning the city and enslaving its inhabitants (*B.J.* 2.68) does not necessarily mean that the Sepphorites themselves were involved in Judas's movement or the attack on the royal palace. But it is at least conceivable that some of the Sepphorites in 4 B.C.E., like many of the Jerusalemites, were ready to strike out against Herodian-Roman rule, even though they were directly or indirectly dependent on it economically. It is inherently more likely, however, that Judas's movement, like the others, was based in the countryside, as Josephus's framing in the *Antiquities* and his account in the *Jewish War* indicate. In that case, the large number of men that he gathered together may have been "desperate" (*Ant.* 17.271) because of the heavy economic pressures that Herod had placed on the peasantry in order to underwrite his many grandiose building and cultural projects, as well as his elaborate Hellenistic administration, the Galilean center of which was Sepphoris.

We can assume from the general context and the specific targets of their attack that these movements were rebellions against Herodian-Roman rule. Judas and company in particular attacked the royal palace in Sepphoris not simply to obtain arms, but also to take (back) "all the property that had been seized there" (i.e., by Herodian officials; *Ant.* 17.271). This action is parallel to similar actions by Simon's movement, which burned the royal palace at Jericho and plundered "the things that had been seized there" and attacked other royal and aristocratic residences (*Ant.* 17.274). The scope and importance of these movements is indicated by the size of the military forces that the Romans mobilized to reconquer the countryside and by the brutal punitive measures they took in retaliation, such as the burning of Sepphoris and enslavement of its people (*Ant.* 17.286–95).

To draw any connections between Judas and his movement and Jesus of Nazareth would be purely speculative. As we become more concrete in our approach to the historical context of Jesus and his followers, however, it is at least noteworthy that the movement and revolt led by Judas took place in the immediate environs of Sepphoris and Nazareth within a few years of Jesus' birth. Here was a mass movement among Galilean peasants from villages around Sepphoris taking common action under the leadership of a popular figure they recognized as king. This occurrence of a concrete movement that took the social form of popular kingship (messianic pretender) in Galilee as well as in Judea and Perea is all the more significant as we realize that there is little evidence of "messianic expectations" in Palestinian Jewish literature prior to the time of Jesus. The movement, moreover, was brutally suppressed and Sepphoris, the principal administrative city in Galilee, just a few miles from Nazareth, had been sacked and some of its people enslaved by a conquering Roman army that swept through the region, surely leaving vivid memories among the Galilean people in the area.

The Urban Poor in Tiberias

Josephus's accounts of events in Tiberias in 66–67 provide us with at least a fragmentary picture of the behavior of the urban poor in an anarchic time of revolutionary excitement. The principal conflict in the city was between "the respectable men" headed by Julius Capellus, who remained loyal to Rome and Agrippa II, and "the most insignificant persons," who were ready for war (*Vita* 32–35). The conflict thus fell clearly along the main line of political-economic division within the city.[26] The "respectable men," who are elsewhere also clearly the (ten) principal men of the city/council (*Vita* 64–65, 69), are the holders of wealth and power, judging from their names and positions, such as the Roman-sounding Julius Capellus himself, two men named Herod, and Compsus son of Compsus whose brother Crispus, the former prefect under Agrippa I, was busy "on his estates across the Jordan" (*Vita* 33). The other faction consisted "of sailors and the destitute" (*tōn aporōn*) (*Vita* 66). Since their leader, Jesus son of Sapphias, is elsewhere identified by Josephus as the *archōn* of the city (*Vita* 66, 271), it has been speculated that the office was elective or that he became a "demagogue."

Despite Josephus's description of Tiberias as having a council (*boulē*) and a stadium, it was hardly a typical Hellenistic city, but a royal administrative city, as argued in chapter 7. Hobsbawm has pointed out that the people of a royal city, most of whom are dependent economically on the business of the court and administration, will usually be loyal to the king as a symbol of their own identity and involvement.[27] Tiberias, however, had no long-standing heritage as a royal city. It was a new foundation, not even two generations old in 66, and had been the "royal city" and capital of Galilee (and Perea) for only about one generation under Antipas and Agrippa I, before the Romans made other arrangements (see further in chapter 7). Moreover, the people brought in at the founding of the city apparently had different cultural backgrounds and different interests in the situation. The royal court and administrative officers included Hellenized Idumeans (Herodians) and others with Greek and Latin names who were members of or directly dependent on the regime. The ordinary settlers, however, evidently had no special links to the royal administration. They were a disparate lot. Even if we discount the caustic tone of Josephus's account of the founding, some coercion was involved in bringing Galileans or Pereans subject to the king into the city. Some "were even poor men who were brought in to join the others from any and all places of origin" (*Ant.* 18.37). Thus many of the residents of the city had started poor and remained poor.[28] Assuming that some of the settlers were villagers brought in from the immediate area, at least some of the new "Tiberians" must have maintained contacts with (other) villagers in the area. There would have been little opportunity in the brief time since the founding of the city for vertical ties (patron-client) between the Hellenized royal-administrative elite and the poor to develop. Even in Jerusalem, where such ties would have been well developed and where the elite and commoners shared a common religious-cultural heritage, sharp conflict erupted along class lines in 66. Tiberias had no such vertical social-economic ties and no such common cultural heritage to mitigate the structural social conflict inherent in the very founding of the city. The loss of the royal bank and archives to Sepphoris (*Vita* 38) would only have exacerbated the conflict, as the principal families and professional administrators lost their previous political-economic standing and prestige and some of the already marginal poor became unemployed.

Thus it is not surprising that from the outbreak of the rebellion in 66 the party/faction (*stasis*) of the sailors and the destitute took a revolutionary stance at odds with "the principal men" of Tiberias, who continued their loyalty to the king who still had them in charge at least of a toparchy. Indeed, it persisted in its rebellious stance despite Josephus's attempts to control affairs in Tiberias and the several attempts made by the "respectable" elite of Tiberis to bring Agrippa II back into control of the city. It seems unlikely that the Tiberian faction of the poor and sailors had any particular form of organization, although it may well have had leaders besides Jesus son of Sapphias, the *archōn* of Tiberias. In contrast to the movement led by the popular king Judas in 4 B.C.E., there was no traditional social form for such a movement or the urban poor to assume, other than that of the faceless and anarchic urban "crowd."[29] The form taken by this faction at a given point was likely defined by the structure and circumstances of the situation. With the hostile accounts of Josephus as our only source, we can catch sight of the actions and/or alliances of the urban poor of Tiberias at three points in particular.

Attack on the Royal Palace

> Jesus, son of Sapphias, the ringleader of the party of the sailors and destitute class, joined by some Galileans, set the whole palace on fire, expecting, after seeing that the roof was partly of gold, to obtain from it large spoils. There was much looting.... Jesus and his followers then massacred all the Greek residents in Tiberias and any others who, before the outbreak of hostilities, had been their enemies. (*Vita* 66–67)

Here, and subsequently as well, the Tiberias poor took common action in accordance with their shared interests. The Herodian kings had taxed "the Galileans" to build, furnish, and staff their palace, and had put former Galilean peasants whom they forced to move into the new city to work building and servicing the palace. Thus both Galilean villagers and the poor of Tiberias would have had reasons for latent hostility toward the royal palace as a symbol of their recently intensified domination.

This action by the urban poor of Tiberias in collaboration with some Galileans has been misinterpreted previously as primarily a zealous religious action because of a misreading of Josephus's narrative, combined with an oversimplified view of "the Jewish revolt." Josephus indicates quite clearly that there were three (not two) different groups and their interests bearing on the disposition of the royal palace in late 66. He and his colleagues "had been commissioned by the Jerusalem assembly to press for the demolition of the palace erected by Herod the tetrarch, which contained representations of animals — such a style of architecture being forbidden by the laws — and requested permission to proceed at once with the work" (*Vita* 65).

The second group, "the principal men" of Tiberias with whom Josephus was carefully negotiating (without including the ordinary people, as was the usual practice by the ruling elite), staunchly resisted the demand and perhaps the provisional Jerusalem government's authority as well (as suggested in chapter 3). Like Antipas, who had founded the city over a cemetery and had decorated the palace without regard to the "Judean laws" in the first place, they were unconcerned about Judean religious sensitivities. For them, the Herodian royal palace probably represented the principal heritage of the city. They had apparently worked out a compromise, however, that would have preserved the luxurious furniture and other objects of great value in the palace (*Vita* 65–67).

The Tiberian poor, the third group, left unconsulted as usual by the men of affairs, took their action independently. Josephus makes no connection between their attack on the palace and the instruction by the "Jerusalem assembly." Thus there is no basis for attributing zealous religious motives to the urban poor of Tiberias. Moreover, if there was a "halakhic" concern about the palace, it was located in the Jerusalem high-priestly and Pharisaic junta of 66–67, not among the sailors and the destitute of Tiberias, who were highly unlikely to have been well versed in halakhic debates.[30]

That the attack on the royal palace was a strike against a prime symbol of their rulers is confirmed by the subsequent struggle they maintained against the combination of "the leading men" of their city and Josephus. At one point later that struggle focused again on the palace and its luxuries as symbols of their exploitation and resentment. After the initial attack and looting, Josephus managed to recover much of the palace furniture, particularly "some candelabra of Corinthian make, royal tables, and a large mass of uncoined silver" (Vita 68). He makes abundantly clear his own agenda: "I decided to keep all that I obtained in trust for the king [Agrippa II], and accordingly sent for ten of the principal councillors, with Capella, son of Antyllus, and committed the property to their charge" (Vita 69). The popular faction was poor but it was not stupid. At an appropriate moment when matters again came to a head in Tiberias, Jesus son of Sapphias inquired pointedly what had happened to the confiscated furniture and uncoined silver. The sailors and destitute knew their opponents and knew that they were engaged in a holding operation until the traditional political-economic order of life could be restored.[31]

The Tiberias Poor in Alliance with Tarichaeans and Galileans

The Tiberias faction of the poor was in communication and mutual cooperation with Galilean villagers and with the townspeople in Tarichaeae. At one point their leader, Jesus son of Sapphias, took the lead in challenging Josephus's apparent collaboration with King Agrippa II. After some young men had ambushed the king's finance officer, Ptolemy, or his wife, and brought the plunder to Josephus in Tarichaeae, Josephus secretly consigned the spoil to two "friends" of the king to be returned (on the whole incident, B.J. 2.595–607; Vita 126–35). Not trusting "their general" (who all but boasts of his utter duplicity and secret agenda), the young men agitated in the villages around Tarichaeae and Tiberias that Josephus was intending to betray the country (chōra) to the Romans. At the eventual confrontation in the hippodrome in Tarichaeae, says Josephus, the principal instigator of the angry mob was Jesus son of Sapphias (B.J. 2.599 adds John of Gischala). This incident, like the struggle in Tiberias itself over the royal palace, reveals that the fundamental conflict, now manifestly in the open, was between the people, villagers, and townspeople, on the one hand, and the rulers and their dependents, on the other. The people suspected, rightly so, as it turned out, that Josephus's real loyalties were to the king, the royal officer, and ultimately the Roman overlords. The incident also illustrates how the Tiberian party of the poor worked in close cooperation with Galilean villagers as well as the people in nearby Tarichaeae in periodic actions against their rulers and in challenging those who would restore the royal-imperial order.

Resistance to the Roman Reconquest

When the Romans advanced through Galilee in the summer of 67 subduing the rebellion in systematic fashion, "Jesus and his followers" made a valiant attempt to resist the inexorable Roman reconquest, while "the leading men" negotiated submission. In a daring guerrilla attack they managed to capture some horses from Vespasian's forces. They apparently could not control the city, however, which was surrendered by the other faction, whereupon they fled to Tarichaeae where they continued their daring resistance (*B.J.* 3.443–70). One of Josephus's sharp criticisms of Justus may indicate that the "one-hundred eighty-five fellow-citizens" slain in the internal Tiberian civil strife consisted largely of some of these "sailors and poor." It would seem likely, moreover, that many among the "2000 Tiberians found at the siege of Jerusalem" (surely an exaggerated figure) were former followers of Jesus son of Sapphias who, once resistance at Tiberias and Tarichaeae was futile, fled with other Galileans to Jerusalem to continue the resistance (*Vita* 353–54).

CONCLUSION

❧

Galilee was repeatedly subjected by a succession of outside rulers, usually from the great empires. Yet the Galilean people had a keen sense of independence, periodically resisting or outright revolting against those rulers, whose regimes were usually based in faraway capitals. The desire to be left alone to conduct their own lives is rooted in several factors, including the geography-topography and the political-economic-religious structure of ancient agrarian empires. From the earliest evidence through Roman times, Galileans' assertions of their independence appear also to be rooted in Israelite traditions of resistance to oppressive rulers.

Given its rugged terrain and distance from navigable waterways, Galilee was not the prime object of imperial conquest. In the broader politics of empire, it was always something of a frontier area, militarily conquered and administered by outside rulers with other primary objectives, such as the "royal estates" of the fertile Great Plain or the temple-state in Jerusalem or the maintaining of a buffer against another empire. In the political-economic(-religious) structure of ancient empires, rulers generally "administered" an area to the extent necessary to extract the desired economic revenues but otherwise did not interfere much in the relatively autonomous social-religious life of the villages and towns which, along with the patriarchal families of which they were comprised, constituted the fundamental social forms. In the case of an area such as Galilee, those two factors likely provided mutual reinforcement of the desire to be left alone. The sense of being remote from the ruling center and the experience of relatively greater independence among frontier people during times of imperial weakness would have served to sharpen the experience of subjection when an imperial regime tightened control in the area.

In what must have been a series of peasant struggles against attempts by the rulers of the Canaanite city-state to reassert their dominance over upland villages, we catch sight of the early Israelite tribes battling the chariot-forces of kings and commanders such as Sisera in the Song of Deborah. Early Israelite traditions express resistance not only to Canaanite kings, but to the imperial kingship of Solomon based in Jerusalem. Indeed, after only two generations under the monarchy and (first) Temple in Jerusalem, the next eight centuries of Galilean history were shaped over against and then independently of Jerusalem. Particularly noteworthy in this regard are two striking differences in historical experience. During the time that the distinctive Judean institutions of Temple and Torah were developing, Galilee was politically-religiously separate from Judea, under the administration of a different imperial province. Moreover, whereas the rebuilding of Jerusalem and the establishment of the temple-state there provided Judea with an indigenous ruling class and central institutions, the lack of such developments in Galilee, which remained directly under foreign imperial administration, left Galilean villages relatively autonomous with no unifying indigenous leadership. The result was that, while Israelite traditions undoubtedly continued to be cultivated in both Galilean and Judean villages, Galilee had no indigenous high-priestly regime with scribal "retainers" to codify centralized "laws of the Judeans" (Josephus's term), which served as a controlling "great tradition." It also meant that Galilee had no indigenous temple-state and priestly aristocracy to serve as a focal point of discontent for the Maccabean Revolt and then as a machinery of state for the consolidation of power by the Hasmonean leaders of that revolt.

After a "dark" period (with little or no sources), a series of rapid changes in rulers, beginning in the late second century B.C.E., brought prolonged tumult for the Galileans, followed by sudden political-economic and -cultural pressures of more intense control by its rulers. After the Seleucid empire's demise and a brief period of domination by the Itureans to the north, the expansionist Hasmonean regime took control of Galilee in 104 B.C.E. The Galileans were never really conquered by the Hasmoneans. Yet so far as we can tell from available evidence, they were never pressed to conform their local village customs and practices to "the laws of the Judeans," let alone "convert" to "Judaism."

Most striking in the history of Galilee from the Hasmoneans through the end of the second-temple period is the turmoil that a succession of rulers brought to the area. Although the Hasmoneans apparently established fortresses and garrisons in Galilee, most of the forty years of their rule prior to the Roman conquest featured dissension within the regime and virtual civil war. The Roman conquest in 63 B.C.E. combined with civil war between rival Hasmonean factions, as well as empire-wide civil war, to produce a whole generation of repeated military devastations and extraordinary taxation in Galilee. At the end of that extreme turmoil, it is clear that the Galileans were the most vigorous and persistent among Herod's new subjects in resisting the Roman client-king's repeated attempts to take control of his kingdom. While bringing an end to the military upheaval, Herod enforced heavy taxation with tightly repressive security measures in the form of fortresses and garrisons in Galilee and elsewhere. After his death (4 B.C.E.), as at his takeover thirty-some years earlier, revolts erupted in Galilee as well as in Judea and Perea. Judging from the considerable size of the military force deployed to reconquer Palestine, the revolt must have been widespread. The social form taken by the revolt in Galilee as in Judea, moreover, that of popular (as opposed to imperial) kingship, indicates that it had deep Israelite roots.

The turmoil during the hundred years of Jerusalem rule over Galilee was followed immediately by developments that had far greater and more sudden and direct impact on Galilean villagers. Ever since Solomon, the rulers of Galilee had governed and taxed from a distant capital. The Roman division of Herod's realm into districts and the assignment of Galilee and Perea to Antipas led the latter to establish his regime in Galilee itself. For an aspiring Roman client-ruler such as Antipas, this meant the building of an appropriate capital *city*, named after the emperor, as a site for his court as well as revenue-extracting administration. After establishing a court and administration (such as archives and bank) at the rebuilt Sepphoris, Antipas then founded "Tiberias."

Reasons of imperial political economy had led to the maintenance of one administrative city in Galilee, Sepphoris. Roman patronage and the cultural chic of Roman client-rulers now brought about the beginnings of an administratively superfluous and culturally alien Hellenistic-Roman urban overlay in Lower Galilee. The double impact must have been intense as well as sudden: compounding the economic drain on village resources in the now rigorously collected taxes to underwrite the two massive urban building projects within twenty years (4 B.C.E. to no later than 18 C.E.) was the visual as well as political presence of two Roman-Hellenistic–style "royal" cities, at least one of which was within view of most villagers in Lower Galilee. The regime ruling Galilee was now located in Galilee, but it was an alien body imposed on the Galilean landscape.

The Roman takeover of Palestine did not change the basic political-economic structure, but it did multiply the levels of rulers that claimed revenues from the villagers' crops. The Romans' appointment of Herod as client-king combined with the Romans' and Herod's maintenance and even expansion of the priestly aristocracy in Jerusalem obviously increased the numbers of rulers to be supported by the produce of the subject peoples. The installation of Antipas over Galilee terminated the direct jurisdiction of the Jerusalem temple-state over Galilee, reducing its ability to demand revenues, but did not alter the basic political-economic system in Galilee. The revenues that the Romans assigned to Antipas from Galilee and Perea came from the agricultural produce of villages that were now under the watchful eye of a regime immediately on the scene. The lack of evidence for royal estates in Galilee itself suggests that the pattern of land tenure was still predominantly that of freeholders on traditional family inheritances. Both Josephus and archaeological evidence indicate that nearly 200 relatively self-sufficient villages dotted the Galilean landscape. With their local assemblies as the form of self-government as well as communal self-expression, these villages maintained an identity within themselves and perhaps with each other as well, judging from Josephus's report of the hostilities during the revolt in 66–67. In mid–first century C.E., however, arose a number of indications that the social-economic bases of Galilean society were under pressure, and even beginning to disintegrate somewhat. The escalating size and frequency of brigand bands in the decades prior to the great revolt indicate that large numbers of people were being cut loose from their land. The villages communities, however, were still basically intact, as Josephus indicates, suggesting that peasant households were under economic and social pressure, but that most had not yet been driven off the land. Galilean participation in the peasant strike in protest over Gaius's statue was likely an expression of economic distress as well as ideological protest. The intense hostility of the Galilean villagers to Sepphoris and the Herodian elite in Tiberias in 66–67, as reported by Josephus, indicates precisely where the Galilean discontent focused: on the rulers and their officials now located in those cities.

Patterns discernible in the revolt of 66–67 also indicate two other important aspects of mid-first-century Galilean life. Although (as indicated in their delegation of Josephus and others to take over Galilee in 66) the priestly aristocracy in Jerusalem was ready to reclaim Galilee at any time, the Galileans, while yielding tithes to Josephus and other Jerusalem priests, resisted Jerusalem's direction of their affairs. Galilean resistance to Josephus and Jerusalem control, however, was no more unified and organized than their resistance to Roman rule in 66–67. Never having had any unifying institutions, always having been ruled by outsiders, Galileans of various villages and regions, like peasants elsewhere, were jealous of their independence. There does appear to have been a degree of regional cooperation and common cause, focused perhaps largely by or against the ruling city or ruling structure in each major area, Sepphoris and the Tiberias elite in western and eastern Lower Galilee respectively, and more directly against the eventual Roman reconquest in Upper Galilee.

Following the great revolt, we hear of no active resistance by Galilean villagers against direct Roman rule. There is no evidence that Galileans joined with Judeans in the Bar Kokhba Revolt in 132–135. Before long after the revolt of 66–70, the Romans dramatically increased their military presence in and around Galilee. There is nothing in their previous history to suggest a streak of either fanaticism or suicidal impulse among Galileans. It is even conceivable that the reduction of three layers of rulers to Roman rule through the cities constituted a relief in the economic burden for the Galileans. The Roman impact on Galilee continued, however. Sepphoris and Tiberias were expanded and further Romanized as part of a more complete, administratively functional "urbanization" of Palestine in the second and third centuries. Counterpoised to that further Romanization, but also the indirect effect of Roman imperial practice, a large number of Judean refugees relocated in Galilee following the Roman devastation of Judea itself in 132–135. In the aftermath of the Roman destruction of Judea, Galilee became the location of Jewish leadership and eventually the center of rabbinic Judaism, based in the Galilean cities, but in resistance to further Romanization of the culture.

As noted in the introduction, one of the principal motives in pursuing a new investigation into the history of Galilee is to explore the context both of the Jesus movement(s) from which (what became) Christianity developed and of the rabbinic movement(s) from which (what became) Judaism developed. The methods by which the textual sources for both of these movements have been investigated are currently undergoing critical scrutiny. Although there has been increasing attention to the historical social context of the Jesus movement(s), scholars continue to interpret textual fragments that have been taken out of literary context, making it difficult to discern the social context of those text-fragments. Although increasing attention has been paid to the literary context of rabbinic traditions, scholars continue to interpret those traditions without much information on the historical social context. Thus statements with any precision are premature prior to more extensive investigation of sources in both literary and social context. At this point only a few very basic observations can be ventured.

Judging from their supposedly earliest literature, the Jesus movement(s) present themselves as developments of Israelite traditions. In both Mark and the Synoptic Sayings Source "Q" (discourse material common to Matthew and Luke where they are not following Mark) Jesus is portrayed as a (Moses-like and/or Elijah-like) prophet engaged in the renewal of Israel. The traditional (biblical) role or "script" of such prophets included both communication of God's revelation and implementation of God's deliverance, including healings and feedings as well as other wondrous acts. Mark has Jesus habitually healing and teaching in the villages, in particular in their "assemblies." There is no indication that Jesus and his followers have any interest in or interaction with the cities of Sepphoris or Tiberias. Both Mark and Q mock Herod Antipas's court in its luxury and whimsical "justice." The renewed Mosaic covenantal teachings in Luke/Q 6:20–49 and Mark 10 suggest that Jesus was not teaching some sort of new lifestyle to individuals, but addressing local communities about their disintegrating social-economic relations. He addresses people who are suffering poverty, hunger, and despair, but are still part of village community relations, however contentious. Since families and villages were the fundamental social forms, any renewal of Israel would have to focus precisely on the renewal of those basic social forms. Jesus also pronounces God's condemnation not of Israel (let alone "Judaism"), but of the Temple, the Jerusalem rulers, and their representatives, the scribes and Pharisees, who "come down from Jerusalem." As represented in Mark and "Q," therefore, the Jesus movement(s) appear to fit the situation of Galilee in mid-first century. The impact of Roman and Herodian rule, particularly the economic drain of Antipas's regime, is felt in the disintegration of households and local village communities. The movement looks to and builds on Israelite traditions and leadership roles. But Jerusalem institutions and traditions to Galileans meant distant rule, and were evaluated ambivalently, perhaps even negatively. Basic in Israelite traditions was the independence of the village communities living under the direct kingship/rule of God, as Moses had taught.

The first rabbinic academies in Galilee were located in (large) villages in the southwest. Rulings in the Mishnah, moreover, appear to be oriented toward householders, even well-off householders. Of course scribal culture traditionally had been oriented toward householders, and large householders at that. In any traditional agrarian society such as second-temple Palestine, households were the fundamental units of production and consumption, the basis of the economy on which the scribes themselves and their patrons, the rulers of the society, depended for revenues. The usual political allies of the scribal class, moreover, would have been the well-to-do householders. This alliance of the tannaitic rabbis in particular was apparently cemented as many of the rabbis themselves became established as wealthy landowners in Galilee. This does not mean that the rabbinic circles were in origins or remained a village-based movement (beyond the particular villages where those earliest Galilean academies were located in the second century). At least by the generation of Judah the Prince, rabbinic academies and activities were based primarily in the cities, particularly Sepphoris. During the third century the rabbinic academies in Tiberias became prominent, important "decisions" were taking place there, and that city became the most important center of Jewish learning and prestige in Palestine.

Some rabbis were wealthy landowners. Yet they resided in the cities, which were the bases of their social-political influence. To the extent that Galilee remained divided between cities and villages, that would have jeopardized rabbinic influences in village affairs. Nevertheless, there was one major difference between the second/third-century rabbis and the earlier Jerusalem priestly aristocracy in relation to the Galilean villagers. Whereas the Jerusalem high priests were apparently viewed as distant rulers closely allied with the Romans, the rabbis, who did not officially exercise political-economic power, were cultivating Israelite traditions in resistance to the dominance of Roman political culture and were doing so nearby, in close but not necessarily exploitative contact with Galilean villagers who shared those Israelite traditions. Although Jewish historians point out that it took centuries for the rabbis to establish significant influence in local "assemblies," they were working not only from common Israelite traditions but in common opposition to the dominant imperial culture.

As more direct and restrictive Roman imperial rule made any attempt at political autonomy and self-rule impossible after the destruction of Jerusalem and the suppression of the Bar Kokhba Revolt, both the proto-Christian movements outside of Palestine and the rabbinic circles in Palestine made the necessary adjustments. Both the successors of the Jesus movement(s), which had aspired to a renewal of Israel in its basic social form of autonomous village life, and later the rabbinic academies, who appear to have projected a utopian vision of an ideal Israel, yielded control of the political to the empire and its alliance with the cities and became what could be called "religions." Earlier generations of Galileans, however, maintaining insofar as possible their independent village life, had repeatedly resisted attempts by outside rulers at more intensive political-economic exploitation or projections of political-cultural programs.

ABBREVIATIONS

✧

AB	Anchor Bible
ABD	D. N. Freedman, ed., *Anchor Bible Dictionary*
AGJU	Arbeiten zur Geschichte des antiken Judentums und des Urchristentums
AJA	*American Journal of Archaeology*
AJSR	*American Jewish Studies Review*
ANET	J. B. Pritchard, ed., *Ancient Near Eastern Texts*
ANRW	*Aufstieg und Niedergang der römishcen Welt*
AOS	American Oriental Society
ASOR	American Schools of Oriental Research
ATR	*Anglican Theological Review*
BA	*Biblical Archaeologist*
BARev	*Biblical Archaeologist Review*
BARIS	Biblical Archaeology Review International Series
BASOR	*Bulletin of the American Schools of Oriental Research*
BJS	Brown Judaic Studies
BTB	*Biblical Theology Bulletin*
CBQ	*Catholic Biblical Quarterly*
CRINT	Compendia Rerum Iudaicarum ad Novum Testamentum
CSCT	Columbia Studies in Classical Traditions
DJD	Discoveries in the Judean Desert
EncJud	*Encyclopedia Judaica*
HTR	*Harvard Theological Review*
HUCA	*Hebrew Union College Annual*

IDBSuppl	Supplementary volume to G. A. Buttrick, ed., *Interpreter's Dictionary of the Bible*
IEJ	*Israel Exploration Journal*
Int	*Interpretation*
JBL	*Journal of Biblical Literature*
JJS	*Journal of Jewish Studies*
JQR	*Jewish Quarterly Review*
JR	*Journal of Religion*
JRS	*Journal of Roman Studies*
JSJ	*Journal for the Study of Judaism in the Persian, Hellenistic, and Roman Period*
JSOT	*Journal for the Study of the Old Testament*
JSOTSup	Journal for the Study of the Old Testament — Supplement Series
JSPSS	Journal for the Study of the Pseudepigrapha — Supplement Series
NovT	*Novum Testamentum*
NTS	*New Testament Studies*
PEQ	*Palestine Exploration Quarterly*
QDAP	*Quarterly of the Department of Antiquities in Palestine*
REJ	*Revue des études juives*
SBLSP	Society of Biblical Literature Seminar Papers
SJ	Studia judaica
SJLA	Studies in Judaism in Late Antiquity
TDNT	G. Kittel and G. Friedrich, eds., *Theological Dictionary of the New Testament*
VTSupp	Vetus Testamentum, Supplements
WHJP	World History of the Jewish People
ZDPV	*Zeitschrift des deutschen Palästina-Vereins*

NOTES

❧

Introduction

1. With hindsight the "contradictions" involved are now evident. As Max Weber argued, the highly individualistic "Protestant ethic" was hardly unrelated to the emergence of corporate capitalism, and Christianizing missions were hardly unrelated to European and American imperialism. Even in the very stage at which early Christianity was supposedly creating an institutionalized form of religion separate from imperial political life, a "love-patriarchalism" emerged (in the deutero-Pauline epistles — or, some would say, already in Paul's own letters) that provided powerful divine sanction to the political-economic-domestic subordination of wives and slaves.

2. German biblical scholars, for example, J. D. Michaelis, *Mosaisches Recht* (Frankfurt, 1775–76), assuming that their own Christianity was purely apolitical, constructed ancient "Judaism" as a decadent, particularistic, and political religion that had been transcended by a universalist Christianity. Some even used such a construction in arguments against allowing Jews political rights in the modern secular state. Michaelis, review of C. W. Dohm, *Über die bürgerliche Verbesserun der Juden*, in *Orientalische und exegetische Biblioteck* 29 (1782).

3. The continuation of the classical nineteenth-century German scholarly construction of "Judaism" can be seem vividly in the "summary" sections of Martin Hengel's monumental scholarly treatise, *Judaism and Hellenism* (Philadelphia: Fortress, 1974). For example, "Summary: The Reform Attempt, Its Failure and the Far-reaching Consequences of the Jewish Counter-reaction":

> Jewish worship of God, without images, spiritual and appearing rational...
> aroused the positive interest of a number of Greek writers...in the early
> Hellenistic period.... [But] the renegades' "zeal against the law" aroused a
> corresponding counter-reaction, "zeal for the law," and as a result the further
> spiritual development of Judaism was in a remarkable way associated with
> the Torah. The Pharisees, who were primarily involved in this development,
> are in a direct line from the Hasidim of the Maccabean period.... This newly
> awakened "zeal"...which found an expression in the intensive national eschatological expectation...is one of the chief causes of the incessant series of
> rebellions in Judea and the great catastrophes of AD 66–70, 116–117, and
> 132–135....The tendency towards segregation from non-Jews...led to ancient "anti-semitism."...The persecutions and victorious Maccabean revolt
> had aroused not only strong religious but also *political forces*....In this way,
> a tremendous strengthening of Jewish national consciousness came about in

Palestine. Despite its expansion and to a degree its missionary successes, the Jewish religion remained primarily a "national" religion. (303–7)

4. A recent illustration of the standard paradigm with regard to the Pharisees and the synagogue (while also a challenge to one aspect of the standard view of the synagogue as a building) is Howard C. Kee, "The Transformation of the Synagogue after 70 C.E.: Its Import for Early Christianity," *NTS* 36 (1990): 1–24.

5. The treatment of Mark by Werner Kelber, for example, in *Mark's Story of Jesus* (Philadelphia: Fortress, 1979), chap. 2, is typical.

6. E.g., John Dominic Crossan, *In Fragments: The Aphorisms of Jesus* (San Francisco: Harper & Row, 1983), 137–44; John Kloppenborg, *The Formation of Q* (Philadelphia: Fortress, 1987), 227; Eugene Boring, *The Continuing Voice of Jesus* (Louisville, Ky.: Westminster/John Knox Press, 1991), 229–30; and frequently in the literature. Several of the Jewish texts often cited with regard to pilgrimage to Jerusalem, e.g., by Joachim Jeremias in *Jesus' Promise to the Nations* (London: SCM Press, 1958), refer not to Gentiles but to the dispersed people/tribes of Israel being gathered in at the eschatological renewal of Israel. If one steps outside of the dominant paradigm, it is possible to discern in these texts a dispute within Israel at its renewal rather than a condemnation of Israel; see R. A. Horsley, *Jesus and the Spiral of Violence: Popular Jewish Resistance in Roman Palestine* (San Francisco: Harper & Row, 1987; Minneapolis: Fortress, 1992), 201–7; and Horsley, "Q and Jesus: Assumptions, Approaches, and Analyses," *Semeia* 55 (1991): 195–96.

7. See Richard A. Horsley with John S. Hanson, *Bandits, Prophets, and Messiahs: Popular Movements in the Time of Jesus* (San Francisco: Harper & Row, 1987); R. A. Horsley, *Sociology and the Jesus Movement* (New York: Crossroad, 1989), chap. 5, and the articles cited in both.

8. E.g., Marcus J. Borg, *Conflict, Holiness, and Politics in the Teaching of Jesus* (Toronto: Edwin Mellen, 1984).

9. I.e., unrecognized in *Bandits, Prophets, and Messiahs* and in *Jesus and the Spiral of Violence;* finally discerned in *Sociology and the Jesus Movement.*

10. Sean Freyne, *Galilee from Alexander the Great to Hadrian: A Study of Second Temple Judaism* (Wilmington, Del.: Glazier, 1980).

11. Kee, "Transformation of the Synagogue."

12. E.g., Burton L. Mack, *The Lost Gospel: The Book of Q and Christian Origins* (San Francisco: HarperCollins, 1993).

13. See chap. 4 below.

14. See further chap. 10 below. Ironically for such "paradigmatic" readings of Mark, the earliest public building that could be identified as a Jewish synagogue was found in Gamla to the east of the lake, datable to at least mid-first century because of the Roman destruction of the town in 67 C.E. Moreover, by the time public buildings are found with any frequency in the third to sixth centuries, they are located in the Golan as well as in Galilee. Given Josephus's reference to a "prayerhouse" (*proseuchē*) in Tiberias along with the "synagogue" building in the fortified town of Gamla, perhaps Jesus' journeys back and forth across the lake in Mark should be read as a symbolic bridging between the urban "Jewish" communities toward the south end of the lake and the rustic farming and fishing villages at the northern end.

15. Discussion of cities in Galilee has been focused primarily on the questions of (outside) "Hellenistic" influence on (indigenous) "Jewish" culture and the "urbanization" of a (previously) rural ethos. Both of those concepts (dichotomies) are derived from discussions of other historical configurations. "Hellenizing" influence on "Jewish" culture derives largely from standard earlier discussion of the Maccabean defense of "Judaism" against the Hellenizing reform forced on Judean in and around Jerusalem by the emperor Antiochus Epiphanes in 168 B.C.E. "Urbanization" has two somewhat different derivations but often overlapping connotations. The one stems from the early Hellenistic imperial policy of establishing "cities" (*poleis*) as a standard political-cultural form in which the political-economic dominant strata were structured at key locations. The other refers to the later Roman imperial policy of administering the countryside through (thus subordinating it to) the most prominent urban settlements in an area.

16. A comment regarding twentieth-century cultural relations seems equally pertinent to the ancient eastern Mediterranean region as well: "Partly because of empire, all cultures are involved in one another; none is single and pure, all are hybrid, heterogeneous, extraordinarily differentiated, and unmonolithic." Edward W. Said, *Culture and Imperialism* (New York: Knopf, 1993), xxv.

17. The history of "urbanization" in Lower Galilee and its effects do not fit the paradigm any more than do the Pharisees-rabbis and the "synagogues." Although Herod's son Antipas rebuilt one city and founded another in Lower Galilee, neither appears to have been particularly "cosmopolitan" and heavily "Hellenistic" in the early first century C.E. They became more so in the course of the second century. However, it was precisely in those Romanized cities that included Dionysus mosaics and pagan motifs on lamps that the rabbis established their most important academies and compiled the monumental achievement of early rabbinism, the Mishnah. Clearly indigenous culture, including intensive legal activities, could thrive side by side with other cultures.

18. Gerhard E. Lenski, *Power and Privilege: A Theory of Social Stratification* (New York: McGraw-Hill, 1966); John H. Kautsky, *The Politics of Aristocratic Empires* (Chapel Hill: University of North Carolina Press, 1982).

19. Each village was a self-contained community economically as well as politically; see Kautsky, *Aristocratic Empires*, 120. "The peasant community...is politically defined by its own structure of power and customary law": James C. Scott, "Agrarian Revolt and the Little Tradition," pt. 2, *Theory and Society* 4 (1977): 212.

20. Kautsky, *Aristocratic Empires*, 74, 112–14. "The relationship between the aristocrat and the peasant is about as reciprocal as that between the shepherd and his animal. The shepherd will protect it from attack and let it live on and eat from his land; 'in return,' he takes its milk or wool and even its meat" (114).

21. Ibid., 194, 188. While attempting to counterbalance the aristocratic interests and orientation of most of our literate sources for antiquity with some degree of empathy with the peasants and other common people, we can still appreciate the fact that without the rulers' drive for display and demands for "surplus" products from the peasant producers, there would be none of the monumental remains of "high" culture from antiquity such as temples and theaters or floor mosaic in villas

and none of the great literary monuments. So Lenski, *Power and Privilege*, 64–65, n. 19.

22. Cf. Kautsky, *Aristocratic Empires*, 49.

23. Ibid., 117.

24. Cf. E. P. Sanders, *Judaism: Practice and Belief 63* B.C.E. — 66 C.E. (Philadelphia: Trinity Press International, 1992).

25. Kautsky, *Aristocratic Empires*, 73.

26. The phrase/concept is from Ranajit Guha, "On Some Aspects of the Historiography of Colonial India," *Subatlern Studies* 1 (Delhi: Oxford University Press, 1982), 5–7.

27. Kautsky, *Aristocratic Empires*, 13.

28. Particularly helpful for Josephus's accounts of affairs in Galilee are Shaye J. D. Cohen, *Josephus in Galilee and Rome: His Vita and Development as a Historian*, CSCT 8 (Leiden: Brill, 1979); as balanced with the more recent and comprehensive studies, Tessa Rajak, *Josephus: The Historian and His Society* (London: Duckworth, 1983; Philadelphia: Fortress, 1984); and Per Bilde, *Flavius Josephus between Jerusalem and Rome: His Life, His Works, and Their Importance*, JSPSS 2 (Sheffield: JSOT Press, 1988).

29. In publications too numerous to cite; see, e.g., Jacob Neusner, *The Rabbinic Traditions about the Pharisees before 70*, 3 vols. (Leiden: Brill, 1971); and Neusner, *Judaism: The Evidence of the Mishnah* (Chicago: University of Chicago Press, 1981).

30. See the pioneering study based primarily on case laws by Martin Goodman, *State and Society in Roman Galilee*, A.D. *132–212* (Totowa, N.J.: Rowman & Allanheld, 1983); and the even more critically sophisticated studies of Lee I. Levine, *The Rabbinic Class of Roman Palestine* (New York: Jewish Theological Seminary of America, 1989); and Shaye J. D. Cohen, "The Place of the Rabbi in Jewish Society of the Second Century," in *The Galilee in Late Antiquity*, ed. Lee I. Levine (New York: Jewish Theological Seminary of America, 1992), 157–73.

31. Two of the leading archaeologists who, with their colleagues, regularly issue reports of excavations are Eric M. Meyers and James F. Strange. The implications of their findings and other archaeological reports for Galilee are discussed at greater length in R. A. Horsley, "The Historical Jesus and Archaeology of the Galilee: Questions from Historical Jesus Research to Archaeologists," *Society of Biblical Literature 1994 Seminar Papers*, ed. Eugene H. Lovering Jr. (Atlanta: Scholars Press, 1994), 91–135.

Chapter 1. The Roots of Galilean Independence

Epigraph: Fernand Braudel, *The Mediterranean and the Mediterranean World in the Age of Philip II*, vol. 1 (New York: Harper & Row, 1972), 31.

1. "Galilee" is not a widely used geographical term in Hebrew biblical literature. One of the Zenon papyri uses the term *galila*, but our "Galilee" comes from *galilaia* used in the Septuagint (the Greek Jewish Bible) and subsequent literature in Greek (such as Josephus and the Gospels). The handful of occurrences in the Hebrew Bible are notable for their variation of reference. From the lists of "cities of refuge" and "cities" granted to the Levites in Josh. 20:7 and 21:32, "Kedesh

in Galilee" is mentioned in the territory of the tribe of Naphtali. But in 21:32 "Kedesh in Galilee" stands parallel to two other towns which are not explicitly placed "in Galilee." In the account of the Assyrian king Tiglath-pileser's conquest of the northern areas of the kingdom of Israel in 2 Kings 15:29, "Gilead and Galilee and all the land of Naphtali" are mentioned following the northern towns Ijon, Abel-beth-maacah, Janoah, Kedesh, and Hazor. This is likely a conflation of two lists, one by towns, the other by broader areas. But in the latter, do "Galilee" and "all the land of Naphtali" overlap, or are they separate and adjacent? Finally, in 1 Kings 9:11–13, "Solomon gave to Hiram [the king of Tyre] twenty cities in the land of Galilee" to help pay off his debt. Those twenty villages "are called the land of Cabul to this day," indicating that "Galilee" included territory to the west of Naphtali along the Tyrian frontier, perhaps in the territory of Zebulun or even of Asher. Finally, in Isa. 9:1, "Galilee = Circle of the Peoples" appears to include both "the land of Zebulun and the land of Naphtali." See further the discussion, including of extrabiblical references, by Rafael Frankel in the *ABD*, 2:879–81.

2. Hypothesis originally by Albrecht Alt, "Galiläische Probleme," *Kleine Schriften zur Geschichte des Volks Israel* (Munich: Beck, 1953), 2:263–74.

3. Some of the generalizations made by Braudel, *The Mediterranean and the Mediterranean World*, 1:25–60, on peoples in the "Mountains" and "Foothills" are applicable to ancient Galilee as well.

4. El Amarna (=EA) letters are cited according to the numbering in J. A. Knudtzon, *Die El-Amarna-Tafeln* (Leipzig: Hinrichs, 1907–15), and in A. F. Rainey, *El Amarna Tablets 359–379* (Neukirchen-Vluyn: Neukirchner Verlag, 1970).

5. On the *hapiru*, see Moshe Greenberg, *The Hapiru*, AOS 39 (New Haven: American Oriental Society, 1953); Marvin Chaney, "Ancient Palestinian Peasant Movements and the Formation of Premonarchic Israel," in *Palestine in Transition: The Emergence of Ancient Israel*, ed. D. N. Freedman and D. F. Graf (Sheffield: Almond, 1983), 39–94, esp. 72–83; Richard A. Horsley, "'*Apiru* and Cossacks: A Comparative Analysis of Social Form and Historical Role," in *New Perspectives on Ancient Judaism: Religion, Literature, and Society in Ancient Israel, Formative Christianity and Judaism*, vol. 2, *Ancient Israel and Christianity*, Presented to Howard Clark Kee, ed. J. Neusner, P. Borgen, E. Frerichs, and R. Horsley (Lanham, Md.: University Press of America, 1987), 2:3–26.

6. On the hypothesis that Israel found its origin in a prolonged sequence of revolts against or withdrawals from the Canaanite rulers rather than by a "conquest" of or a process of gradual immigration into the land, see George E. Mendenhall, "The Hebrew Conquest of Palestine," *BA* 25 (1962): 66–87; and *The Tenth Generation: The Origins of the Biblical Tradition* (Baltimore: Johns Hopkins University Press, 1973); Norman K. Gottwald, *The Tribes of Yahweh* (Maryknoll, N.Y.: Orbis, 1979); Chaney, "Ancient Palestinian Peasant Movements," 39–90. For alternative reconstructions, see, e.g., Baruch Halpern, *The Emergence of Israel in Canaan* (Chico, Calif.: Scholars Press, 1983); Robert B. Coote, *Early Israel: A New Horizon* (Minneapolis: Fortress, 1990).

7. Yigael Yadin, *Hazor: The Schweich Lectures of the British Academy 1970* (London: Oxford University Press, 1972), 108–9, 129–32.

8. "Of the more than 200 Iron Age sites in Ephraim and Manasseh, 85 percent of them were newly founded settlements; that is, most early Israelite villages

were established on previously unoccupied sites": Lawrence E. Stager, "The Song of Deborah: Why Some Tribes Answered the Call and Others Did Not," *BARev* 15 (1989): 53. Surface surveys in southern Lower Galilee suggest increasing settlement of the area during the early Iron age, i.e., the supposed time of Israelite settlement; see N. Zori, *The Land of Issachar* (Jerusalem: Israel Exploration Society, 1977). More recent analysis of pottery fragments found in surface surveys of Lower Galilee suggests increasing density of settlements during the tenth century, some of them fortified; see Zvi Gal, *Lower Galilee during the Iron Age*, ASOR Diss. Series 9 (Winona Lake, Ind.: Eisenbrauns, 1992).

9. Stager, "Song of Deborah," 54.

10. On the form of "popular kingship," see Richard A. Horsley, "Popular Messianic Movements around the Time of Jesus," *CBQ* 46 (1984): 473–78.

11. On the development and use of Elijah–Elisha traditions, see now the essays in Robert B. Coote, ed., *Elijah and Elisha in Socioliterary Perspective* (Atlanta: Scholars Press, 1992).

12. *ANET*, 283; H. Tadmor, "The Southern Border of Aram," *IEJ* 12 (1962): 114–22.

13. See esp. Gal, *Lower Galilee*, 79–82, 108–9. Gal brings an important collection of archaeological data to bear on a number of key historical issues. Yet, like other archaeologists, he is the first to point out that surface surveys provide a limited basis for definitive conclusions, since not all sites are sampled and since only the pottery fragments on the surface can be utilized, without the further material remains and criteria based in the carefully controlled stratigraphy of actual excavations. More decisive evidence for the hypothesis of near-total depopulation of Galilee under the Assyrian empire would have to come from concrete excavations of Iron II sites not mentioned in the Assyrian annals that could prove a sudden and prolonged break in the occupation of those sites.

14. So Martin Noth, *The History of Israel* (Edinburgh: T & T Clark, 1958), 261. See further H. Tadmor, "Some Aspects of the History of Samaria during the Biblical Period," *Jerusalem Cathedra* 3 (1983): 1–11; and John H. Hayes and Jeffrey Kwan, "The Final Years of Samaria (730–20)," *Biblica* 72 (1991): 153–81.

15. Passages such as 2 Kings 17:6 and 21–23 are prime examples of the ideology of the Deuteronomistic history directed against the "rebellious" and "sinful" northern kingdom of Israel. By no means can they be taken at face value.

16. An inscription of Esarhaddon suggests that virtually the whole military apparatus of a conquered ruler, including the supporting cast of agricultural workers, could be incorporated into the imperial army: "[I enlarged the army] with charioteers of the guard, horsemen of the guard, men in charge of the stables, *sa-resi*-officers, service engineers, craftsmen, light troops, shield bearers, scouts, farmers, shepherds, gardeners." See R. Borger, *Die Inschriften Asarhaddons, koenigs von Assyrien* (Graz: Im Selbstdverlage des Herausgabers, 1956), 106.

17. Bustenay Oded, *Mass Deportations in the Neo-Assyrian Empire* (Wiesbaden: Reichert, 1979), 54–57, 91–109. As Oded states, the Assyrian records attest "mass but not *total* deportations. Not all the residents of a certain city or area were deported, but only a proportion of them." Indeed, the vast majority remained, to be taxed by the empire, almost always under the control of Assyrian imperial officers.

18. Yohanan Aharoni, *The Land of the Bible: A Historical Geography*, rev. ed. (Philadelphia: Westminster, 1979), 374–76.

19. See the judicious analysis by Stuart A. Irvine, "The Southern Border of Syria Reconstructed," *CBQ* 56 (1994): 21–41.

20. Additional evidence for the continuity of the Israelite population in Galilee, albeit indirect evidence, derives from recent analysis of the history of the ancient Hebrew language by Gary A. Rendsburg, "The Galilean Background of Mishnaic Hebrew," in *The Galilee in Late Antiquity*, ed. Lee I. Levine (New York: Jewish Theological Seminary of America, 1992), 225–39, and some of the additional literature listed there. *Mishnaic Hebrew*, the language of the Mishnah, which was compiled around 200 C.E. in Galilee, displays distinctive differences from the *Qumran Hebrew* of the Dead Sea Scrolls and the *Late Biblical Hebrew* written in Jerusalem, which is rooted in the southern regional dialect of *Judahite Hebrew*. Recent analysis indicates that *Mishnaic Hebrew* is (close to) the colloquial dialect spoken in Galilee in Roman times. It has long been noticed that certain biblical texts (narratives, victory songs, and so on) that stem from (ancient) northern Israel, such as the Song of Deborah (Judges 5) and the Gideon cycle (Judges 6–8, cited above as a source for the early Israelites in Galilee), display different grammatical usages from Biblical and Judahite Hebrew. Close linguistic analysis indicates that Mishnaic Hebrew shares many of the distinctive linguistic properties found in the *Israelian Hebrew* of those texts stemming from northern Israel. Despite the gap of textual evidence for nearly a millennium, from the biblical texts in Israelian Hebrew prior to 722 B.C.E. to the Mishnah around 200 C.E., a continuity of language use must be posited to account for the strikingly similar linguistic features. The implication is clear: despite the Assyrian conquest the Israelian Hebrew of popular songs and stories such as the Song of Deborah and the Elijah–Elisha cycle continued to be used by the descendants of northern Israelites in Galilee during the intervening centuries, such that mishnaic materials and even rabbinic language patterns are rooted in the same northern Hebrew dialect.

21. See further Alt, "Galiläische Probleme," 2:374–84.

22. On this complicated problem, see esp. Frank M. Cross, "A Reconstruction of the Judean Restoration," *JBL* 94 (1975): 4–18; James D. Purvis, "The Samaritans and Judaism," in *Early Judaism and Its Modern Interpreters* (Atlanta: Scholars Press, 1986), 81–98; Adam Zertal, "The Wedge-Shaped Decorated Bowl and the Origin of the Samaritans," *BASOR* 276 (1989): 80–82; and some of the essays in A. D. Crown, ed., *The Samaritans* (Tübingen: Mohr/Siebeck, 1989).

23. The Romans perpetuated the arrangement, recognizing the Jews as an *ethnos* under their own indigenous rulers. Were the Samaritans similarly treated? Josephus presents the Samaritans as *ethnos* headed by a *boulē*, council, of *protoi* or *dynatoi*, i.e., principal or powerful ones, in *Ant.* 17.20; 18.85.88; 20.125–36; *B.J.* 2.239.

24. Following the persuasive recent summary reconstruction by Purvis, "Samaritans and Judaism," 87–90; and Purvis, "The Samaritans," in *The Cambridge History of Judaism*, vol. 2, *The Hellenistic Age*, ed. W. D. Davies and Louis Finkelstein (Cambridge: Cambridge University Press, 1989), 591–613, esp. 596–604. As Purvis and some of the scholars he cites make clear, older constructions of these highly complicated and uncertain events in Samaritan history as a religious "schism" from "Judaism" are inappropriate.

25. Sean Freyne, *Galilee from Alexander the Great to Hadrian: A Study of Second Temple Judaism* (Wilmington, Del.: Glazier, 1980), 27–35, finds little Hellenistic impact on the Galileans' populace in his survey of "Galilee under the Ptolemies and Seleucids."

26. Most recent critical discussion of the limited and problematic sources and complex issues, with synthetic reconstruction by Grabbe, *Judaism from Cyrus to Hadrian*, vol. 1 (Minneapolis: Fortress, 1992), chap. 2. On the chronology of the restoration, see Cross, "A Reconstruction of the Judean Restoration," *JBL* 94 (1975), 4–18; reprinted in *Int* 29 (1975): 187–203.

27. Grabbe, *Judaism*, 1:131–38; E. Stern, "The Persian Empire and the Political and Social History of Palestine in the Persian Period," in *Cambridge History of Judaism*, vol. 1, *The Persian Age*, ed. W. D. Davies and L. Finkelstein (Cambridge: Cambridge University Press, 1987), 70–87. Stern says that "Nehemiah stepped into a political vacuum" (82). It was a temporary vacuum of Persian political power, perhaps, but in Judea it was a political power struggle that Nehemiah faced.

28. Convincing critical argument from a variety of sources by Stern, "Persian Empire," 82–86.

29. Cf. Shaye Cohen, *From the Maccabees to the Mishnah* (Philadelphia: Westminster, 1987), 138–39. Even if, doubting the historicity of Ezra's mission, one reads Ezra 7–10 as a legitimation of the victory of a particular priestly faction in struggle for a certain policy and political control in Jerusalem (so Grabbe, *Judaism*, 1:136–38), the effect historically is the same: the Jerusalem priesthood was occupied with maintaining the boundaries of its own power and privilege in Jerusalem/ Judea, and not oriented toward expansion of its influence into distant Galilee.

30. If virtually all Israelites had been deported from Galilee by the Assyrians in 732, then the new, non-Israelite inhabitants of Galilee from Assyrian to Hellenistic times would have had even less in common with Judeans — not even a common Israelite background and cultural tradition.

31. Evidently in reaction to Alexander the Great's transformation of the city of Samaria into a Hellenistic city; see Purvis, "The Samaritans," 596–604; and Nathan Schur, *History of the Samaritans* (Frankfurt am Main: Peter Lang, 1989), 35–38.

32. See, recently, Purvis, "The Samaritans," 610–11.

Chapter 2. Galilee under Jerusalem Rule

1. Recently, e.g., Sean Freyne, *Galilee from Alexander the Great to Hadrian: A Study of Second Temple Judaism* (Wilmington, Del.: Glazier, 1980); Freyne's contention that Galileans were loyal to both Temple and Torah, understood primarily in terms of "Judaism" as a religion, will be examined in later chapters.

2. See Jonathan Goldstein, *I Maccabees*, AB (New York: Doubleday, 1976), esp. 62–89; and the review of recent scholarship by Harold W. Attridge, "Historiography," in *Jewish Writings of the Second Temple Period*, ed. Michael Stone (Assen: Van Gorcum, 1984), esp. 171–76.

3. Most treatments of 1 Maccabees date the book late in the reign of John Hyrcanus (134–104); Goldstein, *I Maccabees*, 63, prefers early in the reign of Alexander Janneus. Seth Schwartz, "Israel and the Nations Roundabout: 1 Mac-

cabees and the Hasmonean Expansion," *JJS* 42 (1991): 16–38, has recently argued persuasively that the book was addressed to traditionalist circles early in John Hyrcanus's reign, prior to extensive expansion. An earlier date is not necessary simply in connection with the shifts of style and policy during the reign of John Hyrcanus, however. While 1 Maccabees is highly positive toward the Maccabees as the heroes by whom God delivered Israel (1 Macc. 5:62), it is not uncritically pro-Hasmonean. Yet especially if 1 Maccabees was composed as late as the end of John Hyrcanus's reign, it must have been directed primarily to certain traditionalist Judean circles. While the regime had come to power as defenders of traditional Judean ways, it is highly doubtful that Hyrcanus and his sons would have been avid "Judaizers." The regime was increasingly Hellenized in style and substance, perhaps while still representing key traditional interests. John Hyrcanus bolstered his army with foreign mercenaries and gave his sons all Macedonian dynastic names. His son and first successor Aristobulus styled his regime a "kingship" and himself took the title of "Philhellene" (*B.J.* 1.70; *Ant.* 13.301, 318), and the regime included non-Judeans in prominent positions.

4. Seth Schwartz, "A Note on the Social Type and Political Ideology of the Hasmonean Family," *JBL* 112 (1993): 305–9, provides some suggestive parallels to the rise of local strongmen in situations of political turmoil. Judas and his brothers, however, quickly became more than village strongmen, and more analogous to leaders of guerrilla warfare in wider movements of "national liberation." The Seleucid regime, apparently, and certainly anti-Hasmonean Hellenistic and Roman writers continued to view the Hasmonean regime in terms of its origins, i.e., as a "bandit-state," as evident from the Posidonius reference in Strabo, *Geogr.* 16.2.37 C 761.

5. Detailed study of fragmentary textual and other evidence on the Itureans in Willy Schottroff, "Die Ituräer," *ZDPV* 98 (1982): 125–47, esp. 130–37. Aryeh Kasher, *Jews, Idumeans, and Ancient Arabs* (Tübingen: Mohr, 1988).

6. A review of key provisions in the decree is pertinent:

> In the Great Assembly of the priests and the people and the rulers of the nation and the elders of the country, the following was proclaimed to us:...Then Simon rose up and fought for his nation. He spent great sums of his own money; he armed the soldiers of his nation and paid them wages....The Judeans and their priests have resolved that Simon should be their Ruler and High Priest forever, until a trustworthy prophet should arise, and that he should be governor/general over them and that he should take charge of the sanctuary and appoint officials over its tasks and over the country and the weapons and the strongholds,...and that he should be obeyed by all, and that all contracts in the country should be written in his name, and that he should be clothed in purple and gold. None of the people or priests shall be permitted to nullify any of these decisions or to oppose what he says, or to convene an assembly in the country without his permission. (1 Macc. 14:28–49)

7. On the consolidation of power by the Hasmoneans, amid the decline of the Seleucid regime, see generally T. Fischer, *Seleukiden und Makkabäer: Beiträge zur Seleukidengeschichte und zu den politishen Ereignissen in Judaea während der 1. Halfte des 2. Jahrhunderts v. Christus* (Bochum: Brockmeyer, 1980); and

"Hasmoneans and Seleucids: Aspects of War and Policy in the Second and First Centuries B.C.E.," in *Greece and Rome in Eretz Israel*, ed. Arye Kasher, Uriel Rappaport, and Gideon Fuks (Jerusalem: Israel Exploration Society, 1990), 3–20. For the ways in which the Hasmoneans from the outset also consolidated an economic base, see Shimon Applebaum, "The Hasmoneans — Logistics, Taxation, and the Constitution," in *Judea in Hellenistic and Roman Times: Historical and Archaeological Essays*, SJLA 40 (Leiden: Brill, 1989), 10–11, 15.

8. On Eupolemus, see further Doron Mendels, *The Land of Israel as a Political Concept in Hasmonean Literature* (Tübingen: Mohr, 1987), 29–45.

9. For consolidation of economic power by Simon and John Hyrcanus, see further Applebaum, "The Hasmoneans," 18–22.

10. While Josephus places Hyrcanus's destruction of Shechem and the temple on Mount Gerizim early in his reign, the excavators of the site date the destruction of Shechem after 112 B.C.E.: G. E. Wright, *Shechem: The Biography of a Biblical City* (New York: McGraw-Hill, 1965), 172; R. J. Bull and G. E. Wright, "Newly Discovered Temples on Mt. Gerizim in Jordan," *HTR* 58 (1965): 234–37. The later date would be much closer to the subsequent year-long siege and destruction of Samaria toward the end of Hyrcanus's reign.

11. A concise treatment of Alexander's wars of expansion in the wider Near Eastern political context is Menahem Stern, "Judaea and Her Neighbors in the Days of Alexander Jannaeus," *Jerusalem Cathedra* 1 (1981): 22–46.

12. Doron Mendels, *The Rise and Fall of Jewish Nationalism* (Garden City, N.Y.: Doubleday, 1992), 61–62.

13. See further Mendels, *Land of Israel as Political Concept*, and Mendels, *Rise and Fall of Jewish Nationalism*, chap. 4.

14. Ironically, it is just these decrees that Freyne (*Galilee from Alexander the Great to Hadrian*, 61–62) takes as evidence that Galileans could claims the rights of Jews. Such a reading is rooted in a misunderstanding of the structure of Roman imperial rule.

15. "The interior above Phoenicia as far as the Arabians, between Gaza and Antilibanus, is called Judea": Strabo, *Geogr.* 16.2.21.

16. Stern, "Judaea and Her Neighbors."

17. "How and why was the new territory acquired? In what sense were the inhabitants judaized, and what did this imply? These are among the most difficult and significant questions in Jewish history, and among the least studied": Seth Schwartz, "The 'Judaism' of Samaria and Galilee in Josephus's Version of the Letter of Demetrius I to Jonathan (*Antiquities* 13.48–57)," *HTR* 82 (1989): 384 n. 17. I enter the discussion with considerable trepidation, with apologies for the frequently tentative tone.

18. In the appendix, "The Beginning of Jewish Settlement in Galilee," to "Manpower, Economics, and Internal Strife in the Hasmonean State," in *Armées et Fiscalité dans le Monde Antique* (Paris: Editions du Centre National de la Recherche Scientifique, 1977), 191–94, Bezalel Bar-Kochva sharply criticized both views, suggesting that the view which "assumes that Galilee was already densely populated by Jews before the Hasmonean State" is not based on critical assessment of the sources.

19. See further Joseph Sievers, *The Hasmoneans and Their Supporters* (Atlanta:

Scholars Press, 1990), 49–57; Schwartz, "Israel and the Nations Roundabout," esp. 21–27.

20. The highly schematic 1 Maccabees 5 has been patterned after biblical passages such as Josh. 9:12; Ezra 4:1; Neh. 2:10, 19; 3:33; 4:1–2 ("the nations roundabout") and Deut. 20:13–14 (Judas's treatment of towns in Gilead). Along with this Deuteronomic scheme, 1 Maccabees portrays as Gentile persecution what 2 Maccabees (12:2; 10:14) represents as Seleucid officials' repression, suggesting that 1 Maccabees is at least as tendentious as 2 Maccabees in this case.

21. The letter from the Seleucid Demetrius to the Judeans in 1 Maccabees 10 mentions "three districts" added (to Judea) from Samaria and Galilee (10:30), but this is subsequently clarified as the three toparchies of Aphairema, Lydda, and Ramathaim, all "from the *chōra* of Samaria" (10:38; 11:34), indicating that Galilee was not involved. Similarly, caution is necessary in drawing inferences from certain passing references to Galilee in our sources. For example, the report in 1 Macc. 12:47–51 that when Jonathan advanced on Ptolemais he left two-thirds of his troops in Galilee, who subsequently stood their ground against Seleucid troops, suggests nothing about "support" for Jonathan from Galileans. Ironically some of the passages mentioned as evidence for Galileans being Jews turn out instead to illustrate the basic structure of political-economic-religious domination that the Hasmoneans were assembling over Judea and beginning to extend to other areas of Palestine: e.g., in 1 Macc. 10:38 the three annexed toparchies are to "obey no other authority than the high priest"; and the official letter from Antiochus III in *Ant.* 12.138–44 refer to how those in and around Jerusalem (not Galilee) are to be governed "according to the ancestral laws" as well as to the tax-remission for the imperial regime's client rulers, the Judean priestly aristocracy.

22. E.g., Freyne, *Galilee from Alexander the Great to Hadrian*, 39; Menahem Stern, *Greek and Latin Authors on Jews and Judaism*, 2 vols. (Jerusalem: Israel Academy of Sciences and Humanities, 1974–80), 1:225.

23. What Josephus did is transparent: assuming that "Judea" was the territory claimed by Jerusalem rulers in his own time (cf. his similar insertion of "Judea" at *Ant.* 13.174 for "his own country" in 1 Macc. 12:35), he read *Galgala* as Galilee (thus generating the extremely awkward juxtaposition of "coming into Judea" and "encamping in Galilee") and read the dative plural *arbelois* as a reference to Arbela, a hilly area north of Magdala. He then embellished the brief reference in 1 Macc. 9:2 with a bit of "local color" from the famous later exploits of Herod in ferreting out the brigands holed up in the caves near Arbela, *B.J.* 1.304–13; *Ant.* 14.415–30.

24. Bezalel Bar-Kochva, *Judas Maccabaeus: The Jewish Struggle against the Seleucids* (Cambridge: Cambridge University Press, 1989), 552–59, has offered a convincing explanation for this problematic passage along with a telling critique of alternative suggestions.

25. Notwithstanding his anti-Jewish biases and other limitations, E. Schürer's argument a century ago (*A History of the Jewish People in the Age of Jesus Christ*, 3 vols., rev. and ed. G. Vermes, F. Millar, et al. [Edinburgh: T & T Clark, 1973–87], 1:275) that the portion of Iturean-controlled territory taken by Aristobulus was (part of) Galilee was valid. Ironically, Freyne's paragraph (*Galilee from Alex-*

ander the Great to Hadrian, 43) against Schürer on the "Judaization" of Galilee supports rather than weakens Schürer's conjecture.

26. See, with a critical eye, E. M. Meyers, J. F. Strange, and C. L. Meyers, *Excavations at Ancient Meiron, Upper Galilee, Israel 1971–72, 1974–75, 1977* (Cambridge, Mass.: ASOR, 1981), xix, 155, and Appendix C. Some caution is in order since Jannean coins also predominate among Hasmonean coins found in Judean sites as well.

27. Those who believe that Galilee was already heavily Jewish read this passage as referring basically to Upper Galilee, immediately adjacent to the Itureans' base in Lebanon.

28. See the analysis of sources by W. Schottroff cited in n. 5 above.

29. Cf. the earlier argument by Albrecht Alt, "Galiläische Probleme," *Kleine Schriften zur Geschichte des Volks Israel* (Munich: Beck, 1953), 2:406–7.

30. In Stern, *Greek and Latin Authors*, 1:146.

31. U. Rappaport, "Les Idumeens en Egypte," *Revue de Philologie* 43 (1969): 73–82.

32. Mendels, *Land of Israel as Political Concept*, 75–88, argues that Jubilees pertains to the subjugation of the Idumeans in the 120s by Hyrcanus rather than to Judas the Maccabee's attacks in the 160s. Recently, however, Robert Doran, "The Non-Dating of Jubilees: Jub 34–38; 23:14–32 in Narrative Context," *JSJ* 20 (1989): 1–11, has raised compelling questions about such use of Jubilees as a historical evidence.

33. For the continuing "international" struggle Alexander Janneus waged to maintain control of Galilee and other territories, see Stern, "Judaea and Her Neighbors," 22–46.

34. As in the classic study of ancient Mediterranean materials by Arthur Darby Nock (*Conversion: The Old and the New in Religion from Alexander the Great to Augustine of Hippo* [Oxford: Clarendon, 1933]), who defined conversion as "the reorientation of the soul of an individual, his deliberate turning from indifference or from an earlier form of piety to another, a turning which implies a consciousness that a great change is involved, that the old was wrong and the new is right" (7). A sampling of entries on "conversion" in standard dictionaries and encyclopedias (whether in biblical studies and religion or general) provides further indications of how problematic the concept of conversion is for second temple history.

35. Shaye J. D. Cohen, "Crossing the Boundary and Becoming a Jew," *HTR* 82 (1989): 26. In other, related articles, however, Cohen assumes that ancient authors such as Josephus, Strabo, and Ptolemy are writing accounts of the *conversion* of Idumeans and/or Itureans. But that assumes what needs to be demonstrated. Although in one article he claims that "for Josephus 'to be circumcised' and 'to follow Jewish customs' are synonymous with 'to convert to Judaism'" ("Religion, Ethnicity, and Hellenism in the Emergence of Jewish Identity in Maccabean Palestine," in *Religion and Religious Practice in the Seleucid Kingdom*, ed. Per Bilde et al. [Aarhus: Aarhus University Press, 1990], 222 n. 11), Cohen himself had previously made clear that Josephus has no term for "conversion," which is, at best, an "ill-defined concept" ("Respect for Judaism by Gentiles According to Josephus," *HTR* 80 [1987]: 409–30). The ancient authors are writing accounts of the relations among peoples. To be determined is whether we can adequately understand

those accounts and or the historical relations to which they refer with our concept of conversion.

36. Kasher, *Jews, Idumeans, and Ancient Arabs*, chap. 3. Some sources are subjected to highly critical dismissal as propaganda, while others are taken at face value as evidence for seemingly timeless, unchanging social-religious norms and policies. The trust that developed between powerful Idumeans such as Antipater's father and Hasmonean rulers such as Alexander Janneus hardly provides evidence that rural Idumeans voluntarily identified with their Judean counterparts in common opposition to urban Hellenization. See further the critique of particular points of Kasher's arguments by Israel Shatzman, *The Armies of the Hasmoneans and Herod* (Tübingen: Mohr, 1991), 58–59 n. 90.

37. Grabbe, *Judaism from Cyrus to Hadrian*, vol. 1 (Minneapolis: Fortress, 1992), 2:329–31. Similarly, Sievers, *Hasmoneans and Their Supporters*, 143.

38. So also Cohen, "Religion, Ethnicity, and Hellenism," 216.

39. Josephus supplies no basis for the claim that "in the 'war of Varus' Idumea revolted along with Jerusalem" (Grabbe, *Judaism*, 2:329). The Jerusalemites' protest to Varus, according to Josephus's accounts (*B.J.* 2.73; *Ant.* 17.293), that they had not been involved in the revolt, has some credibility, for Josephus makes clear here as well as earlier in his accounts that those besieging the Romans in Jerusalem were from the countryside. The insurrections put down by Varus were themselves based in the countryside in Galilee, Perea, and Judea, with no mention of any in Idumea (*B.J.* 2.56–65; *Ant.* 17.271–84). Josephus also mentions 2,000 veterans of Herod in Idumea (*B.J.* 2.55; had they been settled there?) fighting against Herod's troops under Achiab — i.e., hardly typical Idumeans. Finally, after Varus had suppressed the insurrections in Galilee, Perea, and Judea, 10,000 more rebels surrendered to Varus on the advice of Achiab. Josephus calls the latter *ioudaioi* in *Ant.* 17.297 and locates them *kata tēn Idoumaian*, probably to be translated "against" or "toward Idumea" in *B.J.* 2.76. Probably these last holdouts were fugitives from Varus's sweep southward through the Judean countryside. If they were Idumeans, they were acting parallel to the peasantry in the other districts of Herod's realm, not "revolting with Jerusalem."

40. Certainly the speeches by Jesus the chief priest and Simon the Idumean chieftain (*B.J.* 4.270ff.) provide no evidence for the Idumeans' views of Jerusalem and the Temple since they are written (in good Hellenistic historiographic fashion) by, and from the point of view of, the wealthy and powerful Judean priest, Josephus (vs. Stern, *Greek and Latin Authors*, 1.356).

41. Anticipating fuller discussion in chapter 6 of the garrisoned fortresses which the Hasmoneans and Herod maintained in Galilee, only the initial Hasmonean establishment of such installations are discussed here.

42. So also Eric M. Meyers, James F. Strange, Carol L. Meyers, and Richard S. Hanson, "Preliminary Report on the 1977 and 1978 Seasons at Gush Halav," *BASOR* 233 (1979): 36. Only if the previous inhabitants were pushed out and Gush Halav became exclusively a garrison town could we conclude from such coins that this village had become distinctively "Jewish," i.e., Judean — on the further assumption that Alexander Janneus would have stationed Judean soldiers and not non-Judean mercenary soldiers there (vs. Freyne, *Galilee from Alexander the Great*

to Hadrian, 44; and Meyers, Strange, and Meyers, *Excavations at Ancient Meiron*, xix, 155).

43. For fuller analysis of the textual and archaeological evidence on Hasmonean fortresses and garrisons, see Shatzman, *Armies of the Hasmoneans*, esp. 44, 83–87, 94–97, on Galilee in particular.

44. Victor Tcherikover, *Hellenistic Civilization and the Jews* (New York: Atheneum, 1970), 60–63; Martin Hengel, *Judaism and Hellenism* (Philadelphia: Fortress, 1974), 18–23.

45. That is, not the emergence of a "native" Galilean aristocracy, vs. Freyne, *Galilee from Alexander the Great to Hadrian*, 49–50.

46. Referring to the power struggles within the Hasmonean regime continuing from the reign of Alexander into that of his wife and successor Alexandra Salome (*Ant.* 13:410–24), Bar-Kochva, "Manpower, Economics, and Internal Strife," 178, notes, "At least some of these *dynatoi* were undoubtedly mercenary commanders, as is also indicated by their threat to join the Arab Aretas and other neighboring rulers (414), by the fact that they isolated themselves in the fortresses (417) and by the names of some of them (Diogenes, 410; Galaistes, 424)."

47. So also Steve Mason, *Flavius Josephus and the Pharisees* (Leiden: Brill, 1991), 97–106, with numerous illustrations of synonymous terms and phrases in Josephus's accounts.

48. Originally, by Elias J. Bickerman, "La charte seleucide de Jerusalem," *REJ* 100 (1935): 4–35, reprinted in *Studies in Jewish and Christian History II*, AGJU 9 (Leiden: Brill, 1980), 2:44–85; more recently Pierre Briant, "The Seleucid Kingdom, the Achaemenid Empire, and the History of the Near East in the First Millennium B.C.," in *Religion and Religious Practice in the Seleucid Kingdom*, ed. Bilde et al., 58–59.

49. Stern, *Greek and Latin Authors*, #11. Cf. Cohen, "Religion, Ethnicity, and Hellenism in the Emergence of Jewish Identity in Maccabean Palestine," 218–19. While seeing that the laws of the Judeans were understood as *politeia*, Cohen perhaps underestimates the continuity of this arrangement from the Persian empire. He also appears to dissolve *politeia*, like the laws of the Judeans, into a realm of religion or culture such that a change in one's *politeia* can be called conversion.

50. Following the recent translation by Seth Schwartz, "The 'Judaism' of Samaria and Galilee in Josephus's Version of the Letter of Demetrius I to Jonathan (*Antiquities* 13.48–57)," *HTR* 83 (1989): 381–82. As Schwartz points out (387–90), Josephus's motives for the intentional alterations to his source probably has to do, significantly, with the demise of the political-religious authority of the Judean elite in the late-first century C.E. because of the destruction of the temple-state (along with the Temple).

51. See, e.g., Tcherikover, *Corpus Papyrorum Judaiorum*, 1:4; Stern, *Greek and Latin Authors*, 1:2–4, 2:620–25; Kasher, *Jews, Idumeans, and Ancient Arabs*, 56–57; and for an earlier time, Jer. 9:25–26.

52. A story Josephus tells about pressure to circumcise two Herodian (Gentile) nobles who had come over to the rebel side in 66–67 C.E. indicates that circumcision held broad social-political significance of solidarity and loyalty, and was not simply a religious matter (the political and religious dimensions were inseparable; see *Vita* 112–13, 149–54).

53. On the other hand, it is possible to read the wording by Josephus and Strabo-Timagenes in the sense, respectively, that the inhabitants were to be circumcised (i.e., a new ritual only for those not already circumcised) or that the Itureans' already being circumcised was the bond by which they were joined to the Judeans (*Ant.* 13.318–19).

54. The following discussion draws on a discussion by James Pasto, "Exclusion or Inclusion? The Origin and Expansion of the Hasmoneans in Light of Comparative Ethnographic Studies," in *Second Temple Studies 2: Hellenistic Period*, ed. John Halligan, JSOTSup (Sheffield: JSOT Press, forthcoming), based on several studies: Kwame Arhin, "The Structure of Greater Ashanti (1700–1824)," *Journal of African History* 8 (1967): 65–85; C. M. K. Morrison, *Ethnicity and Political Integration: The Case of the Ashanti Ghana* (Syracuse, N.Y.: Maxwell School of Citizenship and Public Affairs, 1982); Ivor Wilks, *Ashante in the Nineteenth Century: The Structure and Evolution of a Political Order* (Cambridge: Cambridge University Press, 1975); J. Lamphear, "The People of the Grey Bull: The Origin and Expansion of the Turkana," *Journal of African History* 29 (1988): 27–39; Raymond Kelly, *The Nuer Conquest* (Ann Arbor: University of Michigan Press, 1985).

55. Pasto, "Exclusion or Inclusion?" 11–12.

56. For fuller analysis and arguments, see Mendels, *Land of Israel as Political Concept*, chap. 6. As noted above, however, caution is advised on using Jubilees as a source for a particular period of Judean history, such as the reign of Hyrcanus, following Doran, "The Non-Dating of Jubilees."

57. For fuller discussion of the Roman policy of alliance with and rule through native aristocracies, see G. H. Stevenson, *Roman Provincial Administration*, 2nd ed. (Oxford: Blackwell, 1949); F. F. Abbott and A. C. Johnson, *Municipal Administration in the Roman Empire* (New York: Russell and Russell, 1968); with particular reference to the Jewish high priesthood, see R. A. Horsley, "High Priests and the Politics of Roman Palestine," *JSJ* 17 (1986): 23–55.

58. Freyne, *Galilee from Alexander the Great to Hadrian*, 61–62, both misreads the Roman decrees cited by Josephus and misunderstands the character of political-economic relations under ancient empires when he claims that "the rights and privileges" pertained to the Jews generally, in which the Galileans now supposedly shared.

59. On banditry in ancient Palestine, see further Richard A. Horsley, "Josephus and the Bandits," *JSJ* 10 (1979): 37–63; and Richard A. Horsley with John S. Hanson, *Bandits, Prophets, and Messiahs: Popular Movements in the Time of Jesus* (San Francisco: Harper & Row, 1987), chap. 2. Because ancient historians were oriented toward "political" history, a popular disruption had to be of major scope or significance to be mentioned. How the phenomenon of "social banditry" can be generated in just such circumstances of exorbitant taxation and/or chronic warfare will be examined in chap. 12 below.

60. One incident reported by Josephus appears to indicate Galilean attachment to the high priesthood in Jerusalem. The energetic young Herod, upon appointment as commander in Galilee, immediately set about suppressing the banditry along the Syrian frontier, killing the brigand-chief Hezekiah and many of his band. While this action won appreciation among the Syrians, it provoked a dramatic

vocal protest, both by officers of the high-priestly court (literally "those of the Judeans in office," *Ant.* 14.163) and by the mothers of those murdered by Herod. The former, defending their own position and prerogatives, argued that Herod had "violated their law which forbids slaying even an evildoer unless he has first been condemned by the Sanhedrin." The mothers "every day in the temple begged the king and the people to have Herod brought to judgment" (*Ant.* 14.167–68). As Eric Hobsbawm explains in *Primitive Rebels* (New York: Norton, 1959), 115–21, peasants or other ordinary people often appeal to a king against behavior by one of his officials, since the king is the symbol of justice, especially in its absence. Most of the cases he has in mind, however, come from societies in which the kingship, having been in place for centuries, was hedged about with a sacral aura of tradition. By contrast, in the case of the mothers of the bandits killed by Herod, the high priests in Jerusalem had ruled over Galilee for barely two generations. Thus it may be questionable whether this report by Josephus indicates Galilean attachment to the Jerusalem government. The high priest (and Sanhedrin) may simply have been their only "court of appeal." Freyne, *Galilee from Alexander the Great to Hadrian*, 67–68, in effect eliminates the possibility that these mothers appealing to the high priest and Sanhedrin might indicate some attachment to Jerusalem and the temple by his reading of Hezekiah and his brigands as Hasmonean nobility, to whom he attributes virtually all Galilean resistance to Herod.

61. Freyne, *Galilee from Alexander the Great to Hadrian*, 63–68. In his lengthy argument that Galilee was not a hotbed of revolutionary activity, Freyne was still operating with the modern scholarly construct of "the Zealots" as a longstanding and widespread movement advocating armed rebellion against the Romans. One of the principal supports of that construct was the assumption that Josephus ordinarily used the term *lēstai* (bandits) in reference to "the Zealots." Freyne is thus understandably at pains to explain away Josephus's reports about the *archilēstēs* (bandit-chief) Hezekiah murdered by the young Herod in 47 B.C.E. and the *lēstai* dwelling in the caves near Arbela nearly a decade later. Freyne's claim that resistance to Herod was basically by Hasmonean nobility is also dependent on and an important component of a much oversimplified reconstruction of events in Palestine in the 50s and 40s B.C.E. He apparently believes that Herod's murder of Hezekiah "caused the Hasmonean aristocracy that was prepared to go along with Roman rule to join Antigonus rather than Hyrcanus" and uses as an illustration "the second in command [*hypostrategos*] in Jerusalem," Peitholaus, who "fought against Alexander [first son of Aristobulus, rival to Hyrcanus], *Ant.* 14.84, but for Antigonus [other son of Aristobulus], *Ant.* 14.120" (*Galilee from Alexander the Great to Hadrian*, 63, 93 n. 20). The situation and unfolding events in Palestine (focused on the conflict between the Hasmonean rivals Hyrcanus and Aristobulus), however, compounded by the shifting needs and favor of rival Roman leaders, were far more complex than a simple opposition of Hyrcanus, Antipater, and his son Herod, on the one hand, versus the Hasmonean nobles with Antigonus and the Parthians, on the other. In fact, according to Josephus, Hasmonean officials had begun to defect nearly a decade before Herod killed Hezekiah the brigand-chief. Peitholaus had deserted not to Antigonus but to his father Aristobulus with 1,000 men in 56 B.C.E., and was killed by Cassius (in 52?) when he was attempting to rally Aristobulus's partisans (*B.J.* 1.172, 180). Moreover, to complicate matters,

Julius Caesar had sent Aristobulus back to Syria. Evidently the composition of the political sides was constantly shifting and, for the Hasmonean officers, the outcome was utterly unclear, with much maneuvering for position. In 43 B.C.E., several years after the elimination of the Galilean bandit-chief Hezekiah, Malichus, a Hasmonean officer loyal to Hyrcanus, had Antipater poisoned, whereupon Herod avenged his father's death by having Malichus assassinated (*B.J.* 1.223–30; *Ant.* 14.280–93). The next year, in and around Jerusalem (not Galilee), Malichus's brother Helix attacked Herod's brother Phasael (*B.J.* 1.294–96). Thus there had been power struggles going on within the Hasmonean regime, even within Hyrcanus's regime, for some time, quite unrelated to Herod's murder of Hezekiah and his brigands in Galilee. Moreover, the return of Antigonus from exile appears unconnected with these struggles within the Hasmonean regime in and around Jerusalem. It was connected rather with the political schemes of petty rulers in Tyre and Chalcis (*B.J.* 1.297).

62. Freyne, *Galilee from Alexander the Great to Hadrian*, 67.

63. The highest-ranking officers likely enjoyed substantial income from prebendal estates, and they and other officers in charge of tax collection in regional centers surely came into control of additional agricultural and other revenues, perhaps through the credit-debt mechanism. Perhaps these would be what earlier treatments referred to as "large landowners."

64. Perhaps this paucity of direct evidence is why Freyne lacks even a paragraph on Galilee under Herod, despite the obvious importance of Herod's reign for our understanding of Galilee (see *Galilee from Alexander the Great to Hadrian*, 68).

65. Review of literature in James F. Strange, "Archaeology and the Religion of Judaism in Palestine," *ANRW* 2.19.1 (1979): 651–55.

66. Having been disfigured in captivity, Hyrcanus II was (conveniently for Herod) now disqualified for the high-priestly office itself. Meanwhile, Herod systematically eliminated all other Hasmoneans and Hasmonean loyalists, particularly partisans of Antigonus, and confiscated their property (*Ant.* 15.5).

67. *Pace* Jacob Neusner, *From Politics to Piety* (Englewood Cliffs, N.J.: Prentice-Hall, 1973). See further chap. 6.

68. Several decades later they are still active in political affairs, indeed are at the center of political scheming in the aftermath of the initial revolt in the summer of 66 (*Vita* 20–23).

69. See Shimon Applebaum, "Economic Life in Ancient Palestine," in *The Jewish People in the First Century*, CRINT I.2, ed. S. Safrai and M. Stern (Assen: Van Gorcum, 1976), 661–65. E. P. Sanders, *Judaism: Practice and Belief 63* B.C.E. — 66 C.E. (Philadelphia: Trinity Press International, 1992), 157–68, objects to posing the economic burden of Palestinian producers in terms of the layers of rulers' demands. "Nevertheless," he agrees, "the people were hard-pressed. Modern scholars are in one sense right to speak of their 'oppression.' "

70. See further R. A. Horsley, "The Zealots: Their Origins, Relationships, and Importance in the Jewish Revolt," *NovT* 27 (1986): 159–92.

71. See Richard A. Horsley, "Popular Messianic Movements around the Time of Jesus," *CBQ* 46 (1984): 471–95; *Bandits, Prophets, and Messiahs*, chap. 3.

72. See further Horsley, "Popular Messianic Movements."

Chapter 3. Galilee between Roman Reconquests (4 B.C.E.–67 C.E.)

Epigraphs: John Kautsky, *The Politics of Aristocratic Empires* (Chapel Hill: University of North Carolina Press, 1982), 73; Josephus, *Vita* 65–67.

1. Eric M. Meyers, "Roman Sepphoris in the Light of New Archaeological Evidence and Research," in *The Galilee in Late Antiquity*, ed. Lee I. Levine (New York: Jewish Theological Seminary of America, 1992), 323. See further chap. 7 below.

2. Of the now extensive literature criticizing this modern scholarly construct of "the Zealots," see Solomon Zeitlin, "Zealots and Sicarii," *JBL* 81 (1962): 395–98; Morton Smith, "The Zealots and Sicarii, Their Origins and Relationship," *HTR* 64 (1971): 1–19; Richard A. Horsley, "Josephus and the Bandits," *JSJ* 10 (1979): 37–63; and R. A. Horsley, "The Zealots: Their Origins, Relationships, and Importance in the Jewish Revolt," *NovT* 27 (1986): 159–92.

3. Much of Freyne's book, *Galilee from Alexander the Great to Hadrian: A Study of Second Temple Judaism* (Wilmington, Del.: Glazier, 1980), is devoted to arguing that Galilee was not dominated by "the Zealots" movement. Now that we recognize that no such movement existed in the synthetic way imagined by modern scholars (Freyne was influenced particularly by Martin Hengel, *Die Zeloten* [Leiden: Brill, 1961]), it should be possible to discern more precisely the diverse conflicts and movements that characterized Galilee in the first century.

4. Gerd Theissen, *The Gospels in Context* (Minneapolis: Fortress, 1991), 29.

5. Cf. the recent interpretation of this account in Josephus in relation to the story of the Baptist's execution in Mark 6:17–29 by Gerd Theissen, in ibid., 81–97. Theissen is highly trusting of the historian's ability to move directly from a combination of Gospel story and Josephus's report to historical context and assumes that Antipas possessed "legitimacy in the eyes of the people" (which could then be undermined). He also believes that Josephus is citing "the Jews as a whole," hence witnessing to "popular traditions."

6. The story in Luke 23:7–12 of "Herod" Antipas conveniently in Jerusalem so that Pilate might refer the case of Jesus to him is hardly credible historically. Hence it is unwarranted to believe that Antipas made "frequent visits to Jerusalem on occasion of feasts," vs. Freyne, *Galilee from Alexander the Great to Hadrian*, 71.

7. Freyne (ibid., 69–71) argues that the Galilean cities were integrative, not disruptive, forces, that Antipas's realm enjoyed homogeneity since it was all "Jewish," and hence that Antipas's reign offered "Galilean Judaism" the possibility of developing "a political identity of its own," at once Hellenistic and Jewish.

8. See further Horsley, "The Zealots," 159–92.

9. Theissen, *Gospels in Context*, 85, comments that "specifically Jewish features retreat into the background" in Mark 6:17–29. It is difficult to find any Judean features in this story that could have retreated.

10. For example, A. H. M. Jones, *The Herods of Judaea* (Oxford: Clarendon, 1938), 209, except for the reference to the Pharisees, for which there is no textual basis, simply paraphrases Josephus's encomium in *Ant.* 19.331 (cited below): "Agrippa took great pains to cultivate the Pharisees, residing constantly at Jerusalem, paying sacrifice regularly at the temple, and meticulously observing every detail of the Law"; and Menahem Stern, "Herod the Great," in *The Herodian*

Period, ed. Michael Avi-Yonah and Z. Baras, WHJP I.7 (New Brunswick, N.J.: Rutgers University Press, 1975), 144: "His popularity is also reflected in Talmudic passages, where he is represented as the ruler most acceptable to the nation."

11. See the chronology worked out by Daniel R. Schwartz, *Agrippa I: The Last King of Judea* (Tübingen: Mohr, 1990), esp. 67, 107.

12. See the convincing analysis of Jerusalem politics under Agrippa by Schwartz in ibid., 63–66, 116–30.

13. So ibid., 157–71; cf. 132: "No one could — or no one should — imagine Agrippa as a pious Jew of any sort."

14. See further the treatment of these various forms of social unrest and resistance in my *Bandits, Prophets, and Messiahs: Popular Movements in the Time of Jesus* (with John S. Hanson) (San Francisco: Harper & Row, 1987), and *Jesus and the Spiral of Violence: Popular Jewish Resistance in Roman Palestine* (San Francisco: Harper & Row, 1987; Minneapolis: Fortress, 1992), chaps. 3–4, and the more fully documented articles cited there.

15. Herod the Great is a possible exception. His surveillance of the people appears to have been primarily focused on Jerusalem, while his many and massive fortresses provided security around the rest of his realm (*Ant.* 15.267–92, 293–98).

16. See the provisional sketch in Horsley, "Q and Jesus: Assumptions, Approaches, and Analyses," *Semeia* 55 (1991): 192–93, 199–202.

17. The problems of using synoptic Gospel traditions as historical sources are sufficiently complex as to require fuller treatment in a separate context.

18. A great deal of skepticism, moreover, surrounds his claims to have fortified all those Galilean towns in 2.573–75.

19. Shaye J. D. Cohen, *Josephus in Galilee and Rome: His Vita and Development as a Historian*, CSCT 8 (Leiden: Brill, 1979), 183ff., points out that this procedure is misleading, but suggests no alternative for the labels.

20. Cohen's *Josephus in Galilee and Rome* is the touchstone for subsequent criticism of Josephus's accounts of the revolt in Galilee and his own ambiguous role in Galilean events; see further the review of Josephus scholarship by L. H. Feldman, *Josephus and Modern Scholarship, 1937–80* (Berlin: de Gruyter, 1984); H. W. Attridge, "Josephus and His Works," in *Jewish Writings of the Second Temple Period*, ed. Michael Stone (Assen: Van Gorcum, 1984), 187–92; and Per Bilde, *Flavius Josephus between Jerusalem and Rome: His Life, His Works, and Their Importance*, JSPSS 2 (Sheffield: JSOT Press, 1988), chaps. 2 and 4.

21. See (all by Horsley) "High Priests and the Politics of Roman Palestine," *JSJ* 17 (1986): 23–55; *Jesus and the Spiral of Violence*, chaps. 1–4; *Sociology and the Jesus Movement* (New York: Crossroad, 1989), chaps. 4–5.

22. Martin Goodman, *The Ruling Class of Judaea: The Origins of the Jewish Revolt against Rome* A.D. 66–70 (Cambridge: Cambridge University Press, 1987), takes the important step of recognizing that the priestly aristocracy constituted a ruling class. But the situation they faced in the summer of 66 may not have been a choice *between* retaining their accustomed loyalty to Rome, on the one hand, *or* retaining their power and preeminence in Judea, on the other, because those two were not alternatives in the Roman imperial situation.

23. Fuller analysis of the Sicarii in Richard A. Horsley, "The Sicarii: Ancient Jewish Terrorists," *JR* 59 (1979): 435–58.

24. Cohen, *Josephus in Galilee and Rome*, 153–60, sees as distinctive to *Life* and Josephus's later period an apology "that Josephus was sent to Galilee to keep the peace, and that he intended to submit to the Romans as soon as possible" (along with the related notion that the priestly aristocracy remaining in Jerusalem were taking a similar approach). His analysis of the *Jewish War*, focused as it is on the self-portrait of Josephus as the ideal general, does not probe for elements similar to the *Life*. For a critique of Cohen's reading of Josephus's two accounts and a critically established alternative moving in the same direction as my reading here, see Tessa Rajak, *Josephus: The Historian and His Society* (London: Duckworth, 1983; Philadelphia: Fortress, 1984), chaps. 4 and 6; and esp. Bilde, *Flavius Josephus*, chaps. 2 and 5.

25. Josephus's claim to have levied an army of "upwards of a hundred thousand young men" or to have had "sixty thousand infantry and three hundred and fifty cavalry ready for action" in *B.J.* 2.577, 583, is a fiction belonging to his self-portrait as the ideal general, worthy opponent of his later Flavian patrons Vespasian and Titus.

26. A good illustration of this comes later in the revolt, in Josephus's account of the Roman reconquest of Judea; see Horsley, "The Zealots," 159–92.

27. *Pace* Cohen, *Josephus in Galilee and Rome*, 216–21, who simply finds Tiberias's loyalty shifting periodically. I believe Josephus *is* "interested in the political machinations which lay behind these shifting loyalties," hence that precise reconstruction is possible.

28. The city Gabara seems to be identical with the village Gabaroth, judging from Josephus's narrative in *Vita* 229, 235, 240, 242–43.

29. In one of the major occasions on which outsiders such as peasants and Tiberians were assembled in Taricheae (venting their suspicions about Josephus's ultimate intentions!), he is pursued by an armed crowd and, he writes, had "the distinguished ones and the magistrates beaten... and flayed to the bone" (*B.J.* 2.598–612). He does not, however, indicate explicitly that these "distinguished ones and magistrates" are Tarichaeans, and in the parallel account he makes his violent encounter with the crowd into a semi-separate incident, identifies them as "the brigands and the promoters of disturbance," and has the hands of the most stalwart one cut off (*Vita* 145–47). Hence this incident would not seem to contradict the general picture of good relations between Josephus and Taricheae.

30. In this respect he resembles many other figures, such as the young David son of Jesse (1 Sam. 22:2, and so on), or Pancho Villa, who later became one of the principal leaders of the Mexican revolution. See further R. A. Horsley, "Ancient Jewish Social Banditry and the Revolt against Rome, A.D. 66–70," *CBQ* 43 (1981): 409–32, and comparative literature cited there.

31. Could it be that Simon son of Gamaliel and the leading Pharisees were a bit more "moderate," i.e., independence-minded, than the high-priestly duumvirate, Ananus and Jesus son of Gamala, but the latter were trapped and had to agree to remove Josephus because of either ineffectiveness in controlling Galilee or too much conniving with the *prōtoi* of Tiberias, who were Agrippa's men (i.e., the rival regime for control of Galilee)?

32. Sean Freyne, "The Galileans in the Light of Josephus' *Vita*," *NTS* 26 (1979–80): 397–413. Freyne, however, muddles the picture by not discerning that *hoi*

galilaioi can refer to the Galilean peasantry independent of whether or not they are loyal to Josephus, as in *Vita* 30, 39, 66, 143, 177, 351, where he uses the term just as he already had in *B.J.* 2.621–22; 3.110, 199, and so on. Particular meaning of the term, of course, is contextual. From a perspective within Galilee, the Galileans are usually the peasantry in a given area of Galilee as a whole. But from a perspective beyond Galilee, "the Galileans" can refer to all residents of Galilee, including those in Tiberias and Sepphoris.

33. Cf. ibid., 397–413. Freyne has done a traditional "word study" attempting "to allow the text of the *Vita* to speak for itself." What is needed, rather, is first a careful rhetorical criticism and second a critical historical analysis with full attention to other evidence including the *War* and full awareness of ancient social structure.

34. Freyne, "Galileans in the Light of Josephus' *Vita*," simply misreads *Vita* 28–29 to the effect that the Jerusalem government had instructed Josephus "to prepare for war in terms of arms and fortifications"; hence Josephus may have armed the Galileans. *Vita* 28–29 says the opposite: the people already being well provided with arms, Josephus's charge was to disarm them!

35. A skeptical, critical reading of *Vita* 373–80 suggests that if Josephus did take Sepphoris by storm, he used his trained mercenaries. Quite credible in this account, on the other hand, is that the Galileans in his company would have been only too ready to take advantage of the situation to take revenge on some Sepphorites.

36. Josephus's account here of the foraging expedition as the reason his soldiers were absent from Tarichaeae at a crucial point is far more credible than his pious posturing about having dismissed them a day early in order not to annoy the delicate religious sensibilities of the Tarichaeans in *Vita* 159.

37. Cohen, *Josephus in Galilee and Rome*, 208–9, takes these "leading" and "most distinguished" (*prōtoi* and *dokimotatoi*) Galileans, along with "those in office among the Galileans" as "the Galilean aristocracy." That they are elderly and that they are, in effect, hostages suggests that they were not the aristocracy, who would have been resident in the cities, and who would hardly have been good hostages to guarantee the compliance of the peasantry. Josephus must be using *prōtoi* here, like "those in office," in reference to village elders. This would fit with his (fictional) grand scheme of having councils of seven in each village and a region-wide council of seventy for all of Galilee in *B.J.* 2.570–71.

Chapter 4. Galilee after Roman Reconquest

Epigraphs: Rabbi Yohanan b. Zakkai (first century C.E.), *y. Šabb.* 16.15d; Rabbi Yonatan (third century C.E.), *y. Pesaḥ.* 5.3.32a; Lee I. Levine, *The Rabbinic Class of Roman Palestine* (New York: Jewish Theological Seminary of America, 1989), 77.

1. To say that "Galilee did not suffer because most cities quickly capitulated" (Grabbe, *Judaism from Cyrus to Hadrian* [Minneapolis: Fortress, 1992], 2:583) seems overly distrusting of Josephus's accounts.

2. Literature on the Bar Kokhba Revolt and its circumstances includes: Shimon Applebaum, *Prolegomena to the Study of the Second Jewish Revolt (A.D. 132–135)* (Oxford: BAR, 1976); Peter Schaefer, *Der Bar Kokhba Aufstand: Studien zum zweiten Jüdischen Krieg gegen Rom* (Tübingen: Mohr, 1981); Joseph A. Fitzmyer,

S.J., "The Bar Cochba Period," in *Essays on the Semitic Background of the New Testament* (Missoula, Mont.: Scholars, 1974), 305–54; Benjamin Isaac and Aharon Oppenheimer, "The Revolt of Bar Kokhba: Ideology and Modern Scholarship," *JJS* 36 (1985): 33–60; Menachem Mor, "The Bar-Kokhba Revolt and Non-Jewish Participants," *JJS* 36 (1985): 200–209; Mordechai Gichon, "New Insight into the Bar Kokhba War and a Reappraisal of Dio Cassius 69.12–13," *JQR* 77 (1986): 15–43.

3. E. Mary Smallwood, *The Jews under Roman Rule from Pompey to Diocletian* (Leiden: Brill, 1976), 331–32, 340, 546–48.

4. Fergus Millar, *The Emperor in the Roman World* (London: Duckworth, 1977), 420–34.

5. See esp. Benjamin Isaac, "Judaea after AD 70," *JJS* 35 (1984): 44–50; on the older view, and general economic conditions, see Shimon Applebaum's discussions, most accessible being "Economic Life in Ancient Palestine," in *The Jewish People in the First Century*, CRINT I.2, ed. S. Safrai and M. Stern (Assen: Van Gorcum, 1976), 2:692–99.

6. Even if one imagines that Judean peasants became *coloni* after 70, an unnecessary hypothesis of Smallwood, *The Jews under Roman Rule*, 341, that does not appear to have been the case with the Galileans.

7. Such is posited by Michael Avi-Yonah, *The Holy Land from the Persian to the Arab Conquests (536 B.C. to A.D. 640): A Historical Geography* (Grand Rapids: Baker, 1966, 1977), 112.

8. On the special Syrian rate now applied to Palestine, see Smallwood, *The Jews under Roman Rule*, 479, citing Appian, *Syr. 50*.

9. Presumably this tax included Galileans, since they were considered Judeans in the eyes of the imperial administration and had been involved in the revolt. Discussion of "the Jewish tax" in ibid., 371–78.

10. Ze'ev Safrai, "The Roman Army in the Galilee," in *The Galilee in Late Antiquity*, ed. Lee I. Levine (New York: Jewish Theological Seminary of America, 1992), 103–6; S. Applebaum, *Prolegomena*, 6; M. Avi-Yonah, "Newly Discovered Latin and Greek Inscriptions," *QDAP* 12 (1946): 87–91; Martin Goodman, *State and Society in Roman Galilee, A.D. 132–212* (Totowa, N.J.: Rowman & Allanheld, 1983), 142–43; rabbinic stories, *t. Šabb.* 13 (14).9; *t. 'Abod. Zar.* 2.6–7; *y. B. Bat.* 2.11,7b; on epigraphic evidence of soldiers buried in Tiberias, Goodman, *State and Society*, 142 n. 136.

11. For the frequent presence of the Roman military in villages, see Benjamin Isaac, *The Limits of Empire: The Roman Army in the East* (Oxford: Clarendon, 1990), chap. 3; Goodman, *State and Society*, 140–45, 175.

12. Further references and discussion on *annona* and *angariae* in Goodman, *State and Society*, 147–48. Michael Avi-Yonah, *The Jews under Roman and Byzantine Rule* (Jerusalem: Magnes, 1984), chap. 4, connects the escalation of these originally ad hoc demands into onerous regular burdens with the general political and economic crisis of the Roman empire.

13. Benjamin Isaac, "Milestones in Judaea, from Vespasian to Constantine," *PEQ* (1978): 47–59; Benjamin Isaac and Israel Roll, *Roman Roads in Judaea*, vol. 1, *The Legio-Scythopolis Road*, BARIS 141 (Oxford: BAR, 1982).

14. See Goodman, *State and Society*, 132. When Goodman then (133) concludes

that "the role of the cities in the Galilean economy seems very slight," he appears to miss the implication of his own extensive evidence and argument about how the cities collected their own revenues from the villagers in their city's *chōra*. See further chap. 7 below.

15. Among the many statements of the standard view, see, e.g., George Foot Moore, *Judaism in the First Centuries of the Christian Era* (Cambridge: Harvard University Press, 1927), 83–92; and W. D. Davies, *The Setting on the Sermon on the Mount* (Cambridge: Cambridge University Press, 1964), 256–86.

16. Since most of the pertinent critical studies of the origins of rabbinic Judaism have been published only in the last two decades, treatments of "Judaism" or of Galilee published during that period still follow the standard view, although with certain critical qualifications; e.g., S. Safrai, "Jewish Self-Government," in *The Jewish People in the First Century*, CRINT I.1, ed. S. Safrai and M. Stern (Assen: Van Gorcum, 1974), 1:404–12; Sean Freyne, *Galilee from Alexander the Great to Hadrian: A Study of Second Temple Judaism* (Wilmington, Del.: Glazier, 1980), chap. 8.

17. Shaye Cohen, *From the Maccabees to the Mishnah* (Philadelphia: Westminster, 1987), 219, 221, 223.

18. Close analysis of the various rabbinic versions of the story of Yohanan's escape in Anthony J. Saldarini, "Johanan ben Zakkai's Escape from Jerusalem: Origin and Development of a Rabbinic Story," *JSJ* 6 (1975): 189–204; Peter Schaefer, "Die Flucht Johanan b. Zakkais aus Jerusalem und die Gründung des 'Lehrhauses' in Jabne," *ANRW* 2.19.2 (1979): 44–101.

19. In a close detailed study of traditions about tannaitic rabbis, Cohen ("The Place of the Rabbi in Jewish Society of the Second Century," in *Galilee in Late Antiquity*, ed. Levine, 169–70) concludes emphatically that "in the period before Judah the Patriarch the rabbis were well-to-do, associated with the well-to-do, and interested themselves in questions which were important to the landed classes....No tannaitic document (except for *Fathers according to Rabbi Nathan*, in a series of rags-to-riches stories) implies that any second-century rabbi was poor."

20. See the probing analysis of Jacob Neusner, "The Formation of Rabbinic Judaism: Yavneh (Jamnia) from A.D. 70–100," *ANRW* 2.19.2 (1979): 3–42, on which this paragraph is dependent.

21. Full evidence and argument in ibid., 21–42.

22. Goodman, *State and Society*, 32–33, 196 n. 95, citing E. Meyers, C. Meyers, and J. Strange, "Meiron Second Preliminary Report," 74; E. Meyers, T. Kraabel, and J. Strange, *Ancient Synagogue Excavations at Khirbet Shema'* (Durham, N.C.: Duke University Press, 1976), 258; and M. Schwabe and B. Lifshitz, *Beth She'arim* (Jerusalem: Israel Exploration Society, 1974), 1.20. Elsewhere, however, Meyers ("The Cultural Setting of Galilee: The Case of Regionalism and Early Judaism," *ANRW* 2.19.1 [1979]: 701) acknowledged the lack of archaeological evidence for migration from Judea and settlement in Galilee, referring instead rather vaguely to "the lists of priestly courses, Josephus, and the rabbinic literature" but without specifying any particular passages. Josephus, of course, is hardly a likely source for such information for the second century!

23. Goodman's presentation (*State and Society*, 32–33) reveals just how shaky is the basis for the hypothesis:

> But specific attestation is hardly needed: the continued occupation of second century sites into the third century when recognizably Jewish buildings such as synagogues are built makes it clear that the immigrants are not gentile but Jewish, and if some refugees from Judaea were certainly accepted as settlers by the Galileans it would be strange if large numbers did not take advantage of the good land available. The archaeology and, in particular, the shift of the rabbinic schools to Galilee suggest that they did, and I shall proceed on that assumption.

While evidence for massive migration from Judea to Galilee after the Bar Kokhba Revolt may be lacking, there may be indirect evidence for the movement of priestly families to Galilee sometime after the early second century. In a critical analysis of rabbinic traditions regarding priests in Sepphoris, Stuart S. Miller, *Studies in the History and Tradition of Sepphoris* (Leiden: Brill, 1984), 120–27, demonstrates that (only) *y. Ta'an.* 4.68d, attests the priestly course (*mishmar*) of Yedaiah in Sepphoris sometime in the fourth century. Earlier rabbinic traditions, moreover, indicate that in the late second century the earlier participation of priests from Sepphoris in the Temple was taken for granted. Assuming that those priestly families were originally located in Judea itself, in easier access to the Temple where they were expected to serve several weeks a year, these texts suggest a migration at some point, presumably after the destruction of the Temple.

24. Goodman, *State and Society*, 111 and n. 203, citing H. L. Strack, *Introduction to the Talmud and Midrash* (Philadelphia: Jewish Publication Society of America, 1931), 116–18; Aharon Oppenheimer, "Roman Rule and the Cities of the Galilee in Talmudic Literature," in *Galilee in Late Antiquity*, ed. Levine, 120, pointing out that "there is no concrete evidence concerning the activities of the leadership institutions in Shefar'am" (n. 29).

25. So also Cohen, "Place of the Rabbi in Jewish Society," 169, who cites such tannaitic references as *t. Šabb.* 2.5; 13.2; *t. 'Erub.* 1.2; 6.2; *t. Pesaḥ.* 10.12; *t. Sukk.* 1.9; *t. Ter.* 2.13; *t. Ḥag* 2.13. Stuart Miller, "Intercity Relations in Roman Palestine: The Case of Sepphoris and Tiberias," *AJSR* 12 (1987): 12–13, adds the illustrative case of the third-century Rabbi Yohanan who had "sold various fields, vineyards, and olive groves" between Sepphoris and Tiberias so that he could study Torah. On patronage and fund-raising as a means of support, see Levine, *Rabbinic Class of Roman Palestine*, 69–71. It is seems doubtful that the early rabbis in Galilee were "on the whole" artisans (and that they brought new ideas and expertise that helped to reinvigorate the Galilean economy), versus Goodman, *State and Society*, 93, 177–78, who cites S. Applebaum, "Economic Life in Palestine," 2:684. The proof texts listed are only *m. 'Abot* 1:10, which does not indicate what sort of "labor" one is to "love," and *m. Qidd.* 4:14, a lengthy discussion of morality which does not indicate the rabbis' own professions. Goodman does recognize (178) that by the end of the second century the rabbis included wealthy landowners. Menahem Stern, "Aspects of Jewish Society: The Priesthood and Other Classes," in *Jewish People in the First Century*, ed. Safrai and Stern, 2:620, pointing out that the teaching office was traditionally the province of the priests, claims that "the number of priests among the sages in the coming generations continued

to be significant." He believes that "some were laborers," yet on the other hand M. Beer, in *Annual of Bar Ilan University* 2 (1964): 143, n. 57 (in Hebrew), gives examples of well-to-do sages.

26. Stating more precisely what Goodman seems to be after in *State and Society*, 177–78.

27. Goodman, in ibid., chap. 7, "Rabbinic Authority in Galilee," has laid out the evidence convincingly. In an independent study with more rigorous criteria for evidence, Cohen, "Place of the Rabbi in Jewish Society," has made the case even more convincing, including attention to the rabbis' social position, attitudes, and roles.

28. "The animosity between the first- and second-century sages and the *'ammei ha-aretz* is...indicative of the chasm which existed between the rabbis and segments of the population": Levine, *Rabbinic Class of Roman Palestine*, 40, with extended discussion, 112–26. Aharon Oppenheimer, *The 'Am Ha-Aretz: A Study in the Social History of the Jewish People in the Hellenistic-Roman Period* (Leiden: Brill, 1977), believes the rabbis have far more influence on the people.

29. Goodman, *State and Society*, 110–11.

30. See now the critical treatment of sources and reconstruction of the Patriarchate by Lee I. Levine, "The Jewish Patriarch (Nasi) in Third Century Palestine," *ANRW* 2.19.2 (1979): 649–88, on which the following sketch is heavily dependent. More accessible is Levine, *Rabbinic Class of Roman Palestine*, chap. 4.

31. Levine, "Jewish Patriarch," 655–57.

32. For fuller documentation of the following, see further ibid., 657–58, 662–73.

33. See *y. Yebam.* 12.7.13a; *Gen. Rab.* 81, p. 969; *y. Meg* 4.5.75b; *y. Ta'an.* 4.2.681; *b. Ketub.* 103b; *b. Ber.* 55a.

34. Goodman, *State and Society*, 133–34, provides a helpful clarification of Levine, "Jewish Patriarch," 673, on this matter.

35. See *Gen. Rab.* 97, 9, pp. 1219, 1258–59; *y. Ta'an.* 4.2.68a.

36. See further the arguments by Martin Goodman, "The Roman State and the Jewish Patriarch in the Third Century," in *Galilee in Late Antiquity*, ed. Levine, 131–34. "There is no explicit evidence in rabbinic texts that the *nasi* owed his position to Rome in any way" (131). Having argued earlier (*State and Society*, 135–14) that Judah the Prince was a semi-independent ruler, but tolerated by Rome because Galilee was a tiny and unimportant territory, Goodman now presents a third possibility ("Roman State and the Jewish Patriarch," 134–39). To suggest that Judah's "secular power" derived from his "religious authority," however, imposes modern Western categories that do not fit the evidence cited. If anything the development had been just the other way around, with Judah having rapidly consolidated his social-economic power and influence, by such means as political influence with imperial figures or social coalitions and patronage within Galilee. That prominence and power thus achieved in Galilee provided the basis for unprecedented influence on Galilean life and social forms that were inseparably political-economic-religious, such as the village communities, the "Jewish" communities in the cities, and the rabbinic academies.

37. Goodman, *State and Society*, 111–12; arguing against Hugo Mantel, *Studies*

in the History of the Sanhedrin (Cambridge: Cambridge University Press, 1961), 1–53.

38. Goodman, *State and Society*, 113, in direct opposition to Mantel, *Studies in the Sanhedrin*, 176–235.

39. Not surprisingly, the sponsorship or compilation of the Mishnah is attributed to Judah the Prince. Whatever authority the Mishnah initially had probably derived from the patriarch's social-economic power, rather than the patriarch's power having been being rooted in the authority of the evolving and now published Mishnah. See further Jacob Neusner, *Judaism: The Evidence of the Mishnah* (Chicago: University of Chicago Press, 1981), 230ff.

40. Fuller documentation in Levine, "Jewish Patriarch," 678–80.

41. These divisions among the sages according to their loyalty to or agreement with the patriarch thus cannot be dissolved into the supposed continuing rivalry between Sepphoris and Tiberias, which has now been convincingly challenged for the amoraic period by Miller, "Intercity Relations in Roman Palestine," 1–24.

42. One of the basic theses of Levine in *Rabbinic Class of Roman Palestine.*

43. Such as R. El'azar, a colleague of R. Yohanan who had moved to Tiberias from Sepphoris, along with R. Ami, R. Asi, R. Hiyya, and R. Zera, as laid out carefully by Lee I. Levine, "R. Simeon b. Yohai and the Purification of Tiberias: History and Tradition," *HUCA* 49 (1978): 173–74.

44. Lee I. Levine, "Social Aspects of Burial in Beth She'arim: Archaeological Finds and Talmudin Sources," in *Galilee in Late Antiquity*, ed. Levine, 367; and *Rabbinic Class of Roman Palestine*, 47–55.

45. The most sophisticated and systematic critical analysis of the Mishnah and other rabbinic literature is clearly that developed by Jacob Neusner and his students. The following sketch is directly dependent on Neusner, *Judaism*, chaps. 5 and 6.

46. Evidence cited by Levine, *Rabbinic Class of Roman Palestine*, 71, 172.

47. As pointed out by Neusner, *Judaism*, 239–40. "The two principal institutions of rabbinic Judaism [the synagogue and the schoolhouse] thus play no formative or definitive role in the Mishnah."

48. So Cohen, *Maccabees to the Mishnah*, 111–15, 219–21.

49. On the Dionysiac mosaic, see Eric M. Meyers, Ehud Netzer, and Carol L. Meyers, *Sepphoris* (Winona Lake, Ind.: Eisenbrauns, 1992), 38–59.

50. See further Joan E. Taylor, *Christians and the Holy Places: The Myth of Jewish Christian Origins* (Oxford: Clarendon, 1993), 52–55.

51. See further Eric M. Meyers, "Roman Sepphoris in the Light of New Archaeological Evidence and Research," in *Galilee in Late Antiquity*, ed. Levine, 329, and additional references there.

52. See Anthony J. Saldarini, *Matthew's Christian-Jewish Community* (Chicago: University of Chicago Press, 1994); cf. Howard C. Kee, "The Transformation of the Synagogue after 70 C.E.: Its Import for Early Christianity," *NTS* 36 (1990): 20–24.

53. Particularly influential, at least in Christian theological scholarship, have been Davies, *Setting of the Sermon on the Mount*, and J. L. Martin, *History and Theology in the Fourth Gospel*, 2nd ed. (Nashville: Abingdon, 1979). See now the broad criticism of previous scholarship in Steven T. Katz, "Issues in the Separation

of Judaism and Christianity after 70 C.E.: A Reconsideration," *JBL* 103 (1984): 43–76.

54. See further Katz, "Separation of Judaism and Christianity," 63–76; and Ruben Kimelman, "Birkat Ha-Minim and the Lack of Evidence for an Anti-Christian Jewish Prayer in Late Antiquity," in *Jewish and Christian Self-Definition*, vol. 2, *Aspects of Judaism in the Graeco-Roman Period*, ed. E. P. Sanders et al. (Philadelphia: Fortress, 1981), 226–44. The opposing view is argued in Lawrence Schiffman, *Who Was a Jew? Rabbinic and Halakhic Perspectives on the Jewish-Christian Schism* (Hoboken, N.J.: KTAV, 1985), 53–61.

55. A bishop is not attested for Tiberias until the fifth century.

56. Further discussion of the evidence for Christians in Galilee and elsewhere in Palestine in Taylor, *Christians and the Holy Places*, 57–64.

57. Avi-Yonah, *Jews under Roman and Byzantine Rule*, 90, and chap. 4 generally, attempts to place Palestine Jewry in the context of the crisis of the empire in the third century. Cf. W. H. C. Frend, "Town and Countryside in Early Christianity," in *The Church in Town and Countryside*, ed. D. Baker (Oxford: Blackwell, 1979), 25–42.

58. Daniel Sperber, *Roman Palestine 200–400: The Land* (Ramat Gan: Bar Ilan University Press, 1978), 102–18.

59. On the "Gallus Revolt" see now Barbara Geller Nathanson, "Jews, Christians, and the Gallus Revolt in Fourth-Century Palestine," *BA* 79 (1986), esp. 30–34.

60. Archaeologists differ on the cause of the destruction evident in mid-fourth-century Sepphoris. James F. Strange concludes that the evidence from excavations to date suggests the Gallus Revolt as the cause in "Six Campaigns at Sepphoris: The University of South Florida Excavations, 1983–89," in *Galilee in Late Antiquity*, ed. Levine, 352–53. The alternative cause of the earthquake of 363 is preferred by Meyers, Netzer, and Meyers, *Sepphoris*, 17.

Chapter 5. Roman Imperial Rule and Galilee

Epigraphs: Edward W. Said, *Culture and Imperialism* (New York: Knopf, 1993); Agrippa II in Josephus, *B.J.* 2.391.

1. The standard historical treatment of greater Judea under Roman rule is E. Mary Smallwood, *The Jews under Roman Rule from Pompey to Diocletian* (Leiden: Brill, 1976), which can be consulted for fuller treatment of many of the events and sources covered below. Smallwood's history also illustrates how modern scholars, like their ancient sources (with the notable exception of Josephus), mention Galilee only in passing, as somewhat peripheral to more important imperial affairs.

2. See further A. N. Sherwin-White, *Roman Foreign Policy in the East, 168 B.C. to A.D. 1* (London: Duckworth, 1984), 198.

3. Many of the events cited in the following paragraphs to illustrate the effects of Rome's conquest of Palestine on Galilee are discussed at greater length in chapters 2 or 3 and/or in chapter 6.

4. Sherwin-White, *Roman Foreign Policy in the East*, 101–3.

5. The Jewish diaspora communities in Babylon were perhaps also a factor in the pro-Parthian leanings of some Judeans.

6. It is conceivable that as rebels against Roman rule and the Roman client regime of Hyrcanus, Aristobulus and Alexander evoked some popular support among Galileans as well as Judeans, support that the massacres at Mount Tabor and Tarichaeae would have only intensified among Galileans.

7. Some of the following is based on the discussion by Edward N. Luttwak, *The Grand Strategy of the Roman Empire* (Baltimore: Johns Hopkins University Press, 1976), chap. 1.

8. Ibid., 46–47.

9. M. Mor, "The Roman Army in Eretz-Israel in the Years A.D. 70–132," in *The Defense of the Roman and Byzantine East*, ed. P. Freeman and D. Kennedy, BAR 297 (Oxford: BAR, 1986), 575–602.

10. E. Badian, *Foreign Clientelae (264–70 B.C.)* (Oxford: Clarendon, 1958), 1–14.

11. Appian, *Syr.* 50, is about a later time.

12. See further Smallwood, *Jews under Roman Rule*, 28, 33, 41, including other references to ancient sources.

13. Further analysis of these incidents, their background, and significance in R. A. Horsley, *Jesus and the Spiral of Violence: Popular Jewish Resistance in Roman Palestine* (San Francisco: Harper & Row, 1987; Minneapolis: Fortress, 1992), chaps. 3 and 4.

14. The following sketch of the emperor cult depends heavily on S. R. F. Price, *Images and Power* (Cambridge: Cambridge University Press, 1984); and Paul Zanker, *The Power of Images in the Age of Augustus* (Ann Arbor: University of Michigan Press, 1988), esp. chap. 8.

15. Translation from Zanker, *Power of Images*, 297.

16. Susan E. Alcock, *Graecia Capta: The Landscapes of Roman Greece* (Cambridge: Cambridge University Press, 1993), 141.

17. Luttwak, *Grand Strategy*, 32.

18. On revolts and Roman reprisals in northern Europe, see S. L. Dyson, "Native Revolts in the Roman Empire," *Historia* 20 (1971): 239–74. On the varieties of resistance and rebellions in greater Judea, see further Horsley, *Jesus and the Spiral of Violence*, chaps. 2–4, and *Sociology and the Jesus Movement* (New York: Crossroad, 1989), chap. 5.

19. See further Martin Goodman, *The Ruling Class of Judaea: The Origins of the Jewish Revolt against Rome* A.D. 66–70 (Cambridge: Cambridge University Press, 1987).

20. Ze'ev Safrai, "The Roman Army in the Galilee," in *The Galilee in Late Antiquity*, ed. Lee I. Levine (New York: Jewish Theological Seminary of America, 1992), 103–13. During the period between 120 and 300, "Judea contained the greatest number of Roman troops of any province of its size; half of this army was stationed in [near] Galilee, the area of which was only 25% that of Judea [proper]. It is therefore important to examine the impact of the Roman army on the residents of the Galilee" (105).

21. Fergus Millar, "Empire, Community, and Culture in the Roman Near East: Greeks, Syrians, Jews, and Arabs," *JJS* 38 (1987): 145.

22. *T. Šabb.* 13:9. See critical discussion in Stuart S. Miller, *Studies in the History and Tradition of Sepphoris* (Leiden: Brill, 1984), 31–45, esp. 44–45.

23. Safrai, "Roman Army in the Galilee," 105.

24. E.g., *t. Ta'an.* 2.10; *m. 'Abod. Zar.* 5:6; *m. B. Meṣ.* 6:3; *m. B. Bat.* 9:4; see further Martin Goodman, *State and Society in Roman Galilee,* A.D. *132–212* (Totowa, N.J.: Rowman & Allanheld, 1983), 142–43, 147.

25. Brief discussion with citations in Goodman, *State and Society,* 148–49.

26. Smallwood, *Jews under Roman Rule,* 431; M. Kecker, "The Roman Road Legio-Zippori," *Yediot* 25 (1961): 175; Benjamin Isaac, "Milestones in Judaea, from Vespasian to Constantine," *PEQ* (1978): 47–59.

27. Further discussion of this tax in Smallwood, *Jews under Roman Rule,* 371–75.

28. Goodman, *State and Society,* 140–41; vs. Michael Avi-Yonah, *The Holy Land from the Persian to the Arab Conquests (536* B.C. *to* A.D. *640): A Historical Geography* (Grand Rapids: Baker, 1966, 1977), 112.

29. One would presume that the short-lived regional *sanhedrin* set up by Gabinius in Sepphoris consisted of Hasmonean officials/aristocracy, who would have been the principal wealthy and powerful figures in Galilee after forty-five years of rule by the Hasmonean regime.

Chapter 6. Jerusalem and Galilee

Epigraphs: John H. Kautsky, *The Politics of Aristocratic Empires* (Chapel Hill: University of North Carolina Press, 1982), 159; Jesus ben Sira 7:31; James C. Scott, "Protest and Profanation: Agrarian Revolt and the Little Tradition," pt. 1, *Theory and Society* 4 (1977): 1, 7.

1. Although it is clear in the case of Judea, the Persian sponsorship of indigenous temple-communities and law-codes should not be overstated, according to Amelie Kuhrt, "The Cyrus Cylinder and the Achaemenid Imperial Policy," *JSOT* 25 (1983): 83–97.

2. In addition to the portrayal in the structure of the people at assembly before God in Sirach 50, Ben Sira provides a sketch of various social roles and functions, including peasants, artisans, scribes, and the priestly rulers, in Sir 38:24–39:11. On Ben Sira's portrayals of the social structure of Judea, see further R. A. Horsley and Patrick Tiller, "Ben Sira and the Sociology of Second Temple Judea," in *Second Temple Studies 2: Hellenistic Period,* ed. John Halligan, JSOTSup (Sheffield: JSOT Press, forthcoming).

3. Nahman Avigad, *Discovering Jerusalem* (Nashville: Nelson, 1983), 83.

4. Ibid., 77.

5. Ancient descriptions are Josephus, *Ant.* 15.410–20 and *B.J.* 5.184–227, and the Mishnah tractate *Middot,* with Josephus providing the more accurate description of Herod's temple. Modern scholarly presentations are T. A. Busink, *Der Tempel von Jerusalem,* 2 vols. (Leiden: Brill, 1970–80); Meir Ben-Dov, *In the Shadow of the Temple* (New York: Harper and Row, 1985); Benjamin Mazar, *The Mountain of the Lord* (Garden City, N.Y.: Doubleday, 1975). Useful summaries are Strange, "Archaeology and the Religion of Judaism," *ANRW* 2.19.1 (1979): 650–

55; and E. P. Sanders, *Judaism: Practice and Belief 63* B.C.E.–66 C.E. (Philadelphia: Trinity Press International, 1992), 55–69.

6. Fuller presentation and analysis in my *Jesus and the Spiral of Violence: Popular Jewish Resistance in Roman Palestine* (San Francisco: Harper & Row, 1987; Minneapolis: Fortress, 1992), 71–77.

7. On the movement in Galilee, see chap. 12 below, and my *Bandits, Prophets, and Messiahs: Popular Movements in the Time of Jesus* (with John S. Hanson) (San Francisco: Harper & Row, 1987), chap. 3.

8. On these movements, see my *Jesus and the Spiral of Violence*, chaps. 3–4.

9. On the *sicarioi* in particular, Richard A. Horsley, "The Sicarii: Ancient Jewish Terrorists," *JR* 59 (1979): 435–58.

10. Herod's first high priest Hananel was not from a distinguished Jerusalem family but from a high-priestly family in Babylon (*Ant.* 15.22.39–40). Shortly thereafter, Mariamme's handsome younger brother Aristobulus III was appointed, but a year later was "accidentally" drowned, because threatening to Herod (*Ant.* 15.39.50–56; 20.247–48). After the reappointment of Hananel and Jesus son of Phiabi, Herod appointed the Alexandrian Jew Simon son of Boethus so that he could respectably marry his beautiful daughter (*Ant.* 15.320–22). Implicated in court intrigue, Simon was replaced by Matthias son of Theophilus, a native of Jerusalem (*Ant.* 15.78). Toward the end of Herod's reign, Matthias was blamed for being too lenient about the famous protest against the Roman golden eagle over the gate of the Temple, and replaced by the Joazar, brother of Herod's wife Mariamme II (*Ant.* 15.164–67). Symbolic of the subordination of the high priesthood, Herod himself retained custody of the high-priestly robe used for the most sacred festivals (*Ant.* 15.404).

11. See further R. A. Horsley, "High Priests and the Politics of Roman Palestine," *JSJ* 17 (1986): 23–53; Martin Goodman, *The Ruling Class of Judaea: The Origins of the Jewish Revolt against Rome* A.D. 66–70 (Cambridge: Cambridge University Press, 1987).

12. In defining what constitutes "a dwelling in a walled city" the rabbis project what was already old in their own time back to the time of Joshua son of Nun. See the analysis and conclusions of Stuart S. Miller, *Studies in the History and Tradition of Sepphoris* (Leiden: Brill, 1984), chaps. 1–2, esp. 22–30 and 56–59. Josephus, of course, provides a lengthy description of the fortress town of Jotapata, which he supposedly further fortified and defended against the Roman siege (*B.J.* 3.141–339, esp. 158–60).

13. See the dramatic incidence of *Hasmonean* coins in the lists compiled by Richard S. Hanson, *Tyrian Influence in the Upper Galilee*, Meiron Excavation Project No. 2 (Cambridge, Mass.: ASOR, 1980). Whereas Tyrian coins are "read" as direct evidence of trade by Hanson, the team excavating at Gush Halav had earlier suggested the "military reading"; see Eric M. Meyers, James F. Strange, Carol L. Meyers, and Richard S. Hanson, "Preliminary Report on the 1977 and 1978 Seasons at Gush Halav," *BASOR* 233 (1979): 36; and Richard A. Horsley, "Archaeology and the Villages of Upper Galilee: A Dialogue with Archaeologists," *BASOR* 297 (1995): 5–16.

14. A. Schalit, *Koenig Herodes: Der Mann und Sein Werk*, SJ 4 (Berlin: de

Gruyter, 1969), 683–84, suggests these were at Baka, Kedasa, and Chabulon. Gush Halav/Gischala seems more likely than Kedasa, Jotapata as likely as Chabulon.

15. See further Israel Shatzman, *The Armies of the Hasmoneans and Herod* (Tübingen: Mohr, 1991), 310–16, esp. 312.

16. Cf. the similar assessment, on the basis of the Hasmonean coins found at Gush Halav, by Meyers et al., "1977 and 1978 Seasons at Gush Halav," 36: the Hasmoneans were attempting to "reintegrate distant segments of the population into the religious and political life of their kingdom."

17. Extensive discussion in Sanders, *Judaism*, 146–50. A standard earlier presentation of the variety of sources, difficult to assess and synthesize, is E. Schürer, *A History of the Jewish People in the Age of Jesus Christ*, 3 vols., rev. and ed. G. Vermes, F. Millar, et al. (Edinburgh: T & T Clark, 1973–87), 1:257–74.

18. See further Schürer, *History of the Jewish People*, 1:260–61, 267–70.

19. See further Aharon Oppenheimer, *The 'Am Ha-Aretz: A Study in the Social History of the Jewish People in the Hellenistic-Roman Period* (Leiden: Brill, 1977), 33–36.

20. B. Bar-Kochva, "Manpower, Economics, and Internal Strife in the Hasmonean State," in *Armées et Fiscalité dans le Monde Antique* (Paris: Editions du Centre National de la Recherche Scientifique, 1977), 185–86, argues that Hasmonean revenues consisted primarily of a "secular" tax: "It seems logical, therefore, to conclude that Caesar refers not to the Jewish 'first tithe,' but to the Hellenistic *dekate*, which was the main land tax under the Seleucids. This tax may have already been adopted by the Hasmoneans by the time of Simeon, after the declaration of independence, although certainly at a lower rate."

21. J. Liver, "The Half Shekel Offering in Biblical and Post-Biblical Literature," *HTR* 56 (1963): 173–98, concludes that the half shekel offering originated in Roman times. The Qumran community took that position that it was owed only once in a life-time, not once a year (4 Q Ordinances).

22. Freyne's presentation of the Galileans' relation to the Temple takes the form of explaining away "the fact that the Galileans may not have followed Pharisaic regulations concerning the half shekel offering and do not appear to have been too scrupulous in regard to tithing" (*Galilee from Alexander the Great to Hadrian: A Study of Second Temple Judaism* [Wilmington, Del.: Glazier, 1980], 293). The former is explained as "merely an acceptance of the Sadducaean rather than the Pharisaic position" (281). The laxity regarding tithes is not explained (281–87). Nevertheless he comes to the conclusion that, while after the fall of the Temple "the Galileans refused to identify with many of the stringent rules that at an earlier period had bound temple and land together so intimately," they had earlier viewed the Temple as "the source of their confidence in the ongoing struggle for the necessities of life" (295). It is extremely difficult to follow the twists and turns of the argument. The whole presentation, however, is based on the unwarranted assumption, made at the outset, of the Galileans' "continued faithfulness to the Yahweh shrine through the centuries, despite the vicissitudes of history" (295). Ironically, many of the components of Freyne's argument lend credibility to the Galileans' reputation in later rabbinic opinions for ignorance or laxity in their supposed obligations to Temple and priests.

23. Freyne, in ibid., 277–87, attempts to explain away this and other rabbinic

references to Galileans' ignorance of or reluctance to pay tithes and other dues in his effort to find the Galileans loyal to the Temple. In his critique of Freyne's and others' unwarranted trust in later rabbinic discussions as evidence for earlier Judean or Galilean practices and attitudes, Neusner (review of Freyne, *Galilee from Alexander the Great to Hadrian*, reprinted in *Formative Judaism: Religious, Historical, and Literary Studies*, BJS 37 [Chico: Scholars Press, 1982], 68–69) stops short of explaining the point (and substance) of the contrast between the Galileans and the Judeans.

24. S. Safrai, "The Temple," in *The Jewish People in the First Century*, CRINT I.2, ed. S. Safrai and M. Stern (Assen: Van Gorcum, 1976), 901; Freyne, *Galilee from Alexander the Great to Hadrian*, 293. Freyne's discussion of Galileans' pilgrimage (*Galilee from Alexander the Great to Hadrian*, 287–93) is driven by his broader agenda of denying that an anti-Roman revolutionary spirit was prominent in Galilee. He must thus walk a thin line in a chapter devoted to arguing how loyal the Galileans were to the Temple: they were faithful in pilgrimage, but not fired with zeal for the Temple.

25. For example, D. Chwolson, *Das letzte Passamahl Christi* (St. Petersburg: Eggers and Glasounof, 1892); Joachim Jeremias, *Jerusalem at the Time of Jesus* (Philadelphia: Fortress, 1969), 77–84.

26. Safrai, "The Temple," 2:898–902; cf. his less cautious earlier discussion that estimated "hundreds of thousands" in "Pilgrimage to Jerusalem at the End of the Second Temple Period," in *Studies on the Jewish Background of the New Testament* (Assen: Van Gorcum, 1969), 16–17.

27. Safrai, "The Temple," 900; Safrai, "Pilgrimage to Jerusalem," 18.

28. Safrai, "The Temple," 901. Safrai himself critically rejects much of the later rabbinic references to pilgrimages as "totally divorced from reality...miracle stories...and folk tales...[viewing] pilgrimage in the setting of an idealized past" ("Pilgrimage to Jerusalem," 13). Contrary to Freyne's claim (*Galilee from Alexander the Great to Hadrian*, 287–93), the evidence for Galileans' pilgrimage is scarce as well as skewed. Because Josephus provides so little evidence for Galilean pilgrimage, it is misleading to say that "Josephus seems to stress the social and political role of the pilgrimage — especially for Galilean Jews" (288).

29. Josephus's accounts of this incident and of Cumanus's governorship of greater Judea is to be preferred over that of Tacitus. See the detailed discussion of issues by Menahem Stern, *Greek and Latin Authors on Jews and Judaism*, 2 vols. (Jerusalem: Israel Academy of Sciences and Humanities, 1974–80), 2:76–82.

30. For a very rough sense of such Galilean pilgrimage: if by a high estimate, 1,000 Galileans made a pilgrimage each year and, by conservative estimate, there were 100,000 inhabitants in Galilee (with life-expectancy of between twenty-five and fifty years), then well under half would have made a pilgrimage to the Jerusalem Temple once in their lifetime.

31. For particular incidents along with analysis of protests by the "crowd" in Jerusalem, see further Horsley, *Jesus and the Spiral of Violence*, 90–99.

32. The major study of "the Law" in Galilee, the 1973 Duke University dissertation by F. X. Malinowski, "Galilean Judaism in the Writings of Flavius Josephus," was written prior to the development of recent historiographical criticism of Josephus's histories.

33. See chap. 2 above and Steve Mason, *Flavius Josephus and the Pharisees* (Leiden: Brill, 1991), 97–106.

34. For an application of this distinction to somewhat analogous historical situations, see Scott, "Protest and Profanation," 1–39, 211–46.

35. For example, *m. Pesaḥ.* 4:5; *m. Ketub.* 5:9; 13:10; *m. Ter.* 10:8; *m. Ḥul.* 11:2; on other matters, *m. B. Bat.* 3:2; *m. B. Qam.* 10:9.

36. The results of the extensive critical work of Jacob Neusner, *The Rabbinic Traditions about the Pharisees before 70*, 3 vols. (Leiden: Brill, 1971); see also Neusner's *Judaism: The Evidence of the Mishnah* (Chicago: University of Chicago Press, 1981).

37. *Pace* Jacob Neusner, *From Politics to Piety* (Englewood Cliffs, N.J.: Prentice-Hall, 1973). For further exploration of the Pharisees and certain scribes as what comparative sociologists would call "retainers" of the governing authorities in the structure of a traditional agrarian society, see A. J. Saldarini, *Pharisees, Scribes, and Sadducees* (Wilmington, Del.: Glazier, 1988); and R. A. Horsley, *Sociology and the Jesus Movement* (New York: Crossroad, 1989), chap. 4. Josephus's other portrayal of the Pharisees as one of the three or four principal "philosophies" or "parties" of the Judeans (*B.J.* 2.119–66; *Ant.* 18:11–25) is not inconsistent with his principal representation of them as government retainers assisting in the administration of the society. His focus is always on the high-placed people and groups that play a role in political history. And the Sadducees, Pharisees, Essenes (who withdrew) and, for a time, the Fourth Philosophy, as different "political interest groups" among the priestly and/or retainer strata definitely had different "philosophies" of what Judean life under God's revealed will meant and the implications for civil-religious affairs, just as Greek philosophers had views on "polity" and how the state ought to govern society.

38. The following paragraphs are a summary of the implications of the historical explorations in chap. 2 above.

39. It seems historically utterly unwarranted to think that Pharisaic activity and influence was increasing during the first century C.E., as has been stated or assumed in some recent New Testament scholarship. Such an idea is apparently rooted in the historically unwarranted assumptions that the rabbis were placed in charge of Jewish society in Palestine, including Galilee, soon after the destruction of the Temple and that the Pharisees stood in direct continuity with the rabbis. See further chap. 4 above.

40. For example, by Freyne, *Galilee from Alexander the Great to Hadrian*, 309–18.

41. If one did want to speculate about Judas of Galilee's motivation or ideology, it would appear to stem more from an unswerving commitment to the first commandment of the Mosaic covenant, to have no master or king but God, and not specifically from the official Torah, of which the high priests were the designated official interpreters. The official teachers of the Torah in this case opposed Judas and persuaded the people to submit to the tribute (*Ant.* 18.3–5.23.26).

42. See further Martin Goodman, "Kosher Olive Oil in Antiquity," in *A Tribute to Geza Vermes: Essays on Jewish and Christian Literature and History*, ed. P. R. Davies and R. T. White, JSOTSup 100 (Sheffield: JSOT Press, 1990), 227–45. "The widespread custom among Jews of avoiding gentile oil may have been

based neither on biblical exegesis nor on a decision by an accepted authority but on a pervasive religious instinct which was all the more powerful for its lack of rationale.... [and] is best explained by social and cultural changes in the lives of Jews in this period" (240).

43. It is unusual for Josephus to use *hoi ioudaioi* in his accounts of events in Galilee in *Vita*. Are they different from "the Galileans" or "those around John of Gischala/Jesus son of Sapphias/etc."? Does "the crowd" in the resumption of the story, *Vita* 149–54, refer to the same or different people from "the Judeans" in the initial account? The *palin* = "again" in 149 relates to the immediately preceding conflict between the crowd and Josephus, *Vita* 132–44, not to the initial report of the demand to circumcise the foreign nobles, *Vita* 112–13.

44. Compare another incident Josephus reports which suggests that a copy of "the laws of Moses" or "the sacred law" was found even in "a village," albeit near Beth Horon not far from Jerusalem (*B.J.* 2.229; *Ant.* 20.115–16).

Chapter 7. The Cities and Royal Rule in Galilee

Epigraphs: James C. Scott, "Protest and Profanation: Agrarian Revolt and the Little Tradition," pt. 1, *Theory and Society* 4 (1977): 10; John H. Kautsky, *The Politics of Aristocratic Empires* (Chapel Hill: University of North Carolina Press, 1982), 188.

1. For example, J. Andrew Overman, "Who Were the First Urban Christians? Urbanization in Galilee in the First Century," and Douglas Edwards, "First Century Urban/Rural Relations in Lower Galilee: Exploring the Archaeological and Literary Evidence," in SBLSP, ed. David Lull (Atlanta: Scholars Press, 1988), 160–68 and 169–82; Eric M. Meyers, "Roman Sepphoris in the Light of New Archaeological Evidence and Research," in *The Galilee in Late Antiquity*, ed. Lee I. Levine (New York: Jewish Theological Seminary of America, 1992), 321–38.

2. Martin Hengel, *Judaism and Hellenism* (Philadelphia: Fortress, 1974), 18–23.

3. Versus Sean Freyne, *Galilee from Alexander the Great to Hadrian: A Study of Second Temple Judaism* (Wilmington, Del.: Glazier, 1980), 105–6. Moreover, it is difficult to understand how one can conclude on the basis of a list of produce from *Syria* generally in a Zenon Papyrus that such products were "exported" from *Galilee* in particular simply because the same items were also produced in Galilee.

4. A. H. M. Jones, *The Cities of the Eastern Roman Provinces*, 2nd ed. (Oxford: Clarendon, 1971), 242.

5. Victor Tcherikover, *Hellenistic Civilization and the Jews* (New York: Atheneum, 1970), 102–3.

6. For *ioudaioi* in Scythopolis, see, e.g., 2 Macc. 12:30; see further Freyne, *Galilee from Alexander the Great to Hadrian*, 109–11; cf. Gideon Fuks, "The Jews of Hellenistic and Roman Scythopolis," *JJS* 33 (1982): 407–9.

7. Of the inscriptions from Jerusalem ossuaries containing the remains of Scythopolitan Jews, some are only in Greek, others are bilingual, Hebrew and Greek; see Fuks, "Jews of Hellenistic and Roman Scythopolis," 409–10.

8. Eric M. Meyers, introduction to Richard S. Hanson, *Tyrian Influence in*

the Upper Galilee, Meiron Excavation Project No. 2 (Cambridge, Mass.: ASOR, 1980), 2, and in many related publications.

9. Hanson, *Tyrian Influence in the Upper Galilee*, 53, 69 n. 5; Y. Meshorer, "A Hoard of Coins from Migdal," '*Antiqot* 2 (1976): 54–71.

10. I address this question with provisional analysis in R. A. Horsley, "The Historical Jesus and Archaeology of the Galilee: Questions from Historical Jesus Research to Archaeologists," SBLSP, ed. Eugene H. Lovering Jr. (Atlanta: Scholars Press, 1994), 105–6.

11. Meyers, introduction to Hanson, *Tyrian Influence in the Upper Galilee*, 3.

12. Eric M. Meyers, Ehud Netzer, and Carol L. Meyers, *Sepphoris* (Winona Lake, Ind.: Eisenbrauns, 1992), 10.

13. Meyers, "Roman Sepphoris," 330.

14. The standard historical interpretation that Antipas "rebuilt" the city as his capital appears to be confirmed by the findings of the University of South Florida archaeological investigations. In excavations of building after building, they discovered the founding on bedrock in the early Roman period; see James F. Strange, "Six Campaigns at Sepphoris: The University of South Florida Excavations, 1983–89," in *Galilee in Late Antiquity*, ed. Levine, 339–55. On the other hand, Meyers et al. say that the Joint Expedition found "no trace of violent destruction in the Herodian period" ("Roman Sepphoris," 323; Meyers, Netzer, and Meyers, *Sepphoris*, 11).

15. Thomas Longstaff, "Nazareth and Sepphoris: Insights into Christian Origins," *ATR* 11 (1990): 12.

16. The respective dating of the theater illustrates the different interpretations given to the rebuilding of the city by Antipas, with Strange et al. opting for an early date ("Six Campaigns at Sepphoris") while Meyers et al. prefer a date in the late first century C.E. ("Roman Sepphoris").

17. Considering the Latin names of the "Herodian" officers who still comprised the "principal men" in Tiberias in 66 also fit such a picture, one must project a similar set of names among the original Herodian elite in Sepphoris as well (*Vita* 30ff.).

18. So also Meyers, "Roman Sepphoris," 326. On the military presence, see Ze'ev Safrai, "The Roman Army in the Galilee," in *Galilee in Late Antiquity*, ed. Levine, 103–13.

19. A milestone with the legend "Diocaesarea" dating to 130 was found on the newly built road from Acco to Tiberias (Meyers, "Roman Sepphoris," 326).

20. Meyers, Netzer, and Meyers, *Sepphoris*, 38–59.

21. Meyers, "Roman Sepphoris," 329; Meyers, Netzer, and Meyers, *Sepphoris*, 19–24. For a further indication that such finds do not seem to shake the confidence of archaeologists that Sepphoris was "an otherwise Jewish city," cf. Strange, "Six Campaigns at Sepphoris," 353.

22. Sean Freyne, first on the basis of literary sources (in *Galilee from Alexander the Great to Hadrian*, 195), then incorporating archaeological evidence as well (in *Galilee, Jesus, and the Gospels: Literary Approaches and Historical Investigations* [Philadelphia: Fortress, 1988], 145), had concluded that

> literary and archaeological sources combine to confirm a picture of an essentially rural Galilee, whose inhabitants are committed to the peasant way of

life and live in villages, though surrounded by a circle of Greek-style cities on the periphery.

In a pendulum-like reaction against what they viewed as a perpetuation of the late nineteenth-century idyllic portrait of an exclusively rural Galilee, some interpreters of recent archaeological explorations in Galilee constructed an opposing picture: Lower Galilee, at least, was heavily urbanized, indeed as urbanized as anywhere else in the Roman empire! For example: Overman, "Who Were the First Urban Christians?" 160–68, and Edwards, "First Century Urban/Rural Relations in Lower Galilee," 169–82. Cf. the earlier sketch of Lower Galilee in contrast with Upper Galilean villages in Meyers, "The Cultural Setting of Galilee: The Case of Regionalism and Early Judaism," *ANRW* 2.19.1 (1979): 686–702. Interestingly enough, the advocates of an urbanized Lower Galilee cited some of the same archaeological reports and Josephus references and used the same commercial economic model for Galilee as did Freyne. Although the presentations of Overman and Edwards were clearly provisional and suggestive, some Jesus scholars have already used them as building blocks for sketches of a relatively urbane Jesus: e.g., F. G. Downing, *Christ and the Cynics*, JSOT Manuals 4 (Sheffield: JSOT Press, 1988); Burton L. Mack, *The Lost Gospel: The Book of Q and Christian Origins* (San Francisco: HarperCollins, 1993).

23. James F. Strange, "Some Implications of Archaeology for New Testament Studies," in *What Has Archaeology to Do with Faith*, ed. James Charlesworth and Walter Weaver (Philadelphia: Trinity, 1992), 31–35.

24. Meyers, "Roman Sepphoris," 322–24, 326.

25. For example, Eric M. Meyers and James F. Strange, *Archaeology, the Rabbis, and Early Christianity* (Nashville: Abingdon, 1981), 58. Such estimates are reminiscent of the ancient Judean historian Josephus — "at least 15,000" per village!

26. Magen Broshi, "The Population of Western Palestine in the Roman-Byzantine Period," *BASOR* 236 (1980): 1–7.

27. Discussion and citations in Jonathan L. Reed, "The Population of Capernaum," Occasional Papers of the Institute for Antiquity and Christianity, no. 24 (Claremont: Institute for Antiquity and Christianity, 1992), 11–14.

28. Given Broshi's still generous calculations for all of Western Palestine, a million at most at its late Roman-Byzantine height ("Population of Western Palestine"), the population of Galilee as a whole would probably have been under 150,000 in the first century, even if it were one of the more densely populated districts. Recent estimates of population in Galilee seem far more realistic, in particular, a recent well-informed critically calculated estimate for the Capernaum, which moves the population closer to the earlier picture of a village of around 1,000; see Reed, "Population of Capernaum"; cf. James F. Strange, "Capernaum," *IDBSuppl* (Nashville: Abingdon, 1976).

29. Jonathan L. Reed, "Population Numbers, Urbanization, and Economics: Galilean Archaeology an the Historical Jesus," in SBLSP (1994), esp. 212, 214.

30. Strange, "Some Implications of Archaeology for New Testament Studies," 33.

31. See ibid., 23–59, esp. 32–41. Strange's development of this scheme, however, requires some serious qualification, particularly in connection with how the

dominant "overlay" would have stood in relation to the dominated society and its culture. To say that the relation of particular Jewish cultural components to the Roman overlay would have varied by component (38) simply takes them out of the overall context of political-cultural subordination. To say that Jewish culture was already urban as well as rural and therefore prepared for Roman domination (32) suggests that Galilee was already urbanized prior to Antipas. Moreover, if we are trying to understand Sepphoris in historical context, then the relation of the Roman urban overlay to the indigenous society cannot be considered apart from the dynamics of a history that included widespread popular insurrections against the Roman conquerors and/or their client rulers in 40–37 and 4 B.C.E. and 66–70 C.E. as well as several other protests and resistance movements. To say that the idea 'city' was not a foreign idea, but "expressed what the locals had in mind" and that "the citizens of the city...gave expression to their idea of a city by planning a city, building it, and living in it" (34) seems to neglect the fact that, as the ruler, Antipas would have determined the forms and hired the builders. Strange also does not appear to take into account the degree to which the very indigenous basic "Jewish symbols" he mentions had already been dramatically affected by Hellenistic-Roman influences and political domination; e.g., the Temple had been massively rebuilt in Hellenistic style by the client king Herod.

32. Meyers, "Roman Sepphoris," 324; Meyers, Netzer, Meyers, *Sepphoris*, 12. Besides the fact that there is as yet little or no archaeological evidence for this claim, it is appropriate to note that other archaeologists find that, generally speaking, "ethnicity is difficult to recognize from the archaeological record" (Colin Renfrew and Paul Bahn, *Archaeology: Theory, Method, and Practice* [London: Thames and Hudson, 1991], 169). The further claim that "the considerable first-century remains that have been uncovered...point to a Torah-true population" (Meyers, "Roman Sepphoris," 325) is based on extremely limited evidence: "ritual baths" (*miqva'ot*) in a number of houses and evidence of burial outside the city precincts.

33. It is often simply assumed that Sepphoris was a "Jewish" city, at least in the first century C.E. That assumption, along with other standard assumptions, then creates certain difficulties for understanding literary and other evidence, including that for Sepphoris's "pro-Roman" stand in the great revolt, over against the presumably anti-Roman stance of the rest of the Jewish "nation." For example, Sean Freyne (*Galilee from Alexander the Great to Hadrian*, 123) finds Sepphoris's pro-Roman stance "most surprising given the general anti-Roman approach of Galilee...as a whole." Moreover, assuming that Sepphoris and the Galileans shared "similar religious loyalties" (since both were presumably Jewish), Freyne (128) reaches for economic (separated from the political and cultural factors) class conflict to explain the Galileans' detestation of the city. Meyers ("Roman Sepphoris," 324), assuming that the Sepphoreans were "fellow Galileans" (something which Josephus never even suggests), then assumes also that the Galileans have "anti-Roman sentiments," which the two Josephus texts he cites (*B.J.* 3.32; *Vita* 348) do not indicate.

34. Eric Meyers seems to be suggesting just such a connection between social-structural position and cultural style in his suggestion that the "pagan" motifs

found in what were otherwise identified as "Jewish" houses in the western residential section of the site indicate an "upper class lifestyle"; "Roman Sepphoris," 329.

35. Eric Meyers refers repeatedly to a mass migration of Judeans to Galilee following the revolts of 66–70 and 132–135 (e.g., "The Cultural Setting of Galilee," 700–701). The literary evidence offered, however, is late and shaky at best, especially considering the absence of any archaeological evidence. That many, especially upper-class, "Jewish landed aristocracy" moved to Sepphoris after the great revolt is simply speculation; cf. Freyne, *Galilee from Alexander the Great to Hadrian*, 127.

36. See now Stuart S. Miller, *Studies in the History and Tradition of Sepphoris* (Leiden: Brill, 1984), 62–88, 102, 120–27: rabbinic traditions attest a memory of priestly families in Sepphoris in the second century (whose ancestors had served in the Jerusalem Temple). The one tradition (*y. Ta'an.* 4.68d) which can be used to locate the priestly course of Yedaiah in Sepphoris is paralleled by the dating of the fragmentary inscription of the priestly courses found at Caesarea (on which see further Michael Avi-Yonah, "The Caesarea Inscription of the Twenty-Four Priestly Courses," in *The Teacher's Yoke: Studies in Memory of Henry Trantham*, ed. E. J. Vardaman, J. L. Garrett, and J. B. Adair [Waco, Tex., 1964], 46–57). Prior to Miller's more critical examination of these rabbinic traditions, Menahem Stern ("The Reign of Herod and the Herodian Dynasty," in *The Jewish People in the First Century*, CRINT I.1, ed. S. Safrai and M. Stern [Assen: Van Gorcum, 1974], 272 n. 2), trusting these rabbinic traditions as good evidence for the prominence of the Sepphorean Joseph ben Ellem (who served as high priest for an hour!) at the time of Herod, then drew the conclusion that, because Josephus (in *Ant.* 17.166) describes Joseph as his "relative," the high priest Matthias was also from Galilee. Freyne (*Galilee from Alexander the Great to Hadrian*, 165, 285) takes the implications a logical step further, citing Joseph ben Ellem as an example of "priestly aristocratic landowners in Sepphoris." After Miller's analysis it is clear that Meyers's argument ("Roman Sepphoris," 322) that already from the first century Sepphoris "was a city inhabited by many well-to-do, aristocratic Jews of a priestly background" is supported no more by rabbinic evidence than it is by Josephus or "the archaeological record thus far revealed."

37. Meyers, "Roman Sepphoris," 329. There is strong reason to doubt, however, that "Sepphoris had become the home of Jewish-Christians," as well as of "pagans" and "Jews," according to Joan E. Taylor, *Christians and the Holy Places: The Myth of Jewish Christian Origins* (Oxford: Clarendon, 1993).

38. Meyers, "Roman Sepphoris," 326.

39. Closer study of rabbinic texts with this question in mind may illuminate this issue.

40. In an early essay on the subject, M. Avi-Yonah, "The Foundation of Tiberias," *IEJ* 1 (1950): 160–69, dates the founding in 18 C.E.

41. See F. F. Abbott and A. C. Johnson, *Municipal Administration in the Roman Empire* (New York: Russell and Russell, 1968), e.g., 35, 36, 68, 71, 75, 76, 80, 82.

42. See the important study, "Was Jerusalem a Polis?" *IEJ* 14 (1964), by V. Tcherikover, who comments: "Our chief literary source is remarkably unclear and inaccurate when he uses political-legal terminology" (64). H. W. Hoehner,

Herod Antipas (Cambridge: Cambridge University Press, 1972), 91–102, apparently does not understand the contradiction of claiming, on the one hand, that Tiberias was founded within the framework of a *polis*, and then admitting, on the other hand, that not only the region around Tiberias but the citizens of the city itself were governed by the royal officials rather than by the city's *boulē*.

43. Jones, *Cities of the Eastern Roman Provinces*, 276.

44. See Y. Meshorer, *Jewish Coins of the Second Temple Period* (Tel Aviv: Am Hassefer, 1967), 74–75; Arei Kindler, *The Coins of Tiberias* (Tiberias: Hamei Tiberias, 1961), no. 2. Note also the "uncoined silver" taken as booty from the royal palace at Tiberias and then recovered by Josephus, *Vita* 68.

45. *Eparchos;* the *hyparchoi* mentioned in *B.J.* 2.615 (cf. *Vita* 86) appear to be Josephus's appointees as temporary military governors of Tiberias, although they may well already have been some sort of office holders in Tiberias.

46. Archaeological explorations make it increasingly clear that such "prayer-houses" were typical of diaspora communities but not yet built in Judea and Galilee before the first century C.E.; see further chap. 10 below.

47. Even if these are dismissed as discreet steps taken by a Jewish aristocracy fearful of offending the Roman authorities after the Bar Kokhba revolt, and therefore choosing the safe types favored by neighboring cities (Martin Goodman, *State and Society in Roman Galilee, A.D. 132–212* [Totowa, N.J.: Rowman & Allanheld, 1983], 129), the point is somewhat the same.

48. Goodman (ibid., 46) dismisses this as a "shaky indication of respect," while Taylor, *Christians and the Holy Places*, 53, takes it more seriously on the grounds that "the gods were depicted on coins... because the authorities in charge of the mint thought Zeus and Hygeia fitting symbols for the city of Tiberias."

49. Goodman's claim (*State and Society*, 129) that the inhabitants of both Tiberias and Sepphoris "were mostly Jews" is typical of scholarly statements. Such statements, however, are both based on shaky evidence and framed with an imprecise conceptual apparatus, given this transitional period in Galilee. The presence of rabbis and inscriptions are hardly representative samples, and indicate that some Judeans/Jews lived there. Goodman's reference back to p. 31 is apparently to the statement that "in Josephus' time Galilee was almost entirely Jewish," for which he cites Josephus, *B.J.* 3.41, which says nothing about the composition of the population — beyond his usual term "the Galileans." The further statement that "Tiberias [was] ruled entirely by Jews before 70" (129) obscures the clear political-cultural differences between Antipas (and his court/administration) and the Jerusalem priestly authorities, on the one side, and the Galilean populace, on the other. The wealthy Jerusalem priest Josephus provides several indications of the sharp conflicts in both directions.

50. See Gideon Foerster and F. Vitto, "Tiberias," in *The New Encyclopedia of Archaeological Excavation in the Holy Land* (New York: Simon and Schuster, 1993), 4:1464–73.

51. As classical archaeology refines its categories of analysis, further manifestations and parallels to this general observation are likely to emerge. Already, for example, analysis of baths at royal and royal urban sites in Palestine indicate an indigenous style or "regime" that has adapted Hellenistic-Roman patterns to local culture. But shifts are discernible, suggesting the hypothesis that as Roman

domination moved from "imperialistic," through client kings, to direct "colonial" rule, the provincial elite acculturated more completely. A more subtle stage in that shift, but nevertheless discernible as well as explicable, is the increased acculturation sponsored by a client ruler raised and educated in Rome, such as Antipas and Agrippa I, compared with the relatively more limited assimilation of Hellenistic-Roman cultural forms by the first generation of client ruler, such as Herod. See further David B. Small, "Late Hellenistic Baths in Palestine," *BASOR* 266 (1987): 59–74.

52. See further Daniel R. Schwartz, *Agrippa I: The Last King of Judea* (Tübingen: Mohr, 1990), 137–40.

53. See ibid., 18–23, 77–89, for a convincing case that Josephus depends upon Philo's report of the event in *Legatio ad Gaium*, but that Josephus inserted additional materials that do not contradict but supplement Philo's account. Important for present purposes is Josephus's portrayal of the network of political-economic relationships, not the historicity and chronology of particular incidents and persons.

54. Agrippa II also had such "nobles," clearly non-Judeans from and/or in charge of Trachonitis (*Vita* 112, 149). That this is not a typical Hellenistic *polis*, but a semi-"oriental" petty kingship can be seen by comparison with other texts, such as *Ant.* 11.37; Tacitus, *Ann.* 15.27; see A. N. Sherwin-White, *Roman Law and Roman Society in the New Testament* (Oxford: Oxford University Press, 1963), 137.

55. The following is from Peter Garnsey and Richard Saller, *The Roman Empire: Economy, Society, and Culture* (London: Duckworth, 1987), 34, 56–57.

56. Douglas Edwards, "The Socio-Economic and Cultural Ethos of the Lower Galilee in the First Century: Implications for the Nascent Jesus Movement," in *Galilee in Late Antiquity*, ed. Levine, 63, apparently does not consider that the "growth economy" in which "workers on Antipas' building projects needed shelter, food, and other support services" had to be supported from Antipas's economic base, the Galilean and Perean villagers. Another generalization by Garnsey and Saller (*The Roman Empire*, 51) is pertinent to political-economic relations in Galilee:

> The first century and, even more so, the second have been considered prosperous by observers ancient and modern, and for the rich few this was doubtless the case: they became richer. But for the vast majority of the population the situation was otherwise. To take agriculture, the basis of the economy, for subsistence farmers the margin of surplus production was narrow and was largely siphoned off by the imperial authorities and city-based landlords in taxes and rents.

A generalization by John Kautsky (*Politics of Aristocratic Empires*, 194) is also pertinent:

> There is, then, no alternative to luxury consumption and display, but they, like other elements of aristocratic ideology, also serve the positive function of keeping the aristocracy in its dominant position. Anyone must be struck by the contrast between aristocrats and lower classes in aristocratic empires who

sees the immense treasures accumulated and displayed in the palaces and religious edifices of the aristocracy and recalls the poverty of the peasantry and even the townspeople who lived when this wealth was being assembled — and, indeed, produced it.

57. See chap. 2 above, and Shaye Cohen, "Religion, Ethnicity, and Hellenism in the Emergence of Jewish Identity in Maccabean Palestine," in *Religion and Religious Practice in the Seleucid Kingdom*, ed. Per Bilde et al. (Aarhus: Aarhus University Press, 1990), esp. 212.

58. So Meyers, "Roman Sepphoris," 333.

59. M. T. Boatwright, "Theatres in the Roman Empire," *BA* 53 (1990): 184–92.

60. See the discussion and evidence in Goodman, *State and Society*, 81–82.

61. So Goodman in a review (*JJS* 28 [1977]: 206–7) of H. A. Harris, *Greek Athletics and the Jews* (Cardiff: University of Wales Press, 1976).

62. Goodman, *State and Society*, 131.

63. So Goodman (ibid., 88), as part of an argument that Galilee, in contrast to other areas of the Eastern Mediterranean (and in contrast to what I have argued above), displays "a cultural continuum from city to country." His argument, however, involves the questionable assumption that we can separate the cultural from the political-economic dimensions in our sources and a misreading of key secondary literature (S. Applebaum, "Judaea as a Roman Province: The Countryside as a Political and Economic Factor," *ANRW* 2.8 [1977]: 370–72). The cultural forms established in Tiberias by the "wealthy strangers under royal patronage" were inseparable from their political-economic domination of the Galileans.

64. Lee I. Levine, "The Jewish Patriarch (Nasi) in Third Century Palestine," *ANRW* 2.19.2 (1979): 655, 658.

65. Goodman, *State and Society*, 139.

66. Some possibilities are "the judges of Sepphoris," *m. B. Bat.* 6:7; "the court of Tiberias" and *S. Deut.* 355. Cf. Shaye J. D. Cohen, "The Place of the Rabbi in Jewish Society of the Second Century," in *Galilee in Late Antiquity*, ed. Levine, 163, somewhat indefinitely: these judges were Jews but not necessarily rabbis, and backed by the power of the state.

67. What manner of relationship between Sepphoris and Rome can be found in the legend on the coins of Caracalla is a matter of dispute. What degree of Jewish prominence in Sepphorean politics, particularly membership on the city *boulē*, can be inferred from *y. Pe'a* 1.1.16a; *y. Šabb.* 12.3.13c (*bouletai*) and *b. Sanh.* 8a (Jewish majority on the *boulē?*) requires further critical examination of those rabbinic traditions. Cf. F. Manns, "An Important Jewish-Christian Center: Sepphoris," in *Essais sur le Judeo-Christianisme*, Analecta 12 (Jerusalem: Franciscan Printing Press, 1977), 165–90.

68. Cf. Levine, "Jewish Patriarch," 661.

69. A fourth-century inscription from a synagogue building in Sepphoris refers to a *scholasticus* who, like his father, ranked as a *comes;* B. Lifshitz, *Donateurs et Fondateurs dans les synagogues juives* (Paris: Gabalda, 1967), 59, no. 74.

70. So Levine, "Jewish Patriarch," 650.

71. See *Gen. Rab.* 80, 1, pp. 950–53; *y. Sanh.* 2.6.20d; following Goodman's reasoning in "The Roman State and the Jewish Patriarch in the Third Century," in *Galilee in Late Antiquity*, 133–34.

72. See further Levine, *Rabbinic Class of Roman Palestine*, chap. 4. Goodman, "Roman State and the Jewish Patriarch," 135–36, argues that the Romans' acceptance of the patriarchate was somewhat analogous to their recognition of the power of bishops in their dioceses. Whatever the Roman understanding and attitude toward "religion," however, the power and functioning of the Jewish patriarch in Sepphoris and Tiberias require reconceptualization along the lines of both a sort of unofficial shadow government in an imperial situation and a network of patron-client relations.

73. Levine, "Jewish Patriarch," 661–62, 678–83.

74. Ibid., 659, 662, 667. Levine points out that since the very existence of the Sanhedrin in late Roman times remains an open question, it is best to understand this as a court convened by the *nasi* himself (667).

Chapter 8. Village and Family

Epigraph: James C. Scott, "Protest and Profanation: Agrarian Revolt and the Little Tradition," pt. 1, *Theory and Society* 4 (1977): 18.

1. A recent example of the combination of social history based on literary sources with reconstruction of household life in a village in the Golan is Ann Killibrew and Steven Fine, "Qatzrin: Reconstructing Village Life in Talmudic Times," *BARev* 17 (1991): 44–56. Such reconstructions also draw on comparative studies, such as Carol Kramer, *Village Archaeology: Rural Iran in Archaeological Perspective* (New York: Columbia University Press, 1982).

2. Josephus sometimes uses the term *polis* very loosely in reference to what were clearly villages, such as Asochis or Besara (*Vita* 118–19, 207, 233, 384). Although Josephus refers to Gabara as a city, even as one of "the three chief cities of Galilee" (*B.J.* 3.132; *Vita* 123), it must be the same place as "the village of Gabaroth" (*Vita* 229–43). Tarichaeae, clearly very populous, is perhaps the one ambiguous case, referred to several times as a *polis*. On the other hand, by comparison with his usual references to Tiberias or Sepphoris, it would appear that Josephus often avoids referring to Tarichaeae explicitly as a *polis*.

3. See Z. Yeivin, "Survey of Settlements in Galilee and the Golan from the Period of the Mishnah in the Light of the Sources," Ph.D. diss., Hebrew University of Jerusalem, 1971; Eric M. Meyers, James F. Strange, and Dennis E. Groh, "The Meiron Excavation Project: Archaeological Survey in Galilee and Golan, 1976," *BASOR* 230 (1978): 1–8; W. Praisnitz, "The First Agricultural Settlements in Galilee," *IEJ* 9 (1959): 166–74, esp. 167–68 on Khirbet Kharruba in Upper Galilee; cf. G. Tchalenko, *Villages Antiques de la Syrie du Nord*, 3 vols. (Paris, 1953–58), 1:25–46, on agriculture. More than fifty villages have been identified for the rabbinic period in Galilee. The assumptions and results of archaeological surveys, of course, must be critically scrutinized, as in the recent critique by Michael Fotadis, "Modernity and Past-Still-Present: The Politics of Time in the Birth of Regional Archaeological Projects in Greece," *AJA* 99 (1995): 59–78. The whole issue will soon be updated by the publication of Mordechai Aviam, *Survey of Sites in the Galilee* (Jerusalem, 1995).

4. Meiron and the neighboring villages of Khirbet Shema' and Nabratein have been the subjects of well-published excavations: E. M. Meyers, J. F. Strange, and

C. L. Meyers, *Excavations at Ancient Meiron, Upper Galilee, Israel 1971–72, 1974–75, 1977* (Cambridge, Mass.: ASOR, 1981), with further list of previous publications.

5. D. H. K. Amiran, "Sites of Settlements in the Mountains of Lower Galilee," *IEJ* 6 (1956): 71–74.

6. Martin Goodman, *State and Society in Roman Galilee*, A.D. *132–212* (Totowa, N.J.: Rowman & Allanheld, 1983), 28; J. Percival, *The Roman Villa: An Historical Introduction* (London: Batsford, 1976), 31. Ze'ev Safrai, *The Economy of Roman Palestine* (London: Routledge, 1994), 17–19, noting that the sages did not adhere to consistent use of terminology, outlines his own scheme of three sizes of "towns" and two types of "villages" (or villas).

7. Shimon Applebaum, "Economic Life in Ancient Palestine," in *The Jewish People in the First Century*, CRINT I.2, ed. S. Safrai and M. Stern (Assen: Van Gorcum, 1976), 641–44.

8. Information on different sites, soils, fields, and so on, can be found in numerous articles; e.g., D. H. K. Amiran, "The Pattern of Settlement in Palestine," *IEJ* 3 (1953): 65–78; "Sites of Settlements in the Mountains of Lower Galilee," *IEJ* 6 (1956): 69–77; B. Golomb and Y. Kedar, "Ancient Agriculture in the Galilee Mountains," *IEJ* 21 (1971): 136–40; cf. for the Gaulanitis to the east, D. Urman, *The Golan: A Profile of a Region During the Roman and Byzantine Periods*, BARIS 269 (Oxford: BAR, 1985).

9. Yeivin, "Survey of Settlements in Galilee," xx.

10. As noted in chap. 7 above, recent archaeological discoveries at Sepphoris and elsewhere stimulated scholarly excitement about the degree of "urbanization" in Lower Galilee in Roman times: e.g., J. Andrew Overman, "Who Were the First Urban Christians? Urbanization in Galilee in the First Century," in SBLSP, ed. David Lull (Atlanta: Scholars Press, 1988), 160–68; Eric M. Meyers and James F. Strange, *Archaeology, the Rabbis, and Early Christianity* (Nashville: Abingdon, 1981), 58 (estimating Capernaum at 12,000–15,000).

11. See the critical discussion and application of methods of estimating population in cities and villages of the ancient world by Jonathan L. Reed, "The Population of Capernaum," Occasional Papers of the Institute for Antiquity and Christianity, no. 24 (Claremont: Institute for Antiquity and Christianity, 1992), esp. 11–15.

12. E. Meyers, "The Cultural Setting of Galilee: The Case of Regionalism and Early Judaism," *ANRW* 2.19.1 (1979): 700, estimates most villages in Upper Galilee at between 30 and 50 dunams (7.5–12.5 acres). Cf. the slightly higher estimates for population of various sized villages in Safrai, *Economy of Roman Palestine*, 42.

13. Comparisons can be made with settlements in the Golan and in Samaria: Dan Urman, *The Golan* (Oxford: BAR, 1985), 87–88, 93, found four towns of 30–50 acres, fourteen settlements of 10–30 acres, twenty-eight sites of 5–10 acres, fifty-four sites of 2.5–5 acres, and thirty-three with less than 2.5 acres; and *Landscape and Pattern*, ed. S. Dar (Oxford: BAR, 1986), 36, 42, 47, 51, 53, found several villages between 2.4 to 7.5 acres in area, with one at 10 acres. Yeivin, "Survey of Settlements in Galilee," discusses mostly towns and large villages among his ten sites.

14. See Joan E. Taylor, *Christians and the Holy Places: The Myth of Jewish Christian Origins* (Oxford: Clarendon, 1993), chaps. 11–12.

15. Gellarmino Bagatti, *Excavations at Nazareth* (Jerusalem: Franciscan Printing Press, 1969), 29–32.

16. James A. Strange, "Nazareth," in *ABD*, 4:1051, recently pushed the supposed "refounding" back to the third century B.C.E., well before the Hasmonean takeover of Galilee. Meyers and Strange, *Archaeology, the Rabbis, and Early Christianity*, 57, implying discontinuity with the earlier settlement, suggested that "the village was less than two-hundred years old in the first century C.E."

17. On Capernaum generally, see Vassilos Tzaferis, *Excavations at Capernaum*, vol. 1 (Winona Lake, Ind.: Eisenbrauns, 1989); V. Tzaferis, "New Archaeological Evidence on Ancient Capernaum," *BA* 46 (1983): 198–204; John C. H. Laughlin, "Capernaum. From Jesus' Time and After," *BA* 56 (1993): 54–61.

18. The plan of the bathhouse suggest that "it was built for Roman bathers rather than Jews"; Laughlin, "Capernaum," 57.

19. Meyers and Strange, *Archaeology, the Rabbis, and Early Christianity*, 58, estimated Capernaum at 12,000–15,000.

20. More realistic recent estimates on Capernaum, such as by Reed, "Population of Capernaum," thus return to the earlier estimates by Stanislao Loffreda, *A Visit to Capernaum* (Jerusalem: Franciscan Press, 1972), 20; Strange, "Capernaum."

21. James F. Strange, "The Capernaum and Herodium Publications," *BASOR* 226 (1977): 65–73; cf. Gideon Foerster, "Notes on Recent Excavations at Capernaum," in *Ancient Synagogues Revealed*, ed. Lee I. Levine (Jerusalem: Israel Exploration Society, 1981).

22. Taylor, *Christians and the Holy Places*, chaps. 12–13.

23. Cf. Meyers and Strange, *Archaeology, the Rabbis, and Early Christianity*, 59.

24. Among the numerous reports: Meyers, Strange, and Groh, "The Meiron Excavation Project," 1–24; Eric M. Meyers, James F. Strange, Carol L. Meyers, and Richard S. Hanson, "Preliminary Report on the 1977 and 1978 Seasons at Gush Halav," *BASOR* 233 (1979): 33–58; Eric M. Meyers, James F. Strange, and Carol L. Meyers, "Preliminary Report on the 1980 Excavations at en-Nabratein, Israel," *BASOR* 244 (1981): 1–25; Meyers, Strange, and Meyers, *Excavations at Ancient Meiron*. Since these archaeological reports on excavations carried out in the 1970s still rely on some of the principal assumptions and interpretative categories being challenged in this study, there will be discrepancies between their interpretations of data and the interpretations offered here.

25. Meyers et al., "1977 and 1978 Seasons at Gush Halav," 35–36; Meyers, Strange, and Meyers, "1980 Excavations at en-Nabratein, Israel," 5, 11–13.

26. As explained in chap. 2 above, this is evident from the combination of the second-century rabbinic reference to "old" fortresses at Gush Halav, Jotapata, and Sepphoris (*m. 'Arak.* 9:6), and Josephus's reference to the already existing wells that John of Gischala built up and Titus ordered torn down (*B.J.* 4.117).

27. Vs. Meyers, Strange, and Meyers, *Excavations at Ancient Meiron*, 3, 157–58; Meyers, introduction to Richard S. Hanson, *Tyrian Influence in the Upper Galilee*, Meiron Excavation Project No. 2 (Cambridge, Mass.: ASOR, 1980), 1–4; fuller critique in Horsley, "Archaeology and the Villages of Upper Galilee,"

BASOR 297 (1995): 5–15; with a response by Meyers. On the economy of these villages, see chap. 9 below.

28. Vs. Meyers, Strange, and Meyers, *Excavations at Ancient Meiron*, 157. Gideon Foerster, "Excavations at Ancient Meron," *IEJ* 37 (1987), is skeptical about "trying to impose Roman concepts of urban town-planning on a small settlement" (266).

29. So Meyers, Strange, and Meyers, *Excavations at Ancient Meiron*, 155–57.

30. A general survey of sources pertinent to the Jewish family in antiquity are S. Safrai, "Home and Family," in *The Jewish People in the First Century*, CRINT I.2, ed. S. Safrai and M. Stern (Assen: Van Gorcum, 1976), 728–92. Among the many recent treatments of the Roman family, see K. Bradley, *Discovering the Roman Family: Studies in Roman Social History* (Oxford: Oxford University Press, 1991); and Richard Saller and D. Kertzer, "Historical and Anthropological Perspectives on Italian Family Life," in *The Family in Italy from Antiquity to the Present*, ed. D. Kertzer and R. Saller (New Haven: Yale University Press, 1991), 1–22.

31. See Neusner, *Judaism: The Evidence of the Mishnah* (Chicago: University of Chicago Press, 1981).

32. Max Weber, *Ancient Judaism* (Glencoe, Ill.: Free Press, 1952), 61–70; N. P. Lemche, *Early Israel*, VTSup 37 (Leiden: Brill, 1985), 245–85; Naomi Steinberg, "The Deuteronomic Law Code and the Politics of State Centralization," in *The Bible and Liberation*, ed. N. Gottwald and R. Horsley (Maryknoll, N.Y.: Orbis, 1993), 369–70.

33. Judith Romney Wegner, *Chattel or Person? The Status of Women in the Mishnah* (Oxford: Oxford University Press, 1988), chap. 6, argues that the exclusion of women from certain cultic activities was a major factor in their confinement to the domestic sphere.

34. Such critical procedural assumptions are articulated and followed, for example, by Goodman, *State and Society*, 132–312; and Shaye J. D. Cohen, "The Place of the Rabbi in Jewish Society of the Second Century," in *The Galilee in Late Antiquity*, ed. Lee I. Levine (New York: Jewish Theological Seminary of America, 1992), 157–73.

35. While qualifications and "extrapolations" must be made to move from rabbinic and Hellenistic Jewish literary sources to village customs and practices in Galilee, two recent studies are very helpful in locating and evaluating pertinent sources: Leonie J. Archer, *Her Price Is Beyond Rubies: The Jewish Woman in Graeco-Roman Palestine*, JSOTSup 60 (Sheffield: JSOT Press, 1990); and the more critical analysis of Mishnaic texts in particular, Wegner, *Chattel or Person?*

36. Much previous historical and anthropological treatment of the family has been androcentric and patriarchal in presuppositions and viewpoint. Critiques include *Rethinking the Family: Some Feminist Questions*, ed. B. Thorne and M. Yahon (New York: Longman, 1982); D. Herlihy, "Family," *American Historical Review* 96 (1991): 1–16; J. E. Smith, "Review Essay: Family History and Feminist History," *Feminist Studies* 17 (1991): 349–64. Marianne Sawicki, "Archaeology as Space Technology: Digging for Gender and Class in Holy Land," *Method and Theory in the Study of Religion* 6 (1994): 319–48, points out that archaeological excavations in Galilee and their interpretation do not yet reflect recent advances

in archaeology of gender relations. Sawicki's own interpretations of archaeological reports and Miriam Peskowitz, " 'Family/ies' in Antiquity: Evidence from Tannaitic Literature and Roman Galilean Architecture," in *The Jewish Family in Antiquity*, ed. Shaye J. D. Cohen (Atlanta: Scholars Press, 1993), 9–36, take important first steps in re-forming archaeological methods.

37. Wegner, *Chattel or Person?* 71, suggests that these rulings reflect preexisting customary law incorporated into the mishnaic system.

38. The Hebrew biblical and Mishnaic subordination of women to men is now highly problematic for a culture concerned for more egalitarian values and social practices. The Hebrew biblical and "Jewish" representations of gendered social positions and roles, however, are no more (or less) patriarchal and misogynist than other major literate cultural traditions, such as that of classical Athens (cf. Aeschylus, Oresteia trilogy). If the teachings of Jesus as represented in the Gospels seem more egalitarian, it may be because they are rooted in a popular agrarian ethos, in which the division of labor and specialization of roles was not as highly developed as among the rabbinic sages or the slave-holding "democracy" of classical Athens. To a modern Western understanding of social relations in terms of individual rights and private property, the rulings of the Mishnah appear to represent women as a conflicting combination of the chattel of their fathers/husbands with regard to sexuality and persons with certain rights and responsibilities with regard to the division of labor and economic sustenance (see Wegner, *Chattel or Person?*). Feminist theorists, particularly anthropologists, have offered suggestive explanations for the subordination, confinement, and anomalous representations of women in most societies. The different positions and roles of women and men in societies can be (partly) explained as rooted in the opposition between their respective domestic and public orientations, which in turn are (partly) rooted in women's nurturant capacities (Michele Z. Rosaldo in *Women, Culture, and Society*, ed. Rosaldo and Louise Lamphere [Stanford, Calif.: Stanford University Press, 1974], 23–24). A complementary explanation is that, in distinguishing culture from nature, the usually patriarchal framers of culture feel the need to confine and control women, whom they sense have affinities with nature (Sherry Ortner, "Is Female to Male as Nature Is to Culture?" in *Women, Culture, and Society*, ed. Rosaldo and Lamphere, 69–73). It may also facilitate our understanding, in the cases of ancient Galilean villages and rabbinic rulings, to realize that, in contrast with modern Western individualism and private property, individuals as well as economic resources were embedded in the fundamental social form of the patriarchal family/household. Both the appearance of the treatment of women as chattel with regard to their sexuality/fertility and the husband's control of the *usufruct* of the wife's dowry-property can thus be explained from the customary vesting of authority and responsibility for the management of the traditional family inheritance and other productive and reproductive resources in the patriarchal head of the *bet 'av* (house of the father).

39. See Peskowitz, " 'Family/ies' in Antiquity," 31.

40. J. Kelly, "Family and Society," in *Women, History, and Theory* (Chicago: University of Chicago Press, 1984), 128, comments more generally on how work and home and the labor of women and men, adults and children were bound together.

41. For a critique of the model that correlated public and private/domestic with a division of gender roles, see D. O. Helly and S. M. Reverby, *Gendered Domains: Rethinking Public and Private in Women's History* (Ithaca: Cornell University Press, 1992).

42. Peskowitz, " 'Family/ies' in Antiquity," 33–34; Douglas Oakman, *Jesus and the Economic Questions of His Day* (Lewiston, N.Y.: Mellen, 1986), 23.

Chapter 9. Galilean Village Economy and the Political-Economic Structure of Roman Palestine

1. This is enshrined in the monumental works of Michael Rostovtseff: *The Social and Economic History of the Hellenistic World*, 3 vols. (Oxford: Clarendon, 1941), and *The Social and Economic History of the Roman Empire* (1926; rev. ed., Oxford: Clarendon, 1957). In many ways, Rostovtseff simply projected the nascent capitalism of Russia with which he was familiar back onto the Hellenistic-Roman world. Contemporary with the revised edition of the latter work was a book of essays critically questioning the application of modern "market" assumptions to the ancient world, *Trade and Market in the Early Empires: Economies in History and Theory*, ed. Karl Polanyi, Conrad M. Arensberg, and Harry W. Pearson (Glencoe, Ill.: Free Press, 1957), including the fundamental article by Polanyi, "Aristotle Discovers the Economy," 64–96.

2. Phrases taken from Sean Freyne, *Galilee from Alexander the Great to Hadrian: A Study of Second Temple Judaism* (Wilmington, Del.: Glazier, 1980), chap. 5, esp. 170, 172, 175–77. Even the (formerly East) German scholar Kreissig worked with similar assumptions about the ancient world having basically a market economy; see Heinz Kreissig, *Die sozialen Zusammenhänge des Jüdischen Krieges* (Berlin: Akademie, 1970). Ze'ev Safrai, *The Economy of Roman Palestine* (London: Routledge, 1994), revives the market model in an attempt to understand largely late-Roman and Byzantine Palestine as an "open economy," in contrast to the Roman empire at large.

3. Freyne, *Galilee from Alexander the Great to Hadrian*, 176–78; following Kreissig, *Die soziale Zusammenhänge des Jüdischen Krieges*, 36–51. Shimon Applebaum, "Economic Life in Ancient Palestine," in *The Jewish People in the First Century*, CRINT I.2, ed. S. Safrai and M. Stern (Assen: Van Gorcum, 1976), 662–63, 668, criticizes Kreissig's assumption of a countrywide market or price structure, but accepts the hypothesis of "progressive commercialization" and the basic assumption of a market economy in which the peasants also participated.

4. Freyne, *Galilee from Alexander the Great to Hadrian*, 195.

5. Martin Goodman, *State and Society in Roman Galilee*, A.D. *132–212* (Totowa, N.J.: Rowman & Allanheld, 1983), 19, 54, 60–62.

6. The following sketch of the local Galilean village market is taken from Goodman, *State and Society*, 54–60. Safrai, *Economy of Roman Palestine*, also claims that the local as well as overall economy in Roman Palestine in late antiquity was an "open" trading network, yet repeatedly makes particular statements that contradict such a picture. For example: "There are not many traditions which specifically mention the direct marketing of agricultural goods from the village region in the city or the direct marketing of city goods in the village" (237). "The

descriptions of the market-days above reflect a rather undeveloped commercial and judicial framework" (240). Donkey-drivers, important to his model as "middle-men" and "merchants," are attested in rabbinic texts as hired workers (265–66). Rabbinic texts idealize self-sufficiency and rail against commerce (304–9). Taxes were paid/collected in kind — from the threshing floors! (350, and passim). Most decisive against an "open" market economy locally: "The accepted reality was usu-ally that the farmer also functioned as an occasional artisan or laborer and at least part of his time was devoted to non-agricultural work." Such statements or admis-sions by Safrai only serve to make clear that rabbinic sources represent villagers as peasants in a traditional agrarian society.

7. Indeed, it has been extraordinarily difficult to document such a market econ-omy for Galilee. Goodman has recently attempted it primarily on the basis of case law from the Mishnah and Tosefta. The results are highly problematic and un-reliable. Illustrations can be taken from several key aspects of his portrayal of "Galilean Village Trade," chap. 5 in *State and Society*. None of the Mishnaic texts cited by Applebaum (687 n. 8) and Goodman (54, 211 n. 4) to illustrate market day(s) have to do explicitly with markets or market days, but to (days of) assem-bly and court sessions (*m. Meg* 1:1; 3:6; *m. Ketub.* 1:1; *m. B. Meṣ.* 4:6). Are the *agorai* in the Gospel of Mark markets? or "squares" or "gates" = places of as-sembly? As Goodman admits, "no archaeology has yet revealed in Galilee an open central place on the model of those in the contemporary *polis* (*State and Society*, 54). The only text cited on "bringing in the produce for sale" (*m. Ma'aś. Š.* 4:1, 54 n. 19) concerns redemption of "the second tithe," hence a small percentage of the produce, and that on only the first, second, fourth, and fifth years of the seven-year cycle. No evidence is given that "villages as local trading centers encouraged the establishment of permanent shops... apart from the periodic markets" (55). *M. B. Bat.* 2:3 indicates that shops were simply parts of residential courtyards; is there any evidence for permanent shops in a market place? Does *m. B. Bat.* 2:2 refer to a "craftsman's furnace" or simply to any oven? Goodman admits that "no forge has yet been uncovered in any Galilean site" (56). Mendelsohn's evi-dence on "Guilds in Ancient Palestine" (19; cited in Goodman, *State and Society*, 56 n. 62; cf. Josephus, *B.J.* 2.530 [timber market] and 5.331 [woolshops, brazier smithies, clothesmarket] in Jerusalem) pertains to... Jerusalem, and can hardly be extrapolated to Galileans villages. The evidence for "monetarization" is weak and ambiguous, largely hoards of coins *and weights* (my emphasis); literary evidence (offered from DJD 2, not from the Mishnah) suggests monetary valuation, but not payment in coin. *M. B. Meṣ.* 4:6 has moneychangers in "large towns" but not in villages. The texts cited on scribes (e.g., *m. B. Bat.* 10:3) indicate neither the extent to which scribes were used nor that it "was a profitable profession" (59). The usual text offered for evidence that "the Galilean farmer could rely on a market for his oil" is the story of John of Gischala's sale of oil to Caesarea Philippi in the unique conditions of the great revolt in 66–67, hardly a regular occurrence. Similarly, the evidence cited by Safrai, *Economy of Roman Palestine*, indicates a traditional agrarian society and not the "open" market that he claims for the economy of Palestine generally.

8. Again attempting to be careful not simply to impose a social scientific "model" onto ancient Palestine or to illustrate such a "model" from ancient Pales-

tinian "data," I am relying upon while critically adapting the constructions of traditional agrarian societies based on comparative study of appropriate societies by Gerhard E. Lenski, *Power and Privilege: A Theory of Social Stratification* (New York: McGraw-Hill, 1966), and John Kautsky, *The Politics of Aristocratic Empires* (Chapel Hill: University of North Carolina Press, 1982). For a critique and adaptation of Lenski in connection with pre-Hasmonean second-temple Judea, see R. A. Horsley and Patrick Tiller, "Ben Sira and the Sociology of Second Temple Judea," paper delivered to the Sociology of the Second Temple Group at the 1992 Annual Meeting of the Society of Biblical Literature (in *Second Temple Studies 2: Hellenistic Period*, ed. John Halligan, JSOTSup [Sheffield: JSOT Press, forthcoming]). Thomas Carney, *The Shape of the Past: Models and Antiquity* (Lawrence, Kan.: Coronado, 1975), is useful for comparison because based heavily on evidence from ancient Rome, yet for that same reason cannot be simply "applied" to ancient Palestine, which had a very different political-economic history and heritage from that of Rome.

9. While recognizing that the framers of the Mishnah themselves were articulating not a market economics but a redistributive economics, Jacob Neusner, *The Economics of the Mishnah* (Chicago: University of Chicago Press, 1990), appears to assume that the rabbis were in their own preferred theoretical world, while simply omitting adequate references to "most of the Jews, on the one side, and the economic activities and concerns of labor and capital alike, on the other," and ignoring "most participants in the economy" (52, 68). That is, Neusner apparently not only takes market economics as normative, but believes that once it originated in the sixth century B.C.E., "market economics" had become "well established as the economics of the world economy in which...the Jews of Palestine had been fully incorporated" (8). One might consider, however, merely what percentage of goods being transported across the Mediterranean Sea under Roman imperial rule would have belonged to the "market economy" and what percentage were being moved by "traders" "in response to political commands." Neusner's stated agenda is exposition of the "economics" of the Mishnah, not the economy of Galilee. But one suspects that the former is more reflective of the latter than appears from his thesis of how abstracted the rabbis were from concrete economic realities.

10. Safrai, *Economy of Roman Palestine*, 357. Cf. *Landscape and Pattern*, ed. S. Dar (Oxford: BAR, 1986), 73–76, 237–45, on what may have been plots of tenants on large estates.

11. See David Adan-Bayewitz and Isadore Perlman, "The Local Trade of Sepphoris in the Roman Period," *IEJ* 40 (1990): 153–72.

12. David Adan-Bayewitz, *Common Pottery in Roman Galilee: A Study of Local Trade* (Ramat-Gan, Israel: Bar Ilan University Press, 1993), 229–30.

13. Ibid., 232, referring to this study, "The Itinerant Peddler in Roman Palestine," *Jews in Economic Life*, ed. N. Gross (Jerusalem, 1985; in Hebrew). Similarly, Safrai, *Economy of Roman Palestine*, 87–88, portrays "the traveling salesman (rochel)" as more of a peddler bringing easily carried items such as cosmetics, and not a merchant engaged in more fundamental trade.

14. Safrai, *Economy of Roman Palestine*, 365–69, and passim, claims specialization of production by region (e.g., olives "for the most part in the Galilee" and "the grape especially in Judaea"). However, he does not distinguish whether

his sources focus on the quality or quantity of production, nor does he raise the question of the relations of production that may have lain behind any specialized production (e.g., production of wine on large estates for trade by wealthy landowners).

15. E.g., Richard S. Hanson, *Tyrian Influence in the Upper Galilee*, Meiron Excavation Project No. 2 (Cambridge, Mass.: ASOR, 1980), esp. the introduction by Meyers. Critique of the hypothesis and its basis in incidence of coins found in Richard A. Horsley, "Archaeology and the Villages of Upper Galilee: A Dialogue with Archaeologists," *BASOR* 297 (1995); and more broadly, in Horsley, "The Historical Jesus and Archaeology of the Galilee: Questions from Historical Jesus Research to Archaeologists," SBLSP, ed. Eugene H. Lovering Jr. (Atlanta: Scholars Press, 1994), esp. 105–8.

16. D. Urman, *The Golan: A Profile of a Region During the Roman and Byzantine Periods*, BARIS 269 (Oxford: BAR, 1985), 145.

17. E.g., the separation of discussion of the village economy as "trade" from discussion of Roman taxation and control of land by Goodman, *State and Society*, chaps. 5 and 9 respectively. Z. Safrai, *Economy of Roman Palestine*, focuses separately on production and taxes and trade, never raising the question of "the relations of production" in an overall political-economic system.

18. This political-economic(-religious) relationship in "class societies" among rulers, producers, and the land has been conceptualized as "redistribution," in contrast to the "reciprocity" of relations among the producers in pre-state societies and local communities subject to rulers. But such a seemingly neutral or "objective" concept seems to obscure the differential power in the relationship. Generally the "surplus" is not generated in the first place until power-holders demand it, and the movement of products is basically one way, an expropriation of produce from the peasant producers by the rulers in order to support their artisan and other dependents as well as to underwrite their own, often luxurious lifestyle. See Kautsky, *Politics of Aristocratic Empires*.

19. The compilers of the Mishnah simply assume, articulate, and apply the same understanding of the relations of people, land, and rulers (temple/high-priesthood) expressed, e.g., in the book of Leviticus. Indeed a whole division, "Agriculture," "centers on the designation of portions or the crop for the use of the priesthood ... and so provides for the support of the Temple staff," as is further explained by Neusner, *Economics of the Mishnah*, 17–18.

20. Freyne, *Galilee from Alexander the Great to Hadrian*, chap. 5: "Economic Realities and Social Stratification," provides an alternative treatment, with separate sections on "The Distribution of Wealth," "Taxation," and "Social Stratification." It seems, however, that in the fundamental political-economic structure of ancient Palestine, those "topics" are inseparable insofar as the ruling families and their auxiliaries were wealthy and powerful by virtue of extracting resources from the peasant producers by means of taxation.

21. On the spiral of peasant indebtedness, see R. A. Horsley, *Sociology and the Jesus Movement* (New York: Crossroad, 1989), 88–90.

22. The evidence of royal land has been discussed with considerable confusion in relation to land tenure in Palestine in general and in Galilee in particular. The principal reason is that the standard previous treatments have not considered the

possibility of a political-economic system that does not operate with modern Western assumptions of private property and a market economy. There thus seems little point in engaging those treatments directly, since disagreements on particulars are rooted in the different models of political-economy being used.

23. E. Mary Smallwood, *The Jews under Roman Rule from Pompey to Diocletian* (Leiden: Brill, 1976), 436.

24. See *Landscape and Pattern*, ed. Dar, 88–112, 120, 230–45.

25. See further the assembly of recently augmented evidence and analysis by David Fiensy, *The Social History of Palestine in the Herodian Period* (Lewiston, N.Y.: Mellen, 1991), 32–43.

26. On "prebendal domain" in comparison with other ways of arranging power relations over land, labor, and produce, see Eric R. Wolf, *Peasants* (Englewood Cliffs, N.J.: Prentice-Hall, 1966), 48–59.

27. See esp. Benjamin Isaac, "Judaea after AD 70," *JJS* 35 (1984): 44–50; on the older view, and general economic conditions, see Shimon Applebaum's discussions, most accessible being "Economic Life in Palestine," 692–99.

28. See the analysis by Shimon Applebaum in "Judea as a Roman Province: The Countryside as a Political and Economic Factor," in *ANRW* 2.8 (1977): 386–95; and an alternative interpretation by Moshe Gil, "Land Ownership in Palestine under Roman Rule," *Revue internationale des droits de l'antiquité* 3, no. 17 (1970): 40–44.

29. Such is posited by Michael Avi-Yonah, *The Holy Land from the Persian to the Arab Conquests (536 B.C. to A.D. 640): A Historical Geography* (Grand Rapids: Baker, 1966, 1977), 112.

30. See further R. A. Horsley, "The Zealots: Their Origins, Relationships, and Importance in the Jewish Revolt," *NovT* 27 (1986): 159–92.

31. Safrai, *Economy of Roman Palestine*, 95, speaking apparently of archaeological explorations, comments that "no farmsteads [large estates] have been found yet in Galilee."

32. Albrecht Alt, "Hellenistische Staedte und Domanen," in *Kleine Schriften* (Munich: Beck, 1953–59), 3:384–95; apparently followed by Freyne, *Galilee from Alexander the Great to Hadrian*, 157–58.

33. Avi-Yonah, *Holy Land*, 141–44. The judgment that Beth Anath was not royal land in the possession of a government official but a private estate fits the modern model being followed by M. Rostovtseff (*Social and Economic History of the Hellenistic World*, 1:345 and 3:1403 n. 149).

34. See Stuart Miller, "Intercity Relations in Roman Palestine: The Case of Sepphoris and Tiberias," *AJSR* 12 (1987): 1–24; Lee I. Levine, "R. Simeon b. Yohai and the Purification of Tiberias: History and Tradition," *HUCA* 49 (1978): 173–74.

35. A. H. M. Jones, "Urbanization of Palestine," *JRS* 21 (1931): 78 and passim; and Jones, *The Cities of the Eastern Roman Provinces*, 2nd ed. (Oxford: Clarendon, 1971).

36. A. H. M. Jones, *The Greek City* (Oxford: Clarendon, 1966), 80n, reached a similar conclusion: Sepphoris and Tiberias "fell short of full city status in that they had no territorial jurisdiction, the surrounding districts remaining toparchies and being administered as before by royal officials" — until the time of Hadrian.

37. Jones, "Urbanization of Palestine," 84. See further Freyne, *Galilee from Alexander the Great to Hadrian*, chap. 3, sec. 5. This happened probably under Hadrian.

38. In a traditional agrarian society, the officers of the state, albeit to a lesser degree, were in a position similar to that of the rulers themselves: "To win control of the state was to win control of the most powerful instrument of self-aggrandizement found in agrarian societies. By the skillful exercise of the powers of the state, a man or group could gain control over much of the economic surplus, and with it at his disposal could go on to achieve honor and prestige as well." Lenski, *Power and Privilege*, 210.

39. See the outline of how wealthy aristocrats expanded their wealth and/or control of land through loans to the impoverished people in Martin Goodman, "The First Jewish Revolt: Social Conflict and the Problem of Debt," *JJS* 33 (1982): 418–26. Goodman appropriately focuses on the surplus wealth being accumulated in Jerusalem during Herodian times, but does not correlate the "surplus wealth" of the aristocracy with the overtaxation (by those same aristocrats) that made the people desperate for loans in the first place.

40. Versus Freyne, *Galilee from Alexander the Great to Hadrian*, 45, 49; and his apparent source, Abraham Schalit, "Domestic Politics and Political Institutions," in *The Hellenistic Age: Political History of Jewish Palestine from 332 B.C.E. to 67 B.C.E.*, ed. Schalit, WHJP 6 (New Brunswick, N.J.: Rutgers University Press, 1972), 283–84.

41. The occasional "wealthy" peasant such as the one who, in the story in Luke 12:16–20, built bigger barns to store his abundant crops belongs in a more modest and different category of political-economic relations. Moreover, note the "use-value" expressed in the story: he neither sells on the market nor loans at interest to his neighbors!

42. Assuming that we do not continue to read this parable through modern capitalist assumptions. See now Richard Rohrbaugh, "A Peasant Reading of the Talents/Pounds: A Text of Terror," *BTB* 23 (1993): 32–39.

43. Discussion and documentation in Martin Hengel, *Judaism and Hellenism* (Philadelphia: Fortress, 1974), 1:6–29, 2:3–21, with certain questionable assumptions and generalizations and an inappropriate overall political-economic model.

44. See the discussion by Menahem Stern, "The Province of Judaea," in *The Jewish People in the First Century*, CRINT I.1, ed. S. Safrai and M. Stern (Assen: Van Gorcum, 1974), 331–32.

45. Because Goodman (*State and Society*) assumes a market economy in ancient Galilean villages, he does not consider that Roman tribute (or earlier the Herodian taxation and priestly and temple dues) would have been a major factor for the Galilean peasants, seriously affecting debts, land-tenure, and so on. On peasant indebtedness and its correlation with the wealthy and powerful in Jerusalem, see rather Goodman, "The First Jewish Revolt," 418–27.

46. A. Ben David, *Talmudische Ökonomie: Die Wirtschaft des Jüdischen Palaestina zur Zeit der Mischna und des Talmud* (Hildesheim: Olms, 1974), 293.

47. See further the sketch of Herod's enormous expenditures and income by Magen Broshi, "The Role of the Temple in the Herodian Economy," *JJS* 38

(1987): 31–37; and fuller documentation of taxation under Herod by Schalit, *König Herodes*, 262–98.

48. Freyne, *Galilee from Alexander the Great to Hadrian*, 191.

49. Various estimates of the closely interrelated matters of minimum caloric intake per person to sustain human life, family size, size of plot, yield per seed sown, and percentage of crop taken in taxes, and so on, have been made for areas in ancient Palestine and related places such as (republican) Rome. See Fiensy, *Social History of Palestine*, esp. 87–89, 92–95, for a recent summary and critical correlation of such estimates made on the basis of fragmentary archaeological and literary evidence.

50. Broshi, "Role of the Temple in the Herodian Economy," 31 (citing Schalit, *König Herodes*, 262–98), says one-third or one-quarter of the grain and one-half of the fruit was taken in taxes under Herod. Does this include all three layers? Safrai, *Economy of Roman Palestine*, 332, 341–52, 358, estimates the tax rate for Palestinian peasants generally at around 30%, with rent for tenant farmers at around 50%. For fuller discussion of the levels of taxation (and their relationship to peasant households' economic viability and indebtedness) see Douglas Oakman, *Jesus and the Economic Questions of His Day* (Lewiston, N.Y.: Mellen, 1986), chap. 2; and Fiensy, *Social History of Palestine*, chap. 3.

51. Freyne (*Galilee from Alexander the Great to Hadrian*) articulates a very different assessment of Galilean economic life: "At no time in Galilee's history do we find traces of the outside political agents who might have been instrumental in initiating widespread economic reform or change in the social fabric of life there" (177). The peasants' "life-style and occupation did not bring them into any kind of meaningful contact with the real agents for social change...there was no sense of unrest or frustration" (195). What is "invisible" without an appropriate understanding of the political-economic system operative in ancient Palestine, however, is that "the real agents for social change" were the heavy economic burdens placed on the Galilean peasantry by the multiple layers of tribute and taxation, burdens under which the fundamental social fabric began to disintegrate.

52. See chap. 3 above, chap. 12 below, and Richard A. Horsley with John S. Hanson, *Bandits, Prophets, and Messiahs: Popular Movements in the Time of Jesus* (San Francisco: Harper & Row, 1987), chap. 2.

53. What Applebaum does, in effect, in "Economic Life in Palestine," 658–60. Safrai, *Economy of Roman Palestine*, 328, points out that most tannaitic sources deal with owners of small farmsteads. Further: "Agriculture on Jewish farms and most likely in the entire rural sector was small-scale...and dependent upon self-labor" (358). Daniel Sperber, *Roman Palestine 200–400: The Land* (Ramat Gan: Bar Ilan University Press, 1978), 119–35, 177–86, finds an increase in amount of land held by rich in talmudic sources.

54. A. Ben-David, *Talmudische Ökonomie*, 63.

55. For comments on Latin and Greek equivalents of these types of tenants and the evolution of their status in late antiquity, see F. Heichelheim on "Roman Syria," in Tenney Frank, *Economic Survey of Ancient Rome* (Baltimore: Johns Hopkins Press, 1936–38), 4:146–48.

Chapter 10. Synagogues: The Village Assemblies

1. Martin Hengel, "*Proseuchē* und *Synagōgē:* Jüdische Gemeinde, Gotteshaus, und Gottesdienst in der Diaspora und in Palaestina," in *Festschrift für K. G. Kuhn,* ed. G. Jeremias, H. W. Kuhn, and H. Stegemann (Göttingen: Vandenhoeck & Ruprecht, 1971), now in *The Synagogue: Studies in Its Origins, Archaeology, and Architecture,* ed. J. Gutmann (New York: KTAV, 1975), 169, 172, 181; H. J. Leon, *The Jews of Ancient Rome* (Philadelphia: Jewish Publication Society of America, 1960), 139; W. Schrage, "*Synagōgē,*" *TDNT* 7.806ff; and A. T. Kraabel, "The Diaspora Synagogue: Archaeological and Epigraphic Evidence since Sukenik," in *ANRW* 2.19.1 (1979): 447–510. Richard E. Oster, "Supposed Anachronism in Luke-Acts' Use of *Synagogê,*" *NTS* 39 (1993): 185, demonstrates this point in a chart that lists thirty instances of *proseuchē,* compared with four of *amphitrēatron,* four of *hieron* (Josephus), four of *topos* (three in Josephus), and nine of *synagōgē* (six in Josephus's accounts of only three different cases, on which see below).

2. See A. T. Kraabel, "Unity and Diversity among Diaspore Synagogues," in *The Synagogue in Late Antiquity,* ed. Lee I. Levine (Philadelphia: ASOR, 1987), 51–55, points out that the associations which the Jewish *synagōgai* resemble socially were not particularly "of a religious nature," even though they usually had a patron deity. As Kraabel's own discussion indicates, moreover, these Jewish communities were far more than a "voluntary association."

3. E.g., Hengel, "*Proseuchē* und *Synagōgē,*" 181; Martin Goodman, *State and Society in Roman Galilee, A.D. 132–212* (Totowa, N.J.: Rowman & Allanheld, 1983), 84.

4. Paul V. M. Flesher, "Palestinian Synagogues before 70 C.E.: A Review of the Evidence," in *Approaches to Ancient Judaism,* vol. 6, ed. J. Neusner and E. Frerichs (Atlanta: Scholars Press, 1989), 75–80. For the supposed "synagogues" at Masada and Herodium, "there is no proof of piety or of a definite place of worship": S. B. Hoenig, quoting his own review of Y. Yadin, *Bar Kokhba,* in "The Ancient City-Square: The Forerunner of the Synagogue," *ANRW* 2.19.1 (1979): 453 n. 32.

5. Lee I. Levine, "The Second Temple Synagogue: The Formative Years," in *The Synagogue in Late Antiquity,* ed. Levine, 10–12, eager to demonstrate that "synagogue" buildings were ubiquitous in later second temple times, even finds the evidence at Gamla inconclusive. On the "private houses," see Eric M. Meyers and James F. Strange, *Archaeology, the Rabbis, and Early Christianity* (Nashville: Abingdon, 1981), 141. The attempt by Gideon Foerster ("The Synagogues at Masada and Herodion," *Journal of Jewish Art* 3, no. 4 [1977]: 6–11) to argue for "a well-defined group of synagogues dated to the Second Temple Period" has been ably refuted by Marilyn J. Chiat, "First-Century Synagogue Architecture: Methodological Problems," in *Ancient Synagogues: The State of Research,* ed. J. Gutmann, BJS 22 (Chico, Calif.: Scholars Press, 1981), 50–58.

6. Joseph Gutmann, "The Origins of the Synagogue: The Current State of Research," in *The Synagogue,* ed. Gutmann, 76; Eric M. Meyers, "Galilean Regionalism as a Factor in Historical Reconstruction," *BASOR* 221 (1976): 99; and, for the building at Capernaum previously dated in the first century but now dated in the fourth century, see the review essays of the archaeological reports, Gideon

Foerster, "Notes on Recent Excavations at Capernaum," in *Ancient Synagogues Revealed*, ed. Lee I. Levine (Jerusalem: Israel Exploration Society, 1981), 207–11; and James F. Strange, "The Capernaum and Herodium Publications," *BASOR* 226 (1977): esp. 69–70.

7. Compare references to assemblies in the Psalms of Solomon, with attention to parallel phrases in which the local assemblies are clearly particular manifestations or extensions of the overall congregation of Israel:

> The devout shall give thanks in the assembly of the people,... the synagogues of Israel will glorify the Lord's name. (10:6–7)

> Those who loved the assemblies of the devout fled from them. (17:16)

> He will judge (redeem) the peoples in the assemblies, the tribes of the sanctified... to see the good fortune of Israel which God will bring to pass in the assembly of the tribes. (17:43–44)

It is pertinent to note further that the originally almost interchangeable term *ekklēsia* is also used for both the overall movement or "assembly" and (predominantly) for particular local communities as component local "assemblies" of the larger "assembly" both for Paul and in Acts.

8. See Meyers and Strange, *Archaeology, the Rabbis, and Early Christianity*, 141.

9. See Sidney B. Hoenig, "Historical Inquiries: I. *Heber Ir.* II. City Square," *JQR* 48 (1957–58): 132–39; "The Ancient City-Square: Forerunner of the Synagogue," *ANRW* 2.19.1 (1979): 448–76, esp. 448–54. Although Hoenig is still pursuing the origins of a religious building, he has gathered evidence that clarifies the relation between the *knesset* in early rabbinic literature, which "applied to 'assembly' and designated all communal activities," and its gathering place.

10. Z. Ma'oz, "The Synagogue of Gamla and the Typology of Second-Temple Synagogues," in *Ancient Synagogues Revealed*, ed. Levine, 41.

11. Gideon Foerster, "Architectural Models of the Greco-Roman Period and the Origin of the 'Galilean' Synagogue," in *Ancient Synagogues Revealed*, ed. Levine, 47–48.

12. Similarly, except for continued focus on the place, S. Safrai, "The Synagogue," in *The Jewish People in the First Century*, CRINT I.2, ed. S. Safrai and M. Stern (Assen: Van Gorcum, 1976), 908–9. That synagogues (as places) were concerned with community affairs in general was seen by S. Krauss, *Synagogale Altertum* (Berlin-Vienna, 1922).

13. Anthony Giddens, *The Nation-State and Violence* (Berkeley: University of California Press, 1987), chap. 2.

14. Goodman, *State and Society*, 120.

15. Safrai, "The Synagogue," 933.

16. *Pace* Howard C. Kee, "The Transformation of the Synagogue after 70 C.E.: Its Import for Early Christianity," *NTS* 36 (1990): 12–15.

17. Safrai, "The Synagogue," 919. Ze'ev Safrai, *The Economy of Roman Palestine* (London: Routledge, 1994), 239–40, ironically in a section entitled "The Market on Mondays and Thursdays," provides several Mishnaic or Talmudic ref-

erences to the days of *assembly* and the prayers, recitations of scripture, fasts, and court-sessions that take place then.

18. It is anachronistic for Goodman (*State and Society*, 121–22) to read "money" into such texts where agricultural produce subject to tithes are under discussion. Neither local charity nor the local economy was highly "monetarized," although money may have been involved in certain connections. Is money implied in the "bags" carried by the *gabbaim* in *m. B. Qam.* 10:1?

19. Goodman, *State and Society*, 131.

20. DJD 2.155–59, no. 42; and 124, no. 24B.

21. Goodman, *State and Society*, 122–23.

22. Related by Rabbi Judah in *t. Sukk.* 4.6; Goodman, *State and Society*, 123–24.

23. This parallels the context in Matt. 5:25–26, except that the municipality concerned would have to be fairly large to have a prison; hence the reference may be to a royal or city court, i.e., a level of jurisdiction above the village level.

24. So Goodman, *State and Society*, 124: "It would seem that community control over the synagogue was exercised by officials selected for that purpose, but that there is no reason to assume that they had any considerable secular power."

25. As stated by Goodman himself, *State and Society*, 119, 123.

26. G. McL. Harper, *Village Administration in the Roman Province of Syria* (Princeton: Princeton University Press, 1928), 27–38.

27. Goodman, *State and Society*, 124.

28. Goodman even found one Tosefta passage (*t. B. Bat.* 10.5) "that introduces the *apamalatos* as an official similar to the *gabbai*" — obviously a loan word, the *epimelētes* of Syrian inscriptions.

The information and references gathered by Safrai, *Economy of Roman Palestine*, 46–48 and 54–55, under the separate headings of "Community Activities in the Town" and "Religion," fall into place far more satisfactorily if it is understood in the way outlined above. Thus the local assemblies are led by a sort of council of "seven town elders" and a smaller group of three "archons" led by a mayor. "The town assembly was an active participant in municipal affairs and voted not only on matters of great importance, but occasionally on more mundane affairs" (47). "The major function of the synagogue [building] was not prayer.... Many of the municipal institutions and the functionaries attached to them operated from the synagogue" (54). The synagogue was the local village assembly and its functions were local self-government and community celebrations and cohesion.

29. E.g., Kee, "Transformation of the Synagogue," 12–14, who even suggests that the Pharisees were responsible for the origins of the synagogues as worshipping communities; S. Freyne, *Galilee, Jesus, and the Gospels: Literary Approaches and Historical Investigations* (Philadelphia: Fortress, 1988), esp. 202–10. The traditional assumptions about "Judaism" involving scribes and Pharisees as leaders of activities in the synagogues as religious buildings determines Freyne's whole approach: Since there is little or no direct evidence for "the social role of the scribe in Galilee" he examines instead the evidence for the role of "the synagogue" on the assumption that the latter was the "natural focal point" for the activity of "the scribe with his torah scroll," who supposedly controlled "the various media of education, including the synagogue."

30. Goodman, *State and Society*, 101, 119, 128–29; Safrai, "The Synagogue," 935–36. Although we would not necessarily expect it to be reflecting the situation in Galilee, it is worth noting that the Theodosian Code, which lists synagogue functionaries (including priests, elders, and *archisynagōgoi*), never mentions rabbis (*Codex Theodosianus* 16.8.4, 8, 13, 15). See further A. Linder, *The Jews in Roman Imperial Legislation* (Detroit: Wayne State University Press, 1987), 186–89, 201–4, 220–22.

31. E.g., Lee I. Levine, "The Sages and the Synagogue in Late Antiquity: The Evidence of the Galilee," in *The Galilee in Late Antiquity*, ed. Lee I. Levine (New York: Jewish Theological Seminary of America, 1992), 220. Since the "academies" were basically a teacher and a few pupils, one would assume that they were therefore concentrated in a very few towns or villages in Western Galilee before concentrating in the cities after around 200.

32. Shaye J. D. Cohen, "The Place of the Rabbi in Jewish Society of the Second Century," in *The Galilee in Late Antiquity*, ed. Lee I. Levine (New York: Jewish Theological Seminary of America, 1992), 167.

33. Ibid., 169. This is also one of the main conclusions of the extensive study of the Mishnah by Jacob Neusner. See, e.g., *Judaism: The Evidence of the Mishnah* (Chicago: University of Chicago Press, 1981).

34. Cohen, "Place of the Rabbi," 173; and *From the Maccabees to the Mishnah* (Philadelphia: Westminster, 1987), 221; and Levine, "Sages and the Synagogue," 212. Levine finds the "minimal involvement" of rabbis in synagogue affairs in the second century increasing from mid-third century on, e.g., in "the adjudication of halakhic matters" (206–10). Perhaps the rabbis eventually became members of more local communities and thus had a basis for becoming officers or leaders. Goodman found a passage in the Tosefta (*t. Dem.* 3.4) that points to just such a transition later on: "In the past any *haver* accepting a post as treasurer was excluded from his *havura*, while a new ruling permitted a *haver* to become a treasurer but temporarily suspended him from his *havura*. Something about being a treasurer, perhaps consorting with all those impure poor, would have rendered any man unclean" (Goodman, *State and Society*, 126). Or perhaps by the third or fourth century it began to work the other way around, i.e., perhaps prominent local *parnasim* wanted to become rabbis.

35. *Pace* Halvor Moxnes, *The Economy of the Kingdom: Social Conflict and Economic Relations in Luke's Gospel* (Philadelphia: Fortress, 1988), 18–19.

36. See chap. 6 above for a fuller exploration of "the social role" of the scribes and Pharisees. A. J. Saldarini, *Pharisees, Scribes, and Sadducees* (Wilmington, Del.: Glazier, 1988), 172, following one of his many assertions that the scribes and Pharisees were retainers serving the governing class, adds somewhat ambiguously that "in Galilee, they were … influential in the local village leadership, according to Matthew's account" (172). A survey both of all the references to scribes and/or Pharisees in Matthew and of Saldarini's discussion turns up nothing to indicate that either scribes or Pharisees are represented as themselves being local village leaders.

37. Recently, e.g., Kee, "Transformation of the Synagogue," esp. 14–16. "The chapter is filled with detailed references to what by the end of the first century C.E. were in process of becoming normative practices in the emergent institutional synagogue" (15). In this paragraph and section, however, Kee has shifted his focus

to "Pharisaic Judaism" into which he has subsumed "the synagogue," a shift completed in the last section (20–24), in which *Synagōgē* and *Ekklēsia* mean Pharisaic Judaism and early Christianity, respectively.

38. On the seat of Moses as a symbol of authority, see I. Renov, "The Seat of Moses," *IEJ* 5 (1955): 262–67.

39. Matthew had combined smaller clusters of material from the Synoptic Sayings Source "Q" to form a larger discourse here, just as he did to form the "Sermon on the Mount" in chaps. 5–7 and his long "mission discourse" in chap. 10.

40. Cf., B. L. Mack, *A Myth of Innocence: Mark and Christian Origins* (Philadelphia: Fortress, 1988), 43.

41. Wegner, *Chattel or Person?*; Ross Shepard Kraemer, *Her Share of the Blessings* (Oxford: Oxford University Press, 1992), 93.

42. See especially Bernadette J. Brooten, *Women Leaders in the Ancient Synagogues*, BJS 36 (Chico: Scholars Press, 1982); and Kraemer, *Her Share of the Blessings*, chap. 9.

43. Wegner, *Chattel or Person?* 147.

44. The following is dependent on the analysis and argument of Wegner in ibid., chap. 6.

45. Brooten, *Women Leaders in Ancient Synagogues*, 27–55, 103–38.

46. This is likely to have been the case for Judean village communities as well. Although certain functions would have become priestly prerogatives during the second-temple period in Judea, the villages still retained their semi-autonomous community life in most respects.

Chapter 11. Diversity in Galilean Village Culture

1. Eric M. Meyers, while pursuing a long-overdue *regional* strategy in some of the first archaeological explorations of villages, pioneered analysis of "regionalism" in Galilee in a series of articles: Eric M. Meyers, "Galilean Regionalism as a Factor in Historical Reconstruction," *BASOR* 221 (1976): 93–101; "The Cultural Setting of Galilee: The Case of Regionalism and Early Judaism," *ANRW* 2.19.1 (1979): 286–702; "Galilean Regionalism: A Reappraisal," in *Approaches to Ancient Judaism*, vol. 5, ed. William S. Green (Atlanta: Scholars Press, 1985), 115–31.

2. Meyers, "Cultural Setting of Galilee," 697–98.

3. Apart from the "tentative conclusions," which apply anachronistic categories to ancient Galilean agrarian life, Freyne provides a good description of the geographical characteristics of these three different areas of Galilee, in *Galilee from Alexander the Great to Hadrian*, 9–15.

4. D. H. K. Amiran, "Sites of Settlements in the Mountains of Lower Galilee," *IEJ* 6 (1956): 70–71.

5. The *Greek-English Lexicon* of Liddell-Scott-Jones translates *methorios* as "border area," but "frontier area" seems more appropriate insofar as it refers to the countryside, *chōra*, between major cities or other political jurisdictions, control of which historically would often have been contested.

6. Martin Goodman, *State and Society in Roman Galilee*, A.D. *132–212* (Totowa, N.J.: Rowman & Allanheld, 1983), 20 n. 253, claims close relations with

Scythopolis, citing Michael Avi-Yonah, "Scythopolis," *IEJ* 12 (1962): 123–24. Avi-Yonah, however, cites rather evidence for tensions and hostilities between Galilean villages and Scythopolis, esp. 128–31.

7. Again I am attempting to move behind or underneath the highly generalized term "the Jews" to greater precision regarding differences within Palestine. An interesting illustration is that in tannaitic case law after case law where Goodman (*State and Society*, chap. 4: "Jews and Gentiles in Galilee") writes "Jews," the Mishnah or Tosefta has "Israelites." As laid out in chapters 1–3 above, between Solomon and the Mishnah, the Judeans and the Galileans had divergent histories.

8. See further *The Jewish People in the First Century*, CRINT I.2, ed. S. Safrai and M. Stern (Assen: Van Gorcum, 1976), 756–60, on Galileans' laxity of concern for blood purity, and *t. Ketub.* 1.4.

9. Goodman (*State and Society*, 43) appears to be arguing just that, but then presents evidence of numerous cases which cannot be explained except as taking place in the same village (43–44).

10. A selection of appropriate references: *t. Pe'a* 3.12; *t. 'Abod. Zar.* 7.1; *m. Šabb.* 1:7; *t. B. Meṣ.* 2.27; *m. Šabb.* 16:6, 8; *t. Pesaḥ.* 2.14; *m. B. Meṣ.* 5:6; *t. 'Abod. Zar.* 7(8).5; *m. Giṭ.* 5:9; *m. Nid.* 9:3.

11. Although apparently non-Israelite Syrians were also circumcised, according to Goodman, *State and Society*, 53, citing *EncJud* 13:1183. See also the recent survey by M. Hadas-Lebel, "Le paganisme a travers les sources rabbiniques des IIe et IIIe siècles: Contribution a l'etude du syncretisme dans l'empire romain," *ANRW* 2.19.2 (1979): 397–485; and see Saul Lieberman, *Hellenism in Jewish Palestine*, 2nd ed. (New York: Jewish Theological Seminary of America, 1962), 128–38, on paganism.

12. E.g., Goodman, *State and Society*, 72: "The general rabbinic tendency to assume literacy." Yet it is not clear that the rabbinic texts cited "assume literacy." What "must be discounted," of course, is modern interpreters' "tendency to assume" that, in any given case, a rabbinic text reflects social reality beyond "the highly literate group within which the rabbinic texts were formed."

13. Note the modern assumption about literacy in the appended footnote 6, in Herbert Danby, *The Mishnah* (London: Oxford University Press, 1933), 177: "That he has not learnt to read."

14. It is highly questionable whether much of Goodman's discussion of "Education" (in *State and Society*, 71–81) is pertinent to "Galilean Village Culture" except insofar as the rabbinic traditions he relies upon for some of his evidence may have been cultivated in rabbinic circles that happened to be located in certain villages (in southwestern Galilee). As Goodman himself notes,

> The preoccupations of rabbinic schools were sufficiently esoteric to mark off the student from the rest of the population. The texts assume that the details of law would be known only to a select few (citing *m. Dem.* 2:3 and 4:6)....Above all, all tannaitic texts assume a division of Jewish society into *haverim*, who keep the purity and tithing laws, and *amme haaretz* ("people of the land"), who do not. (76–77)

15. E.g., John 2:1–10; Mark 2:19, 5:38; *m. Šeb.* 7:4; *m. Mo'ed Qaṭ.* 1:5, 3:7; *m. Ketub.* 7:5; *t. B. Qam.* 8.11; *t. Mo'ed* 2.13. See further *Jewish People in the First Century*, ed. Safrai and Stern, 2:757.

16. For a critical survey and assessment of the evidence as of 1970, see Joseph A. Fitzmyer, S.J., "The Languages of Palestine in the First Century A.D.," *CBQ* 32 (1970): 501–31. A recent survey of literature is Martin Hengel, *The Helleniza-tion of Judaea in the First Century after Christ* (Philadelphia: Trinity, 1989), 7–18. As suggested by Fitzmyer's title, most discussions of languages deal with Palestine generally, not Galilee in particular.

17. On the multilingual situation in Palestine generally, Ch. Rabin, "Hebrew and Aramaic in the First Century," in *Jewish People in the First Century*, ed. Safrai and Stern, 2:1007–39; B. Spolsky, "Jewish Multilingualism in the First Century: An Essay in Historical Sociolinguistics," in *Readings in the Sociology of Jewish Languages*, ed. J. A. Fishman (Leiden: Brill, 1985), 1:35–50; *New Documents Illustrating Early Christianity*, vol. 5, ed. Gregory H. R. Horsley (North Ryde, Australia: Macquarrie University, 1989), 40–50.

18. Ben Zion Wacholder, *Eupolemus: A Study of Judaeo-Greek Literature* (Cin-cinnati: Hebrew Union College, 1974), 259–306; Tessa Rajak, "The Sense of History in Jewish Intertestamental Writing," *Old Testament Studies* 24 (1986): 124–45; Doron Mendels, *The Land of Israel as a Political Concept in Hasmonean Literature* (Tübingen: Mohr, 1987), 29–46.

19. See M. Schwabe and B. Lifshitz, *Beth She'arim*, vol. 2, *The Greek Inscrip-tions* (Jerusalem: Israel Exploration Society, 1974), and N. Avigad, *Beth She'arim*, vol. 3, *Catacombs 12–23* (Jerusalem: Israel Exploration Society, 1976).

20. Isaiah Gafni, "Reinterment in the Land of Israel: Notes on the Origin and Development of the Custom," *Jerusalem Cathedra* 1 (1981): 96–104.

21. Hengel, *Hellenization of Judaea*, 9–10, citing a letter from L. Y. Rahmani concerning burial inscriptions in Jerusalem and Jericho.

22. See Fitzmyer, "Languages of Palestine," 513–15, 522–23, for discussion and references to reconstructions and analyses by Lifshitz et al.

23. James F. Strange, "Archaeology and the Religion of Judaism in Palestine," *ANRW* 2.19.1 (1979): 661; Eric M. Meyers, James F. Strange, Carol L. Meyers, and Richard S. Hanson, "Preliminary Report on the 1977 and 1978 Seasons at Gush Halav," *BASOR* 233 (1979): 55–57.

24. See Rabin, "Hebrew and Aramaic in the First Century," 1007–39, esp. 1008–9.

25. For the following, see especially Gary A. Rendsburg, "The Galilean Back-ground of Mishnaic Hebrew," in *The Galilee in Late Antiquity*, ed. Lee I. Levine (New York: Jewish Theological Seminary of America, 1992), 225–40; E. Y. Kutscher, *A History of the Hebrew Language* (Leiden: Brill, 1982), 32.

26. E.g., *b. Ta'an.* 23a; *b. B. Qam.* 92b; *Gen. Rab.* 86:7; and the analysis and ar-gument in Avigdor Shinan, "The Aramaic Targhum as a Mirror of Galilean Jewry," in *Galilee in Late Antiquity*, ed. Levine, 241–51. It should be possible, furthermore, with increasingly sophisticated methods of comparative analysis, for specialists to the discourse of traditional Galilean folk stories in the Targums. One attempt is D. Noy, "Galilean Folk Stories," *Mahanaim* 101 (1968): 18–25 (in Hebrew).

27. On the practice of targum, see especially Steven D. Fraade, "Rabbinic Views on the Practice of Targum, the Multilingualism in the Jewish Galilee of the Third–Sixth Centuries," in *Galilee in Late Antiquity*, ed. Levine, 256–65.

28. Inscriptions collected and interpreted by J. Naveh, *On Stone and Mosaic* (Jerusalem, 1978).

29. Meyers, "Cultural Setting of Galilee," 697–78; Goodman, *State and Society*, 88–89.

30. *Pace* Goodman, *State and Society*, 88.

31. *Pace* Eric M. Meyers, "Roman Sepphoris in the Light of New Archaeological Evidence and Research," in *Galilee in Late Antiquity*, ed. Levine, 333.

32. *Pace* Goodman, *State and Society*, 83–84.

33. Unless archaeological excavations turn up more than .one or two "ritual baths" (*miqva'ot*) in a given village such as Meiron, and depending on assessment of the houses in which they are found, it may be that such "ritual baths" were primarily in the houses of well-off families. If they are also found at agricultural processing installations, then they may reflect certain social-economic relations between workers and landowners.

34. In a different connection, Seth Schwartz, "The 'Judaism' of Samaria and Galilee in Josephus's Version of the Letter of Demetrius I to Jonathan (*Antiquities* 13.48–57)," *HTR* 82 (1989): 390–91, seems to point to the same mixture of cultural-religious influences in Galilee: it is reasonable to suppose that local varieties of "Judaism" incorporated "elements of local pre-Jewish religions and perhaps also of the religions of the surrounding cities and peoples."

35. See M. Avi-Yonah, "Mount Carmel and the God of Baalbeck," *IEJ* 2 (1951): 118–24; Martin Hengel, *Judaism and Hellenism* (Philadelphia: Fortress, 1974), 1:295; 2:172 n. 27, 198 n. 245.

36. See Javier Teixidor, *The Pagan God* (Princeton: Princeton University Press, 1977), 53–54; M. Avi-Yonah, "Syrian Gods at Ptolemais-Accho," *IEJ* 9 (1959): 1–12.

37. Hengel, *Judaism and Hellenism*, 2:172 n. 27, 198 n. 245.

38. Moshe Fischer, Asher Ovadiah, and Israel Roll, "The Roman Temple at Kedesh, Upper Galilee: A Preliminary Study," *Tel Aviv* 11 (1984): 146–72, esp. 168–71; cf. Jodi Magness, "Some Observations on the Roman Temple at Kedesh," *IEJ* 40 (1990): 173–81.

39. Quantitative and configurational analysis of the motifs found in synagogue buildings of Galilee in late-Roman and Byzantine times in Ruth Vale, "Literary Sources in Archaeological Description: The Case of Galilee, Galilees, and Galileans," *JSJ* 18 (1987): 220–26.

Chapter 12. Bandits, Messiahs, and Urban Poor: Popular Unrest in Galilee

1. On Josephus as a source, see the introduction above. Shaye J. D. Cohen, *Josephus in Galilee and Rome: His Vita and Development as a Historian*, CSCT 8 (Leiden: Brill, 1979), concluding that Josephus's accounts of events in Galilee are utterly unreliable, then constructs a highly simplified alternative history based selectively on some of Josephus's statements, yet with no clearly consistent criteria of selection. Cf. review by H. R. Moehring, *JJS* 31 (1980): 240–42. The more recent study of Josephus by Tessa Rajak, *Josephus: The Historian and His Society* (London: Duckworth, 1983; Philadelphia: Fortress, 1984), provides a clear discussion

of the historical context in which Josephus must be read and suggests that, with a continually critical and somewhat skeptical eye, we can utilize Josephus's accounts for cautious historical reconstruction of circumstances and events in ancient Galilee.

2. Cf. Sean Freyne, "Bandits in Galilee: A Contribution to the Study of Social Conditions in First-Century Palestine," in *The Social World of Formative Christianity and Judaism: Essays in Tribute to Howard Clark Kee*, ed. Jacob Neusner et al. (Philadelphia: Fortress, 1988), 50–68, who uses Hobsbawm more like a social scientific model, attempting to "apply the criteria for social banditry" to Josephus's accounts of Galilean groups. See further the response to Freyne's use of Hobsbawm in R. A. Horsley, "Bandits, Messiahs, and Longshoremen: Popular Unrest in Galilee around the Time of Jesus," SBLSP, ed. David Lull (Atlanta: Scholars Press, 1988), 185–86.

3. The key work was Martin Hengel, *Die Zeloten* (Leiden: Brill, 1961).

4. Given the extent to which this synthetic construct of "the Zealots" dominated scholarly discussion of Galilee, it is understandable that the major recent study of Galilee was dominated by the recurrent argument that Galilee was not a hotbed of revolutionary agitation, i.e., Sean Freyne, *Galilee from Alexander the Great to Hadrian: A Study of Second Temple Judaism* (Wilmington, Del.: Glazier, 1980).

5. See Solomon Zeitlin, "Zealots and Sicarii," *JBL* 81 (1962): 395–98; Morton Smith, "The Zealots and Sicarii, Their Origins and Relationship," *HTR* 64 (1971): 1–19; Richard A. Horsley, "Josephus and the Bandits," *JSJ* 10 (1979): 37–63; "Ancient Jewish Social Banditry and the Revolt against Rome, A.D. 66–70," *CBQ* 43 (1981): 409–32; and R. A. Horsley, *Jesus and the Spiral of Violence: Popular Jewish Resistance in Roman Palestine* (San Francisco: Harper & Row, 1987; Minneapolis: Fortress, 1992), chaps. 3–4.

6. R. A. Horsley, "The Zealots: Their Origins, Relationships, and Importance in the Jewish Revolt," *NovT* 27 (1986): 159–92.

7. Eric Hobsbawm, *Primitive Rebels* (New York: Norton, 1959), chap. 2, and Hobsbawm, *Bandits*, rev. ed. (New York: Pantheon, 1981).

8. Recognition of the actual prepolitical (and nonrevolutionary) character of ancient Palestinian brigands would provide strong support for Freyne's contention that Galilee was not especially rebellious (as would recognition that the whole picture of a long-standing revolutionary movement in Jewish society lacks historical evidence). However, in a subsequent publication ("Bandits in Galilee," 50–68), Freyne appears to have understood the concept of "social banditry" in terms of the old construct of "the Zealots," as if it were a political or even revolutionary phenomenon with a "religious component." Ironically, then, the phenomenon of banditry in Galilee becomes subsumed into his earlier concern to deny that there was revolutionary ideology and activity in Galilee.

9. E. Mary Smallwood, *The Jews under Roman Rule from Pompey to Diocletian* (Leiden: Brill, 1976), 44; Freyne, *Galilee from Alexander the Great to Hadrian*, 68, with the claim simply reasserted without further argument of documentation in "Bandits in Galilee." Ironically, to reconstruct Hezekiah and the cave-dwelling brigands as the remnants of Hasmonean nobility injects a special religious-political dimension back into resistance groups in Galilee, whereas to al-

low the brigands to be brigands would support Freyne's own principal contention that Galilee was not full of religiously motivated revolutionary activity.

10. Freyne (*Galilee from Alexander the Great to Hadrian*, 63, 93 n. 20) believes that Herod's murder of Hezekiah "caused the Hasmonean aristocracy that was prepared to go along with Roman rule to join Antigonus rather than Hyrcanus," and uses as an illustration "the second in command (*hypostrategos*) in Jerusalem," Peitholaus, who "fought against Alexander, *Ant.* 14.84, but for Antigonus, *Ant.* 14.120."

The situation and unfolding events in Palestine (focused on the conflict between the Hasmoneans rivals Hyrcanus and Aristobulus), however, compounded by the shifting sides of the Roman civil war, were far more complex than a simple opposition of Hyrcanus, Antipater, and his son Herod siding with Rome versus the Hasmonean nobles siding with Antigonus and the Parthians. In fact, according to Josephus, Hasmonean officials had begun to defect nearly a decade before Herod's appointment as governor of Galilee. Peitholaus had deserted not to Antigonus but to his father Aristobulus with a thousand men in 56 B.C.E., and was killed by Cassius (in 52?) when he was attempting to rally Aristobulus's partisans (*B.J.* 1.172, 180). Moreover, to complicate matters, Caesar himself had sent Aristobulus back to Syria. Evidently the political sides were constantly shifting and, for Hasmonean officers the outcome was utterly unclear, with much maneuvering for position. See further Horsley, "Bandits, Prophets, and Longshoremen," 186–88.

11. Freyne, *Galilee from Alexander the Great to Hadrian*, 67.

12. See further Horsley, "Josephus and the Bandits," 44, 53.

13. On the escalation of banditry in situations of decline of effective governmental power, see Eric Wolf, *Peasant Wars of the Twentieth Century* (New York: Harper and Row, 1969), 107–15.

14. See Horsley, "Josephus and the Bandits," 46, 54.

15. Not so large that it was the brigands who nearly defeated Herod's troops, yet were driven across the Jordan. Both the awkwardness of Josephus's accounts and the geographical location of the pursuit after the battle suggest that Josephus has, in effect on the reader, fused accounts of battles against two quite different foes, one probably the remnants of Antigonus's forces (or possibly general opposition), and the other the cave-dwelling bandits.

16. Freyne, "Bandits in Galilee," lumps this incident together with instances of banditry.

17. See Marvin Chaney, "Ancient Palestinian Peasant Movements and the Formation of Premonarchic Israel," in *Palestine in Transition: The Emergence of Ancient Israel*, ed. D. N. Freedman and D. F. Graf (Sheffield: Almond, 1983), 39–94, esp. 72–83; and Richard A. Horsley, "'Apiru and Cossacks: A Comparative Analysis of Social Form and Historical Role," in *New Perspectives on Ancient Judaism: Religion, Literature, and Society in Ancient Israel, Formative Christianity and Judaism*, vol. 2, *Ancient Israel and Christianity*, Presented to Howard Clark Kee, ed. J. Neusner, P. Borgen, E. Frerichs, and R. Horsley (Lanham, Md.: University Press of America, 1987), 3–26.

18. Josephus's insinuation that Jesus became loyal to him does not seem credible (*Vita* 110). But another possible "reading" of this highly problematic account of Josephus's facile subjugation of both Jesus and the Sepphoreans (*Vita* 104–11)

is that Jesus and his band were making common cause with Sepphoris against Josephus whom *they* saw as pro-Roman and/or a representative of Jerusalem's unwelcome attempt at domination, and that Josephus invented the payment as mercenaries aspect.

19. In the initial suggestion that these brigand groups hired as mercenaries may have comprised some of the force commanded by Josephus ("Bandits, Prophets, and Longshoremen," 190) I was taking as cue Josephus's ostensible exhortation to his "army" to "abstain from their habitual malpractices, theft, banditry, and plunder," in *B.J.* 2.581. Besides being addressed to the whole army, however, this may well be standard exhortation from a general to his troops, and not particular to Josephus's situation in Galilee.

20. To assert that they were "militantly nationalist, but not essentially revolutionary" (Sean Freyne, "The Galileans in the Light of Josephus' *Vita*," NTS 26 [1979–80]: 412) involves both an anachronism and a narrow picture of what would have constituted revolution in antiquity.

21. Translations by Hanson, in Richard A. Horsley with John S. Hanson, *Bandits, Prophets, and Messiahs: Popular Movements in the Time of Jesus* (San Francisco: Harper & Row, 1987), 112.

22. Fuller explanation in Richard A. Horsley, "Popular Messianic Movements around the Time of Jesus," *CBQ* 46 (1984): 471–93.

23. See further, e.g., Ps. Sol. 17:5–8; many passages in the DSS; the general opposition to Herod, and Horsley, "Popular Messianic Movements," 473–83.

24. Prior to the recent discernment of the Israelite tradition of popular kingship, Freyne (*Galilee from Alexander the Great to Hadrian*, 215) recognized that "in realistic terms Judas son of Hezekiah would have had to represent himself as carrying forward some recognizable tradition of kingship." Without considering either the "little tradition" or biblical narratives, then the two options were the Herodian or the Hasmonean. Considering that Judas's rebellion was against Herodian kingship, Freyne then argues that since Judas was in Sepphoris and Sepphoris was a Hasmonean stronghold, he must have been attempting to restore the Hasmonean kingship. The underlying assumption is that Judas is a surviving member of a Hasmonean "noble" or "landowner" family. The argument is farfetched. As Freyne himself points out, some of the Hasmonean officers went over to the rival Hasmonean side and were killed by the Romans, others were drowned in the Lake in resurgent popular uprising, and Herod had most of those remaining killed when he finally obtained a firm grip on power in Jerusalem.

25. See further Richard A. Horsley, "Menahem in Jerusalem: A Brief Messianic Episode among the Sicarii — Not 'Zealot Messianism,'" *NovT* 27 (1985): 334–48.

26. Although the different stances toward Rome and Agrippa II corresponded to the principal class division in Tiberias, the situation both in Tiberias and in Galilee as a whole was more complex than can be comprehended by the standard but simplistic scheme "war party" versus "peace party" (*pace* Cohen, *Josephus in Galilee and Rome*, 217). For example, in Tiberias itself "the principal men" are not necessarily the same as the council (*boulē*). *Vita* 167–68 ‖ *B.J.* 2.638–641 and *Vita* 381, concerning an appeal to Agrippa, do not necessarily mean that the whole council was pro-Roman; in 381 Josephus writes that only *hoi protoi ton ek tes boules* had invited the king to take over the city. Actions taken by the principal

factions in Tiberias, moreover, must be understood in the historical context that involved not simply Roman imperial rule, but other political-economic-religious-ethnic relationships, such as with Galilean peasants, cities of the Decapolis, the Roman client ruler Agrippa under whose rule they had recently been placed, and the rivalry with Sepphoris.

27. Hobsbawm, *Primitive Rebels*, chap. 7.

28. It is unclear what might have constituted "the opportunities of the hellenistic city environment" of which these poor could have availed themselves in order to achieve "social mobility." See Freyne, *Galilee from Alexander the Great to Hadrian*, 236.

29. See the discussion of "the Jerusalem crowd" in Horsley, *Jesus and the Spiral of Violence*, 90–99, and comparative studies listed there.

30. Vs. Freyne, *Galilee from Alexander the Great to Hadrian*, chap. 8, esp. 234–35, 311–12, who finds the attack against the royal palace an "obvious act of zealotism" perpetrated by "a pocket of zealotism in Tiberias and its region" and inspired by "Zealot ideals" emanating from Jerusalem. Of course, the Jerusalem provisional government that sent Josephus was not the same as the rebel coalition that drove out the Romans in the summer of 66, but the "moderate" high-priestly and Pharisaic council attempting to control the volatile situation. Also, it seems inappropriate to draw conclusions about the motives of the Tiberias poor from the supposed motives of the Jerusalem *koinon* which are themselves unclear, given the lack of evidence.

31. Cohen, *Josephus in Galilee and Rome*, 118, reads Josephus very differently, reconstructing the parties, principal figures, and events in Tiberias in such a way that Josephus is leader of both the destruction of the royal palace and the massacre of the Greeks, and "the respectable" elite join with the sailors, paupers, and peasants in pillaging the palace. It is unclear why those who supposedly implemented what had been commissioned by the Jerusalem assembly (led by the priestly aristocracy) should be called "criminals."

INDEX